PAT WELSH'S SOUTHERN CALIFORNIA GARDENING

A Month-by-Month Guide

PAT WELSH'S SOUTHERN CALIFORNIA
GARDENING

A Month-by-Month Guide

Illustrations by PATRICIA CURTAN

Photographs by PAT WELSH, MELINDA HOLDEN, *and* FRANCESCA FILANC

CHRONICLE BOOKS   SAN FRANCISCO

Printed in the United States

Cover photograph of Pat Welsh by Melinda Holden
Cover and text design: Christine Taylor
Composition and production: Wilsted & Taylor

All photographs in this book were taken by Pat Welsh, with
the exception of photo pages: 1, 3, 6 (bottom),
9 (background), 10 (top), 11, 14, 20 (inset), 23 (inset) by
Melinda Holden; and 9 (inset) by Francesca Filanc.

LIBRARY OF CONGRESS CATALOGING-IN-PUBLICATION DATA
Welsh, Patricia.
Pat Welsh's Southern California gardening :
a month-by-month guide / by Patricia Welsh.
p. cm.
Includes bibliographical references (p.).
ISBN 0-87701-629-1
1. Gardening—California, Southern. I. Title.
SB453.2.C3W454 1991
635'.09794'9—dc20 91-23947
CIP

Distributed in Canada by Raincoast Books,
112 East Third Avenue, Vancouver, B.C. V5T 1C8

10 9 8 7 6 5 4 3 2 1

Chronicle Books
275 Fifth St.
San Francisco, CA 94103

To Louis

Acknowledgments

This book couldn't have been written without the help and cooperation of many people. I'm deeply grateful to all who so generously gave of their time to help bring it to completion. First, I thank my wonderful family: my husband Louis, my children Peter and Francie Filanc and Larry and Wendy Woolf, my grandchildren Yvette, Erica, Rebecca, David, and Rachel, and my mother Ruth Begley for their encouragement and for patiently putting up with my diverted attention.

I also thank the many people, including self-styled "chief nagger" Evelyn Weidner of Begonia Gardens, and her late husband, Bob, who kept at me until I finally sat down to write. I'm grateful to them and to innumerable other friends, experts, and growers, as well as plant collectors, home gardeners, and University Extension scientists—too many to name—for sharing their special growing techniques with me and my viewers and readers through the years.

If this book is as helpful and factual as I hope, much of the credit goes to a veritable "walking encyclopedia," the San Diego Home-Horticulture Farm Advisor Vincent Lazaneo. When Vince heard I was writing a book he offered to read and correct the rough draft for technical errors. I'll always be grateful to him for that generous offer. Vince spent much valuable time reading and correcting the first drafts and answering my questions over the phone. If there are errors left in the book they are mine and not his. I'm indebted also to Dorothy Redwine and other members of the Braille Transcriber's Guild of San Diego for recording the book for Vince's perusal and to the several people who shared in the task of writing down Vince's comments and corrections.

A large number of people with special expertise kindly and generously took time out of their busy lives to read this book and make suggestions and additions: Chuck Kline, Horticulturist Emeritus of Sea World and lecturer at UCSD Extension, read the entire manuscript and made many corrections and suggestions. Betty Newton, garden columnist for the San Diego Union, read the chapters and the glossary and made suggestions and corrections for interior climate zones. Susan Locke, Director of Landscaping of Sea World, and Stephanie Bise, Horticultural Supervisor of Sea World, also read all the chapters and made suggestions for coastal gardening. Gilbert Voss, former Horticulturist of Quail Botanical Gardens, read the chapters and corrected the glossary.

Dr. Bill Nelson, owner of Pacific Tree Farms, and Tom del Hotal, manager of Pacific Tree Farms and past president of the California Rare Fruit Growers, gave generously of their time and information on fruit trees. The treatment of strawberries in this book is based on the work of Victor Voth, University Extension scientist and strawberry wizard. Richard Streeper, President of the San Diego Rose Society and rose columnist for the San Diego Union, allowed me to use his year-round schedule for roses. Tom Cooper, macadamia grower, owner of Rancho Nuez Macadamia Nursery in Fallbrook, contributed the system of harvesting the nuts from Beaumont macadamia trees and of roasting macadamia nuts in a convection oven. Karen Kees, Poway garden designer, shared her knowledge of gardening in areas hit by frequent winter frosts.

Others whose expertise contributed to this book include Ernie Chew, Horticulturist Emeritus of the San Diego Zoo; Michael MacCaskey, Southern California Editor of *Sunset* magazine; Bob Dale, veteran TV weatherman at KNSD; Bill Teague, commercial grower, daylily hybridizer, and past Vice-president of the American Bamboo Society; Linda Teague, flower arranger and plant expert; Neil Cassidy, Jim Halda, and Craig Miller of C&M Garden Supply Store in Solana Beach; the manager and employees of Grangetto's Farm Supply in Rancho Santa Fe; Karen O'Toole, manager of Nurseryland in Del Mar; Chuck Badger, Rancho Santa Fe citrus grower and grove manager; the late Alice Menard, home-gardener extraordinaire; Dale Kolaczkowski, manager of Stallings Ranch Nursery; and Richard A. Haubrich, President of the American Bamboo Society.

While I was writing this book events often fell into place in a miraculous way, and people came to my aid just when I most needed them. First, a chance meeting led me to Sandra Dijkstra, a literary agent who goes all out for her writers. Then on the very day Sandra telephoned to say that Chronicle had decided to publish this book, Pam Jones Minchin also phoned to see if I could use her research and garden skills. Pam organized stacks of notes and files I'd accumulated over many years, and helped me to keep up with garden tasks while I was involved with writing. Another miracle occurred when I found myself under a tight deadline. Rebecca Johnston, my copy editor at *San Diego Home/ Garden Magazine*, phoned to tell me she was now freelancing. Within a week Rebecca was helping me type editorial changes onto disk.

It's been a pleasure to work with the good people, both staff and freelance, at Chronicle Books. My sincere thanks to Nion McEvoy, Editor-in-Chief, for his faith in this book; to Bill LeBlond, Senior Editor, for his advice and help; to Charlotte Stone, Assistant to the Editor-in-Chief, for shepherding this work through its final phases; to Mary Ann Gilderbloom, for her creative publicity; and to designer Christine Taylor, of Wilsted and Taylor, for giving the book its visual style.

Finally, I couldn't have had a more conscientious editor or one more devoted to clarity than Carey Charlesworth. Carey is an appropriate name for Ms. Charlesworth since she cared about every detail and lavished attention on this book while patiently enduring my infinite changes and additions.

Contents

For the purposes of this book Southern California means one large swath of the southernmost third of the state. The map shows that third to be a huge area, and most of it sparsely populated. This book addresses the relatively narrow band of heavily populated coastal plains and adjacent inland valleys that begins at the Mexican border, on the south, and extends northward all the way to the Gaviota Pass, north of Santa Barbara. Throughout this region, where more than 80 percent of the state's population lives, approximately the same wide array of plants is grown.

North of the Gaviota Pass the climate differs from that in Southern California, and a somewhat different array of plants is grown on a schedule that's not the same as ours. Mexico also has a different climate and differing conditions. Even so, many of the plants discussed in this book can also be grown in the central and northern areas of California and in Baja California. Mountains and desert areas are not themselves subjects here, but they are treated in discussions of plants and methods.

Though this book is written specifically for Southern California, parts of it may be of help to gardeners everywhere who have greenhouses. It can also help those who live in Mediterranean or subtropical climates throughout the world who can use it like an encyclopedia of subtropical gardening. (Gardeners in other parts of the world will need to vary the month-by-month schedule to fit their climate. Temper-

ature requirements will apply anywhere, but some specific recommendations, such as the ingredients of planting mixes and names of products, must be altered to fit what's locally available.) Many of the "quick tips" and step-by-step planting and growing directions can be helpful to gardeners anywhere.

Our Unique Schedule for Garden Tasks. Gardening in Southern California offers endless adventures. It can be a delight, but in order to garden here successfully you have to understand the many problems and solutions that are unique to our region. If you don't have a certain amount of local know-how you won't be able to avoid the pitfalls and reap the rich rewards. Of all the conditions and problems that make gardening in Southern California quite different from anywhere else, there's none more characteristic than our scheduling. Given our climate and our soil, when, what, and how should we plant, propagate, fertilize, and prune?

That's why this book is arranged month by month and is meant to be used as a handbook—really to hold your hand as you garden. You'll find step-by-step how-tos and special gardening techniques for the particular plants you grow, and as you apply them, develop the local savvy every Southern California gardener needs.

Special Helps in This Book. While organizing the month-by-month chapters I found that some topics could only be covered in one specific month—pruning roses in January, for example—but other topics could have been discussed in any one of several months. For instance, planting and harvesting bananas is discussed in August because it's a hot month, but I could have covered that subject in June or July. So each chapter begins with a brief table of contents and ends with a checklist of what to do in that month, and the page number next to each item tells where that topic is discussed in detail, so you can refer to it easily no matter which month's chapter it's in. Also use these lists to check off jobs after they're completed. Remember as you consult the checklists that no gardener is likely to grow every plant mentioned, and don't be overwhelmed by the number of jobs they recommend.

For topics of special interest to you, by all means consult other books—guides to native and drought-resistant plants, say, or to pruning. A number that I recommend are listed in the bibliography. This book wasn't designed to aid in plant identification. If you don't know all the plants that are mentioned, the best way to learn them is to search them out at nurseries and botanical gardens or look them up in reference works. Some good aids to plant identification, too, are included in the bibliography.

Many horticultural terms are defined briefly where first used, as well as more fully in the glossary at the back of the book. Since a number of these terms are commonly misunderstood, or incompletely understood, just browsing through the glossary may answer many questions. Additionally, for rose growers, there is a chart of the Rose-Pro method at the end of the monthly chapters. It gives those who choose this highly effective method a one-page summation of the tasks throughout the year. The index will help you refer to any topic at any time of year.

Gardening is different in Southern California. Anyone who's ever gardened elsewhere will tell you that. It's not like back East where so many of us came from and I once gardened. It's not like England where I was born and began gardening at the age of three. It's not even like Florida, that other state that attracts retirees with year-round warm weather. Even people who've never gardened anywhere else soon realize how different Southern California gardening is; all you have to do is flip through any book on basic gardening to realize that much of the advice just doesn't apply here.

The Nature of Our Climate

What It Means to Live in a Mediterranean Climate.
Southern California is blessed with a Mediterranean climate, one of the most salubrious growing climates in the world. The main characteristics of a Mediterranean climate are mild winters with enough rain to support plant growth and warm and dry summers with virtually no rain. The factors that create our climate are much like those that create similar climates in other parts of the world: the Mediterranean basin, South Africa, central Chile, and southwestern Australia. Our distance from the equator makes our temperatures subtropical but our position on the southwest corner of a great land mass—in our case the North American continent—keeps our summers dry.

The Pacific Ocean, with its relatively even temperature, also keeps our climate mild. In general, the closer to the ocean your garden is the cooler it will be in summer and the warmer in winter. The farther inland you live the more extreme temperatures your garden will undergo.

What's a Climate Zone?
Within our overall Mediterranean climate there are many geographical variations. These are called plant climates or, more commonly, *climate zones*. Each of these is a geographical area in which the yearly temperature range, length of seasons, average precipitation, humidity, amount of sunshine, and other factors combine to make certain plants grow better than others. Climate zones are caused by masses of air moving over our varied topography of coastal plains, hills and valleys, central uplands, high mountains, and deserts.

Much study has been done on plant climates by the University of California Agricultural Extension and others. But because of the technical aspects of agricultural plant climates, many of which overlap, most California home gardeners rely on the zones and maps in the *Sunset Western Garden Book*. When I mention a specific zone in this book by number or name I'm referring to the zones found in this widely respected work. Usually, however, areas are described here in more general terms, such as "coastal" versus "inland" or, in some cases, a little more specifically as "gardens in inland valleys" contrasted to "right along the beach."

How to Recognize Microclimates in Your Garden.
In addition to major climate zones there are also minizones, called *microclimates*. (Microclimates are small areas within a climate zone: wherever conditions favor the growth of some plants and not others because of factors of climate particular to that spot.) Every neighborhood, every yard has physical characteristics that produce slightly varying climates. Some plants may flourish on the east side of your home but die or do badly on the west. South-facing hillsides collect warmth and are especially good places for growing tropical plants; north-facing hillsides are cooler and thus good for camellias and azaleas.

Gaps on slopes let cold air drain off, while depressions, solid hedges, and walls catch or hold it. Garages, bushes, and walled patios can trap cold air in winter and warm air in summer, creating a more extreme climate than in the rest of the garden. Places that are open to the sky are more likely to be hit by frost than covered areas, because heat absorbed by the earth and by plants during the day radiates up to a clear open sky and is absorbed by the atmosphere.

How Santa Ana Winds Affect Our Weather.
One climate factor that cuts across several zones in Southern California, and determines the condition of the weather temporarily in any it touches, is the Santa Ana wind. (A *Santa Ana* is a dry wind, at its worst a gale force, that blows from a vast interior region to the sea and may strike several times a year, most often between October and March. Santa Anas usually last from one to three days.) Though Santa Anas disrupt what we think of as "normal" weather patterns, they're as natural to our climate as

winter rainstorms. Similar winds are not unknown in other Mediterranean climates.

Santa Ana winds damage plants by their force, drying out their leaves through excessive transpiration and sometimes killing new plantings. When these winds strike, gardeners should make sure plants are well watered. Hanging baskets and delicate container-grown plants should be misted and moved to areas protected from sun and wind.

Plant Choice

The Varied Palette. One of the things that makes gardening in Southern California so much fun—yet also a challenge—is the wide range of plants we can grow. Although we can't grow plants that need a long period of winter chill in order to bloom, such as peonies, Bing cherries, or most Eastern lilacs, we are able to grow a great many plants common to cold-winter climates, such as wisteria and privet. Among flowers and vegetables, most annuals and selected perennials flourish here. Native plants and those that hail from Mediterranean climates similar to ours broaden the palette still further. We can also grow many tropicals and subtropicals from all over the world, especially those from higher elevations. This mix of plants from many regions, with strong tropical and subtropical accents, is what gives our gardens their characteristically Southern California look. It's almost impossible to take a photograph of a local scene without a palm tree, an orange tree, a hibiscus, or some other exotic-looking plant in the background.

The Specialty Plants. Among the many species we grow are groups often called *specialty plants*

because they require special attention and
know-how. These plants and classes of plants
include camellias, ferns, fuchsias, begonias,
daylilies, hibiscus, geraniums, irises, roses,
orchids, epiphyllums, cacti and succulents,
bromeliads, palms, bonsai, vegetables, bamboo,
rare and tropical fruits, and California native
plants.

Specialty plants engender such enthusiasm
among hobbyists that they have fan clubs called
plant societies made up of people—beginners and
old-timers alike—devoted to their culture.
One of Southern California's most valuable
botanical resources is its incredible number of
active chapters of plant societies, and the emi-
nent experts who are members. One of the best
ways to learn how to grow specialty plants is to
join a plant society or simply attend one or
two meetings.

Most of us grow some or all of the specialty
plants in our homes and gardens. You'll find
advice as to their care throughout this book.

Soil Problems and Solutions

How Plants Depend on Soil. Good gardening
begins with good *soil*, the surface layer of earth
that supports plant life. Soil is made up of
particles of weathered rock, organic matter, air,
water, and microorganisms. Plants anchor
their roots in it and get most of their nourishment from it; thus the health of your plants
is largely dependent on the condition of your
soil. *Fertile soils* contain many elements and
properties, like minerals, organic matter, and
good drainage, that make plants thrive, while
poor soils are low in them. If you live in Southern
California and have poor soil, you're not alone;
that's what many of us have to begin with.

The Improvements Humus Makes in Soil. The best
way to improve almost any soil is by working in
organic soil amendments. For small areas use a
spade to dig the amendments into the ground;
for large areas, rent a machine and rototill
the amendments into the ground. As organic
matter decomposes in the ground it becomes
humus, or largely decomposed animal and vegetable matter. The decomposition of organic
matter, including the chemical properties of
humus, improves soil's fertility and structure.
Without humus, minerals can be chemically
locked up so plant roots can't use them. Humus
helps sandy soils hold water and it helps clay
soils to drain.

In the West, where rainfall is sparse, our soils
are generally very low in humus, while in the
East, where rainfall is greater, most soils contain
a high percentage of it. Humus doesn't stay in
the ground forever; it gradually breaks down. So
nature constantly replenishes her rich organic
soils with fallen leaves, rotted twigs, grass, and
animal matter. In your Southern California
garden, it's up to you to do this job.

Some organic materials that have a low
nitrogen content, including hulls, nut shells, and
wood or bark chips, are suitable only as *mulch*
(a layer of organic matter that's applied to
the surface of the soil to reduce evaporation,
cool the soil, and discourage the growth of
weeds). These should not be dug into the soil
until fully decomposed, or they'll rob nitrogen
from the soil as they rot.

Sawdust can be either worked into the soil as
an organic amendment or used as mulch, but it
does rob nitrogen from the soil as it rots. In
order to safely counteract this process, add
nitrogen to the sawdust prior to digging it into
the ground. To use sawdust safely follow this

☞ **Rule of Thumb**: *Add 1 to 1½ pounds actual nitrogen to every 100 pounds of raw shavings*. For a layer of sawdust you've spread 1 inch deep over 100 square feet, the nitrogen required would be that in approximately 1 pound of ammonium sulfate. (The specific recommended ratio by weight is 1.75 parts of nitrogen to 100 parts of unrotted organic matter.)

Besides the nitrogen you supply when you apply the sawdust, so it can decompose without robbing the soil, add nitrogen fertilizer regularly to feed plants. When using raw sawdust as mulch you must compensate by feeding plants more often. The ☞ **Rule of Thumb** is: *When using sawdust as mulch, increase the nitrogen fertilizer you would regularly give your plants by one-fourth and feed them at more frequent intervals.*

You'll find many other ☞ **Rules of Thumb** scattered throughout this book. They're designed to help you do things right the first time instead of learning by making mistakes. Of course you may think rules are meant for breaking, and there's some sense to that. No rule fits every occasion; an experienced gardener knows when and if a particular rule can safely be broken. But unless you're experienced, rules are like helpful guideposts on the road to successful gardening.

Your Soil's pH Value. Another factor that determines how well plants grow in soil is its *pH* value, its degree of acidity or alkalinity. The pH scale is numbered from 0 to 14, with 7.0 neutral. As values decrease, soil is increasingly acid; as they rise above 7.0, the soil is increasingly alkaline. For most plants a soil pH of 6.0 to 7.0 is ideal, because the elements that are essential for plant growth have their maximum availability

in this range. However, a soil pH between 5.0 and 8.0 is usually satisfactory. Certain plants, like azaleas and camellias, are called acid loving because they grow best at a soil pH of about 5.0.

In the eastern part of the United States most soils are too acid for cultivated plants, so farmers and gardeners add lime to make them more alkaline; in other words, they raise the pH level. Many Western soils are too alkaline, so when necessary we make them more acid by adding soil sulfur, or such acidifying organic soil amendments as leaf mold, pine needles, peat moss, or wood shavings—to put it another way, we lower the pH level.

Your Soil's Texture. Before beginning any program of soil improvement, find out what type of soil you're dealing with so you can assess its strengths and weaknesses. Soil is usually classified according to its *texture*, which means the size of the particles that are in it. The three basic particle sizes from largest to smallest are called sand, silt, and clay, and a mixture of all three of them is known as loam. All of these basic soil types can be found in Southern California; often more than one occurs in a single garden. Soils with particles larger than sand are often called gravelly soils. Decomposed granite is a gravelly soil with unique qualities and is found in many parts of Southern California. (Some decomposed granite soils might almost as well be called sand or loam; what distinguishes the granitic soils is some particles that are larger than sand.)

• **Sandy Soil.** Sandy soil is a loose earth mainly composed of tiny particles of rock between 2 and .05 millimeters in size. It feels scratchy or gritty to the touch. If you grip a damp handful, it won't hold together. Water and nutrients drain right out before plants can take a gulp. Sandy soils are often called light because they're easy to work. Their best qualities are their ease of digging and good drainage. Their worst problems are their failure to hold water and nutrients. Another vice of sandy soil is its apparent "hunger," since it eats up organic materials so rapidly. When completely dry some sandy soils are difficult to get wet because the individual grains of sand have become coated with organic fats and waxes from decomposing organic matter, such as eucalyptus or acacia litter.

If you have sandy soil dig in copious organic amendments, apply mulch, and where necessary, use chemical penetrants (surfactants) to wet dry soils and aid water penetration. Don't let sandy soils dry out completely. Use slow-release chemical fertilizers or organic fertilizers, since these won't wash out of the soil as quickly as other types. Mixing polymer granules into the soil under the roots of plants at planting time can also help sandy soils retain water. (Polymer granules, such as Broadleaf P4, are tiny free-flowing particles made up of synthetic organic molecules that can hold up to 170 times their weight in water. When used as a soil amendment they can greatly increase the water-holding capacity of sand and other growing media. Plant roots penetrate the water-filled granules and thus receive a continuous supply of water on demand.)

• **Silt.** Silt is a fine-grained earth mainly composed of particles that are rounder and more weathered than sand particles, and intermediate in size between sand and clay particles.

If you rub it between your fingers when moist, it feels smooth, slippery, and soapy, but not sticky. Silt holds more water than sand but less than clay. It's often found in river bottoms and on valley floors. Silt drains better than clay, yet holds more water than sand. It retains humus and nutrients a little longer than sand. On the other hand it compacts when walked on to a much greater degree than sand. When wet it becomes almost like quicksand. Cultivating when it's too wet can make silt dense and restrict the free passage of air and water.

If you have silty soil fork in organic amendments at regular intervals, never walk on your vegetable rows or flower beds, and dig and cultivate only when your garden soil is moist and not soggy.

• **Clay.** Clay soil is a firm, fine-grained earth containing a large amount of tiny mineral particles—less than .002 millimeters in size—that have negatively charged surfaces. The electrical charge helps clay retain positively charged minerals, like ammonium, potassium, calcium, and magnesium. Clay feels slippery and sticky when wet. If you grip a damp handful it will hold together in a solid lump. Clay soils bake hard in hot weather and hold moisture when wet. Their color varies from white, gray, and greenish to dark brown (*adobe*) or red (*terra-cotta*). Clay soils are often called heavy because they're difficult to work. Their best quality is their mineral richness, and their worst problem is poor drainage.

If you have clay soil work in organic amendments, apply gypsum, install drains, and build raised beds.

- **Loam.** Loam is a combination of clay, silt, and sand. There are many types of loam, depending upon the percentages of the components. Clay loams (those containing more clay) are heavy soils. Sandy loams are light. The best qualities of loam are that it's fertile and, whereas it holds water, it also drains well. Its worst problem is that it's easily compacted when moist.

  If your soil is loam maintain it with regular additions of organic soil amendment, and don't walk on your garden soil when it's moist.

- **Decomposed Granite.** Decomposed granite is a grayish or light brown, granular, and sometimes flaky soil mainly composed of variously sized particles of granite rock, some of which are larger in size than grains of sand. It feels loose, gritty, and abrasive to the touch. The unevenly sized particles are easily seen with the naked eye. On bulldozed ground and mesa tops decomposed granite is often packed down hard as rock, but when it's *alluvial* (deposited by water), in canyons and valleys, it's often loose and friable. The best qualities of decomposed granite are its excellent drainage, aeration, and mineral richness. Some alluvial types are easy to work. Water and nitrogen leach out of all decomposed granite soils quickly.

  If you have decomposed granite soil that is loose and friable, rototill it and add large quantities of such organic matter as nitrolized wood shavings, mushroom compost, green manures, or various animal manures—for example, poultry manure. But if you have the type of decomposed granite that is hard as rock plant in raised beds or, alternatively, use

a back hoe to plow up the surface of these hard areas, then mix in organic amendments and some topsoil; finally cover this with a foot of topsoil.

Finding and Solving Difficult Problems and Conditions. Regardless of which type, or types, of soil you have, you may have to overcome several frustrating problems and negative conditions before you can grow a good garden. The problems most often encountered in local gardens are hardpan, rock-filled soil, root-filled soil, and saline soil. Some of these problems may not be obvious at first glance so it's important to know how to recognize them, as well as how to deal with them if they appear.

- **Hardpan.** Hardpan is a layer of hard compacted soil of any type cemented together by minerals and almost impenetrable by roots or water. Often it's buried beneath a layer of good soil. This is typical of housing developments where a layer of topsoil has been applied over bulldozed subsoil. The problem with hardpan is there is no drainage. Roots go down, hit bottom, and are stopped cold.

  If you have hardpan install French and conventional drains, or plant in raised beds. In some localities, you can dig down in the bottom of each planting hole and break through to a porous layer before planting individual shrubs and trees. When adding a layer of topsoil over hard subsoil, rototill and amend the bottom layer first.

- **Rock-filled Soil.** Rock-filled soil is any type of soil that's largely filled with pebbles and rocks or shallowly based on rocky outcroppings. Rocks often have beauty, practical value, and design potential, but rocky soil is difficult to dig, may have poor drainage, and may not contain enough soil to support plant life. Roots of trees may not be able to penetrate the rock substrate.

If your garden suffers from rock-filled soil build raised beds and terraces, and fill them with topsoil or organic materials such as nitrolized wood shavings and mushroom compost. Use hardscape, container plants, and hanging baskets. Grow rock-garden plants and *epiphytes*. (Epiphytes are plants that grow on other plants but don't sap nourishment from them, as do parasites.) In some areas, holes that drain can be blasted for trees.

• **Root-clogged Soil.** In many old gardens the soil is made hard, dry, and impenetrable by the roots of such invasive trees as eucalyptus, Monterey cypress, and melaleuca. Old trees offer charm and their shade is helpful for some plants, but often water won't penetrate the root-clogged soil. Additionally the ground can't be spaded, tree roots invade planters from below, and new plants can't get started.

One solution is to plant in raised beds; in some cases they work indefinitely. If eventually they too fill with roots, grow plants known for their ability to survive despite competition from tree roots, such as ivy, periwinkle, leather leaf fern, asparagus fern, yuccas, agaves, aloes, and succulents. Cover bare ground with river rock and paving stone. Add hardscape and plant in containers. (Place stepping stones under containers to prevent tree roots from invading them from below.)

• **Saline Soils.** Saline soil can be soil of any type that contains enough salt to be injurious to plants. This is a frequent problem in desert areas where salts accumulate in the soil from salty irrigation water, fertilizers, and manures, and rainfall is insufficient to leach salts to lower levels. Salt injures roots and burns foliage; it may even kill plants. Sometimes evaporation lifts salts into the top layers of soil. Then capillary action pulls the water to the surface, where it evaporates and deposits a white salt crust.

When irrigating saline soil be sure to apply a volume of water adequate to wash the salts out of the top levels of earth down into the ground. Use the furrow system for vegetables but don't plant in the middle of the top of the mound, because salts accumulate there; plant close to the edge of the mound. Construct watering basins for larger plants. Use mulches to reduce evaporation of water from the soil surface. An application of gypsum followed by heavy watering may leach away enough salts to reclaim some salty soils.

When You Begin with Bare Ground. In many cases, new home owners start out with nothing but bare bulldozed ground. All *topsoil*, the uppermost, more fertile layer of soil, has been scraped away. This leaves nothing but bare *subsoil*, the lower layer that usually has lower fertility and a different texture and color than topsoil. In some cases what's left can hardly be called soil at all. But don't give up in dismay. By working in large amounts of organic soil amendments that will gradually break down in the soil, most subsoils can be eventually turned into topsoil. Additionally, the cycles of wetting and drying of the soil that are a natural part of gardening can actually improve the soil's structure. The very process of growing plants with fibrous roots that penetrate the ground can also help to break it apart.

There are two main ways to fix up a bare, bulldozed yard of rock-hard subsoil so plants can grow in it, and either will work if done right. The first method is to add topsoil. But when adding topsoil it's important to avoid creating interfaces. Don't just layer it on top; amend the subsoil first. Remove and haul away at least a foot of the existing soil. Create a proper marriage of soils by rototilling the subsurface and mixing into it soil amendments and some topsoil. Then replace the removed foot of soil with high-quality amended topsoil. Also, if the soil is clay add agricultural gypsum (as discussed below) according to package directions.

The second way to make bulldozed ground into real garden soil is to amend the earth you've got. This method is the less expensive and is used on most commercial and residential sites. First have a soil sample tested. Next, unless you plan to fill depressions or mound the ground, haul away several truckloads of the native soil to make space for the amendments. Rototill 8 inches deep, or—better yet—use a backhoe or plow to loosen the ground a foot deep. Add chemicals and fertilizers as indicated by your soil test, plus organic amendments measuring between 25 percent and 50 percent of the volume of soil you're amending. This means working a 4-inches-deep and preferably 6-inches-deep layer of well-rotted or nitrolized organic amendment, such as nitrolized wood shavings, into the top 8 to 12 inches of ground. Don't skimp on the organic amendments!

How Gypsum Helps Some Clay Soils Drain Better. Sodium pulls clay particles closer together. This makes the soil denser and less easily penetrated by water. When clay particles in the soil have accumulated a high level of exchangeable sodium (alkali), gypsum or calcium sulfate ($CaSO_4$) can loosen the soil and help it drain. Gypsum added to soil releases soluble calcium, which replaces some of the sodium on the clay particles and thereby produces a more open soil structure. Gypsum will not correct poor soil drainage when it is caused by physical conditions, such as fine texture or compaction. Soils that have these problems can be improved by incorporating large quantities of organic matter.

Gypsum is a relatively inexpensive soil amendment. Adding it to clay soil often helps and won't hurt. In most cases, apply enough to make it look as though a light snow has fallen (between 2 and 5 pounds to 100 square feet), and then work it into the ground. As much as 10 pounds per 100 square feet can be used on clay soil prior to seeding or sodding lawns.

How to Check Drainage Prior to Planting. Most plants need good drainage, so after digging a planting hole and prior to planting use this method to check the drainage. First, fill the hole with water and let it drain out. Then fill the hole a second time. Place a yardstick across the hole with its side touching the surface of the water, and make a note of the time. Return several hours later and measure how far the water level has dropped below the yardstick. The ☞ **Rule of Thumb** is: *If the water level in the planting hole drops one fourth of an inch or more per hour, drainage is adequate. If the water level* *drops less than one tenth of an inch per hour, drainage is too poor for most cultivated plants.* In that case, install a drain, construct a raised bed, or choose another spot.

If you're planting on a slope you can install a *sleeve drain* (a pipe, often covered by gravel, that drains water from the bottom of a planting hole and releases it further down on the slope). If hardpan is a problem try to break through to a level that drains and then install a *chimney drain* (a narrow hole filled with fir bark or sand that extends below the planting hole into a layer that drains). If you can't penetrate all the way through hardpan, it's better not to dig a hole into it as this only creates a basin that will fill with water.

Raised beds need only be 8 or 12 inches high. Build the sides of the bed of rock, brick, concrete, or wood, loosen and amend the subsoil under the bed to create a marriage of soils and fill with good amended topsoil. For large trees dig the planting hole down through the raised bed into the lower level. Roots will reach down and out, and your tree will eventually get established in the native soil beneath.

Fertilizer Basics

Plants not only need humus, they need *fertilizer.* A fertilizer is any material, either organic or inorganic, that supplies elements essential to plants for growth. Our native Southern California soils contain only small quantities of nitrogen, which is probably the most important element plants need. Thus we must add it in some form or our plants will go hungry. (Specific recommendations for feeding particular plants are given throughout the month-by-month chapters.)

The Meaning of the Numbers on a Package of Fertilizer. Every package of fertilizer has a trio of numbers on the label. The first number is the percentage (by weight) of nitrogen in the product; the second is the percentage of phosphorus; the third is the percentage of potassium. These three elements, known simply by their chemical symbols as N, P, and K, are found singly or in combination in many fertilizers. For example, fertilizer labeled 16-8-4 contains 16 percent nitrogen, 8 percent phosphorus, and 4 percent potassium. The remaining 72 percent is made up of other chemicals, such as calcium, sulfur, and oxygen, and some filler, which is added to the product in order to make it less concentrated and more easily measured and spread.

A high first number (nitrogen) means the product will give plants a lot of top growth, green leaves, and fast growth. Formulas with a high second number or second and third numbers (phosphorus and potassium) give plants the elements essential for flowering and fruiting. Both phosphorus and potassium promote overall plant health and stimulate growth of strong healthy roots, though in different ways.

Irrigation and Water Conservation

Our Dependence on Imported Water. In Southern California our rainfall is seasonal and the water we use for irrigation is imported, scarce, and expensive. During the last thirty or forty years our population has exploded while our water supplies have dwindled until the inevitable has at last become a reality; there's not enough water to go around. In good years when rains are adequate—and if we carefully conserve water—we can continue to keep our landscapes properly irrigated. But when there's a severe drought that lasts several years, like the drought of the late eighties and early nineties, water prices escalate, cutbacks are common, and in some areas it's against the law to water, or at least to water certain plants, such as lawns. These problems are likely to persist unless the state of California changes its priorities. (At the time this book is written agriculture uses almost 80 percent of California's irrigation water; homes and industries use 12 percent, and a relatively small amount—only 4 percent—is used for landscapes.)

But most Southern Californians deeply appreciate the value of plants and gardens and their importance to our quality of life. There's a growing awareness that landscape plants— especially trees—absorb carbon dioxide, give off oxygen, trap dust, muffle sounds, moisten and cool the atmosphere, and save power by reducing temperatures in buildings. Trees, shrubs, and— yes—even lawns make our cities and suburbs pleasant places in which to live instead of cheerless concrete jungles. Under the right conditions there's still a place for a few of the old favorites that need regular watering, includ-ing camellias, azaleas, roses, and hibiscus. How-ever, when water supplies are cut back painful choices must sometimes be made between plants worth saving and those that are expenda-ble. In such times use the precious water you have to save the larger plants and let the smaller and younger plants go. Lawns, flower borders, vegetables, ground covers, and young shrubs can be quickly replaced. But the mature and graceful trees, shrubs, and vines that add character to the landscape are irreplaceable.

When water supplies are cut back many garden plants, even deep-rooted camellias and roses, can stay alive with much less irrigation

than usual. (They'll just pull in their horns, produce no flowers, and stop growing; don't feed them.) But when water supplies are ade-quate remember that all garden plants need to be watered in order to survive, at least during the summer months. (Some native plants are exceptions.) Most plants need irrigation from time to time during the winter, too, and all plants, even drought-resistant ones, need plenty of water when they're first planted in order to get started.

Right and Wrong Ways to Irrigate. The many methods and the equipment for irrigating are about as varied as the plants we grow, but— aside from an old-fashioned watering can—it all falls into three basic categories. There are conventional underground irrigation systems, drip systems, and plain old garden hoses.

All automatic systems need to be regularly checked for leaks and malfunctioning parts. Also be sure your sprinklers are installed for proper overlap, to keep all plants evenly watered. A frequent problem with overhead sprinklers is that they can cause water to pour off slopes and dry ground and run into the street. Control clocks that pulse water, applying it in short bursts separated by timed intervals, can help prevent this problem by allowing adequate time for the water to sink into parched soil.

One of the best and newest ways to water plants is by using a drip, mist, or trickle system. Most of these systems feed water at controlled low pressure into an approximately ½-inch-diameter hose, or "header," which in turn feeds smaller spaghetti-sized hoses, or "microtubing," leading to individual plants. At the plants, "emitters" release a measured amount of water to root zones or mist the foliage. Some systems emit water through hoses buried in the ground. These include hoses made from recycled auto tires, which weep water from pores—gardeners call this "leaky-hose"—and perforated plastic Bi-Wall, a type of drip tubing especially made for watering row crops. Other systems allow you to convert your existing sprinklers to a drip operation. You simply unscrew the sprinkler head from the top of the riser, screw on the new drip attachment, and then connect up microtubes leading to specific plants. It's even possible to convert overhead irrigation of a small existing lawn; you remove strips of grass, install drip hoses a few inches under the soil surface, and replace the sod.

The worst way to water is to stand around, hose in hand, squirting water on bare ground. This only wets the surface, digs up the ground, and does more harm than good. If you must water with a hose, make watering basins around the root zones of shrubs and young trees, and build dikes of earth or bender board (wooden or plastic lawn edging) around flower beds. Lay the hose on the ground inside these areas and flood them.

How Your Soil Type Affects Watering. Some plants with shallow roots, including cool-season lawns, many annual flowers, and vegetables, need approximately an inch of rain weekly for optimum performance. Precise amounts and the intervals between watering can vary according to several factors; for example when the weather is windy, or hot plants lose moisture from leaves, they need more water. On an everyday basis soil type is the most important factor in how much to water.

Once clay soil has gotten thoroughly wet it hangs on to water much longer than sandy soil, which soon dries out. If you have clay soil you should water less frequently but for a longer time than a gardener living in the same area who has sandy soil. The percentage of humus in the ground can also affect water penetration and retention. Organic soil amendments help water penetrate clay soils faster and drain more quickly. The amendments do the exact opposite for sandy soil, making water penetrate slightly more slowly and helping soil retain water longer.

In general water penetrates sandy soil much faster than clay soil, so for sandy soil less is required to reach a given depth. The ☞ **Rule of Thumb** is: *One inch of water will penetrate sandy soil about 12 inches, loam about 7 inches, and clay soil only 5 inches, perhaps less.*

How to Measure Inches of Irrigation Water. An inch of water from an overhead sprinkler can be measured by setting out empty juice cans here and there, both close to and far away from a sprinkler. Measure the time it takes to fill the cans with an inch of water. (This technique can also be used to test a new irrigation system and locate dry spots in your sprinkler pattern.)

How to Find Out the Depth of Water's Penetration. You can't tell whether plants have enough water by looking at the surface of the ground. Sometimes the ground can look like a swamp on top but be dry as a desert underneath. At other times the ground may look dusty dry on top but still be soggy wet below. How do you really know whether water reached those roots? The best way is to dig down with a trowel or spade and take a look; if the soil is saturated with water below the roots of plants, there's water enough.

Other ways to test soil moisture are with a

soil probe (awl) or with a *tensiometer*. Though expensive, these instruments are a means to quantify moisture at specific depths of soil. A soil probe is a metal tube with handles on the top and a cut-out section on one side of the lower portion. Wind it manually into the ground a few inches at a time, then pull it up and remove the earth trapped in it. Keep repeating the process until eventually you get a soil sample from the required depth. A tensiometer consists of a dial attached to a long metal probe, usually with handles at right angles so it can be thrust deeply into the ground.

How Shallow Watering Harms Plants. Shallow watering makes roots grow close to the surface while deep watering encourages them to reach far down into the ground. Deep-rooted plants go through winds and drought much better than shallow-rooted ones. Always water deeply and infrequently rather than shallowly and often. For trees and shrubs this means watering until moisture reaches 2 to 4 feet into the ground; for vegetables and perennials, 1 to 2 feet; for annuals, 6 to 12 inches; for cool-season lawns, also 6 to 12 inches; and for warm-season lawns, such as Bermuda, perhaps as much as 1 to 2 feet.

Why Overwatering Is as Bad as Underwatering. When plants are underwatered they show such signs of stress as wilting, browning, drying, and dropping of leaves, buds, and flowers—and eventually they die. It's equally as bad to overwater them. Too much water deprives roots of the oxygen they need to function and grow. Overwatering causes root rot and crown rot,

which in turn lead to softening, drooping, yellowing, and dropping of leaves. The plants become stunted and weakened, and often they die.

How Frequently Plants Need Irrigation. Most cool-season lawns, vegetables, and annual flowers have shallow roots and need to be watered more frequently than deep-rooted plants—at least once a week in warm weather, more often in hot, dry weather and in sandy soils. Some shade plants, such as container-grown fuchsias and impatiens, may need water every day. Most shrubs are able to go longer between irrigations, perhaps as many as ten or fifteen days. Many mature trees growing in clay soil can go several weeks between irrigations. But when you do water them water slowly for a long time, so it sinks deeply into the ground. Some established drought-resistant plants may need only one or two irrigations in summer; some native plants must have no irrigation in summer, or they may die from root rot.

How to Conserve Water by Using Your Local Evapotranspiration Rate (ET). Gardeners with lawns can conserve water by using an ET chart based on your local evapotranspiration rate (ET). (The ET rate is a number that stands for the inches of water that evaporate from the soil plus the amount of water that transpires through the blades of grass during a certain period of time.) The philosophy behind ET is that if it's possible to figure out the amount of water that leaves the soil and evaporates from leaves you can then determine how much must be replaced by annual rainfall combined with irrigation. ET rates are calculated by University of California scientists, and they vary by geographical area, and from year to year and even from day to day. Because of the variables involved they aren't perfect, but when used they do help eliminate over- and underwatering. ET rates can't be used in their pure form without doing some fairly complicated mathematics. Fortunately gardeners can benefit from ET rates without dealing with any of these difficulties. Charts designed for home gardeners are based on ET, but they are easy to understand and don't require you to do any figuring.

To obtain an ET chart telephone your County Cooperative Extension office or your local member agency of the Metropolitan Water District and ask for the current ET chart for the area in which you live. These charts tell you when you should water your lawn and for how long. You can then save water by basing the irrigation of your lawn on your local ET chart for the appropriate time of year. Also check the lawn for signs of drying. If your lawn goes dry prior to the next suggested watering, you should water cool-season grasses slightly more frequently and warm-season grasses for a slightly longer time at each irrigation. Also, water less when the weather is cool and cloudy and more when it's hot, dry, and windy. Water much less in winter than in summer.

How Planting in Zones Saves Water.

Group plants according to their need for water. Grow plants with low, medium, and high water requirements in separate zones. This permits intelligent programming of watering to entire areas. If you mix plants with dramatically different water requirements, either the high water users will die of thirst or the low water users will die from rot.

How Plant Choice Can Save Water.

Choose drought-resistant plants for your basic landscape. Place plants that need more water in containers attached to a drip system, or grow them in the ground in small areas close to the house. Use drip systems for irrigating vegetables and annual flowers that need regular water. Grow these plants during years when rains are heavy and water supplies are adequate; cycle them out during drought years. If you need a lawn, plant a drought-resistant grass and keep the lawn area small. Most lawns, other than Bermuda and zoysia, use more water than many shrubs, trees, and flowers, and they're far more labor intensive. When properly designed, small lawns can be just as pleasing as large ones.

How to Make Artificially Softened Water Safe for Plants.

Many apartment dwellers have no water for irrigating plants other than artificially softened water. Long-term use of softened water is bad for plants. The sodium in softened water gradually builds up in containers, and eventually it makes the soil less permeable. The accumulated salts also harm plant roots and burn the tips and edges of leaves, turning them brown. To make artificially softened water safe to use on your houseplants, mix in ½ teaspoon of gypsum per gallon of water. In most cases this is enough gypsum to replace the calcium that was removed by the softening process.

How to Make Gray Water Safer for Plants.

Like water that's been artificially softened, gray water can also burn plants and tie up nutrients in the soil so the plants can't use them. (Gray water is the name given to water from sinks and bathtubs and from the rinse cycle of dishwashers and clothes washing machines.) As with softened water, gypsum can be used to treat gray water so it is less injurious to plants. First apply gypsum to the ground according to the directions on the package. If you use gray water often reapply gypsum occasionally—at least once every year or two. (Local regulations may allow you to use gray water for watering your garden in times of drought, but it can be hazardous to health if it is not applied properly. For various reasons it is against the law to use gray water in some areas. Ask your county health department for instructions as to its safe and legal use and follow them closely.)

No pastime is better exercise than gardening or is more rewarding, especially in Southern California—if you know what to do and when to do it. After a year or two of combining the information in the month-to-month chapters of this book with practical application in your own home garden, you'll be a seasoned, experienced, and knowledgeable gardener. What's more, you'll be getting results and having fun. And isn't that what it's all about?

JANUARY

JANUARY

The Bare-Root Month

In cold-winter climates gardeners rest from their labors in winter, but in Southern California we garden year-round. Our gardening year starts in January, and it begins with a flurry of activity. Many tasks throughout the year are seasonal, so if you don't get to them one month you can do them the next. But January's jobs can't be put off. The main tasks—prune deciduous fruit trees if you haven't already done so, prune roses, dormant spray, and put bare-root plants into the ground—must be done now. February will be too late. Coastal gardeners can start this month to feed their citrus trees. (If you live in an inland valley wait until March.) There are also many flowering plants to care for and, as in every month, chores for keeping up lawns and vegetable gardens.

Despite the fact that January is our coldest and sometimes our wettest month, it's often one of the nicest times to work outdoors. Good days are crisp and clear, perfect for gardening and for making the gardener feel even more optimistic than usual. So rejoice that the holidays are over, dig in, and enjoy the promise of a New Year, which to the true gardener is always the same: this year the garden will be better than ever before.

Bare-Root Planting

January is often called the bare-root month because a great many plants are available at local nurseries during January in bare-root form. *Bare-root* describes a plant that has had all the soil taken off its roots before shipping. Only plants that go dormant in winter can be bare-rooted. In our region the major items sold this way are roses (discussed in a separate section, below); cane berry bushes; deciduous fruit trees; ornamental deciduous trees and vines; strawberries; and a few vegetables, including artichokes, asparagus, horseradish, and rhubarb.

There are definite advantages to buying plants bare root. Not only are they usually cheaper than plants in containers but the selection of plant material, especially of roses and fruit trees, is far greater. (See the accompanying boxes for how to plant bare-root trees and roses.) But before you dash out and start recklessly filling your car with bargains, a word of caution: more mistakes are made in plant choice now than at any other time of year. Unfortunately, some local nurseries, discount houses, and do-it-yourself centers still carry bare-root varieties that are poor choices for our climate. Asking for help may do no good, because the salesman may know less than you do about gardening and in particular may never have heard of a chilling requirement.

Choose Low-Chill Varieties. A *chilling requirement* is the number of hours between 45°F (7°C) and 32°F (0°C) that a deciduous plant needs in order to grow, flower, and fruit. It applies particularly to deciduous fruit, nut, and ornamental flowering trees and to berries. It's not the depth of cold that does the job but the length of time in hours that the plant undergoes the cold temperatures. Lengths of time necessary for proper performance may vary, according to variety, from hundreds to even thousands of hours.

If a plant suffers lack of its required winter chill buds won't open properly or will open unevenly. Leaf buds need even more winter chill to break their dormancy than flower buds. If a tree doesn't have enough leaves it won't grow well, and its fruit will sunburn. Fortunately there are many fine varieties of deciduous plants with low chilling requirements, those that need few, if any, hours of cold in order to bloom and bear. Refer to the lists in the encyclopedia section of the *Sunset Western Garden Book*.

Choose Cane Berry and Blueberry Bushes Adapted to Our Climate. Bare-root cane berries, grape vines, and blueberries are available at many nurseries now, but again, some nurseries still sell varieties that won't bear fruit in Southern California. Look especially for Rabbiteye blueberries. These were developed in Florida and Georgia and bear delicious berries here. You'll need at least two bushes, for cross-pollination. Plant them so the root ball is slightly high. They need acid soil mix, acid fertilizer, good drainage, and ample moisture; in short, care and planting much like that for azaleas, except with full sun.

Check Whether You Need a Pollinator. *Pollination* is the transfer of pollen from the *anthers* (the male part of flowers) to the *stigma* (female part). Some fruit plants are self-pollinating; bees and other insects carry the pollen from flower to flower on the same plant. Others are cross-pollinating; they need another plant, called a pollinator, in order to bear fruit.

Don't Let Bare-Root Plants Dry Out. Purchase bare-root plants early in the month. The early shopper gets the best plants. If you buy them with roots wrapped by the shipper leave them in their containers, and keep them in a shady

How to Plant a Bare-Root Deciduous Fruit Tree

- Choose a spot in full sun with good drainage and adequate space for the tree to grow. (If space is limited choose a dwarf tree, or plant so you can espalier, training it on wires; on an arbor; or against a preferably east-facing wall.)

- Prune off any damaged or broken roots, and plunge the remaining roots into a bucket of water to soak while you dig a hole.

- Dig a planting hole and check the drainage (as described on p. 10).

- If the soil is heavy clay work at least 2 pints of gypsum into the soil in the bottom of the hole. It will do no harm, and it may improve drainage.

- If gophers are a problem line the hole with a basket made of poultry wire to protect the roots while the tree is young.

- Hold the tree in the hole so that the bump on the *bud union* faces north, to shade it from the sun, and the original soil line (look for it below the bud union) is 2 inches higher than the surrounding ground. (The bud union is the location where the variety was grafted onto the rootstock; on trees it usually appears as a slight bend in the trunk or a change in its width.)

- Backfill the hole by sifting the native soil you took from it back into the hole around, through, and over the roots. (Don't add soil amendment unless you're planting in pure sand.) Plant high, so that as the tree grows the area where the trunk meets the ground is high and dry.

- Press down with your hands to compact soil around and over the roots.

- Make a watering basin. Mulch the ground around the plant and in the basin.

- If the tree does not already have a good branching habit prune it immediately after planting: cut the tree to a height of 30 inches to 36 inches above ground. Remove most of the side branches (if side branches are present) except those needed for main-scaffold limbs. You can produce a low-branching tree by choosing to keep three low branches that are not exactly opposite each other.

- To protect the trunk from sunburn paint it with flat white latex paint (not enamel) that you've slightly diluted with water.

- Water deeply by allowing the hose to lie on the ground and trickle into the hole until it penetrates around the roots. In fast-draining sandy or decomposed granite soil, water often until the tree is established. If drainage is poor or if the soil is heavy clay, check once a week and water when the soil begins to dry out. Gradually lengthen the intervals between irrigations.

place until you're ready to plant. The packages usually contain enough moisture to keep the roots in good condition until the end of the month, but the sooner you plant, the better. (Beware of packaged plants on display in full sun, since the roots may be dried out or damaged by heat.)

If you purchase your bare-root plants at a nursery that sells them loose in a bin of shavings you have the benefit of choosing specimens with good, strong root systems but also the responsibility to keep them moist. Once you get the plants home soak the roots in a pail of water for an hour or two and then plant right away. If that's impossible heel the plants in. To *heel in* means to dig a shallow trench in a shady spot, lay plants on their sides with their roots in the trench, cover the roots thoroughly with soil up to the soil line, and water well. It takes only a few minutes to heel plants in, and it can save them from ruin if you don't get around to planting as soon as you'd hoped. Heeled-in plants can survive at least six weeks, though it's best not to leave them that long because by then they'll have started to grow.

Deciduous Fruit Trees

All deciduous fruit trees need to be pruned for good shape from "childhood" up, and to bear well they need to be pruned at least once a year. The time to do the major pruning is January (unless you already did the job in December). The ☞ Rule of Thumb is: *deciduous fruit trees should be pruned during winter while the trees are dormant and after the leaves have fallen to the ground but before new buds have swelled.*

Each type of fruit tree needs to be pruned

differently, so it's important to know which kind of tree you're pruning and how to prune it properly. For example, apples bear their fruit on spurs that bear again and again, sometimes for as long as twenty years. If you whack off all the spurs you'll have no fruit. In general apple trees need very little pruning once a main framework of branches has been established.

Plums also bear on spurs. The pruning of mature European plums is minimal, as for apples, but Japanese plums grow so vigorously that they need heavy pruning of new growth. Apricots bear partly on one-year-old wood and partly on spurs that continue to bear well for four or five years. They must be pruned so as to replace one-fifth of the bearing wood by heading back older branches. Peaches and nectarines need the heaviest pruning of all: their fruit is borne on one-year-old wood. By pruning them hard, you encourage new growth to replenish fruiting wood. Figs need very little pruning at all except to control tree size and foliage density.

Not only different varieties but individual trees vary in the pruning they need. And no two trees can be pruned exactly alike; basic guidelines will apply differently according to the placement of their branches, their age, and their overall vigor.

Only an expert can keep all the complications of pruning clearly in mind. If you're not an expert follow a pruning manual that applies to mild climates and contains charts. (Martin's *How to Prune Fruit Trees* is one; I often consult more than one book, because each one says things differently.)

After pruning deciduous fruit trees, clean up the ground under the tree and follow up with dormant spray, as explained on page 28.

* ✳ *

The Basic Categories of Roses

Hybrid Teas are the most popular garden roses. They usually produce one flower per stem, on plants from 2 to 6 feet high. Grandifloras are bigger and taller, sometimes 8 to 10 feet high. Floribundas produce quantities of flowers in clusters on bushy plants usually shorter than Hybrid Teas. Polyanthas have smaller flowers than Floribundas carried in larger bunches on many canes.

Climbing roses come in several types. Some, such as climbing *sports* (mutations exactly like the parent except for growth habit) of Hybrid Teas, are everblooming. Many old-fashioned climbing types bloom mainly in spring. Climbing roses send up long bendy canes that usually don't end with a flower bud like standard roses; most of the flowers occur on side shoots that spring from the canes. Some types of climbers can be used as ground covers, and some can be grown as large free-standing shrubs, but most need support, such as a large tree, a fence, or an arbor. Pillar roses are similar to climbing roses. They have tall canes that are less bendy than those of climbing roses. They can be trained straight up a post or pillar or the corner of your house and will bloom all the way from the ground to the tops of their canes.

Miniature roses are natural dwarf versions of all the above types of rose. The only difference is that their canes, stems, flowers, and leaves are scaled down in size. There are other types of roses, including many fine old-fashioned varieties, but those listed here are the ones most frequently grown today. Though Hybrid Teas are still the local favorite, Floribundas, climbers, and old-fashioned roses are gaining popularity because they give more color and charm. Many old-fashioned roses and modern shrub roses (those with a more graceful shape than the stiff Hybrid Tea rose bush) are disease resistant and easy to grow.

* ✳ *

Roses

January is an important month for rose care because this is the time to choose and plant bare-root roses, prune the ones you've already got, and spray with dormant oil. It's also the time to choose a method of fertilizing your plants, though not to feed with nitrogen.

Choose a Method of Fertilizing. Most gardeners don't fertilize roses this month, because the ☞ **Rule of Thumb** for beginning to fertilize roses is: *wait until the leaves unfurl and change from red to green before feeding roses with nitrogen.* However, throughout the monthly chapters you'll find a choice of two fertilizing systems for roses. One system is to purchase a commercial rose food and use it according to package directions. This is the easiest method and requires no thinking other than remembering to feed your roses monthly throughout the growing season. Your other choice is to feed your roses with generic fertilizers according to a system I call the Rose-Pro Method (based

✳ ✳ ✳

How to Plant a Bare-Root Rose

· Examine the roots. Prune off any broken or damaged portions. Then stick them in a bucket of water to soak while you dig a hole.

· Choose a spot in full sun, and dig a hole approximately 1½ feet deep and 2 feet wide.

· Be sure to check the drainage (as described p. 10) and make sure it's adequate. It's possible to grow roses in red clay or adobe—they thrive in heavy soil—but they won't grow in a swamp.

· Unlike tree planting, rose planting calls for amending the soil, because the root system is smaller. So unless your soil is superior loam you'll need some good organic soil amendment, either a bagged commercial type or homemade compost, to mix with the earth you take from the planting hole. (Manure can be used as mulch but not in the hole.)

· Build a cone of mixed soil on the bottom of the hole, firming it with your hands. Set the plant on top, and spread the roots out over the cone. They shouldn't bend on the bottom of the hole. If they do, start over and dig deeper.

· Check your soil level with a stick. The bud union should end up 2 to 3 inches *above* ground level. Most roses do better with the bud union (that knob at the base of the plant) aboveground, so don't bury it, as they do in the East or Midwest. Plant high, because if you add mulch yearly, as you should, the bud union can get buried.

· Backfill the hole to the correct planting depth, firm the ground around the roots with your gloved hands, mulch the ground over the roots, and build a watering basin.

· Place the hose into the watering basin and let the water trickle in slowly, to water the roots thoroughly. In fast-draining soil, water daily for the first three days and twice a week for the next three weeks. In moist, heavy soils, check the soil twice a week and water when needed. Thereafter apply adequate water—preferably by means of a drip system—to saturate the root zone once or twice a week, depending on the weather, your climate zone, and your soil.

✳ ✳ ✳

largely on the work of San Diego rosarian Richard Streeper, and summarized for the whole year in the Rose-Pro table on p. 319). You'll find this system slightly more complicated and time-consuming than using rose food, but it's very effective and much less expensive, which can be a help if you grow many roses.

If you plan to use commercial rose food don't fertilize this month. But if you opt to follow the Rose-Pro Method feed your roses this month as follows. Give all plants 2 tablespoonfuls of Epsom salts (magnesium sulfate) to provide magnesium. Also give all newly planted roses 1 cup of superphosphate and all established plants ¼ cup of superphosphate. (Phosphorus is longer lasting in soil than nitrogen; this is the only time during the year when you'll need to give your plants this nutriment.) Sprinkle the Epsom salts and superphosphate on the ground over the roots and water them into the soil. (When planting bare-root work the superphosphate into the soil under the roots at planting time.)

Select Bare-Root Roses. To get the best choice of rose varieties and plants go to the nursery as soon as possible this month, but study a good handbook first (such as Ray and MacCaskey's *Roses: How to Select, Grow and Enjoy*). Choose not only for color and fragrance but for basic categories of growth habit (see accompanying box), disease resistance, vigor, and your climate zone. Some roses are more heat resistant than others. Roses with fewer petals generally do better along the coast than those with many petals, because there isn't enough heat for

many-petaled roses to open completely. It's possible to save money by purchasing old varieties that are no longer patented, but it's not wise to skimp on grade, which is determined by law and labeled on each plant. Always buy No. 1 grade plants. They have more roots, bigger canes, and a better shape, so you end up with a healthier and more vigorous plant.

Also consider water conservation. Limit the number of roses you plant by the amount of irrigation you'll be able to give them. Grow roses in a zone devoted to plants that have similar high requirements for water; don't put them close to drought-resistant plants. Install a drip irrigation system to water your roses, and place at least three emitters around each bush in order to soak the entire root zone. Or make a circle of any soaker tubing, including leaky-hose, that can be curved. (Don't use Bi-Wall; it works only for straight rows.) If you plant roses close to the house you can supplement their irrigation in times of severe drought with gray water.

Prune the Roses You Already Have. Prune your rose bushes in January before new growth starts. (See the large box for directions.) Choose a day after a good rain, or irrigate the day before you prune. Assemble your tools. You'll need pruning shears (the blade type that slice like scissors, not the snap-cut type that can squash the bark), long-handled shears, a keyhole saw, pruning compound or a white latex glue, a pair of leather gloves, and some knee pads. You'll also need to know what kind of roses you've got.

✳ ✳ ✳

How to Prune a Rose

The Basic Principles

If you moved to Southern California from a cold-winter climate forget what you may have learned there about rose pruning. In the East and Mid-west, roses are pruned hard in fall—down to 12- or 18-inch stubs—so they'll survive the winter. Here we should never shorten a healthy, productive cane. The more good wood left on the plant, the earlier it flowers and the longer it lives—so don't cut your plants way down. Try never to cut lower than your knee. Many of our roses can be left 4 feet tall after pruning, but the canes that remain should be thick and healthy ones.

Bush Roses

· Start by removing all wood that is dead, damaged, or diseased.

· Remove all twiggy growth (smaller than the thickness of a pencil). It simply won't produce.

· Remove all old, spent canes. These are the ones that look tired and woody and produced nothing but spindly wood and inferior flowers last year. Get down on your knees and saw off the old canes right at the bud union—here's where your keyhole saw and knee pads come in handy. Saw off any old stubs, too. Sawing is not only easier than cutting, it stimulates production of new canes. However, if you have a great many roses and not much strength it's better to use a ratchet-type pruner than not to take off old stubs and canes. (Ratchet-type pruners are long-handled blade-cut pruners with a built-in ratchet device that makes it easy to cut through thick, hardwood branches. They're expensive and usually only available by mail order.)

· Leave all the good strong canes in place, at least four or five per plant (five to seven for plants over five years old; more for some Floribundas).

· For all bush roses remove all branches that cross. Try to open up the centers so each plant takes the shape of a vase. In interior valleys it's a good idea to leave a few branches that cross the center in order to give shade, but gardeners elsewhere should cut off all branches that cross the center.

· For Floribundas cut out the center branch from each cluster of branches, and cut the other ones back to three or four *eyes* (undeveloped buds). On Floribundas leave more twiggy growth—you can even use hedge shears on them to get the right shape.

· For tree roses cut back the branches to be between 1 foot and 18 inches in length, depending on the age of the rose. (As tree roses age leave their branches longer.) Remove all sprouts arising from the roots or trunk. Aim for symmetry: a rounded bush on top of the upright trunk.

· Miniature roses resemble large roses in every way except size, so for these follow the instructions for full-sized roses but scaled down proportionally. Shape ground-cover types with hedge shears.

· For full-size roses remove about one-third of all growth that was new last year, but don't cut into any new growth that's thicker than your thumb.

Make Clean Cuts. When making all cuts, in order to slice cleanly, put the blade of the pruner, rather than the anvil, next to the part of the plant that's going to remain. Cut closely above a promising outside bud, so new growth will point outward. Cut ¼ inch above the bud; even closer if you can do so safely. Make your cut straight, not slanted. A sharp angle can dry out wood and kill the bud.

Remove the Suckers. *Suckers*, on roses, are canes that spring from below the bud union. Instead of growing from the bud union like the canes of the variety you want, they grow from the rootstock. Suckers are usually easy to recognize because they're thinner and more prickly than the canes that arise from the bud union, and their leaves are usually smaller and shaped differently from the other leaves on the plant. If allowed to persist they'll sap strength from your varietal rose.

Suckers are easiest to reach after the major pruning is complete. The best way to get rid of one is to grasp it firmly with a gloved hand, work it back and forth and around and around to loosen it, then pull it off with a mighty yank. If you can manage this you'll get the bud cells along with the stalk, but if instead you cut it off two or three more suckers are likely to spring from the same spot.

Let Them Stand Tall. Finish the major pruning by cutting the tops of the canes so they're roughly equal in height. If any leaves remain on your plants when you are through pruning clip— don't pull—them off. Removing the leaves prevents the buildup of disease.

After pruning:

· Your Hybrid Teas should stand 2 to 3 feet tall.

· Grandifloras should be 4 to 5 feet tall.

· Floribundas and Polyanthas should end up about knee high with a round, bushy shape.

· Miniature roses should be between 6 inches and 3 feet tall, depending on their age and variety. (These roses vary greatly in size according to type and age.)

Finish Up. Paint all cuts on the bud union with pruning compound or white glue to protect them

from rot. (This treatment is unnecessary for cuts higher on the plant.)

Clean up the ground under and around the plants. Destroy all leaves and debris. Then mulch under your plants with steer manure or— better yet—with compost. Follow up with a dormant spray (as discussed below), such as Orthorix. Wait until new growth unfurls and turns from red to green before feeding.

Climbing and Pillar Roses

Young climbing roses (particularly those less than two years old) should be pruned little or not at all. Do prune all everblooming climbing roses that are more than three years old now.

Climbers that bloom only once a year should be pruned when they finish blooming, but if this task was neglected old spent canes and all sucker growth should be removed now. Clean up and dormant spray those that drop their leaves in winter. (Before spraying, clip off any leaves that remain except from species roses that are evergreen in mild climates, like *Rosa banksiae*, 'Lady Banks' Rose'.)

Climbers that are arranged sideways on arbors and fences and espaliered on walls can bloom for many years on the same old canes. If this is the method you choose then be sure to remove unwanted canes as they arise throughout the year. Eventually, if the roses decline in vigor, allow new canes to grow and replace the old ones. With pillar roses it's better to cut out one or two old woody canes yearly and allow new, vigorous canes to replace them.

Here's the procedure.

· Remove all dead or twiggy growth extending from the bud union.

· Leave all good, well-placed canes on the plant.

· Remove any suckers that arise from below the bud union.

· Cut back all *laterals* (side branches) to two or three buds each.

- Clip off all remaining leaves. (In cold climates rose leaves fall in winter. Here we often have to defoliate most or all by hand.)

- Untie the rose and reposition it on its support. Climbing roses bloom mainly on laterals that spring from the canes. In order to encourage them to put out more laterals and thus to bloom more, train the canes as horizontally as possible, either onto a fence, into an existing tree, over an arbor, espaliered on a wall, or with the tips of the canes pegged to the ground, giving the plant the shape of a fountain. Pillar roses are an exception. You can tie all the canes of a good pillar rose in a vertical position, onto a post, say, or the corner of your house, and it will bloom massively all the way from the ground to the top of its canes.

- Clean up and mulch the ground, and follow up with a dormant spray, such as Orthorix.

Dormant Spray

Dormant spray is any insect or disease-control spray—such as horticultural oil, lime-sulfur, or Orthorix—that's applied after a *deciduous* plant has gone dormant and dropped its leaves. (Deciduous plants are those that drop their leaves during dormancy. Many other plants are said to be dormant in winter even though they may not be deciduous. Don't spray these, because strong concentrations of oil sprays are damaging to leaves and can burn them.)

If you grow roses or deciduous fruit or ornamental trees you should dormant spray these plants every winter after their leaves have dropped off, to prevent the buildup of disease. If any leaves are still clinging to the plant in January they should be clipped off prior to spraying.

Even organic gardeners who eschew chemical sprays should use dormant sprays. Since they're applied in winter they don't harm beneficials and can't contaminate fruits; it's virtually impossible to grow certain plants, particularly peach trees, without using them. Of course you should always follow label directions and use safety measures when handling chemical sprays. Wear protective clothes, boots, rubber gloves, goggles, and mask.

What Dormant Sprays Do and How They Work.
Dormant oil sprays are used to control overwintering mites and insects, such as scale and certain caterpillars, by coating their bodies and suffocating them. Various types are available, so choose one that's recommended for the specific plant or plants you want to treat. In the case of peach trees and nectarines it's important to use lime-sulfur, to prevent peach leaf curl. This is a fungus disease that causes the leaves of peaches and nectarines to become curled and misshapen and then drop off the tree. The fruits may have warty areas on them. Severely infected trees that aren't treated for several years will decline and may die. Lime-sulfur also controls certain mites and overwintering spores of other fungus diseases.

Timing of Spray for Peach and Nectarine Trees. Peach trees and nectarine trees should be dormant sprayed twice: once after the leaves fall in November or December and again in January before the buds begin to swell. If you didn't spray in November or December, spray twice in January, once early in the month and again two weeks later. If you use lime-sulfur and rain occurs within forty-eight hours, treat again. It's best not to spray if a heat wave is expected, because if temperatures rise above 90°F (32°C) soon after treatment lime-sulfur may injure buds. Use a proper sprayer—one with which you can aim the spray onto the tree rather than broadcasting it into the air—and go over the tree carefully, reaching all parts.

Dormant Spray for Sycamore Trees. Sycamore trees (*Platanus* species) are hosts to a flock of pests and diseases, among which sycamore scale (*Stomacoccus platani*) is one of the worst. Sycamore scales overwinter on bark as eggs, then in spring attach themselves to the undersides of leaves and suck out plant juices. This creates yellow spots that eventually turn brown and causes leaves to drop prematurely. The scales also feed on young twigs and limbs, causing dieback and weakening the tree.

To find out whether your tree suffers from scale look for cottony white masses of material bulging from cracks and crevices in the bark. This cottony substance protects overwintering eggs. Affected trees must be thoroughly sprayed now with a high-volume, high-pressure spray in order to get rid of these eggs. It's almost impossible for a home gardener to do the job right, since professional equipment is needed. The procedure is to use dormant oil at the rate of 2 gallons of oil to 98 gallons of water, with

Quick Tip

How to Keep Skunks Out of Flower Beds.
Protect your spring bulbs and annual flowers from being crushed by skunks. Don't throw away the thorny canes you prune off climbing roses; bend them around the borders of your flower beds to make a low fence. Peg them in place with bent sections cut from coat hangers. The canes will soon be hidden by foliage and flowers, but skunks won't cross the thorny barrier.

How to Fertilize Citrus Trees

- Determine how much fertilizer a tree will need during the year and divide this quantity by the number of applications you want to make during the year.

- Use a coffee can and a bathroom scale to weigh the amount needed for each application. (Mark the level and poundage on the can and keep it to use again. That way you won't need to weigh the fertilizer each month.)

- Scatter the contents of the can evenly on the ground in a 3- to 4-foot wide, doughnut-shaped band centered under the drip line (an imaginary line directly under the branch tips). The main feeder roots of a mature citrus are in the top 2 feet of soil beginning 2 or 3 feet from the trunk and extending out twice as far as the drip line. You can, if you wish, distribute the fertilizer over this entire area.

- Water the fertilizer deeply into the ground, right away. (Don't work it into the soil.)

a wetting agent (surfactant) also mixed into the spray. Make sure all precautions are followed during the spraying, and finish by cleaning up fallen leaves, twigs, and debris. (See p. 51 for more about sycamores.)

Citrus Trees

Start Fertilizing Citrus in Coastal Zones. If you live in a coastal zone January is the time to start feeding your citrus trees. (See the accompanying box for directions.) By fertilizing your trees now you'll promote more blossoms in February and thus a more abundant crop. If you live in an interior zone where frosts continue through February and sometimes into March, don't start feeding your citrus trees until March. Feeding too early might encourage a flush of growth that could be damaged by frost.

Citrus trees are heavy feeders. A mature tree growing in clay soil needs 1 pound of actual nitrogen per year, but that's not the same as a pound of dry fertilizer. Let's say you choose a balanced granulated fertilizer such as 16-8-4 or a slow-release fertilizer such as 17-6-10. Since the first number stands for the percentage of nitrogen in the mix you'll need to feed about 6 pounds of either of these products to each full-grown tree. Feed young trees proportionately less. For example, a one-year-old tree could be fed ¼ pound of actual nitrogen per year. A three- or four-year-old tree can use ½ pound of actual nitrogen per year. When a tree is six or eight years old it can usually be given the full amount. In fast-draining soils, such as sand or loose decomposed granite, use more fertilizer—up to 1½ pounds of actual nitrogen per year.

If you live in a coastal zone, divide the total

amount of granulated fertilizer needed for each tree into six equal doses. Give one feeding per month from January through June. If you live in an interior climate zone, divide the total amount of granulated fertilizer needed into four equal doses. Apply the first dose in March and the remainder at monthly intervals through June. Slow-release fertilizers are more expensive but more convenient, since they require less-frequent application. Divide slow-release fertilizer into two equal applications. Apply the first in January if you live in a coastal zone, late February inland, and the second in June if you live on the coast or July in the interior.

Correct Chlorosis. Give iron and zinc to citrus trees now if they show signs of *chlorosis* (iron deficiency). Plants suffering from chlorosis have light green leaves with dark green veins. Don't use iron sulfate. It can't be absorbed by the tree, because it combines with minerals in the soil and becomes insoluble. Get the chelated kind that's combined with zinc. Apply it, according to package directions, evenly to the ground around the tree, along with the fertilizer when you apply it. For faster results purchase a product for foliar application and spray it onto your tree. Overwatering can cause chlorosis, so proper irrigation is often the best treatment.

Irrigate Citrus. Water mature citrus deeply and infrequently—perhaps once every two or three weeks depending on the weather and your soil type and drainage—rather than shallowly and often. Frequent shallow watering can harm citrus; it encourages shallow rooting and causes root and trunk rot.

Make sure sprinklers don't hit the trunk of any citrus tree. A wet trunk can lead to gum-mosis (oozing sap and sunken lesions on the trunk, caused by fungus disease). The ☞ **Rule of Thumb** for watering citrus is: *Apply water so it sinks into the ground around the tree in a broad doughnut-shaped band beginning one third of the distance from the trunk to the drip line and extending an equal distance beyond the drip line.* The area of ground next to the trunk of the tree should be kept high and dry, with no soil pushed up against the trunk. If water is collecting in the wrong places build a wide double-walled watering basin around the tree at the drip line to keep the irrigation water there and away from the trunk.

Control Citrus Pests. Check trees for insect and disease damage (as described on p. 49). Be on the lookout for snails. In inland valleys snails often spend the winter snuggled together in the crotches of orange trees. You can clean your entire tree of snails now by picking them off, tying them into a plastic bag, and tossing them into the trash. Once snails have been removed clip off bottom leaves that brush the ground. Some gardeners find that surrounding the trunk of each tree with a copper band prevents snails from crawling back up it. (These and further snail and slug controls are discussed on p. 73.)

Camellias and Azaleas

Plant and Clean. Camellias and azaleas are two of our most prized plants for permanent winter color in semishade. Both camellias and azaleas have a long bloom cycle that starts in fall and lasts through spring, but not all varieties flower at the same time. Some varieties may open as early as October; others don't flower until April or May.

✳ ✳ ✳

How to Plant Camellias and Azaleas

- Choose an area in semishade. Most camellias and azaleas need some sun in order to bloom. Morning or evening sun is best—not midday. Good spots are in dappled light under lath, shade cloth, or an open tree, or to the north of a house, hedge, or wall.

- Choose an area with good drainage, especially for azaleas. If you don't have such an area, use raised beds or tubs filled with an acid-type potting mix.

- Slide the plant out of the container, hold the root ball over a bucket or wheelbarrow, and wash off the top inch or two of soil. (It might have picked up petal blight in the nursery.) Pour a little bleach in the removed soil and water and discard this away from the garden, preferably in a deep hole.

- Dig a planting hole 1½ times as deep as the root ball and twice as wide.

- Amend the soil from the hole by mixing it with one-half acid-type soil amendment, such as commercial camellia-azalea mix, leaf mold, or premoistened peat moss. (Be sure to moisten peat—see tip—because dry moss sheds water. If you plant with dry moss it will stay dry and kill your plants.)

- Plant camellias and azaleas high. They can't stand to have soil collecting around their trunks. Measure the height of the root ball and the depth of the hole. Add as much amended soil as needed to bring the top of the original root ball 2 or 3 inches higher than the surrounding soil.

- Gently lift the plant into the hole, face it with the best side to the front, and backfill the hole with amended top soil.

- Use your hands to press the soil mix firmly around and over the roots. Replace the layer of soil you previously washed off, but don't make it thicker than it originally was.

- Form a watering basin, and mulch the ground over the entire bed with an acid mulch, such as pine needles.

- Place the hose, running gently, into the watering basin and allow the water to thoroughly penetrate the root ball and the surrounding ground, while you go on to the next plant.

- Water daily for the first three days and frequently thereafter until the plants are established. Then lengthen the periods between irrigations.

✳ ✳ ✳

As a general rule you can safely plant any camellia or azalea during a cool winter month, including this one (see the accompanying box for directions). But the best time to plant a specific variety is while it's actually bearing flowers. This is because the roots and branches of camellias and azaleas rest rather than grow during their bloom cycle, and the minute they finish blooming they start a spurt of growth. If you plant them while they're in bloom they get off to a good start, but disturbing roots by planting later interferes with their normal development.

When you shop for azaleas, don't just fall for a pretty face; select good varieties. To find them, refer to lists in the *Sunset Western Garden Book* and ask experts for recommendations. Belgian Indicas, developed for florists, are often difficult to grow. Alaska, Phoenicia, and Formosa are easy for beginners. (The last two, sometimes taken to be identical, are not the same. Formosa has larger leaves and is often used as under-stock.) Don't be misled by the term "sun azalea." These varieties can take more sun and interior heat than most azaleas, but they will die if you put them in full sun. The exception is in the fog belt along the coast. Some camellia and azalea varieties can stand full sun along the coast if grown in the ground, not pots.

Protect Camellias from Petal Blight. Pick up dead and fallen petals and flowers from camellias, daily if possible, in order to prevent petal blight. *Petal blight* is a fungus disease that causes brown, discolored, rotting blooms—not just at the petal tips, as can be caused by wind or rain, but brown to the center. Blighted blossoms that fall to the ground permit the fungus to live and

Quick Tip

How to Get Peat Moss Wet.
Pour a soup pot full of boiling water on a wheelbarrow full of peat moss, add water from a hose, and mix with a shovel. Let this sit several hours to cool. When using a lot of peat moss wet it in batches, and cool the batches by spreading them on a paved area such as the patio or driveway.

Quick Tip

A Time-Saving Way to Foil Petal Blight.
Cut shade cloth in circles, with a hole in the center and a slit from the outside of the circle to the center hole. Place under potted or ground-grown camellias during the flowering season. When blossoms fall pull out the fabric, shake it into a waiting trash can, and replace it under the bush.

Quick Tip

Prune Camellias as You Pick Them.
Whenever you leave the house break off a few blossoms, each with a short piece of stem and a few leaves. Give them to whomever you meet at work, the bank, the store, you name it. It's all the pruning most camellias need.

reproduce in the soil for years. Spores can be carried by the wind from nearby gardens.

Cleanliness is the best way to avoid petal blight, but if you're troubled with a serious outbreak the chemical spray Bayleton can be an effective control. Add a spreader-sticker such as Spraymate, according to package directions, when you mix the spray. (A *spreader-sticker* is an additive that decreases surface tension of water, making sprays cover plant surfaces more evenly and effectively.)

Protect Azaleas from Petal Blight. Petal blight also attacks azaleas. To control it remove dead and brown blossoms—and while you're about it, snap off the little seed capsule inside each flower with your thumbnail rather than leaving it on the plant. Long-blooming varieties, such as Alaska, California Sunset, and Nuccio's Happy Days, will be stimulated to produce even more flowers.

Watering

It's tempting to neglect watering chores when the weather's cool and plants aren't growing, but properly irrigated plants stand up better to frost than plants with dry roots. Even when it rains don't forget those specimens under the eaves that aren't getting a drop. Many a poor camellia or tree fern has died an untimely death just because the gardener forgot that while Mother Nature will gladly rain on everything she can reach, she doesn't own a garden hose.

Coping with Frost

Move Container Plants to Safety. Many a balmy December is followed by a sudden cold snap in

January. Protect tender container-grown plants such as impatiens, fuchsias, and cymbidiums from frost by moving them under the eaves of your house or beneath a sheltering tree. Injury is more likely for plants exposed to an open sky. Cold air can often be trapped in an atrium or courtyard surrounded by walls, or even hedges. So don't choose these spots for sheltering treasured tropicals. Move them to places from which cold air can escape.

Cover Plants in the Ground. Protect tender plants growing in the ground, such as agaves, aloes, Natal plum, bougainvillea, and cineraria, by throwing old sheets, towels, canvas drop cloths, car covers, or cardboard boxes over the plants. In interior zones use tall pea stakes (as described on p. 258) or hoops of heavy-gauge wire to support cloth above the plants, since the fabric may sometimes become cold enough to damage foliage it touches. Dash out first thing in the morning and uncover the plants before sun strikes. Heat builds up quickly under covers and can burn foliage as badly as frost.

Don't Prune Off Frost Damage. If, despite all your care, some tropicals are damaged by cold, resist the urge to prune off the unsightly dead parts. The frost-burned portions will protect the rest of the plant. Removing frost-burned leaves and twigs now can be disastrous, causing the plant to grow and then be hit again, worse than ever, if more cold follows. So hold off until the weather warms up and all danger of frost has past. (Then, you may find plants not as badly damaged as you think.) The ☞ **Rule of Thumb** is: ***Wait until you see signs of regrowth, before cutting off frost-damaged growth.*** Large branches may not recover until summer. (Paint bare limbs with whitewash to protect them from sunburn.)

Epiphyllums

Start feeding epiphyllums with 0-10-10 or 2-10-10 liquid fertilizer every two weeks to encourage spring and early summer bloom. Even if you've neglected them and they look scruffy don't feed with higher than 2 percent nitrogen now, or you'll trigger growth instead of flowers.

Don't prune epiphyllums until after the bloom cycle. It's all right to cut off badly diseased or rotted branches, but like excess nitrogen, extensive pruning will make your plants grow rather than bloom. Plants should have some sun now, not solid shade.

Cymbidiums

Purchase cymbidiums now, while they're in bloom. Continue to feed those that haven't yet bloomed with a high-bloom formula (p. 229). Stake bloom spikes, and protect the plants from snails and slugs. Once blooms open stop feeding the plants but keep them well watered. Put plants that are blooming in a cool, shady spot to lengthen flower life.

Enjoy some cymbidiums in the house, too, but don't let them sit in puddles. Put gravel in plant saucers and cachepots to hold roots safely above water that drains out the bottoms of the pots.

Color from Permanent Plants

A well-planted garden in our area can have perennial color year-round. If your garden needs some pepping up consider adding one or more of the following January-blooming plants. Among drought-tolerant plants that give color now are many named varieties of New Zealand tea tree (*Leptospermum scoparium*), Bailey's acacia (*Acacia baileyana*), Kaffirboom coral tree (*Erythrina caffra*), and many species of aloe. By choosing aloes with care you can have varieties in bloom any month of the year, but most of the aloes we grow here are from South Africa so they flower in winter, a time when the insects that pollinate them are most active.

Less drought resistant but still beautiful are deciduous magnolias, such as *Magnolia soulangiana* or *M. stellata*. These trees stay small for a long time and are good in flower and bulb beds, entryways, and small-space gardens; against a dark wall; or in Oriental gardens. A striking plant for winter bloom is the pink powder puff bush (*Calliandra haematocephala*), at its best espaliered on a sunny wall. Orange marmalade bush (*Streptosolen jamesonii*) needs plenty of water but gives bright orange bloom at this time of year in frost-free zones. (It's lovely when planted above a retaining wall and allowed to cascade down it.) Outstanding choices for purple bloom are the vine *Hardenbergia violacea* 'Happy Wanderer' and the Brazilian shrub called princess flower (*Tibouchina urvilleana*).

Flower Beds and Containers

Plant Cool-Season Flowers. If you planted winter and spring bedding flowers in September and October you can congratulate yourself now because many should be flowering, especially in coastal zones. But in January nurseries are brimming with *cool-season flowers* (annual and perennial bedding plants that bloom in winter) already in bloom. These include cyclamen, English primroses, malacoides primroses, obconica primroses, calendulas, pansies, johnny-jump-ups, violas, stock, and snapdragons. So if you didn't plant before and your flower beds and pots need sprucing up, or if you have bare patches in your beds, use nursery transplants to fill them with instant color.

Fertilize Cool-Season Flowers. The trick with cool-season flowers, other than wildflowers, is to give them plenty of nitrogen for strong growth, as well as high phosphorus for bloom and some potassium for general plant health. The reason for the extra nitrogen is that it tends to leach from the soil during the rainy season. Also, fungi and bacteria in the soil are less active in cooler weather, so nutrients are not released as quickly from organic matter. This is especially true of plants growing in containers. (In general use liquid or slow-release fertilizers for winter flowers in containers, pellet or liquid fertilizers for plants in the ground.)

Feed Cineraria. Feed cineraria (*Senecio hybridus*) once every two weeks for growth, with a liquid fertilizer high in nitrogen. Once buds show switch to a high-bloom fertilizer such as 2-10-10, to stimulate production of large flowers. Watch for leaf miners; if necessary, spray with a systemic such as Orthene to control them. (Mix it with a spreader-sticker such as Spraymate in order to increase effectiveness. Also check that your bottle isn't outdated.)

Should You Plant Seeds? January isn't one of the best times for planting seeds, but that doesn't mean it's impossible to plant. Seeds of California poppies and other wildflowers, gaillardia, clarkia,

godetia, and sweet alyssum (*Lobularia*) will sprout and grow if sprinkled onto well-prepared ground and raked in prior to rain. It's better, however, to plant wildflowers in fall (as described on pp. 256, 259). (Water seeded areas daily to keep them damp, when rains aren't adequate.)

Seeds of summer flowers started indoors late this month and *potted on* can give you an abundance of bedding plants to fill pots and borders in March or April in frost-prone inland areas. Use of a heat cable followed up by light from a fluorescent lamp (as discussed on p. 61) will help speed germination and grow stocky plants.

Coral Trees

Prune Naked Coral Trees. The naked coral tree (*Erythrina coralloides*) is one of the best coral trees for local gardens in Zones 21 to 24. Though slower to start it's a much better choice for home gardens than Kaffirboom coral (*Erythrina caffra*). It blooms spectacularly in spring on tip growth. Once a tree has become established prune it judiciously in January (heavily, when specimens get out of hand), during its brief dormancy, in order to bring out its artistically bizarre shape and stop it from becoming a tangled mess. Cut out branches that cross. Control size by cutting out unwanted branches. A word of caution: don't whack off all the tip growth or you'll lose all the flowers.

Don't Prune Kaffirboom Coral Trees Now. Many Kaffirboom coral trees (*Erythrina caffra*) are pollarded in winter—all branches are cut back so hard that only stubs are left at the top of a bare trunk. Pollarding coral trees permanently ruins their shape, makes them subject to rot, and prevents them from ever blooming. Prune

Kaffirboom coral trees, if necessary, by thinning out a few unwanted branches back to a main scaffold branch or trunk while leaving all desired growth in place, and do the job after rather than before bloom.

Kaffirboom coral trees eventually become giants, 30 feet high and 40 feet wide. Plant them in places where they'll have room to grow to full size, and don't plant them on lawns. The frequent watering lawns need is bad for Kaffirboom coral trees; it causes overly rapid growth with dangerously brittle, top-heavy branches. Most coral trees do better and bloom more beautifully when subjected to benign neglect, once established. When winter rains are adequate, and depending on the soil, mature trees in coastal zones can often go without irrigation until late summer before showing stress and needing a deep application of water.

Jobs for a Cold or Rainy Day

Start a Garden Notebook. If you don't know much about gardening keep a notebook to help yourself learn. If you're a seasoned gardener keeping notes can help you remember things you'd otherwise forget. There are several printed diaries on the market, but any notebook or calendar will do as long as there's plenty of room to write. Here are some ideas for items to include:

- Names of plants in your garden; new plants you learn about and hope to get some day
- Diagrams of the vegetable garden
- Sowing and planting dates and when plants first came up
- Dates of transplanting and harvesting

- Yields of vegetables and fruits plus the varieties grown
- Heights of perennials; times and durations of bloom
- Where you planted bulbs, plus how they did and where you got them
- Ideas, newpaper and magazine clippings, empty seed packets, tasks to remember to do
- Disease and bug problems and how (or if!) you overcame them
- If you watered automatically, how long you set the timer

Clean Out the Potting Shed. Another good task for a rainy day is to clean out the potting shed or tool shed, if you have one. If you don't, this is a good time to consider building one and getting the messy accumulation of garden supplies and equipment out of the garage. A serviceable shed for supplies and tools can often do more to promote domestic harmony than flocks of psychiatrists.

Order Seeds from Catalogues. Most seed catalogues arrive in January. Order now so you'll have the seeds in time for spring planting. If you've ever gardened in a cold-winter climate you probably remember the joy and temptations of poring over a seed catalogue on a snowy day.

The danger of ordering from catalogues when you live in Southern California is ordering not only too much but the wrong items for our climate zones. Check all new-to-you ornamentals by looking them up in the encyclopedia section of the *Sunset Western Garden Book*, so you won't be disappointed by trying to grow something that isn't suited to your climate zone or that needs to go through a freezing winter in order to perform.

The plus side of catalogue buying is that you can sometimes find rare items that aren't locally available. If you care about color schemes and don't always want a mixed packet, you can get flowers in specific colors. Many gardeners order vegetable seeds because they're fussy about varieties and enjoy growing gourmet varieties that they can't buy in the grocery store. Don't forget to add a package of nitrogen-fixing bacteria, such as Legume-Aid, to your order. If you plan to plant beans in March you'll need this product, which usually isn't available in local nurseries.

Studying seed catalogues can help beginners learn about annuals and vegetables, but be forewarned; many cool-season plants and flowers that are planted in early spring in the East are planted in fall here. When you live in Southern California you should think ahead and order seed for fall planting now along with the seed for spring. (Keep the seed cool and dry during the summer.) Or, if you prefer, order from catalogues again in summer for fall planting, though by then some items may be sold out.

Lawn Care

Cool-Season Lawns. Cool-season lawns, such as bluegrass, tall fescue, and ryegrass, are at their best now, so keep mowing them regularly and feeding them, at intervals of one month to six weeks with a soluble lawn fertilizer or with other products as directed. (Bluegrass, bentgrass, and ryegrass are bad choices for Southern California but, unfortunately, they're still planted.) Water all cool-season lawns when rains aren't adequate.

A healthy, well-fed lawn is more resistant to disease. If you notice unsightly red-brown pigment on grass leaves plus red dust on your feet after walking across your lawn, it's suffering from rust. This is a sign it needs feeding. You don't need to spray—just fertilize with nitrogen and mow regularly to remove the older, infected portion of the grass blades. The rust will disappear and the lawn green-up like magic.

Choose a Good-Quality Fertilizer. Low-cost soluble fertilizers containing nitrogen alone or in combination with other nutrients will give your cool-season lawn a quick green-up. Slow-release fertilizers are more expensive, but they last longer and are less likely to burn the grass. Heavy rains won't wash them out of the soil. Regardless of the type you choose spread the fertilizer carefully, according to directions, and beware of dumping when going around corners with a push-type feeder. Burn patterns are ugly and difficult to eradicate.

Warm-Season Lawns. Warm-season grasses, such as Bermuda, St. Augustine, and zoysia, are dormant now. They need no feeding or mowing. But watch dichondra for signs of insect damage and fungus in cool wet weather. Treat it if necessary with products that are recommended for dichondra pest and disease control.

Control Crabgrass with a Preemergent Herbicide. If annual weeds such as crabgrass were a problem last year, use a preemergent herbicide now or in early February to stop seeds in their tracks. Generally you'll be safe if you treat during the last half of January in coastal zones and in early February inland. Treat twice, with the second treatment two weeks after the first. You can, if you wish, be highly scientific about this task and use a soil thermometer. When the soil temperature reaches 63° to 65°F (17° to 18°C), that's the time to treat the lawn with a preemergent herbicide. If in the past you've had a terrible crabgrass problem, treat a third time in late March along the coast and in early April inland and catch the plants that come up later. Not all the seeds germinate at the same time, and even long-lasting products can wash out of the soil.

Some products have to be sprayed on. Others come in dry form. Always read the label carefully and follow directions exactly. Rate and time of application and safety precautions (such as keeping children and dogs off treated areas) differ from product to product. But be aware that most of the timing directions are aimed at gardeners in cold-winter climates. Thus many local gardeners make the mistake of treating too late for local conditions.

Check the Lawn Mower. January is also a good time to check over the lawn mower and make sure the blades are sharp. If necessary, have them sharpened.

Vegetable Gardening

Fill In with Transplants or Seeds. If there's any room available in your vegetable garden fill it with winter vegetables; use either transplants of broccoli, Brussels sprouts, cabbage, cauliflower, celery, lettuce, parsley, peas, and Swiss chard or seeds of beets, carrots, lettuce, peas, radishes, and turnips. Artichokes, asparagus, strawberries, rhubarb, and horseradish can be bought bare root. I list the last three with reservations. November's a better time to plant

strawberries (p. 288), and rhubarb is difficult in Southern California. I don't recommend growing it, because along the coast it doesn't get the frost it needs to develop good flavor, and inland it usually succumbs to root rot during the summer. (See pp. 93 and 64 for artichoke and asparagus planting directions.) Horseradish grows like a weed here. It's well worth growing but needs ample water plus room to grow. Confine it in a special place, such as a raised bed, or it can become a noxious and invasive pest.

Plant Lettuce. This is the best time for lettuce. It's easy to grow and a money saver. Plant either from transplants, which will give you a faster harvest, or from seeds (see box), which will give you more lettuce over a longer period of time. Lettuce seeds germinate within a wide range of soil temperatures (from 35° to 80°F; 2° to 27°C) but sprout quicker at cooler temperatures than warm ones, so this is a good time to plant them. Growing from seeds also gives you more interesting varieties to choose from, such as Rouge d'Hiver, a red Romaine, or "mesclun," the French-termed mix of red and green lettuces with herbs—especially pleasing to the gourmet.

Force Fava Beans to Bear a Crop. If you planted fava beans last October, by now they should be waist height. Protect them from being pushed over by rain or wind by adding a few bamboo stakes and connecting them with twine.

In some climate zones fava beans will bear crops without the aid of the gardener, but for a variety of reasons (including too much shade, water, or fertilizer) they may bear flowers but no beans. If that happens pinch off the growing tips of the stems. It's all right then to side-dress the rows with vegetable fertilizer

How to Plant, Grow, and Harvest Lettuce from Seeds

· Plant in full sun. (Lettuce can take some shade in summer, but not in winter.) Don't plant it in the same spot twice, or it may succumb to wilt.

· Dig deeply prior to planting. Mix in organic soil amendment and add fertilizer that's recommended for vegetables to the top 6 inches of soil, according to package directions.

· Distribute the seed down a wide row, or broadcast it on a raised bed at the approximate rate of 3 seeds for every 2 square inches of soil surface.

· Cover the seed very lightly with potting soil (about ¼ inch), and water by sprinkling lightly. Use a misting valve. Continue to keep the seed bed damp by sprinkling daily until the seeds sprout—three to seven days. Then lengthen the watering times and water more deeply. (If your lettuce seeds don't germinate, your soil may be too salty. Give the soil a long deep soaking to leach out salts. Plant again with fresh seed.)

· Stimulate fast growth with plenty of water and fertilizer. (Fast growth means sweet, crunchy lettuce, while slow growth makes it tough and bitter.)

· Protect the plants from slugs (p. 73).

· Thin seedlings according to package directions. Either eat the little thinnings or transplant them to an adjacent row.

· If you'd like to grow lettuce but don't have space, plant it in pots and half-barrels filled with potting soil. Feed every two weeks with liquid fertilizer recommended for vegetables.

· Harvest whole heads of lettuce, leave the roots in the ground, feed and water them, and they will grow new heads. Or lengthen your harvest by taking off only the outside leaves as needed.

according to package directions; gently cultivate it into the ground, and water deeply. Within a week of pinching the favas will start to bear beans. Wait until the pods are between 5 and 8 inches long and filled with beans before you begin to harvest.

Harvest Cole Crops. Here's how to harvest cauliflower, cabbage, and Brussels sprouts. When it's done correctly all but cauliflower will continue to produce.

As soon as you see the white *curd* (head) beginning to form on cauliflower, tie the leaves together over the top to protect it from sunshine. Sun turns cauliflowers green. (Even "self-blanching" types are best treated this way in our strong sun.) Untie and check them every few days. Suddenly a head will start to fill out. Then check that one daily for readiness.

A head of cauliflower is a flower in the bud stage. Harvest it just when the snowy white buds are all filled out but before they open. When you see the sections just beginning to loosen up and separate around the outside, cut the head with a knife below the curd. If you wait too long it will be overdone and ricey.

Homegrown cauliflower cooks more quickly than bought. Steam the whole head for three to five minutes, then test with a fork. No need for sauces; straight from the garden it's a tasty treat, one of the best vegetables.

After harvesting pull out and compost the plant. Replace it with something else, such as carrots or lettuce, not another *cole crop* (member of the cabbage family)—they all share the same diseases.

Broccoli is another edible flower bud that needs checking daily. Harvest by cutting stalks with a knife when the buds are filled out but still tight. Don't pull up the plants when you harvest; leave them in the ground and side dress the row with fertilizer. Unlike cauliflower, broccoli will branch and give you more crops. The farther down on the stalk you cut the fewer but the fatter will be the side branches you get. Many home garden varieties—Bonanza is one—are known for their ample manufacture of such second, third, and fourth crops.

Harvest cabbage as soon as the heads fill out and feel firm to the touch. If they give when you squeeze them they're not quite ready. As soon as they feel hard as a bowling ball pick them by cutting just below the head. If you wait too long they'll split.

To keep the plants going cut off the outer leaves but let the roots remain in the ground. Fertilize and water them and they'll form three or four baby heads, though these have a stronger flavor than the first harvest.

There's a trick to harvesting Brussels sprouts, and unless you practice it you may not even get a crop: As soon as the plant begins to manufacture sprouts pull off its lower leaves with a downward twisting motion, and take off a few of the tiny sprouts at the bottom of the stalk. This stimulates sprouts farther up on the stalk to grow faster. As the sprouts grow pull off all the remaining lower leaves that have sprouts above them, leaving a top knot of leaves at the peak of the stalk rather like a mini palm tree. This provides more room for sprouts and forces the energy of the plant into sprout production.

Harvest Brussels sprouts as soon as they're big enough to eat. Always take them from the bottom to the top. Side-dress the row with fertilizer and continue to water the plants when rains aren't adequate. They'll grow and continue to produce sprouts throughout cold weather.

Purchase / Plant

- ☐ Purchase and plant bare-root **roses, trees, vines, berries,** and **vegetables,** 19
- ☐ Choose and plant **camellias,** and **azaleas,** 31
- ☐ Purchase **cymbidiums,** 35
- ☐ Purchase and plant **cool-season flowers** to fill in bare spots, 35
- ☐ Plant seeds of **warm-season flowers** for transplants to put out in spring, 36
- ☐ Continue to plant **winter vegetables** from transplants and seeds, 39
- ☐ Many **succulents,** including **cacti,** bloom in winter and spring; purchase new types now, 185

Trim, Prune, Mow, Divide

- ☐ Prune **deciduous fruit trees,** 22
- ☐ Prune **roses,** 25
- ☐ Pick **camellias,** 33
- ☐ Deadhead **azaleas,** 34
- ☐ Don't prune off **frost damage,** 34
- ☐ Prune **naked coral trees,** 36
- ☐ Mow **cool-season lawns.** Most **warm-season lawns** are dormant now and don't need mowing, 38

Fertilize

- ☐ Choose a system for fertilizing **roses.** (Rose-Pro gardeners feed with Epsom salts and superphosphate.) 24
- ☐ Begin to feed **citrus trees** in coastal zones only, 30
- ☐ Treat **citrus trees** to correct chlorosis, 31
- ☐ Start feeding **epiphyllums** for bloom with 0-10-10 or 2-10-10, 35
- ☐ Continue to fertilize **cymbidiums** that have not yet bloomed with a high-bloom formula, 35
- ☐ Feed **cool-season flowers** (other than wildflowers), 36
- ☐ Feed **cineraria,** 36
- ☐ Fertilize **cool-season lawns,** 38

Water

☐ When rains aren't adequate water **all garden plants** according to their individual needs. (**Succulents** don't need water now, but **native plants** will perform better if given water in dry weather during their growing season.) 12

☐ Irrigate **citrus trees,** 31

☐ Remember to water **plants under eaves** where rains can't reach them, 34

☐ Water **cool-season lawns** when rains aren't adequate, 38

Control Pests, Diseases, and Weeds

☐ Dormant spray **roses** and **deciduous fruit trees,** 28

☐ Dormant spray **sycamore trees,** 29

☐ Check **citrus trees** for pests, 31

☐ Pick up dead **camellia** blossoms to prevent petal blight, 33

☐ Protect **cymbidiums** from slugs and snails, 35

☐ Control rust on **cool-season lawns,** 38

☐ Control **crabgrass** with preemergent herbicide, 38

☐ Watch **dichondra** for insect and disease problems, 38

☐ Check **trees, shrubs,** and **ice plant** in coastal zones for overwintering whiteflies. Control by spraying, 160

☐ Pull **weeds,** 170

☐ Spray **peach** and **apricot trees** for peach leaf curl, 286

Also This Month

☐ Protect **tender plants** from frost, 34

☐ Stake **cymbidium** bloom spikes, 35

☐ Start a **garden notebook,** 37

☐ Clean out the **potting shed,** 37

☐ Order **seeds** and **supplies** from seed catalogues, 37

☐ Check the **lawn mower;** have the blades sharpened if necessary, 39

☐ Pinch tips of **fava beans** if they fail to bear crops, 39

☐ Harvest **cool-season vegetables** as they mature. Harvest cole crops by individual methods, 41

☐ At month's end begin to check **bamboo** in coastal zones to see if it's time to propagate, 85

FEBRUARY

FEBRUARY

A Month for Waiting

In Southern California February feels like spring. Acacias decorate the roadsides, orange blossoms scent the air, the first bulbs come into bloom, and gardens smell inviting after rain. Native plants are in a season of growth, and cool-season garden flowers such as primroses, cyclamen, linaria, annual African daisies, and cineraria are at the height of their beauty. But despite appearances it's still winter. Most plants are growing slowly now, and the wise gardener knows never to rush the seasons. February is not a major planting month. If spring is in your blood concentrate on putting in those few items that can be planted now.

Though there are many interesting jobs to be done in February it's also a time for waiting. Certain plants can be pruned now, but wait until the weather warms up before cutting off frost-bitten branches. In cold low-lying gardens and interior valleys, wait until all danger of frost is past before you move those tender plants safely sheltered under eaves. Fertilize deciduous fruit trees—and avocados too, in coastal zones—but wait until next month to feed most

How to Feed an Avocado Tree

· Weigh the total poundage of fertilizer
you need for each monthly feeding on your
bathroom scale and divide it equally into
four coffee cans.

· Using gypsum as a marker divide the
ground under the tree into four equal pie-
shaped areas. Place one coffee can in each
pie-shaped section.

· Sprinkle the contents of each can evenly
over the ground under the tree from about
1 to 2 feet away from the trunk to the
branch tips, or drip line. (Avocados have
feeder roots just under the soil surface
beneath their entire leaf canopy.)

· Water deeply immediately after fertilizing.

of the landscape. Throw off your coat, dig in the
garden, prepare the soil, spread manure, start a
compost heap, but wait until March to put in
summer vegetables and flowers.

Avocado Trees

If You Use Commercial Fertilizer. A mature avocado tree needs at least 2 pounds of actual
nitrogen per year and varying amounts of other
nutrients, like phosphorus and zinc, periodically.
For the home grower the easiest way to go is to
use a commercial fertilizer specifically recommended for citrus and avocados that contains
nitrogen, phosphorus, potassium, and zinc.
If you do opt for bagged "citrus and avocado
food" follow the package directions, which
usually tell you to measure the girth of the tree
24 inches up from the ground and feed ½ to 1
pound per inch of girth. But if you have several
trees it may be less expensive to purchase a
large bag of generic fertilizer, with a formula
such as 25-18-10 or 16-8-4 or slow-release
17-6-10—good formulas for avocados, but not
magic numbers you absolutely must find.

When you use a product with 25 percent
nitrogen, you need to give 8 pounds of it to
each mature tree (eight or ten years of age) per
year. Give 12 pounds if you have selected a
product with 16 or 17 percent nitrogen. Give
young trees proportionately less. (For example,
you could give a three-year-old tree one-quarter
the total amount, a five-year-old tree half the
total amount, and a large tree over fifteen years
old—especially if it is growing in fast-draining
soil—as much as 3 pounds actual nitrogen
per year.)

Gardeners in coastal zones should divide the

total amount of fertilizer for the year into five equal applications and give one feeding each month from February through June. Interior gardeners should divide the total amount into four monthly applications and give one feeding per month from March through June. With slow-release fertilizers you can divide the fertilizer into two equal doses. Give the first dose early this month if you live along the coast, late this month if you live inland, and give the second dose in June.

If You Use Organic Fertilizer. Organic gardeners can feed avocados by spreading 25 pounds of aged chicken manure (available bagged under the name EZ Green in some Southern California nurseries) under each mature tree in February. Beginning in March, give each mature tree one trowelful of bloodmeal and one of bone meal every six weeks, through August. If mulch is thick sprinkle food underneath, and then replace the mulch on top.

Other Basic Requirements of Avocados. The main requirements of avocados are rich soil, excellent drainage, and a thick layer of mulch over the roots. Allow the leaves that fall to remain under the tree; don't rake them up. (Avocados are best planted at the back of the garden where their large leaves won't look untidy.) Add additional mulch to young trees.

Never cultivate or dig under avocado trees, because that would damage the roots and all your fruit might fall off. It's best not to grow anything under an avocado tree, especially if it needs frequent irrigation. Wet soil promotes root rot of avocados.

Citrus Trees

Feed Citrus in Coastal Zones. If you live in a coastal zone, fertilize citrus trees again this month (and every month through June, as described on p. 30). If you live in an interior zone, hold off fertilizing until March.

Control Citrus Pests. Citrus pests often step up their activity now. Books such as *Citrus, How to Select, Grow and Enjoy,* by Richard Ray and Lance Walheim, and the *Ortho Problem Solver* contain colored photographs to help you recognize specific pests and diseases. Use a magnifying glass to identify such pests as aphids, which cause curly leaves and sooty mold; mealy bugs, which also cause sooty mold; and woolly whitefly, which can be recognized by fuzzy white residue under leaves. Rust mites (the same pest as silver mite on lemons) cause reddish-brown fruit that spoils easily. Various scales attach themselves to trunks, twigs, and fruit.

Wash Citrus Trees. Of course you could have your trees professionally sprayed with chemicals specific to whatever pests you find. But one of the pleasures of growing your own fruit is knowing it hasn't been sprayed. Fortunately many calamities can be avoided by keeping trees clean. It's been proved that beneficial insects can't reach the harmful ones if the latter are hidden beneath a layer of dust. If the trees are dusty even after rain spray them with soapy water made with an insecticidal soap, such as Safer's, or a solution of 1 to 2 tablespoons of dishwashing liquid—the kind you use in the sink, not in a machine—per gallon of water. (Before spraying cut off the tips of branches that brush the ground, as described below, because they're a ready highway for ants.)

Washing trees can also help rid them of certain pests directly. Aphids, woolly whiteflies, and mealy bugs can be washed to the ground with a soapy spray. An even better job can be done if you're willing to get right under the leaves and manually scrub off aphids and other pests with a sponge or paint brush. I've done this myself and it doesn't rank high on my list of favorite jobs, but rubber gloves, a rain suit, and boots can make it bearable.

Cut Ants Off at the Pass. Although washing and sponging under the leaves can get rid of most pest problems on citrus, the problems will come back if you don't get rid of ants. Ants are determined little dairy farmers who manage immense herds of sucking insect "cows," such as aphids, mealy bugs, woolly whiteflies, and scale. Ants protect pests from predators, carry them from plant to plant, and milk them for honeydew. If you can get rid of ants your pest problems will be almost completely gone. This requires a special strategy.

Before washing the trees, carefully cut away any branches that are lying on the ground. Don't cut up too high. It's good for a citrus tree's branches to hang low, not only because of all the extra fruit they bear but because this "skirt" of low branches protects the trunk from sunburn. Now the only avenue left for ants will be up the trunk. You can cut off that route by applying a sticky product such as Tree Tangle-foot—or Stickem, which is even stickier and longer lasting. (Stickem is available in some local nurseries and from Seabright Enterprises, Ltd., 4026 Harlan Street, Emeryville, CA 94608, 415/655-3126.)

Don't put these products directly onto bark. Wrap a nylon stocking around the trunk (so that ants can't climb under it), cover it with a strip of paper, and apply the substance to that. Renew the coating frequently to keep it sticky. You can also spray the ground with diazinon to control ants. (Regular professional spraying is best.) Once you're rid of ants the beneficials can go to work to clean up your grove.

Protect Honeybees. When gardeners tell me their citrus trees were loaded with flowers but they got no fruit I always ask, "Did you spray with malathion?" Invariably the answer is "Yes, I was told it would get rid of the aphids." Malathion will indeed kill aphids. It will also kill honeybees, and if you don't have any bees you won't get any fruit. A good ☞ **Rule of Thumb** is: ***Don't spray citrus with insecticides like malathion when the trees are in bloom.***

Cooperate with Beneficials. It's remarkable that even difficult pests such as scale insects and rust mites will be killed by beneficial insects on a clean, well-kept tree. However if your trees are in such bad shape that you feel you must spray against rust mites then spray twice a year—spring and fall—with a miticide. Be sure to choose one recommended for citrus. If scale is also a problem, mix the miticide with oil, then your spray will control scale at the same time.

Deciduous Fruit Trees

Feed deciduous fruit trees when the weather warms up in February and the flower buds swell just prior to bloom. The reason for fertilizing now rather than throughout the spring and summer months, as is done in cold-winter climates, is that fertilizing in summer could produce unseasonal flowering, irregular fruiting, or a spurt of growth that could shorten or prevent winter dormancy.

Feed no more than 1 pound of actual nitrogen per year to each mature deciduous fruit tree growing in fast-draining soil. Feed less to trees in clay soil, and feed young trees very lightly. Too much nitrogen can overstimulate growth. Most experts say deciduous fruit trees need only nitrogen, not phosphorus or potassium, when grown in deep fertile soils, but my own experience indicates that they respond well to a complete formula like 16-8-4, or whatever the gardener may have used to feed citrus and avocados. Vary the amount and formulas depending on local conditions, the fertility of your soil, the size of your tree, and the results you get after the first yearly feeding.

Water deeply and well after fertilizing. If you are an organic gardener spread a deep layer of aged horse manure over the tree roots at this time. If rains are inadequate watch the leaves for brown edges indicating possible salt burn. Water to flush salts to deeper levels.

Sycamore, Ash, and Alder Trees

Continue control of pest and disease problems on sycamore (*Platanus*) trees, and now include ash (*Fraxinus*) and alder (*Alnus*). Refer to the *Ortho Problem Solver* and ask your Farm Advisor for advice on applicable fungicides and pesticides in your area. The best solution is to clean the ground, prune out dead and diseased wood, and have your trees professionally sprayed. Problems are worse in some areas than others. Don't plant without prior investigation.

Spray Sycamores. Sycamore anthracnose (*Gnomonia platanus*), a fungus disease often called sycamore blight, can completely ruin the appearance of sycamores unless controlled now. If you wait for damage to occur there's no solution. Anthracnose causes dieback of young shoots and leaves; brown, scorched-looking mature leaves; and cankers on stems and branches that can girdle and kill them. Spray with a fungicide containing *chlorothalonil* (Daconil 2787) three times: once when buds begin to swell, again when leaves reach full size, and finally two weeks later.

Use oil sprays when trees are dormant to control scale and sycamore lacebug (*Corythucha*), which overwinters in bark and branch crotches and later causes whitening and dropping of leaves. (Spray later with a systemic at the first signs of any damage.)

Spray Ash Trees. Ash anthracnose (*Gloeosporium aridum*) can infect some ash trees, such as Modesto ash, so severely that all the leaves sometimes go brown and drop off after the tree leafs out in spring. Usually new leaves grow in summer, but if the disease isn't checked large portions of the tree can die. Clean up all debris under the tree. Cut out dead branches. Spray three times with Benlate or captan: once when leaves unfurl, again two weeks later, and once more two weeks thereafter. Fertilize just prior to leaf emergence to promote vigorous growth.

Spray Alders. The main pests are aphids and alder flea beetles (*Altica ambiens*), which overwinter in debris. Clean up the ground. Follow up by spraying with a product such as Sevin (*carbaryl*).

Kiwi Vines

Prune kiwi vines in February, during dormancy. Kiwis bear mostly on new canes arising as laterals from fat buds on canes that grew last year. Prune young kiwis lightly, to develop a primary trunk and to create a structure on a pergola, overhead wires, or espalier. Head back canes to create fruiting wood. Prune mature kiwis hard, to remove old wood and produce fresh fruiting growth. Here are the basic steps for mature plants.

- Remove all twiggy, dead, diseased, and tangled growth.
- Remove a few 2- or 3-year-old branches each year, to reduce crowding and encourage growth of new branches for the future. (These cuts won't produce much fruit this year but are necessary for renewal.)
- Cut off all but twenty-eight or thirty canes with smooth wood (those that grew last year). Shorten the remaining canes to four or five buds.
- Shorten fruiting spurs (short side branches) to two buds each.

Camellias

Continue to buy, plant, and transplant camellias now, while they're still in bloom and before they start to grow. (See the box on camellias on p. 32 for how and where to plant.) Most people choose camellias simply by picking out something that looks pretty. It's better to select them for your climate zone and ease of growing. Some are slow growers, others vigorous. Some are good along the coast, others better inland. Many varieties need extremes of temperature in order to open their blooms and thus do better in inland valleys than they do along the coast.

Among varieties that do well inland but have difficulty opening in coastal gardens are Mathotiana, Ballet Dancer, Mrs. Charles Cobb, Chandler Elegans, C.M. Wilson, and Chiro-Chan. Easy to grow either on the coast or inland are Debutante, Pink Perfection, Herme (Jordan's Pride), Professor Sargeant, Lady Claire, and Ace of Hearts. The last can take full sun when grown close to the coast.

As a general rule, singles and semidoubles do best in milder areas, though many formal doubles will open. Anemone-form and peony-form camellias usually won't open in coastal gardens, because the winters are too warm. Get more information from knowledgeable gardeners, nurseries that specialize in camellias, and your local camellia society.

Chinese Magnolias

Purchase Chinese magnolias that bloom on bare branches now, while they're in bloom. Saucer magnolia (*Magnolia soulangiana*) and star magnolia (*M. stellata*) eventually become large, but they grow so slowly they're good choices for small gardens. Use them as focal points in corner beds. They're best against a dark background. They grow best in interior valleys or the Los Angeles basin where they get some winter chill. A pink saucer magnolia underplanted with spring-flowering bulbs can be breathtaking.

Clivia

Purchase clivia now while they're in bloom to get the shade of orange and the size of flowers you want. Belgium hybrids are more handsome than chance seedlings, and recently several Californians have come up with exciting new varieties—there's even a white one. Flame, developed by a local nurseryman, has unusually wide, shiny foliage and brilliant, flaming orange-red blooms, with twenty-four individual flowers in each cluster compared to the usual fourteen. (Your local nursery can order it from Monrovia Nursery.)

Clivia are easy to grow in pots or the ground and are good multipliers. They flower most when crowded, and they'll bloom in northern exposures under overhangs with too much shade for most other winter flowers. If you grow enough of them they make dramatic, long-lasting cut flowers.

Bait now for slugs and snails. They don't often damage the leaves but do like to hide in them and sneak out at night to eat the flowers. A time-honored ☞ **Rule of Thumb** is: ***Don't plant clivia next to red or pink tones of azalea. They clash.*** (White azaleas are beautiful near clivia.)

Gerberas

Plant Transvaal daisies (*Gerbera jamesonii*) now through April. New varieties are freer blooming and have a wider range of colors than older types.

Gerberas are easy to grow in pots or the ground but need good drainage, sun along the coast, and part shade inland. When planting take care to bury all the roots but not the crown (the place where the roots join the leaves). They rot if planted too deeply. Allow gerberas to dry out slightly between waterings. Protect them from snails and feed often with a complete fertilizer.

Gladioli

Start planting gladioli early this month. By continuing to plant a few more every week between now and the end of March you can have a continual display lasting from early June through summer. The ones that go in now will be less subject to thrips, and you may not need to spray them. This rasping insect that disfigures leaves and flowers particularly favors gladioli, but it's most active in hot weather.

Gladioli are easy to grow if you give them what they need: full sun; light, sandy loam; bone meal worked in under the corms and covered with a handful of earth; plenty of water; and good drainage. Buy the best corms and plant them in drifts at the backs of beds—they look gawky in rows. Or use dwarf types up front. Plant small corms 3 to 4 inches deep, larger corms 4 to 6 inches deep. (Mark the spots so you won't plant something else on top.) They do well in pots if you shade the containers from burning sun. A few giant red ones can spark up a patio.

Roses

Water and Fertilize Roses. Keep roses irrigated with 1 inch of water per week beginning at midmonth when rains aren't adequate.

If you've chosen to fertilize your roses with a commercial rose food, wait for the leaves to unfold before feeding them. As soon as the leaves lose their reddish hue fertilize your roses with a complete fertilizer recommended for roses, and mark the date on your calendar so you can feed them again on approximately the same date next month. Do this fertilizing just prior to a regular irrigation or heavy rainfall.

You can, if you wish, choose a fertilizer that contains a systemic pesticide as discussed below under pest control.

Throughout this book I also recommend an alternative method for fertilizing roses, the Rose-Pro Method (as summarized on p. 319). If you've chosen to feed your roses according to the Rose-Pro Method, apply 1 cup of gypsum to the ground over the roots of each rose in early February. Follow up with deep watering to leach accumulated salts down into the ground. Later, in mid-February, give each of your rose bushes and young climbing roses 1 cup of Milorganite (6-2-0), an organic fertilizer, to contribute to a good organic soil. Give established climbers (over 3 years old) 2 cups of Milorganite. Sprinkle this over the root zone and follow up with irrigation. (If you didn't start your Rose-Pro regime last month it's not too late to begin; early this month, feed Epsom salts and phosphorus fertilizer to your roses as recommended last month. Follow the directions on p. 25.)

Protect Roses from Pests and Diseases. It's an unfortunate fact that roses, one of our most loved garden plants and the national flower of the United States, are also host to a flock of pests and diseases. It's almost impossible to grow healthy roses without spraying them with chemicals. It can be done—I've done it myself for years—but to do so you have to grow only the most disease-resistant roses and be content with somewhat ratty looking plants for the second half of the year.

If you're not satisfied by anything less than pristine rose plants unblemished by pests or diseases, you simply have to use chemical sprays.

In that case, start spraying this month against fungus diseases with Funginex. It will control mildew and rust, but since it controls rust only as a preventative you must start spraying before the onset of the problem. The best times to spray are either in the early morning or late in the evening when the wind's died down. Whenever you spray with chemicals be sure to wear protective clothing, including a shower cap, boots, face mask, and waterproof gloves. After spraying put your clothes into the wash and immediately take a shower, washing not only your body but also your hair; even perfect roses aren't worth taking chances with your health. Most rose pests aren't active yet, so it's not necessary to start pesticides until next month. (If aphids are a problem, wash them off with a squirt of the hose.)

If you too prefer not to spray roses with toxic chemicals, plant such disease-resistant varieties as many of the old-fashioned roses plus the modern roses Duet, Queen Elizabeth, Fragrant Cloud, Prominent, and Peace, and the climbing roses Butterscotch, America, and Lady Banks' Rose. The last is also resistant to pests, including aphids. (There are many more resistant varieties; refer to the lists in rose handbooks, such as Ray and MacCaskey's *Roses: How to Select, Grow and Enjoy.*)

You can, if you wish, control sucking pests (those, like aphids or scale, that attach themselves to plants and suck out their juices) by using a systemic pesticide in the soil. This practice kills few if any beneficials, with the possible exception of bees; observe them in your own garden to make sure they aren't being killed. Some commercial rose fertilizers, such as Green Light Rose and Flower Food, contain systemic pesticides along with the fertilizer.

In general, systemics are safer than sprays but their use nonetheless requires certain precautions. Never use systemics close to food plants, such as herbs, fruit trees, or vegetables, because the poisons could be picked up by their roots; don't breathe in the dust, and wear rubber gloves while measuring them. Mildew can often be controlled with WiltPruf, a product designed to be used as an antitranspirant. Spraying once or twice a season is usually sufficient, but be sure to spray at the first sign of powdery mildew.

Bulbs

When rains aren't adequate keep spring bulbs well watered. Dryness can damage flowers.

After ranunculus are 3 or 4 inches high remove the netting that's covering them. Birds love the sprouts when they're young and tender but turn up their beaks at them later.

Try growing lilies of the valley (*Convallaria majalis*). You can buy prechilled roots, called pips, at nurseries now. Plant the pips in pots of high-quality potting mix, water them, and keep them in a warm east window. Give the pots a quarter turn daily. They'll bloom fragrantly in three weeks.

Fuchsias

Fuchsias bloom only on new wood. They need to be cut back annually to stimulate growth (see directions in boxes). In mild, frost-free coastal zones you can cut them back in November and allow regrowth during the winter, but for most other Southland gardeners February's the time to cut them back. Wait until you see some green growth begin, then prune.

How to Cut Back Hanging-Basket Fuchsias

- Cut fuchsias growing in hanging baskets back to pot level or 4 inches above the soil. If the plant is young and vigorous take off all green growth.
- Turn the basket on its side and, with your gloved hand, clean off the surface of the soil. Remove all old leaves and debris, including dead bodies of slow-release fertilizer.
- Dig out and remove about ¼ of the old potting mix, roots and all. Replace it with fresh fast-draining acid soil mix. Press it down firmly. Rehang the plant in semishade.
- Water well after pruning. Don't let the roots dry out.
- Start to fertilize immediately, and fertilize regularly thereafter, with a balanced fertilizer high in growth ingredients. For example, use 1 tablespoon slow-release 14-14-14 or 18-18-6 on the top of the soil once per month or use 20-20-20, 18-24-16, or 30-10-10 liquid every two weeks.
- As plants regrow pinch them to make them bushy; when a sprout has made three pairs of leaves, clip off the top pair. This makes the plant branch. When it's really full, stop pinching and let it bloom.

＊ ＊ ＊

How to Cut Back Standard and Shrub Fuchsias

· Cut back standard and shrub fuchsias into old wood now. Look at the bark. The twiggy growth with smooth bark is what grew last year. The bark with darker color and rougher texture is the old wood. Cut off the twigs along with an inch or two of the older wood.

· Go easy on very old specimens that haven't been pruned in years. Cut back these one-third now. Then wait a month to six weeks for the plants to regrow. When they're leafed out cut back a third more, and wait for that to regrow before finishing the job. (If you cut back a venerable old fuchsia all at once you might kill it.)

· Clean up the ground under the fuchsias. Water, fertilize, and pinch back as described in the box on hanging-basket fuchsias. If you use slow-release fertilizer, increase the amounts proportionately to the size of the plant. For instance, sprinkle ¼ cup of the slow-release type all over the soil under the plant where irrigation water will hit it, or soak the roots with 2 gallons of liquid fertilizer.

· As plants regrow pinch to make them bushy, as described last in the box on hanging fuchsias.

＊ ＊ ＊

The Use of Manure as Mulch

Manure has been much criticized for its high salt content. If you've ever had a problem with salt damage on plants or had a soil test showing a high salt content in your soil, don't use it. But bagged steer manure is an inexpensive and readily available soil amendment that has some good applications when used wisely. On certain plants it can be beneficial, especially when they're growing in fast-draining soil and when the application of manure is likely to be followed by rains. (Some plants, such as asparagus, are more resistant to salt than others.)

Observing these precautions, spread manure over the roots of the following: bananas, ginger, cannas, asparagus, and old clumps of geraniums. Also spread it under bushes, trees, and ground covers, especially gazanias, ivy geraniums, and small-leaved ivy. (Don't use manure on camellias, azaleas, ferns, succulents, or specialty plants other than those listed.) Water thoroughly after spreading.

Pruning Chores for Washington's Birthday

Washington's birthday is the time-honored day for cutting back certain tropical and subtropical plants, including begonias, ginger, and cannas. Gardeners in mild areas, such as Rincon, Malibu, Long Beach, Laguna, and coastal San Diego County, can do these jobs a week earlier, on Lincoln's birthday. But if you live in a low-lying interior valley where you may still get a late frost, it's safer to wait until early March.

Prune Begonias. Cut back *Begonia* 'Richmonden-sis' to pot level or 4 inches above the ground to keep the plants from getting leggy in summer.

Feed lightly with a balanced fertilizer mixed half-strength. They'll soon regrow. Richmon-densis begonias grow best in the ground or in large containers—they dry out too soon in small ones. When ground grown they can be used as a tall ground cover and can go two or three years before being cut back, if desired.

Cut back container-grown cane begonias and angel wing begonias to pot level now, for a bigger flower display in summer. Spectacular varieties such as Irene Nuss, which bears the largest bunches of flowers of any cane begonia, especially benefit from this treatment. Flowers will be larger and plant size more controlled.

Cut back old-fashioned, tall-growing cane begonias lightly to encourage branching. Cane begonias can be grown in moist acid ground away from invasive tree roots or, if trees are a problem, in large tubs.

Prune Ginger, Cannas, Asparagus Fern, Ivy, and Pyracantha. If you live in an interior valley, remember to hold off pruning these plants until the weather has warmed up for good and there's no more chance of a late frost.

Ginger is *monocarpic*, which means it blooms just once on a stalk and then dies. If you don't cut back stalks that have bloomed the clump will tend to stop sending up new growth. You won't get much if any bloom.

- **Kahili Ginger (*Hedychium gardneranum*).** Cut back to ground level now all stalks that have bloomed, to encourage growth of new stalks that will bloom this year. Leave stalks that have not yet bloomed.

- **Shell Ginger (*Alpinia zerumbet*).** Beginning now, cut down to the ground all stalks that have bloomed, when the blooms have finished.

Quick Tip

How to Make a Green Shrub or Tree Bloom with Pink or Red Flowers.
Conceal large tubs of cane begonias under tall informal shrubs, such as Pittosporum undulatum. *Train the begonias into the shrubbery so flowers cascade among the branches in a natural way. The shrub will appear to be blooming with pink or red blossoms for most of the year.*

Continue this throughout the year. After blooms fade, some varieties make little plantlets that you can use to propagate more plants.

• **Cannas.** Cut all stalks that have bloomed down to the ground now, to encourage new stalks to grow and make plants look as good as new. Deadhead them throughout the year (remove individual dead blossoms after bloom).

• **Asparagus Fern (*Asparagus densiflorus* 'Sprengeri').** Renew ratty-looking clumps by cutting them to the ground now. Fertilize for quick bounce back.

• **Algerian Ivy (*Hedera canariensis*).** Renew thick, woody stands by cutting them to the ground by hand or rented machine. Follow up with fertilizer.

• **Pyracantha.** Cut off branches that have borne fruit this year to the base of the plant or to strong side branches. Pyracantha only bears on one-year-old wood, so don't cut off last year's wood that will flower this spring and bear fruit next winter.

Compost

A compost pile can be a great way to use up vegetable wastes from garden and kitchen and return them to the soil. In general there are two ways to go: slow (cold) composting and rapid (hot) composting. Slow composting involves much more time and more space but less effort, and it works eventually even if you don't have the perfect combination of ingredients. (Serious composters should consider purchasing a garden chipping machine, since small particles decom-

pose much faster than large ones.) Rapid composting is indeed fast but takes considerable work; it kills most disease and pest organisms, but you need scientific know-how and a ready supply of the necessary ingredients.

Slow Compost. Choose a hidden area at least 10 feet square. Dig within it a hole 1 or 2 feet deep and 3 or 4 feet square, and pile in such garden refuse as leaves, vegetable peelings, lawn clippings, and chopped remnants of garden plants. If you find you have too many dry materials and not enough wet ones while you are making a pile, sprinkle on some sulfate of ammonia to provide extra nitrogen and speed up decomposition. Wet the pile often to keep it damp.

When adding such wet materials from the kitchen as fruit and vegetable peelings first dig a deep hole in the pile and pour them into it; chop them up a bit with a spade and then completely cover them over with other materials to prevent problems from odors and flies. Topping a cool compost pile with a thin layer of moist earth can also destroy odors and prevent flies from laying their eggs. Technically, the best compost is made without the addition of earth, but if an occasional topping of it saves you from the horror of finding maggots in your compost pile changing the rule in this case is worthwhile.

Keep adding to the pile until it is about 3 feet high and 3 feet wide; then start another. Leave the first for another six months or a year to rot. Slow composting is hit or miss. Some slow compost piles heat up part of the time depending on the ingredients that have gone into them, and they decompose faster than others. Others never go through a hot stage. Many cold compost piles become earthworm factories; the worms slowly devour all the organic materials and eventually turn them into rich soil. Sooner or later you'll end up with a heap of finished compost, and it will be about half the size of the pile you started with. When your compost has become even textured, soft, crumbly, dark brown, and sweet smelling, and you can no longer discern what went into it, then it's sufficiently decomposed to safely add to garden soil. Use homemade compost like any other soil amendment—it's better than most you can buy. (This pit system of making compost is unconventional, but it's an excellent way to make a low-profile compost pile and keep it damp in our dry climate.)

Rapid Compost. Choose an area for composting or build a system of three wooden bins. An excellent plan for bins is included in A. Cort Sinnes' *All About Fertilizers, Soils, and Water*. The University of California Leaflet 21251—*The Rapid Composting Method*—tells you how to make compost in one to two weeks.

Basically, to make a good, active pile it's necessary to mix equal amounts of carbonaceous wastes with nitrogenous wastes, until you have a pile approximately 3 feet square. Carbonaceous wastes are woody materials, such as dry leaves, corn stalks, hay, and wood shavings. Nitrogenous wastes are fresh manure and damp green or wet plant materials, such as grass clippings, green leaves, and kitchen peelings. (Grass clippings do an excellent job of heating up compost, but don't layer them like other materials or they'll stick together in a leathery wet mat that won't properly decompose. Instead, separate them with dry materials; thoroughly mix grass clippings with an equal volume of hay or dry leaves, such as chopped eucalyptus leaves.) Don't add earth to hot compost piles; earth only slows

Suburban and Small-Space "Composting"

Even without room for a compost pile you can have some of compost's benefits. Mix vegetable wastes from the kitchen with unsoftened water, and puree them in a blender. Dig a hole with a trowel, and pour the contents of the blender straight into the garden soil. Cover it with earth to discourage flies. (This is a good way to feed earthworms and increase their numbers.)

You can also chop up vegetable and fruit wastes from the kitchen and bury them in back of flower beds and under the paths in your vegetable garden. They will slowly decompose, adding soluble nitrogen straight into garden soil.

down the composting process and makes the final product too heavy.

Keep the pile damp. Covering the pile loosely with a sheet of black plastic can help hold in moisture and discourage flies from being attracted by odors. (With hot composting flies are usually not a problem; all their eggs are killed by heat.) As soon as the pile heats up to approximately 160°F (71°C) begin to toss and turn it with a garden fork every day or two to keep it from getting too hot. (If the compost heats to over 160°F the microorganisms that break down the organic materials will be killed and the process will have to start over.) As you work try to get the inside portions onto the outside and the outside portions into the middle. Tossing also aerates the pile, which keeps the decomposition process functioning. In two to three weeks, when your compost has thoroughly cooled down and is fine textured, dark, and sweet smelling, stop tossing it and use it in the garden as a soil amendment.

Warning. The following items should *never* be added to compost: dog or cat manure, meat, bones, or fat.

Flower Beds and Containers

Deadhead and Feed Cool-Season Flowers. If you planted cool-season flowers in October they should have started to bloom before Christmas and be in full bloom this month. If you got them in late, they'll start to bloom this month.

Continue to feed with a balanced fertilizer and deadhead or pick them to promote bloom. Nitrogen is less active in cold soil, so choose a fertilizer with a high first number as well as bloom ingredients. Most of the new pansy varieties with smaller flowers don't need deadheading, but larger-flowered varieties look better if seed pods are removed. Older varieties need this care to keep them blooming. Among winter flowers that need to be deadheaded or picked to promote continuous flowering are snapdragons, stock, linaria, Iceland poppies, tall varieties of cineraria, and calendulas.

Plant More Annual Flowers if Necessary. Fill bare patches and containers with transplants of such cool-season flowers as primroses, pansies, violas, calendulas, and perennial candytuft. If you planted these and other cool-season flowers at the right time (September through November) you won't need to plant many flowers now, because all available space will be taken. People who fill whole beds this late don't get their money's worth, because flowers won't bloom as long. But there are some exceptions. Perennial candytuft (*Iberis*) is an admirable plant for edging a bed and is often available only in spring when in bloom. New varieties of viola and pansy are both heat and cold resistant. They go through winter better and last longer in hot weather.

It's too early to plant most warm-season flowers, such as marigolds, salvia, or lobelia. They won't get off to a good start. One exception is petunias. They won't bloom in February but will make strong roots for better bloom later. So if you still have a whole flower bed or tub to fill in a hot spot in full sun, choose petunias. Protect them from frost and snails. Feed for growth.

Switch Fertilizers for Cineraria. Cineraria (*Senecio hybridus*) are growing fast now and, in most gardens, start to bloom before the end of

February. Continue to feed them with high nitrogen until the plants are large in size and begin to show buds. Then switch to 2-10-10 or 0-10-10, and feed every two weeks until the flowers are fully open. Once flowers open stop fertilizing, but continue regular watering. Spray with a systemic for leaf miner, if necessary. Control aphids with Safer soap. Bait for slugs and snails.

Seeds for Flower and Vegetable Transplants

Although February is too soon for planting summer flowers and vegetables in the ground it's not too early for planting seeds. Ambitious gardeners with lots of space to fill can grow their own transplants in flats or peat pots filled with sterilized potting soil. Use bottom heat (70°F; 21°C) from a heat cable to germinate seed. (Alternatively, a 15- or 20-watt bulb in a "trouble light," protected from moisture by several layers of plastic, can be used under flats raised on bricks or flower pots.) Bright light for healthy transplants can be provided by a fluorescent shop light hung 7 to 10 inches above your flats. Leave it burning from fourteen to sixteen hours per day.

Give plants a gentle transition into the garden—first a week in the shade, then one in full sun, during daytime only. The third week leave them out at night, too, to harden them off. Grow varieties, colors, and sizes not found in the nursery.

Lawn Care

Check Warm-Season Lawns for Thatch. Thatch is a layer of partially decomposed leaf sheaths,

➤

Quick Tip

How to Test the Thickness of Thatch.
With a sharp knife cut a small triangle into the soil and pull out the resulting plug of turf. A layer of thatch between ¼ and ½ inch deep is normal. Thatch thicker than ½ inch will harm the lawn.

How to Dethatch Warm-Season Lawns

• Wait until the weather in your area has warmed up for sure and your lawn has greened-up and begun to grow. This is mid to late February in coastal areas and early March in inland valleys.

• Rent a professional renovator or dethatching machine called a *vertical mower*, which will cut down into the thatch. (It may be necessary to reserve one in advance.)

• Mow the lawn short at least twice, first back and forth in one direction and then across it from side to side. Adjust the blades lower each time.

• Drive the vertical mower over the area. Go in both directions and then diagonally. Start on the highest setting, then lower the level of the blades. (If the thatch is very deep don't try to do the job all at once. Renovate it by degrees over one or two years; with each treatment remove ½ inch of thatch.)

• Rake up the thatch, bag it, and send it to the dump. Don't compost it—it would take a blow torch to kill the stolons.

• Follow up by leveling, if necessary. (See directions in the accompanying box.)

• Evenly sprinkle on fast-acting fertilizer at the rate of 6 pounds of sulfate of ammonia for each 1,000 square feet of lawn. Use a spreader if you have one. (There's no need to use an expensive fertilizer at this time.)

• Follow up by watering thoroughly. Keep the lawn well watered until it's completely regrown.

* ✳ *

stems, and roots that forms between the earth below and the grass blades above. It's not made up of grass clippings. Certain subtropical grasses that spread by runners, like Bermuda, make lots of thatch. Bluegrass is intermediate in thatch production, while tall fescue and perennial ryegrass make little if any. If thatch is more than ½ inch thick it harms the lawn by preventing water and fertilizer from passing through. (See the quick tip.) Roots may even "move upstairs" and live in it. Thatch dries out fast, causing dead patches of lawn in summer. A thick layer gives a lawn a springy texture and makes mowers bounce, causing scalp marks.

Dethatch warm-season lawns such as Bermuda (see directions in the accompanying box) every two or three years, when they wake up and start growing again in late winter or early spring. If you dethatch your lawn just after it greens-up it will bounce back quickly. (Dethatch cool-season lawns in early fall, as described on p. 263.)

Mow, Feed, Aerate, and Spread Mulch on Cool-Season Lawns. Cool-season lawns are still growing fast this month. Water them regularly when rains aren't adequate, to keep them growing. Mow them frequently with the mower blades set short, to 1½ or 1¾ inches. Fertilize every six weeks or, with a slow-release formula, less frequently. To increase the humus content of the soil top cool-season lawns with a fine-textured organic soil amendment.

Grass that's mulched now will withstand hot weather better in summer. You'll need about 1 cubic foot of mulch for each 100 square feet of lawn. In fast-draining soils where salt damage has not been a problem it's probably all right to use steer manure, despite its possible high

How to Level Your Lawn

When you mow your Bermuda lawn in summer do you end up with brown, scalped areas? These mower marks may result from the machine bouncing on a thick layer of thatch, but many times they result from dips and bumps in the grade. One method for keeping golf courses smooth and their hills so gently rolling is to top them with sand at least once a year, and let the grass grow up through it. You can correct bumpy lawns in the same way, and you won't need to do it as often. Do this job just after the grass begins to grow, and your lawn should bounce back fast and won't have scalp marks after mowing. Here's how.

- Measure the lawn and order sand and soil amendment. For each 200 square feet of lawn you'll need at least 1 cubic foot of good washed plaster sand and 1 cubic foot of dark-colored, fine-textured soil amendment, such as ground nitrolized wood shavings or ground bark. (The dark color attracts heat and speeds growth.)

- Totally scalp and, if necessary, dethatch the lawn (as also described in this section).

- Mix your sand equally with soil amendment by putting a shovel of one, then a shovel of the other into a wheelbarrow and mixing the contents.

- Arrange the sand mixture in piles all over the lawn. (This will look like the attack of a giant gopher.)

- Attach a 4-foot piece of 1 × 4 lumber to a garden rake (not a grass rake) to construct a leveling device. (Drive half a dozen nails into the lumber and bend them over the teeth of the garden rake.) Push and pull your leveler evenly over the lawn, filling in the depressions.

- Sprinkle a fast-acting fertilizer over the top. Use a spreader if you have one. Apply 6 pounds of sulfate of ammonia for each 1,000 square feet of lawn. (There's no need to use an expensive fertilizer at this time.)

- Water thoroughly and continue to keep the lawn well-watered, if rains aren't adequate, until the grass comes through.

How to Plant Bare-Root Asparagus

- Put the plants in a bucket of water to soak while you prepare trenches in well-drained soil 1 foot deep, 1 foot wide, and 3 feet apart. (Amend the soil with organic amendment if necessary.)

- Put 4 inches of well-aged manure mixed with one handful bone meal per linear foot in the bottom of each trench, or mix in 15 to 20 pounds of 5-10-10 or 5-10-5 fertilizer per 100 feet.

- Cover the bone meal with 2 inches of soil, and form mounds 4 inches high and 18 inches apart in the trench.

- Place the plants on the mounds with their roots arranged out over the sides. Cover them with soil so that each crown is an inch below the soil surface.

- Water the plants well when rains aren't adequate. As they grow, add more soil to cover them until the trench is filled.

- Mulch with manure in February. Wait two years before starting to harvest.

salt content. If you have clay soil it's wiser to use fine-textured nitrolized wood shavings or nitrolized ground bark. If soil compaction has been a problem rent an aerator prior to mulching, and run it over the lawn to remove plugs of earth and sod. Rake up the plugs, then spread the soil amendment and rake it into the holes. After aerating, mulch with nitrolized ground bark or nitrolized wood shavings, not manure. Water thoroughly after spreading it.

Continue to Control Crabgrass. In inland areas control crabgrass by treating your lawn with a preemergent herbicide in early February and once again two weeks later (as described on p. 38). If you live in a coastal zone and you failed to use a preemergent in late January, it may be too late now for preemergent control. Remember to start earlier next year.

If plants are already up and growing, control crabgrass instead with a postemergent herbicide such as disodium methylarsonate. Use it before seed sets. Follow package directions to the letter, and be especially careful to follow the safety precautions. Keep children and dogs off the area for the recommended period of time. Gardeners who prefer not to use selective postemergent herbicides because of the dangers involved can still win the war against crabgrass. By pulling up the plants in fall (as described on p. 263), using preemergent herbicide earlier next year and applying it again in April, you will eventually be able to get rid of the problem.

Vegetable Gardening

February offers the last chance for planting winter crops. Whether to plant more at this time depends on how much ground you have, how close to the ocean you are, and how much your family likes winter vegetables. If you're crowded for space it's much easier this month to continue to pick and eat the winter vegetables you have, and hold off major planting until March. That way most of the garden can be dug up, the soil prepared, and the first planting of summer vegetables put in all at one time. But if your family adores a specific winter vegetable, such as peas, a last crop could be put in now, especially if you live near the coast. Hot temperatures will ruin peas, but cool coastal conditions will permit much later harvesting. (When planting peas this late, be sure to choose a disease-resistant variety. Mildew problems increase as the weather gets warmer.)

Other vegetables that can be planted now are lettuce, curly cress, beets, broccoli, cabbage, carrots, cauliflower, celery, kale, kohlrabi, potatoes, radishes, spinach, Swiss chard, and turnips. Asparagus, artichokes, horseradish, and rhubarb can be put in bare root. With asparagus, equally good and sometimes better results can be had from planting in early spring from seeds. To do so, dig and prepare the trench as described in the accompanying box for bare-root planting, plant the seeds in the bottom of the trench according to package directions, and fill in with soil as the plants grow. The difference is you'll have to wait three years instead of two before starting to harvest.

Purchase / Plant

- [ ] Continue to purchase and plant **camellias** and **azaleas**, 31, 52
- [ ] Choose and plant **Chinese magnolias**, 52
- [ ] Purchase **clivia**, 52
- [ ] Plant **gerberas**, 53
- [ ] Begin to plant **gladioli**, 53
- [ ] Plant **lilies of the valley**, 55
- [ ] Fill in beds and pots with **cool-season bedding plants**, if necessary, 60
- [ ] Start seeds for **flower** and **vegetable transplants**, 61
- [ ] Plant more **winter vegetables** if desired, 64
- [ ] Plant **asparagus** from bare-roots. (Wait until March to plant from seeds.) 64, 65
- [ ] Many **succulents**, including **cacti**, bloom in winter and spring; continue to purchase colorful types, 184

Trim, Prune, Mow, Divide

- [ ] Prune **kiwi vines**, 52
- [ ] Cut back **fuchsias** after they begin to grow, 55
- [ ] In coastal zones prune **begonias**, **ginger**, **cannas**, **asparagus ferns**, **ivy**, and **pyracantha**, 56
- [ ] Deadhead **cool-season flowers** to keep them blooming, 60
- [ ] Mow **cool-season lawns**, 62
- [ ] Check **warm-season lawns** for thatch. Dethatch if necessary but wait until the lawn begins to grow, 64
- [ ] Level **Bermuda lawns** that need it, to prevent scalp marks from mowing, 63
- [ ] Propagate running (usually hardy) **bamboos** in coastal zones, 85

Fertilize

- [ ] Continue to feed **citrus trees** in coastal zones, 30
- [ ] Continue to fertilize **epiphyllums** with 2-10-10 or 0-10-10, 35
- [ ] Begin to fertilize **avocado trees** in coastal zones, 48
- [ ] Feed **deciduous fruit trees**, 50
- [ ] Fertilize **roses**, 53
- [ ] Begin to fertilize **fuchsias**, 55
- [ ] Spread manure over the roots of **bananas**, **ginger**, **cannas**, **asparagus**, and old clumps of **geranium**, 56
- [ ] Feed **cineraria** with 0-10-10 or 2-10-10 to promote bloom, 60
- [ ] Fertilize **cool-season lawns**, 62
- [ ] Fertilize **raspberries** and other cane berries when they begin to grow, 305

Water

- [ ] Water **all garden plants** according to their individual needs; don't water **succulents,** 12 (184)
- [ ] Water **roses,** 53
- [ ] Keep **bulbs** well watered, 55
- [ ] Water **cool-season lawns** as required to keep them growing, 62

Control Pests, Diseases, and Weeds

- [ ] Continue to bait **cymbidiums** for slugs and snails, 35
- [ ] Control pests on **citrus trees,** 49
- [ ] Control pests on **sycamore, ash,** and **alder trees,** 51
- [ ] Bait **clivia** for slugs and snails, 53
- [ ] Protect **roses** from pests and diseases, 54
- [ ] Protect **cineraria** from leaf miners, aphids, and slugs and snails, 60
- [ ] Control **crabgrass** with preemergent herbicide, 61
- [ ] Hand weed **flowers** and **vegetables,** 170
- [ ] Trap **gophers,** 287
- [ ] Protect **celery** from slugs, 73, 312

Also This Month

- [ ] Continue to harvest **winter vegetables,** 41
- [ ] Mulch young **avocado trees,** 49
- [ ] Make a **compost pile,** 58
- [ ] Mulch **cool-season lawns,** 62
- [ ] Aerate **cool-season lawns** if compaction has been a problem, 64
- [ ] Blanch **celery** a month prior to harvesting whole heads, 312

MARCH

MARCH

The First Spring Planting Month

Our spring planting season begins on the first of March, so roll up your sleeves and pitch in. People who set aside extra time for gardening in spring and again in fall find that their gardens require less maintenance during the cool winter and hot summer months. Sometimes weeks go by when the landscape seems to get along all by itself with only an occasional boost from the gardener. At other times, especially in March and April and again during September and October, good gardeners often spend whole days working outdoors. These are the months when most of the planting is done.

During March you can plant most summer annuals and perennials, warm-season and cool-season lawns from seed, some cool-season and most warm-season vegetables, and almost all permanent garden plants, such as trees, shrubs, ground covers, and vines. (Wait a month or two to put in tropicals. They'll take off better in warmer weather.) If you've never gardened before you couldn't choose a better time to start, because you'll soon see results. One of the wonderful things about our sunny climate is how quickly it makes the garden grow. Gardeners with low-lying or mesa-top gardens should still be aware of cool temperatures at night and the possibility of frost until March fifteenth, even late April in some foothill locations, but for most of us the weather has warmed up for sure. Winter is over, spring has arrived.

The Basic Landscape

Fertilize Permanent Plantings. Most ornamental trees, bushes, lawns, and ground covers respond well to fertilizer at this time. In good years abundant spring rains green-up the hillsides and bring out wildflowers, gardeners don't have to water as much, and salts are leached out of our soils. But heavy rains also wash soluble nutrients, especially nitrogen, down to lower levels, sometimes out of reach of roots. So fertilize the basic landscape with a complete granulated fertilizer high in nitrogen. If you have a straggly ground cover that's never quite covered the ground, a sprinkling of granulated fertilizer in early March will do wonders. Water it in thoroughly or apply it when the weatherman says we're going to have rain.

This doesn't mean you should indiscriminately fertilize everything in sight. Many plants fall into the broad category of specialty plants because they require special handling. Some specialty plants, including cacti, succulents, and native plants, have little or no need for fertilizer. Others, such as camellias, azaleas, begonias, fuchsias, ferns, orchids, epiphyllums (orchid cacti), roses, fruit trees, and vegetables, have unique requirements. Follow the directions for them in this and other monthly chapters.

There are other exceptions, too. Old overgrown gardens in rich soil sometimes become virtual jungles feeding on their own refuse. To fertilize such a garden when there's no sign of nitrogen deficiency, such as stunted growth, yellow leaves, or disease, may simply contribute

to more growth, requiring constant pruning. And such invasive plants as blue gum eucalyptus (*Eucalyptus globulus*) and old stands of Algerian ivy, once established, make one wish one had never planted them. Feeding them would make them more rampant.

Plant New Permanent Specimens. March is one of the two best times of year to plant almost anything we grow in the permanent landscape, such as trees, shrubs, vines, and ground covers. The other is October. Planting in fall is traditionally considered to be just a bit better than planting in spring, but after a year or two you'll never know the difference. Now through mid-June is the time to look your garden over, see its strengths and weaknesses, replace troublemakers you don't like, and add permanent specimens where needed. Choose drought-tolerant plants over heavy water users. Be sure to group plants according to their needs for water, for sun or shade, and for soil type. Before purchasing any plant, research its requirements and growth habit.

Frost Damage

If you have a cold, low-lying garden or live in an interior valley, beware; there's always the possibility of a late frost striking suddenly in early March. Keep a garden diary from year to year and listen to the evening news to help anticipate temperatures. Protect tender plants such as tomatoes with caps at night. Remove them during the day. If you grow tomatoes in cages surround them with plastic. On cold nights throw a cover over the top.

Once all danger of frost has passed take tender tropicals out from under eaves and spreading trees where you sheltered them. At last you can cut off the unsightly frost-damaged portions of trees, shrubs, and vines. Control the urge to clean up too soon; damage may not be as bad as you think. As soon as leaves start showing, you can safely cut off dead portions without destroying more than necessary. With bougainvillea in particular wait until you see growth resume, then cut back to it. (Follow up with food and water to hasten its regrowth.) Bougainvillea blooms on new wood, so spring pruning often results in more summer bloom.

Control of Snails and Slugs

Warm spring rains keep snails and slugs on the prowl. Our common garden snail is actually the edible European snail *Helix aspersa*, an important food source since ancient times. One can grow them in cages, purge them, and eat them. (Picart's book, *Escargots from Your Garden to Your Table*, and the UC publication Leaflet # 2222, *Snails as Food: Escargots*, in the bibliography, tell how.) But if you're more interested in simply getting rid of them strike back early and mount a multiflank attack. Here's a selection of controls.

- Go out at night with a flashlight and rubber gloves, and hand pick them; bag them, and dispose of them in the trash. (Look for them by day under leaves of amaryllis, agapanthus, agave, cannas, clivia, daylilies, and dracaena.)

- Wear rubber boots and squash them underfoot (though eggs may survive).

- Clean up the garden; get rid of undergrowth and other hiding places.

- Surround trunks of citrus trees with copper collars. Snails won't cross them. Cut off low-hanging leaves that brush the ground.

- Lay on the ground such traps as upside-down grapefruit rinds, loose lettuce leaves, upside-down flower pots, and flat boards with 1½-inch wooden runners at each end to raise them off the ground. Next morning throw away the lettuce leaves and grapefruit rinds, pests and all. Lift the boards and flower pots daily and dispose of the slugs and snails lurking underneath.

- Fill yogurt cartons with 1½ inches of beer (or a solution of 1 cup water, 1 teaspoon sugar, and ¼ teaspoon baker's yeast). Make entry holes in the side. Sink the cartons upright in the ground up to the holes. (Slugs are attracted, become inebriated, and fall in and drown.)

- Keep ducks; they eat slugs and snails, though they also eat many garden plants. Chickens, guinea hens, jungle fowl, and bantams are also good at cleaning out slug and snail eggs, with varying appetites for plants. Other natural predators include ground beetles, skunks, snakes, starlings, frogs, toads, opossums, and—yes—rats. (If you live in an area free from snails, chances are it's infested with roof rats.)

- Introduce the African *decollate* snail, a carnivorous snail that eats young *helix* snails. (Their best use is in citrus groves rather than in home gardens, since they damage new seedlings and transplants. They aren't legal in all counties.)

- Use a nontoxic spray, such as Plant Shield (not available in all areas).

- Use baits. They come in spray, pellet, powdered, and thick liquid form. Products containing Mesurol, such as Slug-Geta, and products containing a high concentration of

Quick Tip

Make a Homemade Snail Jail.
To protect birds, wild animals, and pets from eating slug and snail bait squash the sides of empty tin cans to leave a 1 ½-inch space— just enough room for snails to enter. Dampen the interiors and sprinkle in bait. Place the traps around the garden and tie them in orange trees. Fully enclosed, strong baits can be used safely.

metaldehyde, such as That's It, are highly effective but also most toxic and must not be used around edible crops. Liquid bait, such as Deadline, is effective and long lasting but may make animals sick if they step in it and lick it off.

Mesurol works better than metaldehyde in cloudy, shady, or overgrown conditions. Metaldehyde works better in open areas, because it works by paralyzing the snails. If they're in the open the sun will kill them, but if they're in a moist shady area they'll hide and recover in a few days. Sprays are effective on ground covers, and they may harm birds less. All baits work better when you switch them from time to time. Products that contain a combination of carbaryl and metaldehyde can be used in the vegetable garden, and they kill sowbugs too, but they should not be allowed to come into contact with edible plant parts. The ☞ **Rule of Thumb** for all baits except liquid types is: ***When using snail and slug baits, bait once thoroughly, wait ten days or two weeks, and bait again.*** (The first treatment gets the parents, the second gets the offspring.)

Flower Beds and Containers

March is the first month to plant warm-season annual and perennial flowers outdoors either by seeds or transplants. If you weren't able to take advantage of fall planting, fill all beds and pots with warm-season flowers now. If you planted last fall, however, most beds are full to overflowing with cool-season flowers. There's little if any room for planting more. The only planting to be done is to plant seeds in flats—for bedding plants to be set out later, to fill bare patches as they occur, and to plant pots and hanging baskets and fill in any area that by month's end may have finished flowering (a bed of cineraria, for example).

Continue to feed container-grown flowers with liquid fertilizer for growth and bloom. Fertilize cool-season flower beds with a granulated fertilizer if you see a slowdown of growth or flowering. Water it in well afterward. Deadhead flowers to keep them blooming.

Though nurseries are filled with such cool-season flowers as primroses, calendulas, nemesia, stock, snapdragons, Iceland poppies, pansies, and violas, wise gardeners remember that these are the flowers that should have been planted in fall. Planted now, for the most part cool-season flowers will give only a short season of bloom, especially inland. The height of their bloom season is April, though in coastal gardens some will last through May. Stock, snapdragons, calendulas, and Iceland poppies are particularly unhappy choices to plant now. Heat or disease knocks them down fast. Pansies, polyanthus primroses, cyclamen, and violas can be popped into blank spots, but don't fill whole beds. Polyanthus primroses and small-flowered cyclamen will bloom through June in cool coastal gardens, however, and can be kept alive to bloom another year. And newer varieties of small-flowered pansies are floriferous and heat tolerant. They may last into August.

If you're filling whole beds, prepare the ground thoroughly and choose mainly warm-season flowers. Good choices among annual flowers to plant now from pony packs for color in sunny spots all summer long include ageratum, marigolds, cosmos, sweet alyssum, verbena, salvia, petunias, and nierembergia. An incredible

number of perennials can be put in now, including achillea, agapanthus, perennial alyssum (*Aurinia saxatilis* or *Alyssum saxatile*), campanulas, candytuft (*Iberis sempervirens*), carnations, columbine, coreopsis, coral bells, daylilies, delphiniums, dusty miller, dianthus, marguerites, gaillardia, geum, penstemon, perennial forget-me-nots (*Myosotis scorpioides*), Pride of Madeira (*Echium fastuosum*), statice, and Shasta daisies. In semishade put in transplants of begonias, lobelia, impatiens, coleus, and fuchsias. (Bedding begonias and lobelia can take full sun along the coast when grown in the ground. Impatiens can take full sun only if they're in a cool breezy spot next to a lawn rather than hot pavement.)

A large number of warm-season flower species can be planted successfully now from seeds. They include achillea, ageratum, alyssum, anchusa, balsam, ornamental basil, browallia, calliopsis, celosia, cleome, coleus, cosmos, gaillardia, gazania, geranium, globe amaranth, gloriosa daisy (rudbeckia), helipterum, hollyhock, lobelia, marigold, morning glory (be sure to nick morning glory seeds with a file, so they'll sprout), salvia, sanvitalia, sunflower, strawflower (helichrysum), thunbergia, tithonia, verbena, and impatiens. (Ageratum, coleus, lobelia, scarlet salvia, and impatiens need light in order to germinate. Sprinkle seeds on top of prepared soil, and anchor them by pressing gently into the soil surface—don't cover them with earth. Keep them moist by frequent misting.)

Desert gardeners can plant vinca rosea, nicotiana, portulaca, solanum (ornamental eggplant) and zinnias from seeds, but the rest of us had better not plant them yet. These heat lovers can't stand cold feet. They'll do much better if we wait for warmer weather.

Roses

Water Roses Deeply. Give roses plenty of water this month so they can grow plenty of leaves, stalks, and buds for next month's flowers. In interior zones they may need as much as 2 inches of water per week at weekly intervals in fast-draining soil.

Fertilize Roses. Continue to fertilize your roses this month according to the system you've chosen. If you're feeding with a complete fertilizer recommended for roses, check your calendar to see when you did the job last month and fertilize one month later; once again mark the date on your calendar. (Fertilizing once every six weeks as recommended on many rose-food packages doesn't provide them with adequate nitrogen.)

If you're following the Rose-Pro Method of fertilizing (as summarized on p. 319) give each rose 1 tablespoon of sulfate of potash (0-0-25) during the first week in March. (This is an annual application. Since potassium is longer lasting in soil than nitrogen, it needs to be added only once a year.) Also, this month start fertilizing each rose regularly—once a week—with 1 tablespoon of sulfate of ammonia (21-0-0). Simply toss these nutriments on the ground under each rose prior to a regular deep irrigation. Using this system a great many roses can be fed in a relatively short amount of time. Try to stick to a schedule and fertilize your roses on the same day each week, but always make sure that the fertilizer is thoroughly watered into the ground.

Additionally, if you're using the Rose-Pro Method, start this month to give your roses micronutrients (trace elements) as a foliar spray.

The easiest way to do this is to mix either Super K Gro or Stern's Miracle Gro into the sprayer along with the fungicide or pesticide when you spray.

Control Pests and Diseases. If you prefer not to spray your roses with chemicals, control pests by handpicking, by spraying with Safer soap, and by introducing beneficial insects. Wash off aphids with the hose, or control them along with other sucking insects by using systemic pesticides in the soil (unless your roses are close to food plants). Disease control can be partially accomplished without spraying by growing disease-resistant roses exclusively and by spraying with an antitranspirant, like Wilt-Pruf or Cloud Cover, against mildew.

If you're growing roses for show or aiming for perfection, however, continue to spray at weekly intervals with Funginex to control fungus diseases. At midmonth start spraying also with Orthene to control pests. Measure the Orthene and Funginex at the rates per gallon given on their labels and combine them in the same quantity of water you would use for only one of them. To each gallon of mixed spray add a squirt of dishwashing detergent, to make your spray cling better. Also add the quantity of Miracle Gro or Super K Gro recommended on the package, as mentioned above, to foliar feed the roses with trace elements and acidify the spray. (Always wear protective clothing and follow all precautions when you spray.)

If you grow just a few roses the above routines will take care of most pest problems, but if you grow many roses they're likely to be attacked by spider mites, a troublesome pest that's difficult to control without a miticide. At the time of this writing Avid is the most effective control, but it's toxic, difficult to find, and comes only in large, expensive quantities. If you choose to use it spray three times at intervals of seven days, and a fourth time twenty-one days later.

Begin Disbudding. If you're interested in growing roses for show or if you prefer your roses to bear only one large flower per stem, begin disbudding your Hybrid Tea and Grandiflora roses early this month. To disbud a rose means to remove the secondary, or side, buds on the flower stem shortly after these appear. Secondary buds sap strength from the primary buds. By removing them you allow the center bud to grow to full size. (An exception is when roses send up new canes. In this case, allow them to "candelabra," to grow naturally without disbudding in order to get maximum height.)

In most cases there are only one or two side buds to remove, and some roses have none, but a few Hybrid Tea and Grandiflora roses make so many secondary buds that none of the flowers can fully open. Nonetheless, most home gardeners never bother to disbud their roses. (Don't disbud roses that are naturally meant to grow in bunches, like Floribundas or Polyanthas.)

Bulbs

Spring-Flowering Bulbs. Unless rains are steady and frequent continue to water spring-flowering bulbs. After they finish blooming cut off the flower pods and feed the plants with a well-balanced fertilizer—it's an investment in next year's performance. Don't cut the leaves off until they go brown and die back. (If their floppy appearance bothers you tie them in knots.)

Tigridias. Bulbs of tigridias, or tiger flowers, can be found at local nurseries now. Plant them 6 inches apart and 3 inches deep in full sun along the coast, or where they'll get afternoon shade inland. Fertile loam or sandy soil is best. If you have clay soil mix in plenty of soil amendment or plant in pots or raised beds. The colorful blooms appear in July and August. Each flower lasts only one day, but others follow on the same branch so the bloom season is quite long.

Gladioli. Tie gladioli planted in February to stakes installed at planting time. Protect them from slugs and snails, and keep them well watered. Feed potted glads with liquid fertilizer. Continue to plant gladioli, though when planted now they will need more protection from thrips in summer.

Dahlias. Prepare planting holes for dahlias by mixing plenty of organic matter into the soil. Some aged chicken manure can be added to the soil now, along with premoistened peat moss, nitrolized wood shavings, or homemade compost, in preparation for planting in April. Dig the organics deeply into the ground—as much as a foot deep—and keep the soil damp.

Tuberous Begonias. Start tuberous begonias this month. If you kept some tubers from last year take a look at them now to see whether they're showing signs of life. If so bring them out of hiding and start watering them. Buy new ones at local nurseries. Some tubers are slow to sprout, so choose those that already have a sprout or two.

Tuberous begonias aren't easy to grow, but if you have rich acid soil in an east-facing area, not

* ✳ *

How to Grow Tuberous Begonias from Tubers

- Fill flats with damp peat moss. Roll the tubers in soil sulfur and sink them into the peat moss so that each one is barely covered, with the bumpy concave side up, the rounded bottom down.

- Place the flats in a warm, shaded spot with early morning sun or in a lath house or gazebo. Keep them damp but don't fertilize them yet.

- When growth is 2 or 3 inches high plant in well-drained acid soil in pots, hanging baskets, or the ground under an eave or noninvasive tree, preferably facing east. (Plant them with leaf points facing the front of the bed; the flowers will face the same direction.)

- Wait until growth is 3 or 4 inches high, then start feeding the plants regularly, every time you water; tuberous begonias are big eaters. Use an evenly balanced fertilizer such as 10-10-10, 8-8-8, or 20-20-20.

- Control mildew with a fungicide—Benomyl or Enid, for example. (Add a spreader-sticker, such as Spraymate, when you mix your spray.) Or try a nontoxic spray such as an antitranspirant—Wilt-Pruf or Cloud Cover, for example—which often controls mildew indirectly.

- Always allow plants to dry out a little between waterings. Begonias are far more drought resistant than they appear.

* ✳ *

too many snails, and a knack for growing begonias they can be one of the most rewarding plants for summer color in semishade. Years ago they were considered suitable for coastal zones only. New heat-resistant varieties such as the Non-Stops have made it possible for gardeners in interior zones to try their hand at this most colorful and exotic-looking garden plant. If growing them from tubers sounds too involved, wait until summer and visit a "dig-your-own" nursery, such as Weidner's Begonia Gardens in Leucadia, San Diego County.

Chrysanthemums, Marguerites, Gamolepis, and Euryops

Chrysanthemums should always be grown from fresh cuttings rooted in March. Also take cuttings now of marguerites, gamolepis, and euryops. They all root easily.

Early in the day take softwood cuttings, 3 to 5 inches long, from the succulent, bendy growth at the tips of branches. (It snaps when bent even though soft and flexible.) On chrysanthemums there should be at least two leaf buds. If you have a lot of cuttings keep them moist in burlap until you can plant. Remove the lower leaves of each cutting, leaving two or three leaves in place, and dip the cut end in RooTone. Knock off the excess. Root chrysanthemums in flats of damp sand and the others in fast-draining potting mix to which you've added about 10 percent perlite. Cover the flats with plastic, and place them in a brightly lit but shady place under a tree.

As soon as the cuttings are rooted plant them in pots or the ground. Feed them for growth. After they start to grow pinch them back to make them bushy. This is a great way to grow enough marguerites, euryops, and gamolepis to fill beds in a new garden. (For more about these yellow shrub daisies, see p. 157.)

Chrysanthemums require more care than the others, but they're capable of rewarding you in fall with a massive display of color. Feed them often during their growth, control rust with Bayleton, and control leaf miners, thrips, and aphids with systemics. Pinch them back often until August to make them bushy, and stake the plants to keep them from falling over as they grow. If you remove all but the top buds during summer you'll have huge flowers. If you leave all or most buds in place you'll have a bigger color display with smaller flowers.

Citrus and Avocado Trees

Now's a good time to plant citrus and avocado trees. They'll have all spring and summer to get established before winter's cooler temperatures slow their growth. Provide them with good drainage and choose varieties that are right for your area. If you wrapped the trunks of young trees last fall, unwrap them now.

In interior zones also begin fertilizing citrus and avocado trees this month (as described on pp. 30 and 48). In coastal zones continue to fertilize them.

Macadamias

As with citrus and avocado trees, this is a good time to plant macadamias and to unwrap the trunks of young trees if you wrapped them for frost protection last fall.

Two species of macadamia are grown here, the integrifolia (*Macadamia integrifolia*) and the tetraphylla (*M. tetraphylla*); both are from Aus-

tralia. These trees are attractive, slow-growing evergreens with glossy green foliage and white flowers. The trees can survive drought well, but in order to bear a good crop they need about the same amount of water that avocado trees require. Overwatering is seldom a problem. Macadamias bear round nuts that are notoriously difficult to crack; a special nutcracker is a necessity. The kernels have a high oil content and delicious flavor; in stores they're a luxury item.

Fertilize Macadamias. The precise requirements of macadamias for fertilizer are not yet known; overfertilization may actually harm the tree. When these trees are grown in fertile garden soil and given adequate water and full sun they'll increase in size and produce crops with no fertilizer whatsoever. However if you're growing a macadamia tree in poor soil, or if it's stunted in size and bears poor crops, feed it very lightly every six weeks from now until June with a complete fertilizer containing no more than 10 percent nitrogen. The safest way to feed a macadamia is to apply a solution of fish emulsion over its roots twice monthly during any month of the year when the average minimum temperature is in excess of 50°F (10°C). Mix 5 tablespoons of fish emulsion into 5 gallons of water, and sprinkle the solution all over the ground under each tree. This will not harm the tree in any way.

Select and Plant Macadamias. When purchasing a macadamia tree don't buy a seed-grown tree, which may or may not bear nuts. Be sure to choose a proven, grafted variety. Most varieties are hardy to 27°F (-2°C), but all grow best in frost-free zones. Integrifolias and hybrids are more cold resistant than tetraphyllas. (Cate

✳ ✳ ✳

How to Harvest, Husk, Dry, and Roast Macadamia Nuts

People who take the time to perform the following tasks can produce homegrown nuts that are every bit as good as those grown commercially. Because of the chemical makeup of macadamias slow drying is essential to a good product.

- **Harvest Ripe Nuts.** If your tree is a Beaumont variety pick all the nuts from the tree during the first week in March. With all other varieties when the nuts start falling from the tree it's a sign that they're approaching ripeness. In the case of varieties other than Beaumont, the first few nuts that fall (during the first two weeks) may not be completely ripe. Open some up; if they're wrinkled or discolored throw them out and wait until good nuts start falling. Once they do, rake them up every day or two and separate the nuts from the leaves. (The nuts are likely to spoil if left lying on the ground more than a week.)

- **Husk the Nuts.** Use a large pair of pliers to remove the husks (the outer coverings of the nut that may or may not remain attached to the nuts). If your tree bears nuts that are difficult to husk, let the unhusked nuts sit several days in shade and then they'll be easier to remove. (It's best to husk the nuts from Beaumont immediately.)

- **Air Dry the Husked Nuts in Their Shells.** To do this, spread them in shallow, screen-bottomed trays and put the trays on a rack or other support in a dry, shady place. Leave them there for two or three weeks.

- **Finish Drying the Nuts in Their Shells over Low Heat.** Do this by placing them in a screen-bottomed container over a furnace register for three or four days. Or, dry the nuts at 100° to 115°F (37° to 46°C) for twelve to forty-eight hours, or more, in a shallow pan in the oven.

and Elimbah are tetraphyllas and Beaumont, a good backyard tree, is a hybrid between tetraphylla and integrifolia.) If gophers live in your vicinity line the planting hole with a basket of poultry wire to protect the young roots from gopher damage.

Harvest Macadamias. The nuts on macadamia trees ripen at different times of year depending on variety. When the nuts are ripe they usually fall off the tree over a period that may last several months—ninety days is common. The nuts from Cate, for example, ripen from September through mid-December, and those of Elimbah ripen from December to April. Beaumont is an exception to this rule; it hangs on to its crop long after the nuts are ripe, so you must pick them off. If you're growing a Beaumont macadamia strip all the nuts from the tree during the first week in March. Unfortunately, most gardeners leave them hanging on the tree because they don't realize that the nuts on Beaumont stick tight. Leaving the ripe nuts on the tree makes Beaumont bloom throughout the year, eventually drop its yearly crop of nuts over about nine months—from October through June—and over several years will make the nuts successively smaller, until all you get are

(The lowest possible setting on an electric oven may dry the nuts in as little as twelve hours. The heat given off by the pilot light in an old-fashioned gas oven is ideal; it will dry the nuts in three or four days.) From time to time crack open one or two nuts to test their progress. When the shells are dry and brittle rather than bendy—even though still hard—and the nuts are loose in the shell and approaching crispness, they're done.

- **Store the Nuts in Their Shells.** Enclose the dried nuts in sealed heavyweight plastic bags to prevent them from absorbing moisture, and store them in a cool place.

- **Remove the Shells.** Crack open the hard nut shells with a special macadamia-nut cracker. These are available, for example, from the Gold Crown Macadamia Society, P.O. Box 235, Fallbrook, CA 92028, 619/728-4532.

- **Store the Nutmeats.** Store the nutmeats in tightly covered containers in the refrigerator or freezer. (Roasted nuts may also be stored this way.)

- **Roast the Nutmeats.** Shelled macadamia nuts are ready to eat or to use in cooking, or you can roast them. In a preheated conventional oven roast whole and half nuts for forty to fifty minutes at 250°F. (To avoid burning don't roast broken pieces that are smaller than halves.) Watch them carefully, and stir them occasionally to prevent burning. Remove them from the oven as soon as you see them start to turn from white to light tan.

To use a convection oven first make a basket from folded ¼-inch hardware cloth. Fill it with shelled nuts of all sizes—whole, halves, and pieces—and roast at 300°F for twenty minutes.

✳ ✳ ✳

"peewees" (undersize nuts). But if you pick the nuts off by hand during the first week in March the tree will put all its energy into the new crop, and you'll get a good harvest of large-sized nuts the following year. With all other varieties wait until the nuts fall to the ground—don't ever pick them or shake them from the tree—and then gather them up at least once a week.

Some varieties of macadamia are self-husking—the husk, or outer covering of the nut, splits open when the nuts ripen. Cate is somewhat self-husking, Beaumont is reasonably self-husking, and Elimbah and some integ-rifolias are less so. But with many varieties the gardener must manually remove the nuts from the husks.

Macadamia nuts require considerable processing. After harvesting and husking it's important to slowly dry macadamia nuts properly; otherwise they'll be sticky or gummy (see the accompanying box for directions).

Epidendrum

Epidendrum orchids are easy to grow in pots or the ground, are inexpensive, bloom almost year-round in frost-free zones, and are almost immune to pests and disease. Grow them in full sun along the coast, part shade inland. They're spectacular in raised beds flanking swimming pools and worth hunting for in specialty nurseries.

Once an epidendrum stem has borne its clusters of cattleya-shaped flowers it won't bloom as well a second time. Cut it back to the second leaf joint from the ground. Stick the cuttings in the ground or in pots filled with potting soil and you'll soon have new plants. Feed them often with liquid fertilizer for growth and bloom.

Camellias

Improve the shape of camellia bushes now by judicious pruning, and bring the cut branches inside to enjoy the pleasure of them with both flowers and leaves intact. Look at the structure of your camellias; cut where you want to increase bushiness. If you look closely at a branch you'll see the bump where last year's growth began. The new wood is a different color. Make your cut in this new wood just beyond the bump. This will produce branching and more flowers next year.

Azaleas

The more vigorous an azalea, the easier it is to grow. But some that are robust and easy to grow—Southern Indica azalea varieties such as Pride of Dorking, Formosa, and Phoenicia; Rutherfordianas such as L.J. Bobbink; and even some heat-resistant Brooks hybrids—sometimes throw out extra growth in awkward places. Don't do all-over pruning yet, but now's the time you can improve an azalea's shape by

cutting out undesirable, crossing, or old woody branches that have ceased to bear well. These unwanted branches make lovely cut flowers to take into the house.

Choose and plant azaleas while they're in bloom, but don't feed them until the bloom season is over. Overfeeding azaleas is a cardinal sin. It's possible to kill them with kindness as well as neglect. They also mustn't be overwatered, but never let an azalea dry out completely or it will die.

Fuchsias

Continue to feed and pinch back fuchsias. They only bloom on new wood. Every tip will produce flowers, so the idea is to make the plant produce as many tips as possible. As soon as each sprout grows three pairs of leaflets pinch out the top pair. Take some of the bendy new unpinched growth for cuttings. (See the accompanying box.)

Hibiscus

Start to prune tropical hibiscus (*Hibiscus rosa-sinensis*). Hibiscus only flowers on new wood; if you never prune it the flowers appear ever farther from the center until they're out of sight on top of a leggy shrub. Young plants need little or no pruning. Plants more than five years old should be pruned a little every month from now until August. Don't chop hibiscus all over like a hedge, because this slices the large leaves in two. Here's what to do.

- Choose only three or four woody branches to remove now. For symmetry, they should be on opposite sides of the shrub. Reach into the hibiscus and prune out the whole branches, back to two or three growth buds from the center of the plant. This will encourage bushiness and regrowth from within. (With very vigorous varieties, such as Agnes Galt, prune harder now, taking out as much as one-third of the old, woody growth.)

· In a month or six weeks remove three or four more old branches in the same way and proceed thus throughout summer. Put it on your calendar. This progressive pruning will result in lots more growth and flowers. (Don't prune hibiscus in winter.)

· To keep hibiscus shaped as a screen or large hedge, head back one-third to one-fourth of the tip growth 1 or 2 feet into the shrub, here and there all over the sides and top of the hedge. Come back in a month and head back another third. Continue throughout summer. When you walk away no one should be able to see you've pruned.

· Follow up with fertilizer and water.

Quince, Guava, and Cherimoya Trees

Quince, guava, and cherimoya not only are ornamental but bear delicious fruit, and they grow well here. However, though they have many flowers they don't always bear much fruit, because we don't have the right insects here to pollinate them efficiently. You can help the local bees and ensure a larger crop by hand pollinating.

With quince and guava choose a warm, dry morning and simply dab the centers of the flowers with a small sable brush to distribute the pollen. If there are too many flowers for this, use a long-handled wool duster. Dust the

How to Start a Fuchsia from a Cutting

· Clip from an established fuchsia a soft, bendy growth tip with two or three pairs of leaves.

· Clip off the bottom pair of leaflets.

· Dip the cut end of the stem, including the *node* from which you have clipped off the leaves, in a rooting compound, such as RooTone, and knock off the excess. (A node is the place on a plant stem from which one or more leaves grow.)

· With a chopstick make a hole in a 4-inch pot filled with fast-draining acid potting mix, such as Bandini #105.

· Take your first "pinch": clip off the top pair of leaves so the plant will begin to branch as soon as it begins to grow.

· Write the variety name on a plant label and stick it in the pot.

· Keep the plant moist in semishade. Begin feeding as soon as growth begins.

· As soon as the roots fill the container, pot the plant on—repot it in a container one size larger—and pinch it back to keep it bushy.

pollen into the flowers all over the outside of the tree.

With cherimoya a two-step technique is necessary because the flowers are both female and male. In the morning hours, when the flowers aren't fully opened, they're in the female stage. In the afternoon the flowers open fully and become male. First collect pollen, in the afternoon; hold a 35 millimeter film cannister under each fully opened flower, and brush the pollen and strawlike anthers into the cannister with a small paint brush. Close the container and keep it in a cool, dry place. The next morning find flowers in the female stage. Spread the petals with your fingers, dip the brush into the cannister of fresh pollen, and apply it to the conelike pistil with an even, swirling motion. It takes cherimoya fruit five months to mature, so if you pollinate ten or twenty blossoms once a week year-round you should have a far more abundant harvest, with fruit ripening throughout the year instead of only in November.

Bamboo

For thousands of years bamboo has been among mankind's most economically useful plants, but modern gardeners prize it most for its serene beauty and for the tropical or Oriental atmosphere it lends to the landscape. Nonhorticulturally-minded people are often surprised to learn that bamboo is actually giant grass and thus, like Bermuda grass, bluegrass, and wheat, bamboo is a member of the *Gramineae* family. There are well over a thousand different species of bamboo (members of the *Bambuseae* tribe of grasses), and these are further divided into numerous genuses, their actual number depending on which botanist you consult. Some bamboos grow 120 feet tall with individual stems (called culms) a foot in diameter; some bamboos are low-growing ground covers—a foot or less tall; and there's every size between these extremes. Most bamboos are evergreen; some are hardy, and others are tropical.

There are two main types of bamboo, those that grow in a clump and those that send out long runners. The ones with runners can eventually spread all over your property, and they often invade your neighbor's garden too. Control these invasive types by planting them aboveground in containers, or grow them in the ground but enclose them in drain tiles, bottomless containers, or a buried barrier of poured concrete or galvanized metal. Or grow them in a raised bed surrounded by a 1-foot-deep trench filled with fir bark; police the trench often to cut off escaped runners as they enter it.

Most bamboos are *monocarpic*: once they bloom and bear seeds they die. Some species flower at various times, and many of this type bloom without dying. But other species don't flower for many years and when they do it's on a specific schedule—perhaps at intervals of 7, 15, 30, 60, or 120 years, or possibly even several hundred years. (Some types have never been known to flower.) Amazingly, when members of many species flower, bear seeds, and die they do so all at one time just as if they were one plant. Sometimes an entire species dies within a year or two all over the world. Eventually this bamboo species will come back from seed, and in some cases the rhizomes stay alive and put out new growth after a few years. This fascinating habit can be a tragedy if you're a panda bear and depend on a particular species of bamboo for food. Also a tragedy if you're a gardener and a species you grow reaches the end of its cycle.

How to Propagate Bamboo from Rhizomes

Bamboos grow from branching rhizomes that have joints on them, called nodes, from which spring the fibrous roots and the bamboo stems or canes, called culms. The rhizomes of running bamboos are elongated while those of clumping kinds are short and thick. The right time to separate bamboo is when new culms are just ready to sprout (when the underground buds have swelled but not yet begun to grow).

Start now from time to time to dig down carefully with a trowel and see when buds are forming. Hardy bamboos (these are mainly the types with runners) usually begin to grow in early March, sometimes as early as late February along the coast. If the new shoots have already emerged from the ground it's too late; they will abort if you separate their rhizomes then. (If you're too late, try again next year.) Tropical bamboos (most clumping types are tropical) tend to sprout a little later. Divide the running and clumping types according to the methods given below.

Divide Running Bamboo. Look for a place where several mature culms emerge from the ground. They should be near each other.

- With a saw or long-handled loppers cut off a section of rhizome that contains at least two nodes and two to four existing culms (plus visible buds that are about to sprout).

- Dig up the rhizome with its roots.

- Cut back the culms by one-third to one-half of their height to compensate for the loss of roots.

- Plant the rhizome immediately in rich organic soil in a container or the ground, positioning it at the same depth at which you originally found it.

- Cover the roots with an inch or two of mulch, stake the culms, if necessary, to prevent them from being pushed over by wind, make a watering basin, and water thoroughly.

- Keep the roots moist until the new plant is well established.

- Beginning one month after planting start fertilizing regularly with a lawn fertilizer.

Divide Clumping Bamboo. Look on the outside of the clump for a bulge of growth containing at least three or four culms and some rhizomes with buds on them. (This can be difficult since growth is often dense.)

- Slice down around the chosen bulge of growth with a sharp spade or cut through the rhizomes with a pruning saw to separate them from the parent plant. Then with a trowel or spade dig up the entire clump with the rhizomes and the roots attached.

- Proceed to cut back, plant, water, and fertilize the new plant as described above for running bamboos.

(Two years ago my prized clump of Mexican weeping bamboo [*Otatea acuminata aztecorum*], a graceful, drought-resistant variety that flowers every thirty-five years, flowered so enthusiastically that all the rhizomes completely died.)

Choose Unusual Bamboos and Feed Them Like Grass. A number of bamboos, including Mexican weeping bamboo, are well suited to Southern California gardens (consult the list and detailed discussion in the *Sunset Western Garden Book*), but only the most common ones can be found in most nurseries. Unusual bamboos can best be found in specialty nurseries, at botanical-garden sales, or through the American Bamboo Society.

Most bamboos require good soil and plenty of water to look their best. They also appreciate a layer of mulch over their roots. Remember they are a type of grass, and feed them occasionally during their growing season—the warm months of the year—with a lawn fertilizer according to package directions.

Divide Bamboo in Spring. The easiest way to propagate bamboo is by separating rhizomes from the parent plant in spring just before the plants begin to grow. Bamboo can be propagated from seeds when those seeds are available, but they aren't always viable. (See the accompanying box for directions using rhizomes.)

Lawn Care

March is the time to feed all types of established lawns and to plant new ones from seed. You can also plant lawns from sod this month. First, though, decide whether it's lawn that you want.

Consider the Lawn-Free Landscape. Before putting in a lawn consider the pros and cons of having one. Water shortages make large lawns inappropriate for modern needs, and you may have to let a lawn of any size go brown in a drought. But there's still a place for a small lawn and there are several good reasons for wanting one. Nothing provides a cooler look, a better contrast for flowers, or a more comfortable play space for people and dogs. You can't play croquet on anything else. But if you don't have a reason for planting a lawn as good as children who need it to play on, choose a landscape of patios, ground covers, flowers, trees, shrubs, and wandering paths. Lawns sap our energy, water, and money—not to mention our patience and peace of mind. A cottage gardener I know says, "Lawns take just as much care and water as flowers; I'd rather have flowers!"

Mow, Feed, and Water All Lawns. Warm-season grasses, such as Bermuda, dichondra, and zoysia, are waking up from winter dormancy in March. As soon as they start growing begin mowing weekly with a reel mower to the correct height for each. Mow common Bermuda to 1 inch, hybrid Bermuda to ½ or ¾ inch, St. Augustine to between ¾ and 1¼ inches, and zoysia to ¾ to 1 inch in height. Cut Adalayd grass with a rotary mower to between ¾ and 1 inch in height. Cool-season grasses, such as fescue, ryegrass, and bluegrass, are still growing fast; mow them weekly with a rotary mower to 1½ inches in height.

Feed all established lawns now with a complete lawn fertilizer—containing phosphorus and potassium as well as nitrogen—to get warm-season grasses off to a good start and keep cool-season grasses going longer. A healthy, well-fed lawn is better able to withstand pests and diseases and choke out weeds. While nitrogen gives your lawn top growth and a healthy green color you can see, phosphorus and potassium feed the roots and growth systems of the plant that are unseen but just as important. Phosphorus and potassium are longer lasting in soil than nitrogen, so one feeding a season with them is often adequate. After this complete feeding you can switch to a less expensive, pure nitrogen fertilizer if desired, and feed warm-season grasses with it once a month for the rest of the growing season.

Feed most turf grasses at the rate of 1 pound of actual nitrogen per 1,000 square feet of turf. Feed dichondra one-half this strength and the new tall, drought-resistant fescues three-quarter strength. (The latter respond best to frequent but light applications of fertilizer.)

Apply fertilizer when the ground is damp and grass blades dry, and follow up by watering deeply. Otherwise you risk burning your lawn. If you're willing to pay the price, coated slow-release fertilizers are available that will feed your lawn for as long as six months from a single application. These are fine to use on warm-season lawns now, but don't make the mistake of using a slow-release fertilizer on a cool-season lawn at this time of year. Cool-season grasses need little or no fertilizer during the warmer months of the year.

Irrigate all lawns now, according to their individual needs, when rains aren't adequate.

Choose the Best Time to Plant. Both warm- and cool-season grasses may be bought as sod, and cool-season grasses can be planted from sod any month year-round. Although you can plant both warm- and cool-season grasses from seed this month, wait if you possibly can to plant cool-season grasses. October is a better time to plant them because fall planting gives cool-season grasses planted from seed more time to establish a root system before summer heat arrives. When planting warm-season grasses, wait until the weather has warmed up in your area. (If you plan to plant zoysia, it's best to wait until June.)

Study Lawn Types Before Planting One. How do you choose which grass is right for you? Begin by looking around your neighborhood. Talk to the owners of good-looking lawns. Don't just choose for appearance, though. Consider how much traffic your lawn will have to take and how willing you are to fuss over it. Also consult your Cooperative Extension Office and reference books on lawns—for example, MacCaskey's *Lawns and Groundcovers, How to Select, Grow and Enjoy*—before choosing a lawn that's right for your area and needs. Experienced nurserymen are another source of information; they usually know which seed or sod has performed well in your neighborhood. Above all, consider drought resistance.

Weigh the Pros and Cons of Warm- and Cool-Season Grasses. If water were plentiful the majority of gardeners would never choose to plant such warm-season grasses as Bermuda and zoysia because of their bad habits; they go brown in winter and they invade borders. Most people like cool-season lawns better, because they stay green all year and look more like eastern lawns. But periodic droughts, dwindling water supplies, and forced cutbacks have made gardeners realize that it's totally unrealistic to expect a lawn to look like a golf green; the ideal lawn is one that can survive. Cool-season lawns aren't invasive, but they take a lot of water—

about 38 inches a year of rain and irrigation—to keep them looking good. If you don't water them they'll die. Warm-season lawns like Bermuda and zoysia can look good on only 18 inches of irrigation a year, and you can cut that amount by two-thirds and still keep them alive. If you're forced to let them go brown in a drought, they'll pull in their horns and may live through it. The very characteristics that make Bermuda invasive and devilishly hard to get rid of are the same that help it live through tough times. (If you want to keep it from creeping into your flower beds, install a continuous concrete curb to keep it in bounds.)

If despite this warning you decide to plant a cool-season grass it's often wise to plant a mix. That way the grass that's best adapted for you will take over; weak ones will die out. But read the label on the mix. Bentgrass is an unacceptable choice. It's thirsty, disease-prone, and ill-adapted to our climate. Kentucky bluegrass—unmixed with other grasses—is also a poor choice. Though it will survive near the coast in fertile, well-drained soil and full sun, it requires a high level of maintenance and a great deal of water. When it's mixed with ryegrass, however, it makes the lawn less susceptible to fusarium blight, a fungus disease that attacks in summer, than a lawn that's planted from ryegrass alone. Tall fescues and finer-textured ryegrasses are somewhat less demanding than bluegrass, but they need almost as much water. Tall fescue varieties are disease resistant and take traffic well, but they don't form a dense sod or fill in bare spots. If they're not planted thickly they can look threadbare. However, two new dwarf varieties, Bonsai and Twilight, have finer blades and form a denser turf than other tall fescues.

Common Bermuda grass, such as NuMex Sahara, can be started from seed, but hybrid Bermudas and many other subtropical grasses are planted from rhizomes, sprigs, plugs, or *stolons* (sections of stem that creep along the surface and root into the ground). A fine hybrid Bermuda grass such as Santa Ana, mown short with a reel mower, will give you a good-looking lawn for most of the year. New varieties of Bermuda such as NuMex Sahara have improved early spring color. New varieties also make zoysia well worth considering, but hold off until June to plant since it takes off much better in summer. (See p. 161 for more about zoysia.) St. Augustine grass can take more shade than any other choice, but it needs a lot of water. Tests have shown that common Bermuda grass and Santa Ana hybrid Bermuda are the two most drought-resistant lawn grasses. You can keep them green with less water than it takes to keep many drought-resistant ground covers alive, including gazaneas, vinca, coyote brush, and Australian saltbush (*Atriplex semibaccata*).

Plant New Lawns. Regardless of the type of grass and method of planting you choose be sure to prepare the site thoroughly. If you're planting an invasive grass, such as Bermuda or an invasive variety of zoysia, first install edging to keep it from creeping into borders.

For all lawns, rototill deeply, add plenty of soil amendment, and level and lightly roll the ground. Sprinkle seeds evenly and cover them with mulch. Either roll stolons with a cleated roller to press them into the soil or partially cover them with topsoil. Keep your freshly planted lawn damp until established. Sprinkle it twice or three times daily, but avoid watering late in the day.

Vegetable Gardening

Start planting summer vegetables now. If you've never before grown a vegetable garden March is the best time to begin. The first week in March is the earliest time for putting in warm-season crops. The sooner you plant the sooner you'll have a harvest.

A wide range of crops can be put in now. Summer vegetables that can be planted in March include artichokes, chayote, corn, green beans, New Zealand spinach, and tomatoes. In coastal zones and warm, south-facing gardens cucumbers and both summer and winter squash can be planted by midmonth. If you have room there's still enough cool weather left to plant a few cool-season crops, such as broccoli, head lettuce, kohlrabi, potatoes, and cabbage. And of course you can plant the crops that go year-round, such as carrots, radishes, beets, chard, and turnips. Wait until April to put in the real heat lovers, such as peppers, lima beans, melons, pumpkins, eggplant, and okra.

Provide Adequate Light. Plant vegetables in full sun. Without it they'll succumb to disease and fail to flower, and you won't get a crop. Lay out your vegetable garden to make the best use of sunlight. The ☞ **Rule of Thumb** is: ***Plant tall crops to the north and short crops to the south, and arrange your rows from north to south so the sun goes from side to side across them***.

If you're dying to grow vegetables but don't have full sun try lettuce, potatoes, asparagus, and herbs—parsley, for example. In a pinch these choices will take partial shade. (For lettuce it's sometimes better.) Tomatoes will bear a crop with just four or five hours of midday sun in a warm, sheltered location, especially if it also provides reflected heat.

Provide Good Soil and Drainage. Vegetables need deep, fertile soil with adequate drainage. Sandy or decomposed-granite loam is best. But if you have red clay, adobe, or almost pure sand, don't despair. Good vegetables can be grown in heavy clay soils or highly sandy soils if plenty of organic soil amendment is added. Don't attempt to grow vegetables in areas clogged with tree roots, since they sap the water needed for healthy growth. If your soil is rock hard or drainage is nil, plant in raised beds that are filled with top soil mixed with organic amend-ments. If roots are a problem, plant in large containers with paving stones underneath.

Install a Drip System. Decide on a watering system. The furrow method is good especially with heavy soils, but it wastes water. Overhead sprinkling can work early in the day, but it can be bad along the coast, where excess mois-ture on leaves, cool temperatures, and a moist atmosphere may encourage the growth of fungus diseases.

The best way for modern Southland gardeners to water vegetables is with a drip system. Most vegetables need the equivalent of an inch of rain per week for healthy growth. Drip systems use 40 to 60 percent less water by putting it where roots are. Choose a system designed for row crops, such as nonclogging agricultural Bi-Wall tubing that can be buried 3 to 6 inches under-ground. The time taken now to install a drip system will save untold hours later.

Plant for Successive Crops. When planting vegeta-bles that mature all at the same time, like

* ✳ *

How Farmers Discovered That Legumes Need Inoculation

All *legumes* (plants such as peas and beans that have a pod shaped like a pea pod) have the ability to take nitrogen out of the air. They do it by means of nodules on their roots and a symbiotic relationship with tiny bacteria called *rhizobia*. Centuries ago farmers noticed that certain patches of peas or beans produced better crops than others. They discovered that a handful of soil from one of these good patches mixed with the seed of legumes could improve growing conditions in less productive areas. Unbeknown to themselves they were actually inoculating their seed.

Modern inoculants are available by mail from seed companies and come with directions for their use. Most kinds can be applied by sprinkling them into the bottom of the furrow before planting seeds. When planting many seeds mix them in a bowl with enough table syrup or honey to make them sticky. Then add inoculant and stir the seeds until each one is thoroughly coated. If you inoculate your seed don't use nitrogen fertilizer; the plant will manufacture all the nitrogen it needs, and adding more will make the inoculant less effective.

* ✳ *

carrots and beets, don't plant the whole package at once. Plant quantities no bigger than your family can eat at one time, and save the rest of the seeds to plant at intervals for continued crops. The same goes for lettuce. If you continually harvest outside leaves you can lengthen the harvest, but if you plan to take out whole heads, plant at shorter intervals.

Make Space for Planting in Established Gardens. If you grow vegetables year-round in an established garden begin now to make space for summer crops. When you plant winter vegetables in fall you can usually pull up just about everything and start out fresh. But in spring when you plant summer vegetables it's not quite that easy, because the seasons for many crops overlap. It's often necessary to plant now among some winter vegetables that are still going strong and to pull out others—even if they aren't quite finished—in order to make enough room for summer vegetables.

The smaller the space the more important it is to schedule your fall planting so that most cole crops, such as cabbage, broccoli, and cauliflower, are finished by now. If they're still going plant them earlier next year. Peas are often getting ratty looking and mildewy by now, so pull them out and replace them with tomatoes and corn. Harvest the last of the fava beans and pull up celery, which by now is usually going to seed. Onions and garlic stay in the ground to mature as the days lengthen. Be sure to weed your onions often; their small root systems can't compete with the rapacious roots of weeds. Replace parsley now or next month. A good place for it is east of a row of trellised cucumbers, where it will get some shade on hot afternoons. By cleaning out most winter crops

How to Grow Pole Beans

- Choose a spot 6 feet square in full sun.

- Dig up and loosen the soil to the depth of 1 foot, and cultivate a 4-inch layer of organic soil amendment (but not manure) into it.

- Sprinkle the ground with 2 pounds of commercial vegetable fertilizer (5-10-10 or 6-12-8, for example). Work this into the top 6 inches. Or, alternatively, you can work in 1 pound bone meal or 2 pounds 0-10-10 and provide nitrogen by inoculating your seed with nitrogen-fixing bacteria. (The accompanying box describes the origins of this technique.)

- Tie together at one end four 8-foot-long bamboo poles or green plastic-covered garden stakes. Set up your teepee with the legs spread about 4 feet apart and the ends shoved 3 to 4 inches into the ground.

- Plant 5 or 6 beans 3 inches apart, with the scar side down, around each pole. Plant 1 inch deep along the coast, 2 inches deep inland. Cover the seeds with commercial potting soil and pat it down gently.

- Water deeply after planting. Don't water again until the beans come up unless the soil begins to dry out. (Sometimes beans rot instead of coming up. If the problem is heavy soil see the box for how best to plant in it. If the problem is cold soil—below 60°F or 16°C—presprout the seed before planting it. See p. 121.)

- Once the plants have emerged keep them well watered and protect them from birds and snails.

- When the plants are 3 or 4 inches tall thin to the best three on each pole. (Snip the others off with scissors.) Give the young plants a helping hand to start them winding around the poles. Once started they'll keep going with no further help from you.

Quick Tip

**How to Protect Bean and
Corn Sprouts from Birds.**
*Birds, especially mockingbirds, love young bean
and sweet corn sprouts. Pop a green berry basket
(the kind that strawberries and cherry tomatoes
come in) over each planted seed. After sprouts
have touched the top of the baskets, you can
safely remove them. Birds will have lost interest.*

How to Plant Large Seeds in Heavy Soil

Heavy soils such as red clay or adobe often bake to a hard crust on top. Large seeds—beans or squash, for example—may not be able to break through. Take these precautions to avoid their rotting under the ground.

- Make a trench to the right planting depth. Soak the trench deeply, at least twice or three times, and let the water drain out.

- Place seeds in the bottom of the trench. (In the case of beans, place them with their scar side pointing down. The root will go straight down and all your beans will come up at the same time.)

- Cover the seed with an inch of dry potting soil, in coastal zones, or with 2 inches of dry potting soil inland. Pat it down gently and don't water again until the beans pop through. The dry potting soil will act like a mulch and draw just the right amount of moisture to the seed for it to sprout.

now, and cultivating and amending the soil, you help prevent a carryover of pests and diseases.

Plant Green, Wax, and Purple Beans. Green beans are often called snap beans or string beans, though modern varieties are almost stringless. Wax beans are similar but turn yellow as they mature and usually have a milder flavor. There's also a delicious purple bean—Royal Burgundy is the improved variety—that turns green when it's cooked. All these beans do best when planted now.

For the earliest harvest plant bush beans—choose a good variety, such as Venture from Park Seed or Pencil Pod, a wax bean. If you have limited space plant pole beans. (See the accompanying box for directions.) You'll get a bigger and longer-lasting harvest and, in most cases, a better tasting bean. Brown-seeded Kentucky Wonder is one of the finest and easiest varieties for our area because it's resistant to rust. White-seeded Kentucky Wonder, also rust resistant, is actually a different strain and not quite as prolific. (Try both and compare.)

Plant Potatoes. Seed potatoes can be bought now at local nurseries. Plant them if you have room; they're fun and easy and delicious when homegrown. Cut seed potatoes in half so there are two or three eyes per section, roll them in RooTone or soil sulfur, and let them stand a day or two for the cuts to callus over before planting. Or, if you prefer, plant the seed potatoes whole. Tests indicate you may get a bigger harvest that way. (Potatoes can also be grown from seed, but until better varieties come along it isn't worth the trouble.) Plant them 3 or 4 inches deep and 12 inches apart.

Potatoes grow best in fertile, sandy, slightly

acid soil. Before planting them amend your soil with acid soil mix—for example, nitrolized redwood shavings or peat moss. Also apply a complete vegetable fertilizer according to package directions and work it into the top six inches of soil. As the plants grow mound the soil up around their stems until you have formed a row that is mounded approximately 6 inches higher than the surrounding ground. Keep the ground moist by giving it an occasional deep watering.

Plant Artichokes to Grow as an Annual Vegetable. Globe artichokes (*Cynara scolymus*) are edible thistles that have been cultivated since the time of the ancient Romans. They grow well in Southern California, particularly close to the ocean. They're usually planted bare root in fall to grow as a permanent plant that will produce a crop the following summer. (Bare-root plants are the commercial variety Green Globe, which are the same kind you most frequently see for sale in your grocery store.) If you plant these in spring you can't be sure of a harvest the first year. Now, however, newer seed-grown varieties of artichoke, plus proper fertilization and care, can guarantee a harvest the same year, even if you plant as late as March. To plant now and grow artichokes as an annual buy transplants already growing in pony packs or 4-inch containers. These are the seed-grown plants, and they'll produce a harvest as early as June. (If you live in a hot interior valley wait until mid to late summer to plant seed-grown plants for a late winter and spring harvest. Flower buds are woody if they mature during hot weather.)

Dig the soil deeply. Artichokes need good drainage, plenty of fertilizer, and deep watering in order to grow rapidly. Add a generous quantity

➤

Quick Tip

How to Keep Seeds Dry.
Fold partially used seed packages securely and place them in a dry screw-top jar. Add a homemade dessicant of 2 tablespoons dried skim-milk powder wrapped in tissue, secured with a rubber band. Seal the jar tightly, and store it in the refrigerator or in a cool, dry place.

* ✻ *

How to Plant and Grow Tomatoes

Tomatoes are the favorite vegetable for home growing. If you want to grow a special variety you can't find in nurseries—Sweet Million, for example—you can sprout the seeds indoors (they germinate readily) and grow your own transplants. But it's easier and quicker to grow your tomatoes from transplants you buy at the nursery, so that's the method given here.

- Select a disease-resistant variety, such as Better Boy, Ace Hybrid, or Celebrity, that's appropriate for your needs and climate zone. For a quick harvest when planting in March, also plant an early variety—Early Girl or Taxi-Yellow, for example.

- Choose a spot in full sun, and prepare the soil by digging it deeply with a spade and adding soil amendment.

- Use either a vegetable fertilizer or one especially recommended for tomatoes—Ross Tomato Boomers, for example. (It's a slow-release type. Stick one into the ground next to each planted tomato.) Take care not to overfeed with nitrogen.

- Plant transplants deeply. If they're leggy snip off the lower leaves, make a little trench with the trowel, lay the plant in sideways, and bend the stem up gently. Roots will form all along the buried stem.

- Choose a staking system. (See the accompanying box.)

- Water deeply and continue to irrigate so the soil stays evenly moist.

* ✻ *

of organic soil amendment and choose a good quality vegetable fertilizer. Measure the dimensions of the ground to be fertilized and follow package directions. Cultivate the fertilizer into the top 6 inches of soil. Space plants 4 feet apart—don't crowd them—and plant high to avoid crown rot. Cover the roots thoroughly with soil, then make a watering basin slightly deeper than the crown of the plant. As the plant grows pile a little more soil around the main stalk, to prevent irrigation water from touching it.

Water artichokes twice a week for the first two weeks and then deeply once a week, or use a drip system that provides ample water. (The ground must be constantly moist, so don't grow them during drought years.) Artichokes grow quickly when watered and fed, and they tend to send up many offshoots or side shoots, sometimes called suckers. Break them off as they occur. If you have room stick them elsewhere in the garden; they'll grow. Or plant them in 5-gallon containers to give to friends. (Artichoke plants in pots are amusing on a patio since they'll bear artichokes, though they'll be small in size.) Protect plants from snails, which love artichokes.

* ✺ *

How to Stake Tomatoes

Don't let tomatoes sprawl on the ground; they'll rot, or pests will get them. Here are three staking methods. Each gives different results and requires different pruning and training. The third method is recommended only for coastal zones.

1. Bend a 6½-foot length of 5-foot-tall, 6-by-6 hardware cloth or cement-reinforcing wire to make a round cage 2 feet across. Place a cage over each plant. Stake it down firmly to withstand wind.

Pruning and Training: Don't prune at all. The tomato will climb up inside the cage by itself and need no staking.

Results: This method will give you the most fruit but the smallest.

Areas for Which Recommended: Any zone, but especially those with hot, interior climates (because the fruit is well shaded).

2. Construct a trellis of 6- or 8-foot-tall hardware cloth or cement-reinforcing wire supported by three or four 8-foot stakes shoved 1 foot into the ground.

Pruning and Training: Prune out most suckers but allow two or three main stems to grow. You don't need to tie up the vines; just weave them gently in and out as they grow. The trellis will support them.

Results: The fruit will be bigger than by the cage-grown method, and more numerous than by the single-stem method that follows.

Areas for Which Recommended: All zones—either coastal or inland.

3. Support each tomato with a single 8-foot stake that you embed 1 or 2 feet in the ground.

Pruning and Training: Tie up the tomato plant as it grows. Remove all suckers (side sprouts growing above leaves), allowing only one main trunk to grow.

Results: This method takes more work but gives enormous fruit and an early harvest.

Areas for Which Recommended: Coastal zones only (because fruit will sunburn inland).

* ✺ *

Quick Tip

How to Foil Cutworms
Save the cardboard tube from inside holiday wrapping paper. Cut it into 2-inch sections to make protective collars. When you plant tomatoes first slip the leaves of each plant gently through a cardboard collar. Last, anchor the sleeve ½ inch into the soil around the transplant. Cutworms won't climb over.

Purchase / Plant

- [ ] Plant **drought-resistant plants**, 15
- [ ] Plant **asparagus** from seeds, 65
- [ ] Don't plant **tropicals**, 71
- [ ] Plant **trees, shrubs, vines,** and **ground covers,** 72
- [ ] Plant flower beds with **warm-season flowers,** if you have space, 74
- [ ] Plant **perennials,** 74
- [ ] Plant **tigridias,** 77
- [ ] Continue to plant **gladioli,** 77
- [ ] Start **tuberous begonias,** 77, 78
- [ ] Plant softwood cuttings of **chrysanthemums, marguerites, gamolepis,** and **euryops,** 78
- [ ] Plant **citrus, avocado,** and **macadamia trees,** 79
- [ ] Purchase **epidendrums,** 81
- [ ] Start **fuchsias** from cuttings, 83
- [ ] Plant **lawns,** 88
- [ ] Start planting **summer vegetables.** Plant more **cool-season crops** if desired, 89
- [ ] Replace **parsley** now or next month, 90
- [ ] Plant **green beans,** 92
- [ ] Plant **potatoes,** 92
- [ ] Plant **artichokes** from seed-grown transplants, 93
- [ ] Plant **tomatoes,** 94

Trim, Prune, Mow, Divide

- [ ] In interior valleys prune **begonias, ginger, cannas, asparagus fern, ivy,** and **pyracantha,** 56
- [ ] Dethatch **warm-season lawns** just after they begin to grow, 62
- [ ] Deadhead **annual** and **perennial flowers,** 75
- [ ] Start to disbud **roses** if you are growing roses for show, 77
- [ ] Tie floppy leaves of **bulbs** in knots. (Don't remove them before they go brown.) 77
- [ ] Tie **gladioli** to stakes as they grow, 77
- [ ] Cut back **epidendrum** stems after bloom, 82
- [ ] Prune **camellias,** 82
- [ ] Take cut flowers from **azaleas** while they're in bloom, 82
- [ ] Pinch **fuchsias** to make them bushy, 82
- [ ] Start to prune **tropical hibiscus,** 82
- [ ] Propagate **bamboo,** 85
- [ ] Mow all **grass lawns,** 86
- [ ] Cut back **blue hibiscus** (*Alyogyne*) progressively from now until fall, 154
- [ ] Pinch back **petunias** when you plant them, 178

Fertilize

- [ ] Begin to fertilize **citrus trees** in interior zones. Continue to fertilize **citrus trees** in coastal zones, 30
- [ ] Continue to fertilize **epiphyllums** with 0-10-10 or 2-10-10, 35
- [ ] Begin to fertilize **avocado trees** in interior zones. Continue to fertilize **avocado trees** in coastal zones, 48
- [ ] Fertilize **fuchsias,** 55
- [ ] Fertilize **ornamental trees, bushes, lawns,** and **ground covers,** 72
- [ ] Feed **container-grown flowers** with liquid or slow-release fertilizer, 75
- [ ] Fertilize **cool-season flowers** if growth or flowering slows, 75
- [ ] Fertilize **roses,** 76
- [ ] Begin to fertilize **macadamia trees,** 79
- [ ] Feed all **lawns,** 86
- [ ] Treat **blue hydrangeas** with aluminum sulfate, 229

Water

☐ When rains aren't adequate water **all garden plants** according to their individual needs, 12

☐ Keep **fuchsias** well watered, 55

☐ Water **roses,** 76

☐ Water **spring-flowering bulbs** when rains don't do the job for you, 77

☐ Don't let **azaleas** dry out, 82

Control Pests, Diseases, and Weeds

☐ Control **slugs** and **snails,** 73

☐ Control pests and diseases on **roses,** 76

☐ Protect **gladioli** from slugs and snails, 77

☐ Control **cutworms,** 92

☐ Be on the lookout for **juniper moths.** (Spray if necessary.) 110

☐ Pull **weeds,** 170

☐ Plant **French marigolds** (*Tagetes patula*) solidly and leave them for a full season of growth to control nematodes, 208

☐ Spray **cycads** for scale, 214

Also This Month

☐ Record last **frost dates** in garden notebook, 72

☐ In interior zones protect **tender plants** until all danger of frost has passed, 72

☐ Once all frost danger is over take out **tender tropicals** you sheltered during winter, 72

☐ When **frost-damaged plants** resume growth, cut off damaged portions, 73

☐ Prepare holes for planting **dahlias** next month, 77

☐ Unwrap trunks of **young citrus** and **avocado trees,** 79

☐ Harvest Beaumont **macadamia nuts** and cure them correctly, 80

☐ Hand pollinate **quince, guava,** and **cherimoya,** 83

☐ Install a drip system for irrigating **vegetables,** 89

☐ Continue to harvest **winter vegetables,** 90

☐ Inoculate **legumes,** 91, 93

☐ Choose a staking method for **tomatoes,** 95

☐ **Desert flowers** begin to bloom in late March. See them now or next month, 101

☐ Make an **herb garden,** 310

APRIL

APRIL

The Height-of-Bloom Month

April is a magic time, the height of spring in Southern California. In the back country native plants deck the hillsides with color. So get out and take an observant walk around an old neighborhood, visit botanical gardens, go on garden tours sponsored by local clubs, and enjoy wildflowers in their moment of greatest glory. Take along a camera and notebook to record ideas. See native plants in bloom at such locations as Rancho Santa Ana Botanic Garden, 1500 North College, Claremont, CA 91711 (714/625-8767) ; Torrey Pines Park [on the Coast Highway immediately south of Del Mar in San Diego County] (619/755-2063); the Theodore Payne Foundation,10459 Tuxford Street, Sun Valley, CA 91352 (818/768-1802); and the Antelope Valley California Poppy Reserve, 15101 West Lancaster Road, Lancaster, CA 93536 [go

15 miles west of Lancaster on Avenue I, which becomes Lancaster Road] (805/274-1180; when not in service phone the California Department of Parks and Recreation, 805/942-0662). For more ideas purchase a copy of Bartel and Belt's *A Guide to Botanical Resources of Southern California.* Or phone the Wildflower Information Hotline in Lancaster (805/948-1322).

At home April is our second spring-planting month but less demanding than the first. Southern California is in full bloom this month. We pride ourselves on year-round flowers, but we have more in April than at any other time of the year. Cool-season annuals planted in September and October reach their zenith early this month and, by midmonth, countless permanent landscape plants are in full bloom. If you did most of your spring planting in March, relax now and enjoy the fruits of your labor. If not, there's still time to catch up on jobs that went undone.

It's warm enough to sprout seeds quickly but not hot enough to scorch seedlings. Stormy days—often bringing heavy rains—alternate with sunny days, speeding growth and opening flowers. Pests also enjoy the warming trend. Cabbage butterflies, thrips, mites, and tobacco budworm speed up activities and need to be controlled. Despite this one negative note April is a month to relish.

Valley and Desert Dwellers

If you live in a hot inland valley or desert area do your last planting this month before the onslaught of summer heat. This is the last moment for you to plant ground covers without risking development of ugly gaps, and it's not too late to plant tropicals and subtropicals— palms and oleanders, for example. Local nurseries have assortments of heat-loving bedding plants that can go into the ground now, including balsam, vinca, marigolds, zinnias, petunias, and portulaca. (In desert areas, plant petunias in fall.)

Mulch plants after setting them out, and protect them from the hot noonday sun until they're well started. A shot of well-diluted liquid fertilizer after planting can get plants off to a good start. Choose a fertilizer that has instructions for new plantings on the label.

Azaleas

April is the best month of the year in which to plant azaleas, though not the first possible. (Precise directions are given for January, p. 32.) The largest number of azaleas are in bloom now, and while they're in bloom their roots are dormant so you can safely plant them. As soon as they finish blooming they'll take off and grow. Above ground they'll start putting out fresh leaves, and below ground they'll sprout tender young roots that shouldn't be disturbed.

Plant azaleas in tubs or the ground and in partial shade—a northern or eastern exposure is best. For easy care water with a drip system adjusted to keep roots evenly moist—neither soggy nor dry.

Wisteria

Choose wisteria vines now while they're in bloom. There are two main types: Chinese wisteria (*Wisteria sinensis*), which blooms all at once on bare branches, and Japanese wisteria (*Wisteria floribunda*), which has a longer period of bloom, more fragrance, and flowers that open from top to bottom as leaves appear. Besides the familiar violet-blue there are white, pink, and purple wisterias, some with 3-foot-long blooms. Named varieties are worth hunting for. Grown from cuttings they have characteristics superior to those of chance seedlings.

Wisteria is one of our most satisfactory vines because, though it's easy to grow and highly drought resistant once established, its blooms are among the most romantic of flowers in color, shape, and fragrance. It's deciduous, so if you grow it on an arbor it can give you welcome shade in summer and sunshine in winter. And it flourishes anywhere from desert to beach. Plant the vines in full sun, provide strong support, and water and fertilize them often for the first year or two to get them started. Once a wisteria is well established you can subject it to benign neglect, but not before.

Epiphyllums

Epiphyllums, or orchid cacti, are true members of the cactus family but native to open jungles rather than deserts. They like semishade, well-drained soil, and, since most are *epiphytes* or tree-dwelling plants (and because they're particularly delicious to snails), they do well in hanging baskets. There are more than nine thousand named varieties to choose from. Real fanciers fill entire backyards with these plants and have blooms year-round, but most gardeners grow them for a spectacular show beginning now and lasting through June. Begin looking for them in nurseries. Watch the newspaper for epiphyllum shows in May. Ask friends to save you a branch of this or that admired variety. They're easy to start from cuttings (the box on p. 104 tells how).

For most of the year epiphyllums are the ugly ducklings of the garden. They can be kept tucked away in a semishady spot, watered once a week in dry weather, pruned of dead branches to encourage growth, and fed occasionally with a complete fertilizer such as 8-8-8 liquid or fish emulsion ("liquid fish") during the summer and with a high bloom formula such as 0-10-10 or 2-10-10 from January until they bloom. Now's the time to move plants to center stage and enjoy the exotic flowers. Make sure you face the plants in the same direction they're used to, or the flower buds may fall off.

Each flower lasts only a day or two, but more keep opening. For best appearance cut off the faded blossoms that have bloomed; otherwise their wilted petals will hang on for a long time. Mist "epis" frequently in dry weather, but don't overwater them. Though less drought resistant than most other cacti epiphyllums use little water, especially if you irrigate them with a drip system instead of a hose. Test whether plants are ready for watering by sticking a finger an inch or two into the mix. If it feels damp don't water. If it feels dry turn on the drip system until you see water drain out the bottoms of the containers; then turn it off. During the rainy season don't water at all.

What's an Epiphyte?

An epiphyte is a plant that lives by attaching itself to another plant, typically to a tree, or in some cases to a rock. They often root in pockets of soil that gather in the crotches of trees and are fertilized by a regular sprinkling of bird droppings, dead insects, and the occasional dead animal. Unlike parasites epiphytes don't take nourishment from the host plant. Most are native to humid tropical or subtropical regions. Many aroids, orchids, ferns, cacti, and bromeliads are epiphytic. They're good choices for our gardens because so many of them have developed built-in reservoirs, thickened leaves, or other devices to see them through drought.

All epiphytes prefer loose, acid, airy, well-drained soil. They're often grown in hanging baskets. Some are grown on slabs of bark, and all can be *naturalized* (made to grow and multiply as they would in the wild) on tree branches and kept moist by misting with an automatic mist system.

* ❋ *

How to Start an Epiphyllum from a Cutting

- Cut off a branch from a plant you wish to propagate, making the cut at the narrow intersection where it joins another branch.

- Use a permanent broad-tip marker to write the variety name in block letters directly on one side of the cutting.

- If the cut branch is wide, trim off excess flesh to make a point. Dip the cut sections in a rooting hormone such as RooTone, knock off the excess, and allow the cutting to dry and "callus off" for a day or two.

- Plant in a 4-inch pot of dry—not wet—potting soil to a depth ½ inch above the two lowest *areoles* or spine cushions. (On epiphyllums these are found in the notches on the stem.) Tamp the soil down firmly around the cutting, stake it with wood or bamboo, and tie it securely.

- Mist the cutting daily, but take care not to water the soil until the cutting has rooted, in about a month. (You can check by pulling gently on the cutting; when roots have sprouted it will resist. Or you can tell by feeling the thickness of the cutting; when the roots begin to grow it will get plumper.) Once it has rooted, start regularly watering. Feed lightly when it has grown 2 or 3 inches tall. When roots fill the container, repot it into a larger size.

- A good soil mix for epiphyllums is light, airy, drains well, and contains agricultural charcoal. The following works well: 1 gallon good quality acid, commercial potting soil mix recommended for "jungle" plants, 1 cup perlite, and 1 cup agricultural charcoal.

* ❋ *

Pruning

Cut Back Poinsettias. After poinsettia flowers have faded, sometime between now and the end of May, prune garden-grown plants back to two or three dormant buds. (These look like swellings or scars close to the bottoms of the branches.) Poinsettia (*Euphorbia pulcherrima*) is best-known today as a Christmas pot plant, but old varieties like Hollywood make easy-care garden plants, requiring only average watering in summer. (Among indoor varieties Annette Hegg grows best outdoors.) Order garden varieties from nurseries, or purchase them at plant sales. They grow easily from cuttings. Fifty years ago, before modern varieties and growing techniques made poinsettias so popular for Christmas, they were a staple of California gardens in frost-free zones, and they're still useful for hard-to-reach sunny spots, such as a south-facing garage wall.

Control Shrubs That Would Like to Be Trees. Hedges and shrubs start fast growth now. Any green shrub that has an eventual size of over 6 feet needs frequent pruning during the warm months if you want to keep it as a shrub. (Remember to prune flowering shrubs that bloom for a specific season after rather than before bloom.) Many shrubs would like to shoot up and become trees; it's all right to let them— some make fine specimens—but when it happens by accident you end up with a crowded garden. (A more sophisticated approach is to use dwarf plants that will always be the right size for the space.)

With shrubs in particular, work for a billowy, flowing form, wider below than above (so lower branches won't die from shade). There are three major ways to prune them.

1. Plants with small leaves can be clipped on the outside like a hedge, with shears or loppers.

2. Plants with large leaves are best cut from the inside, with branches cut out deep within to renew growth from inside out. This gives an informal look and is often necessary to keep heavy trunks from growing taller. (A saw or ratchet pruner can make this job easier; the built-in ratchet in particular increases your strength manyfold.)

3. Plants that grow from the ground in the shape of a fountain, such as oleander and heavenly bamboo (*Nandina domestica*), are best pruned by taking out entire branches to ground level after bloom. Pittosporum, myoporum, and photinia are among the shrubs to prune beginning now.

- **Victorian box (*Pittosporum undulatum*).** This is useful as a somewhat drought-resistant, informal shrub in coastal zones. (It requires more water in interior regions.) It frequently starts as a volunteer. Victorian box rapidly becomes a 15-foot tree if allowed, then gradually grows to 30 or 40 feet in height and width—a nice-looking tree but drippy with leaves and sticky fruit. It can be kept an informal hedge or screen indefinitely by cutting it back, mainly with loppers, beginning in spring and continuing occasionally throughout summer. A 9-foot hedge can be cut to 3 or 4 feet but will take a year or two to recover.

- **Tobira Pittosporum (*P. tobira*).** The standard variety can grow slowly to tree height, but with shears and loppers it can easily be kept small or pruned into artistic shapes. Wheeler's

Dwarf is compact; it grows eventually to only 2 or 3 feet, with a mounded shape and no pruning necessary.

- **Myoporum (*Myoporum laetum*).** To keep myoporum looking good as a shrub, windbreak, or informal hedge, control it from the beginning by cutting it back with loppers several times a year. Left to its own devices it shoots rapidly to 30 feet tall and 20 wide, and the bottom section eventually becomes bare and woody. A full-grown myoporum is an unattractive tree with no virtues; you can't cut it back into old wood and get anything but spindly regrowth.

- **Photinia (*Photinia fraseri*).** This plant naturally grows as a shrub—as tall as 10 feet, if you don't cut it shorter—or you can prune it into a small tree while it's young by choosing a single trunk and cutting out all others. Prune it often with loppers to keep the size you choose and encourage fresh growth. New growth is red—dull when front lit but exciting when planted on the west so that afternoon light shines through the leaves. When grown as a shrub, don't let photinia get wide on top or the bottom section will become bare and ugly. If it gets too tall cut it to the desired size this month. It will soon bounce back.

Deciduous Fruit Trees

Deciduous fruit trees that are overloaded with fruit always drop a lot of it later in the year, in a natural process called June drop (described on p. 156). You can permit your fruit to grow larger with less June drop by starting to thin it now. Thin out the fruit lightly this month,

How to Plant Dahlias

- Choose a spot in full sun along the coast, or afternoon shade inland, in rich, well-drained soil. Work in soil amendment if you didn't prepare planting holes in March.

- Dig holes 7 to 8 inches deep for large tubers or 5 to 6 inches deep for small tubers, and 1 to 3 feet apart according to size. Work into the bottom of each hole a handful of bone meal or 2 tablespoons of 2-10-10 or 2-18-8, or other high-bloom fertilizer. (High nitrogen cuts down on bloom.) Cover this with 2 inches of fast-draining soil or sand.

- Place the tuber on top with the eye (the growth bud) up.

- Cover it with 2 inches of soil. As the plant grows up through this soil, continually cover it with more.

- Stake tall varieties at planting time, with the stake next to the growth bud. Tie them up later. (Bedding varieties don't need it, but a stake will help you remember where the tubers are.)

- When plants are up 3 inches begin to fertilize with diluted liquid fertilizer every two weeks or with a complete slow-release fertilizer according to package directions.

- When the plant has three sets of leaves pinch off the top set to encourage branching. Some gardeners like to pinch again when plants are 1½ to 2 feet high. This will produce more but smaller blooms.

removing one or two fruits from heavy clusters all over the tree. Thin the fruit again four to six weeks later. (Mark it on your calendar so you won't forget.)

Bulbs

Plant Dahlias. Dahlias are the best-kept secret in the garden. With just a little care they're easy to grow and so flamboyant they'll make any gardener look like an expert. Grown in rows they're unpleasantly stiff, so plant dwarf and bedding types in drifts among other flowers and tall ones at the backs of beds.

Feed Irises. Fertilize irises with a low-nitrogen, high phosphorus and potassium plant food—2-10-10 or 2-18-6, for example—to encourage bloom. Solid fertilizers are the easiest to use for plants growing in the ground. Use liquids in containers. Protect irises from slugs and snails, which will ruin the plants if allowed.

Tie Up Leaves of Spring-Flowering Bulbs after Bloom. Continue to water spring-flowering bulbs when rains aren't adequate. Feed those that have bloomed with a balanced liquid fertilizer or solid bulb food watered into the ground. This will help them flower better next year. Don't cut off the green leaves until they go completely yellow; tie them into knots to make them look neater, and plant summer flowers around them.

Roses

Control Pests and Diseases, Fertilize, and Irrigate. Continue to control pests and diseases on roses (as described on pp. 54, 76). If you've chosen to follow a regular spraying routine with chemical sprays, continue to spray with Orthene and Funginex. (Some rose growers may also use a miticide, such as Avid, against spider mites, but Avid is highly toxic, not widely available, and expensive.) If you prefer not to spray with chemicals watch for caterpillars, which step up activity this month, and control them with BT (Bacillus thuringiensis).

Fertilize your roses regularly. Either feed once this month with a commercial rose food or, if you're following the Rose-Pro Method, feed at weekly intervals with 1 tablespoon sulfate of ammonia per rose and foliar feed with micronutrients (as described on pp. 76, 319).

In interior zones and fast-draining soils irrigate roses deeply with up to 1½ inches of water per application, and increase the frequency of irrigations now from once a week to twice a week. (One inch of water applied twice a week may be adequate in coastal climates and water-retentive soils.)

Prune Roses by Picking, Deadheading, and Disbudding. Roses start blooming in April, and when you pick them for cut flowers you're doing a kind of pruning. Roses naturally flower in flushes of bloom, but how you cut them affects both the lapse of time between consecutive flushes and the length of the stems they have. The longer the stems you cut, the more time it will take for the rose to rebloom, though the flowers will be good ones on long, strong stems. If you always cut your roses with short, stubby stems, the bush will bloom again much sooner, but with inferior flowers on short, weak stems. So unless you're growing exhibition roses, choose the middle ground; cut neither down too far nor up too high.

The easiest way to encourage roses to put out strong, healthy growth while allowing them to bounce back into bloom within a few weeks is to follow this general **Rule of Thumb**: *Cut flowers from rose plants that are over 1 year old just above the first 5-leaflet leaf that points away from the center of the plant*. (Leave more greenery on a first-year plant to make the bush stronger.) When flowers have been allowed to fade on the bush, deadhead them at the same point. This method of picking roses brings flowers back quickly on stems long enough for cutting. (An exception should be made for rose varieties that naturally bear long-stemmed roses and are, in

❋ ❋ ❋

How to Keep Cut Roses Fresh

· To Prevent Neck Droop of Cut Roses: In early evening pick full buds that are beginning to open. Wrap them in a black plastic trash bag so no light can enter, and store them overnight in the refrigerator (between 6 and 12 hours). The next morning take out the roses and treat them as follows.

· To Make Cut Roses Last Seven or Eight Days: Immerse them in a sink filled with lukewarm water (100°F; 38°C) for 20 or 30 minutes. Clip off the lower leaves (but not the thorns), then recut the stems *underwater*. Arrange the roses in a vase filled with either of these solutions: 1 quart water, 2 tablespoons fresh lemon juice, 1 tablespoon sugar, and ½ teaspoon bleach; or 1 pint regular 7-Up, 1 pint water, and ½ teaspoon bleach.

* ✳ *

How to Plant a Water Lily

- Purchase a water lily planting tub from a mail order company specializing in water gardening, or make your own from a plastic or cardboard plant container that is 14 or 18 inches in diameter and 6 to12 inches deep. (Both are lightweight and hold up well underwater.) Plug the drainage holes with wads made of two layers of newpaper. Containers can also be made from plastic baskets like small laundry baskets. Line them with polyester quilt batting.

- Plant water lilies in rich garden soil; fertile loam is best. Make sure it contains no manure (which encourages growth of algae) and no peat moss, compost, commercial potting soil, perlite, wood shavings, or other lightweight soil amendment that might float to the surface of the pond.

- According to package directions, mix into the soil a complete, slow-release, granulated fertilizer that's recommended for aquatic plants and contains trace elements to enhance growth and flower color. Or choose a generic complete fertilizer such as 10-20-5, and mix ¼ cup of it into every 3 gallons of soil. Be sure the fertilizer you use contains trace elements but no herbicides or pesticides.

- Fill the container to 2 inches below the top with fertilized soil, and then water it so that it settles. Add more soil if necessary. Plant one lily at a time and keep all others moist and in the shade. Don't let their roots dry out.

- In the case of hardy water lilies plant them when the water temperature is 60°F (15.6°C) or higher. Place the tuber with the bud facing up, and with the end that contains the bud pointing toward the center of the container and the other end of the tuber gently touching the inside of the container. Plant so that the crown or growth bud is ¼ inch below the

any case, more appropriately raised for their cut flowers than for their beauty in the landscape. Cut these types with longer stems, if desired, but always leave at least two leaves on the plant at the bottom of each stem. New growth will arise above them.)

For one-to-a-stem and show-quality roses, continue to disbud Hybrid Teas and Grandifloras (as described on p. 77).

Water Gardening

Fish and lily ponds are one of the most exciting yet tranquil elements of horticulture. Water can provide sound from fountains and waterfalls, movement from fish, birds, dragonflies, and sky reflections, plus a paradisaical atmosphere and colorful flowers. Ponds can be of any size or shape. You can grow a dwarf water lily or dwarf exotic lotus even in a half wine barrel.

Water lilies (*Nymphaea*), among the most intriguing flowers we grow, come in two main kinds. Hardy water lilies, which are easy to grow, bloom during the daytime in summer and have flowers that float on the surface of the water; tropical water lilies, which have a longer bloom season, carry their blossoms high above the water surface. Tropical lilies come in a surface of the ground and the tuber slopes down at a 45-degree angle from the bud end to the place where the tuber touches the container.

- Cover the top of the container with a circle of ½-inch galvanized wire poultry netting that's cut 2 or 3 inches wider than the diameter of the container. Bend it down over the sides to keep out fish. The lily will grow up through the wire. Or, alternatively, cover the surface of the soil with a 1-inch layer of pebbles or sand.

- Immediately after planting, submerge the container in the pond so that the top of the soil is 6 inches underwater. When the plant is thoroughly established, lower it so the soil surface is 12 to 18 inches underwater. Use bricks or cement blocks under the container to adjust the height.

- Plant tropical water lilies when the water temperature is 70°F (21°C) or higher. Place

the round chestnutlike tuber of each tropical water lily upright in the center of the container with its roots buried and its crown, the place from which the foliage emerges, protruding slightly above the soil.

- If your tropical lily has foliage, make your circle of poultry wire 2 inches larger than for hardy lilies. Cut a hole in the center 4 inches in diameter. Then cut the circle of wire straight through the middle from side to side, dividing it into two equal halves. After planting the lily, fit the two halves over the surface of the soil with the plant growing up through the middle and tie the two halves together. Bend down the edges around the sides.

- Immediately after planting carefully submerge the tropical lily in the pond with 4 to 6 inches of water above soil level. When the plant grows to 8 inches in diameter, lower the container so there are 12 inches to 18 inches of water above it.

* ❋ *

rainbow of colors, including blue, with flowers often as big as dinner plates. Some are night blooming. Lotus (*Nelumbo*), an exotic plant sacred to the Hindu and Buddhist religions, requires much the same care as water lilies. There are many other aquatic plants. Some grow like water lilies and lotus do, with their roots in mud or soil and their foliage either floating on the surface of the water or standing above it. (Most aquatic plants that are rooted in soil are best grown in containers for ease of maintenance. See the accompanying box for how to plant water lilies.) A second group of plants floats freely on the surface of the water,

while a third type is completely submerged and adds oxygen to the pond.

The romance and beauty of water gardening, like all other types of gardening, has its practical side. First, the pool should be properly balanced, which means it should contain the right ingredients to prevent the water from becoming stagnant. The ☞ **Rule of Thumb** for balancing a pond is: *For each square yard of water you need two bunches of submerged oxygenating grasses, twelve water snails, two 5-inch-size goldfish or koi, and 1 medium-to-large water lily*. (In water barrels substitute several guppies or mosquito fish for the goldfish or koi.) Don't feed your fish.

If you don't feed them they won't overproduce or grow too large. They'll get all they need from the pond and act as natural gardeners, helping to keep the water clean. In an ecologically balanced pond fish eat bugs, various organic materials floating on the top of the pond, submerged oxygenating grasses, and algae. Even though you don't feed your fish they'll get to know you and they'll come to you when you approach the pond or touch the water.

Once you've provided all the elements for balance the water may turn green with algae, a diverse group of primitive flowerless plants, but it will eventually settle down and be clean and clear most of the time. There are two kinds of aquatic algae: filamentous, which attach themselves to walls and plants, and floating, which turn ponds green. Algae grow fast in unseasonably warm weather, and many balanced ponds go green for a while in spring. If this happens to your pond don't worry, just wait. When the weather cools, or when the water is adequately shaded by lily or lotus leaves, it will clear up by itself. If your pond stays green throughout the warm months it may not be properly balanced, it may need more submerged oxygenating plants, or it may need more water lilies to shade the surface. Sixty to seventy percent of the water surface should be shaded by leaves during summer; less in winter.

Also, once in a while you should feed the plants, which for a pond means getting in there bodily. You'll need to wear hip boots, protective clothing, and long rubber gloves for this job since some forms of algae can be absorbed through the skin and may produce allergic reactions. Fertilize water lilies and lotus in April. They're gluttons for food and won't bloom or grow well without adequate nourish-ment. Beginning now, feed one aquatic plant pellet (the 6-gram slow-release type—10-5-5, for example) to each container per month. Use a wooden dowel to shove each pellet deeply into the soil mix as close to the crown of the plant as possible. While you're about it, scoop up some of the muck from the bottom of the pond. (Some gardeners report good results from using this pond byproduct as a fertilizer on roses and other plants. You can try this if you wish, but use it sparingly at first because it may contain harmful salts.) Don't be concerned about mud-dying the water as you work. It will clear again and the fish won't come to harm.

If you don't have a pond consider the several easy ways to add one to the landscape, including ready-made pond liners, both shaped and flexible. Be sure to put your pond in full sun. For more information, order the magazinelike catalogue from Van Ness Water Gardens, 2460 North Euclid Avenue, Upland, CA 91786. Or refer to books on water gardening—for exam-ple, Sunset's *Garden Pools, Fountains and Waterfalls,* Uber's *Water Gardening Basics,* or Paul and Rees' *The Water Garden.*

Pest Control

Spray for Juniper Moths. During recent years several pests have attacked the tips of many of our most valuable and drought-resistant juniper bushes, juniper trees such as Hollywood juniper (*Juniperus chinensis* 'Torulosa'), and cypress trees including Italian cypress, or *Cupressus sempervirens* (but not Monterey cypress, false cypress [*Cha-maecyparis*] and arborvitae [*Thuja*]). Tip damage severely weakens and disfigures the plants, turning them brown and sometimes killing them. The main culprits are juniper tip moth

(*Stenolechia bathrodyas*), cypress tip moth (*Argyresthia cupressella*), and in interior valleys juniper twig girdler (*Periploca nigra*), which kills not just the tips but entire stems. Most of these insects spend nine or ten months, most of their life cycles, inside the host plants. Until beneficial controls are discovered the best chance we have to control these pests is to catch them when they're out and on the wing, which is sometime between March and May in Southern California. Plants that have been sprayed at the right time show remarkable improvement, but juniper tip moth has three generations a year and thus may require repeated spraying.

To diagnose tip moths (rather than damage by mice, dogs, or salt) begin now to examine the foliage. For cypress tip moth, look for ¼-inch silver-white cocoons. Once you have found these shake the foliage once a week and look for numerous silver-tan moths, which act rather like whiteflies when disturbed, flying up in the air before settling back on the host plant. When you find them it's time to spray with Sevin or diazinon. (Always mix in a miticide when spraying with Sevin.) Spray again in two weeks. In June or July, when eggs are hatching, spray with a pesticide such as Ortho Isotox.

To find out whether twig girdlers are the problem break open the bark under an affected twig, peel it back, and look for the characteristic little runways girdling the wood. Look also for cocoons and moths. The UC publication *Juniper Twig Girdler*, Leaflet 2541, suggests drenching affected junipers thoroughly with a spray of lindane mixed in the ratio of 1 tablespoon per gallon of water. If you do this job yourself do it in April and repeat it in May. Practice all precautions for spraying; wear protective clothing. Personally I recommend having a professional do the spraying because of the dangers involved and the efficacy of professional equipment. (Some licensed companies report success with monthly spraying of Cygon systemic pesticide.) Another way to go is to tear out the troublemakers and replace them with something more pest resistant.

Spray for Caterpillars and Worms. This is the month when caterpillars and worms wake up and begin serious munching. In a shrub-surrounded garden, with many beneficials, tree frogs, and birds in residence, it may not be necessary to spray. But if caterpillar and worm damage is out of control, spray with BT, the bacterial disease that affects certain caterpillars but no other pests or insects. It's sold as a liquid or powder under the Safer and Attack brands and such trade names as Dipel and Thuricide. (Read the labels to make sure it's BT you're getting.) When mixing powders into sprays add a spreader-sticker, such as Spraymate or some Safer soap. It will make mixing easier and increase the effectiveness of the spray.

Spray against Fuchsia Mite. Fuchsia gall mite (*Aculops fuchsiae*) is a relative newcomer that's spread at an alarming rate by means of birds and insects. It attacks new growth, twisting and distorting buds, foliage, and flowers and turning leaves red. Fortunately, predacious mites are keeping this pest under control in many areas, and some fuchsias—Voodoo, Pink Marshmallow, Nonpareil, and Gartenmeister Bonstedt, for example—are resistant, fighting off the problem without assistance. Such varieties as Jingle Bells and Marinka seem more susceptible.

In my garden I put up with some minor damage from fuchsia gall mites, I control them with beneficial insects rather than by spraying, and I grow resistant varieties. If you're dissatisfied with this solution or have a serious infestation, first cut off the infected parts 3 or 4 inches below the damaged area. Tie the trimmings in a plastic trash bag and dispose of them in the trash. Follow up by spraying your plants at least twice at intervals of two to three weeks with Sevin. Remember when you use Sevin to mix it with a miticide because Sevin kills the beneficials that kill mites. Or spray on alternate weeks with Orthene, which gives partial control of mites along with many other pests.

Control Spider Mites. Now through summer watch carefully for spider mites; they're most active in warm weather. Spider mites are members of the arachnid family that live on pine needles and under the leaves of other favored plants, including roses, fuchsias, primroses, and cyclamen. They suck out plant juices and cause whitening, yellowing, stippling, and loss of color in the foliage that can sometimes mean death to the plant. If you think a plant has mites place a white sheet of paper under the foliage and tap the branch. Look with a magnifying glass for tiny black or reddish spiderlike creatures scurrying around on the paper. Another telltale sign, which is easier to see, is fine, hairlike webbing— like spider webs but messier—around, over, and under leaves and twigs. Suspect spider mites on roses when their leaves turn yellow and fall off. Rub a yellowing leaf on a white cloth; if a smudge results mites are to blame.

Some plants, including fuchsias or moosehorn ferns, can be so weakened by spider mites that they die. Roses won't die from them, but they can be set back. Healthy plants are less likely to suffer a bad mite attack. If you fertilize an affected moosehorn fern, for example, at the first sign of damage, it's quite likely to overcome mites without being sprayed. Well-fed and properly watered plants growing in a mixed landscape where beneficial mites have been encouraged to set up housekeeping will usually survive without spraying. Or you might get by with using a nontoxic spray like Safer soap, which kills soft-bodied mites without killing many beneficials. Roses may need to be sprayed with a specific miticide, such as Avid, but it's not widely available and comes only in large quantities. (If you use it be particularly careful to follow the precautions given on p. 54.) Severe mite damage can occur from spraying plants with Sevin (carbaryl) without the addition of a miticide.

Control Eugenia Psyllid. For almost a hundred years eugenia (*Syzygium paniculatum,* also called Australian brush cherry) has been Southern California's most valuable hedge plant for frost-free zones; one can grow it to any needed height and clip it as narrowly as 1 foot. But sometime during the late 1980s the eugenia psyllid (*Trioza eugeniae*) was accidentally imported from Australia, and it has since rendered its namesake practically useless for new plantings. Eugenia psyllid is a small flying insect that lays eggs under new foliage on eugenia shrubs and trees. The larvae suck out the juices from fresh leaves, stunting, twisting, and distorting the foliage, but they don't kill the plants. Young plants show more damage than old ones.

The University of California has dispatched an entomologist to Australia to search for beneficial insects to control eugenia psyllid. Meanwhile, have patience; don't cut down established eugenia hedges or trees. You could try spraying them, if you wish, with Orthene soluble powder once a month or with Mavrik at intervals of once every two months. (Find Mavrik at agricultural supply stores.) Or try Ace caps, a systemic pesticide—you drill a hole in the trunk and insert them. This systemic method has the advantage of not requiring you to go on a neighbor's property to spray. (Warn children not to eat the berries of sprayed or treated trees.) If you're planting a new hedge substitute another plant, like Carolina laurel cherry (*Prunus caroliniana*) or yaupon (*Ilex vomitoria*). Yaupon is hardy and makes a fine smooth-textured hedge in coastal or interior zones, though it grows much wider than eugenia.

Control Ash Whitefly. Sometime in 1988 the ash whitefly (*Siphoninus phillyreae*) hitched a ride into California, and since then the Los Angeles County Agricultural Department has been besieged by more phone calls than for any other single pest. Ash whiteflies are flying insects about one-eighth inch long and look much like any other whiteflies. (Don't confuse them with greenhouse whiteflies that attack tomatoes, fuchsias, and other garden plants, as discussed on p. 159.) They proliferate at an astounding rate and attack members of the olive, rose, and legume families. In Southern California the plants that have suffered most are trees, including ash, ornamental pear, loquat, toyon, pomegranate, apple, peach, and during the winter even citrus.

Ash whiteflies lay their eggs under the leaves of favored plants. The nymphs feed on plant sap and excrete honeydew, a sugary liquid that attracts ants. Heavy infestations of this pest, especially in October, cause blizzardlike clouds of insects and disgusting quantities of sticky honeydew that blackens garden furniture, sidewalks, cars, and other plants with sooty mold. Leaves of stricken plants often fall off.

As with eugenia psyllid, predatory insects are being sought to control this pest. Until these are introduced, refrain from planting the trees that are most affected. Unfortunately, like most whiteflies, ash whitefly is tough to kill, but you can cut down its numbers by beginning now to wash these trees off with soapy sprays at intervals of two or three weeks. Spraying with summer oil (light horticultural oil) can also provide some control, but check the labels carefully; some plants are easily burned by oily sprays, especially in warm weather. (Ace caps, as suggested above, might help on nonfood plants, but results of tests aren't yet known.) Spraying with pesticides is not recommended, because they kill the beneficials that will eventually control this pest. One of the best ways you can help your plants withstand this pest is to water and fertilize them regularly. While you await the arrival of new beneficials also try releasing lacewings (available from some nurseries and also by mail, at intervals of two weeks to one month throughout warm weather).

Release Beneficials and Encourage Animals. Start releasing beneficial insects this month. Ladybugs are available at many nurseries now. Keep the packages damp with a few drops of water and apply the insects by small spoonfuls here and there around the garden at dusk. Fewer fly away when introduced into the garden in the cool evening hours. Put a few on each of your fuchsias. Also send away for other beneficials, including lacewings and predatory mites and wasps. Encourage birds—they eat many insects—and, though it may sound eccentric, also encourage bats, which eat night-flying moths whose larval forms, such as cutworms and budworms, are so destructive in the garden. (Much-needed homes for bats can be purchased from Bat Conservation International, Inc., P.O. Box 162603, Austin, TX 78716-2603, 512/327-9721.) Welcome spiders into the garden; hold back on chemical spraying. Spiders, beneficial insects, and animals can help the gardener keep pests under control better than poisonous sprays. Try to interest your neighbors.

Flower Beds and Containers

A Word about Timing. April is an ideal month to plant warm-season annuals and perennials for summer color. In actual practice, however, most gardeners who planted cool-season flowers last fall have no room to plant in. All sunny beds are filled with flowers at the height of bloom now, at least until midmonth and typically until May. (Maintain these areas by deadheading, staking if necessary, and watering when rains aren't adequate.) The only beds bare of blooms now are those that were filled with cineraria or bulbs, now faded and ready to be replaced. If all your flower beds are bare of blooms in April it's probably a sign you didn't plant the right things at the right time. Don't despair; this fall you'll get another chance. (See p. 232.)

For now, resist the urge to stock up on masses of spring flowers in bloom at the nursery, because they'll soon fade. It's very confusing to first-time local gardeners that in April nurseries are overflowing with cool-season flowers in full bloom. (The correct way to use them is as fill-ins where something has died or faded. Or fill a pot or two for a party or special occasion.) Examples of items *not* to fill beds with now are primroses, Iceland poppies, calendulas, dianthus, foxgloves, snapdragons, stock, cineraria, violas, and pansies except the new heat-resistant varieties, such as the Universal series.

What to Plant Now. Seeds of warm-season flowers to plant now include alyssum, ageratum, anchusa, amaranthus, calliopsis, cosmos, celosia, coleus, marigold, nicotiana, portulaca, scarlet salvia, and verbena. (Except in the hottest areas wait until May to plant zinnias. They languish when planted in cold soil.) Save money by starting your own bedding plants from seeds that are easy to grow, such as cosmos, scarlet salvia, ageratum, and marigolds, in flats of potting soil. Start them in semishade, cover them with a sheet of plastic, and keep them moist until germinated. As soon as they're up remove the plastic, move them to sun, and water daily. When they've made two true leaves start feeding for healthy growth. You'll have plenty of transplants to fill beds.

This is the best time of all to dress up patios with tubs and hanging baskets of warm-season annual flowers from nursery transplants. Flowers to put in now from pony packs and color packs include ageratum, globe amaranth, begonias, campanulas, dusty miller, gaillardia, impatiens, lobelia, marigolds, nierembergia, petunias, scarlet salvia, blue salvia, and vinca. Marguerites can be planted in coastal zones; gamolepis and Green Gold euryops (*Euryops pectinatus* 'Viridis') are good for either the coast or inland. Some flowers, particularly daisy types such as cosmos, tend to shoot straight up on one stem and pop a bud on top. Pinch this bud off to encourage branching. Petunias do better when pinched back at planting time. It takes self-control to do this, because you destroy flowers, but it pays with more bloom on bushier plants later.

Lawn Care

Feed, Water, Mow, and Plant. Feed all lawns this month, and water them thoroughly after feeding. Warm-season grasses are speeding up growth now and will need regular fertilizing throughout the warmer months. Water warm-season grasses deeply and infrequently to encourage deep rooting. Most cool-season grasses need more frequent and shallow watering.

All warm-season lawns can be planted from sod or stolons now, and common Bermuda can be planted from seed. Cool-season lawns can be put in from sod, although it's best to wait until October. (See p. 87 for advice on lawn selection.)

Mow all lawns once a week to keep them at their proper height, as described on page 86.

Encourage Dichondra. Dichondra may look somewhat ratty and thinner than usual in April. This is natural; the plants are creating seed. Look closely—the seeds are large and quite visible. Help the process along and encourage the filling in of bare spots by mulching after the seeds fall. Fertilize lightly with a product containing an insecticide, to get rid of flea beetles and cutworms early in the game.

Despite its lush appearance dichondra is more drought resistant than we give it credit for. Allow it to wilt between waterings; this helps discourage disease. Step on it. If your

➤

Quick Tip

Make an Easy Hanging Basket with a Continental Look.
In each 12-inch redwood basket or plastic container plant one 1-gallon size, heat-resistant ivy geranium with tiny flowers, such as the Balcon or Fischer Cascade series. (These are the ones seen spilling out of window boxes in Europe as far south as Italy.) Fill around them with good potting soil. Sprinkle the top of the soil with a few seeds of trailing blue lobelia, or, for a quicker start, add one transplant of lobelia from a pony pack to each corner of the container. Hang it in full sun or part shade, keep it damp, and feed it occasionally with a complete slow-release or liquid fertilizer (Peters 20-20-20 mixed half-strength or a similar formula).

✳ ✴ ✳

How to Get a Huge Harvest of Sweet Corn

- Choose a good variety, such as the supersweet All American Award winner How Sweet It Is. Buy seeds for successive plantings of twelve to twenty plants at a time.

- Spade the ground deeply in a square area that gets full sun, north of shorter crops. (Corn is pollinated by wind. Pollen from the male flower must fall on the female silks, so plant in a block of several short rows rather than in one long, skinny row.) Mix organic soil amendment into the ground and cultivate a vegetable fertilizer (6-12-6, for example) into the top 6 inches according to package directions.

- Set up a drip system designed for row crops, such as the Rain-Jet Gardening Kit containing laser-perforated drip lines called Hardie Bi-Wall. Run the rows north to south, 3 feet apart (18 inches apart if space is at a premium). Connect one length of Bi-Wall drip line every 3 feet, and bury the lines 3 to 6 inches deep under rows mounded 4 inches high and 8 inches wide between furrows that are to be used as paths.

- Except in the hottest areas cover the entire area with black—not clear—plastic sheeting as mulch, to increase heat and yields.

- In coastal zones presprout the seeds over bottom heat indoors. (The box on p. 121 tells how.) Supersweet varieties have a "shrunken gene" that causes their seeds to be shriveled and difficult to germinate if soil is cool.

- As soon as the seeds sprout plant them 2 inches deep and 12 to 18 inches apart in each row. (If the rows are only 18 inches apart, use the wider spacing within rows for a bigger harvest.) For each, use a razor blade to slit a 4-inch-square X in the plastic mulch, make a 2-inch-deep hole with your finger, and put the

footstep remains clearly impressed, that's your sign it's time to water. Then water deeply and thoroughly. Early in the morning is the best time, rather than in the middle of the day or in the evening. Program your sprinklers to water this way.

Vegetable Gardening

Continue to Plant Summer Vegetables. Did you plant summer vegetables last month? If so you'll get an early harvest. If not, don't be discouraged; it's not too late. Many vegetables prefer being put in now. Among vegetables to plant now from seeds are green beans, beets, carrots, corn, endive, leaf (not head) lettuce, New Zealand spinach, pumpkins, radishes, salsify, squash, sunflowers, Swiss chard, and turnips. Put in transplants of cucumbers and tomatoes.

This is the last month to plant seed potatoes (as described on p. 92; also see the section following on mounding and harvesting potatoes). In hot interior zones plant sweet potatoes beginning this month. This is the first month for putting in the heat lovers: eggplant, peppers, okra, lima beans, cantaloupe, and watermelon. If you live in a fog bank, wait until May to plant cantaloupe. In this case it usually isn't worthwhile to plant watermelons; they grow better inland.

seed in with the root pointing down and the sprout pointing up. Press the soil gently back together. Fold the cut edges of plastic under and slip the lower edge of an upside-down berry basket into the slit area to protect seed from birds. (The berry basket will exactly fit the square space you have cut and be held firmly in place.)

· Water with a drip system—daily in sandy soil or twice or three times weekly in clay soil— until sprouts emerge. Gradually lengthen spacing between waterings until you're watering deeply and well about every three days in sandy soil, once a week in clay.

· When leaves reach the tops of the berry baskets remove baskets. Plant more corn in two weeks, and feed the first batch with fish emulsion.

· When the corn tassels out give it extra water and feed it thoroughly with a balanced liquid fertilizer, for example with 2 tablespoons Terr-O-Vite and 2 of 0-10-10 per gallon of water. Send this through the drip line, pour it around plants with a watering can, or soak the ground under the plastic with it using a water wand attached to a syphon. If you prefer to use granulated fertilizer, apply nitrogen fertilizer when the corn is 12 to 18 inches high and again when it is 24 to 30 inches high. Use 1 to 1½ pounds of actual nitrogen per 1,000 square feet of planted area.

· For full ears in a small plot hand pollinate: when tassels bloom with dusty pollen break off sections and whip them on the silks at the tops of the ears. (To activate growth in every kernel each silk needs one grain of pollen.)

> ➤
>
> *Quick Tip*
>
> **How to Secure Plastic Mulch to the Ground.**
> *With wire cutters cut the bent ends off wire coat
> hangers to make arched sections approximately
> 5 inches long. Shove them through the plastic
> down into the ground all around the edges
> and here and there on the paths.
> These can be used for several seasons.
> (Take care not to spear drip lines.)*

Quick Tip

Vegetable Space Saver.
For three crops in one space, interplant corn with pole or lima beans and one or two pumpkins or the kind of winter squash that grows on a sprawling vine, such as Sweet Mama. The beans will climb up the corn and need no support. The squash or pumpkins will give you another crop on the ground (and incidentally will discourage raccoons from stealing your corn, if these masked bandits live in your neighborhood).

Plant Herbs among Your Vegetables. Plant culinary herbs in April. Put in summer savory, thyme, rosemary, oregano, sage, and parsley from nursery transplants. (You can also plant parsley from seeds.) Herbs are fun, easy to grow, and seem to have a good effect on vegetables when grown among them. Cilantro and arugula can be grown throughout summer in semishade in some gardens, but they prefer cooler weather. Grow French tarragon (*Artemisia dracunculus*), horseradish, and mint in containers; they're invasive. (Don't be fooled into buying tasteless Russian tarragon—*Artemisia dracunculoides*—by mistake.) Mint is supposed to deter tomato hornworm. Dill attracts these voracious creatures. They like it better than tomatoes. Plant Spicy Globe basil from seed and other types from transplants or from seed—basil makes tomato salads a special treat and seems to grow well near tomato plants. (For more about herbs, see p. 310.)

Plant for Successive Crops. If you planted vegetables last month continue to put in seeds now for additional crops. Many gardeners plant too much at one time. Then it all matures at once, and they're swamped. A similar problem is planting too much of one crop; zucchini can easily overwhelm the unwary. Two or three plants are plenty for a family of four. A row will feed an army.

Vegetables to plant successively are those that you harvest over a short period (a week or two), like corn and bush beans, or those in which individuals are harvested wholly, like carrots or beets. Lettuce can go either way; you can take just the outside leaves to extend the harvest or cut whole heads.

When planting successively, use a quarter or

a third of a package of seed at intervals of two to three weeks. Choose interesting varieties. Carrots, for example, come in many sizes, sweetness levels, and degrees of crunchiness. Grow several and taste test them with your family.

Thin Those Rows. Don't forget to keep thinning your vegetable rows according to package directions. When you thin leafy vegetables like lettuce transplant the extras into another row, but don't try this with carrots; they split when they're transplanted. Thinning seed rows—and flower beds, too—is a task too often neglected by first-time gardeners. People hate to do it because it seems so wasteful. Actually the reverse is true. You won't feel sad about thinning rows if you remember that overabundant plants have the effect of weeds; by competing with each other they stunt your crops. This is especially true of plants like onions that have shallow roots.

Prune Tomatoes and Avoid Problems. You can train tomatoes several ways (as described on p. 95). If you plan to grow them on stakes or a trellis prune each plant now to one or two major vines, by pinching off the suckers that grow as side branches above leaf joints. Check them weekly; they grow fast.

Occasionally gardeners complain of getting no fruit. This can happen if the plants are growing in shade. Sometimes plants have green growth but no flowers. This comes from too much nitrogen (treat the ground around the plants with liquid 0-10-10 to correct it). If plants flower but the blossoms drop off without fruiting they may have been allowed to dry out

completely. Other causes of bud drop are temperatures lower than 55°F (13°C) or higher than 75°F at night or 105°F in the daytime (24° and 41°C). Desert dwellers should grow tomatoes during the fall, winter, and early spring months.

If low temperatures are the source of your problem grow early varieties until the weather warms up, or try using a tomato blossom-set spray. Use it exactly according to directions: one slight burst of spray about 10 inches from each bunch of flowers only three times, at intervals of ten days. Sometimes flowers drop off because they weren't pollinated. This can happen in wet weather or in greenhouses. Tomatoes have "perfect" or self-pollinating flowers. The pollen has to go only a short distance within the flower, from the anthers onto the sticky stigma. Wind does the job more than bees, so if there's no wind there won't be any fruit. You can improve pollination of your tomatoes by rapping with a hammer on tomato stakes or cages in the middle of the day, when the weather's warm and dry.

Mound and Harvest Potatoes. Until potato plants have grown 10 inches high, use a hoe to mound soil up around the stalks, but leave the leafy portion sticking out of the top. This increases the harvest and keeps the potatoes cool and dark. (Potatoes' skins turn green if they're exposed to light; all green portions of potatoes are poisonous, including stems, leaves, fruit, and sprouts.) If before mounding soil around the stems you first mix it with nitrolized wood shavings or homemade compost harvesting becomes much easier. Stop mounding the soil when the mound is 5 or 6 inches high or when the plants begin to flower.

When flowers appear some tubers have grown—you can then gently push the soft, amended soil aside and use a trowel to dig up just the number of small new potatoes you want for dinner. Replace the mound so the remaining potatoes will be protected from heat and sunlight. When the leaves begin to turn yellow with age you can harvest as many full-grown new potatoes as desired. Leave smaller tubers in the ground to continue growing. Once the tops of the plant have completely withered and died harvest the remainder by digging up the whole row with a garden fork. Leave these mature potatoes on top of the earth to dry for two or three hours; then store them in a cool dark place at 40° to 45°F (5° to 7°C). If you store them at over 50°F (10°C) they'll sprout and eventually spoil.

Protect Lettuce against Pests. Bait lettuce against slugs and snails with a product recommended for the vegetable garden, or cut them off at the pass by baiting with a long-lasting snail bait, such as Deadline, around the entire perimeter of the garden. Watch for leafhoppers; they spread virus diseases. (Spray for them with Safer soap, or control them with diatomaceous earth if you feel it's absolutely necessary, but the latter will kill ladybugs and other beneficials, including spiders.)

Introduce beneficials, as discussed in the preceding section on control of pests. Ladybugs, lacewings, trichogramma wasps, and other beneficials are even more important in the vegetable garden because most gardeners prefer not to spray vegetables with pesticides. Be sure to put ladybugs where you see whiteflies and aphids. Control caterpillars with BT.

How to Presprout Seed for a Fast Start with No Rot

Some seeds, planted in the ground, may rot instead of growing. Examples are any beans planted in cold, wet soil, some relatively new varieties of sugar peas that have shriveled-looking seeds, and supersweet varieties of sweet corn that also have shriveled seeds caused by the so-called "shrunken" gene that makes them so sweet. In these cases it's easy, timesaving, and worthwhile to sprout seeds indoors. Here's how:

- Wet a paper towel. Squeeze it out and spread it flat. Arrange a few more seeds than you need on half the towel, so they don't touch each other. Bend the other half over. Put the whole thing, flat, in a ziplock plastic bag and seal it up.

- Place the plastic bag containing the paper towel and seeds over bottom heat at approximately 70°F (21°C). Possible heat sources include low-wattage light bulbs, radiantly heated floors, antidampness bars used to keep closets, towels, and pianos dry, heat vents, water heaters, or even the tops of TVs or VCRs. (If a light bulb or heating bar is used elevate the seeds on a cookie sheet or metal tray, to defuse the heat.)

- Check your seeds daily; add moisture if needed. Bean seeds sprout in about three days, corn and peas in four or five. As soon as they sprout plant them in the garden. Handle them gently; don't break their roots.

- To plant make a hole with your finger deep enough for the thin white root to go straight down, with the thicker, yellowish sprout pointing up. (In cool weather plant the seed only an inch deep. After the sprout comes up you can mound the soil higher around it.) Press the soil gently but firmly from the side to make good contact. If some sprouts fail to come up, presprout some more and replant to fill gaps in the row.

Purchase / Plant

- [ ] Continue to plant **drought-resistant plants**, 15, 72
- [ ] Choose and plant **azaleas** while the largest number of plants are in bloom, 102
- [ ] If you live in the desert or in a hot inland valley finish all **spring planting** this month, 102
- [ ] Choose and plant **wisteria** while it is in bloom, 102
- [ ] Purchase **epiphyllums**, 103
- [ ] Plant **dahlias**, 106
- [ ] Plant **water lilies**, 108
- [ ] Plant **warm-season flowers**, 114
- [ ] Plant **tubs** and **hanging baskets**, 114
- [ ] Continue to plant **summer vegetables**, 116
- [ ] Plant **corn**, 116
- [ ] Plant **herbs**, 117
- [ ] Plant **tropicals** in inland valleys, 131
- [ ] Start **perennials** from seeds in interior zones, 158
- [ ] Purchase, plant, and transplant **succulents**, including **cacti** and **euphorbias**, 185
- [ ] Now through summer choose, plant, and naturalize **bromeliads**, 186

Trim, Prune, Mow, Divide

- [ ] Break off suckers from **artichokes**, 94
- [ ] Remove suckers from **tomatoes** and tie up the vines, 95
- [ ] Take cuttings from **epiphyllums**, and root them to make new plants, 104
- [ ] Cut back **poinsettias**, 104
- [ ] Trim **hedges** and **screens**, including **pittosperum**, **myoporum**, and **photinia**, 104
- [ ] Thin out fruit on **deciduous fruit trees**, 105
- [ ] Prune **roses** by picking, deadheading, and disbudding, 107
- [ ] Mow **lawns**, 115
- [ ] Thin **vegetable crops** planted last month according to package directions (including **beans**), 118
- [ ] Stop pinching **fuchsias** when plants are well filled out and bushy. Remove seed pods often after flowers fall, 154
- [ ] Pinch back **petunias** when you plant them, 178
- [ ] Start to prune and train **espaliers** as they begin to grow, 203
- [ ] Propagate **daylilies** by planting their proliferates, 206
- [ ] Divide and plant **dahlia tubers** you lifted from the ground in December, 301

Fertilize

- [ ] Feed **citrus trees**, 30
- [ ] Feed **avocado trees**, 48
- [ ] Feed **fuchsias**, 55
- [ ] Feed **tuberous begonias**, 78
- [ ] Feed **irises**, 106
- [ ] Fertilize **roses**, 107
- [ ] Feed **water lilies**, 110
- [ ] Fertilize **lawns**, 115
- [ ] Fertilize **peppers** when flowers first show, 191
- [ ] Feed and water **cycads**, 213
- [ ] Treat **blue hydrangeas** with aluminum sulfate, 229
- [ ] Do not fertilize **onions** after they begin to make a bulb, 290

Water

- [ ] Water **all garden plants** according to need when rains are inadequate, 12
- [ ] Keep all **vegetables** well watered, particularly **globe artichokes**, 94
- [ ] Water **roses**, 107
- [ ] Water **lawns** (including **dichondra**), 115
- [ ] Don't let **tomatoes** dry out, 119, 144

Control Pests, Diseases, and Weeds

- [ ] Control **crabgrass** with a final treatment of preemergent herbicide, 39, 64
- [ ] Continue to control **slugs** and **snails**, particularly on **irises** and **lettuce**, 73
- [ ] Control **rose** pests and diseases, 106
- [ ] Spray **junipers** and **Italian cypress** for juniper moths, 110
- [ ] Spray with BT against **caterpillars** if necessary, 111
- [ ] Control **fuchsia gall mite**, 111
- [ ] Control **spider mites**, 112
- [ ] Control **eugenia psyllid**, 112
- [ ] Control **ash whitefly**, 113
- [ ] Release **beneficials**, 113
- [ ] Protect **corn** from raccoons, 118
- [ ] Control **leafhoppers**, 163
- [ ] Cultivate to remove weeds among **shrubs** and **trees**, 170
- [ ] Control weeds among **vegetables** and **flowers** by hand pulling, 170

Also This Month

- [ ] Move **tuberous begonias** started in flats into pots or beds, 78
- [ ] Keep **bamboo** from running into your neighbor's garden, 84
- [ ] See **spring flowers** including **wildflowers** and **native plants** in full bloom, 101
- [ ] Continue to tie up leaves of **bulbs** that have bloomed, 106
- [ ] Treat **cut roses** to keep them fresh, 107
- [ ] Consider building a **garden pond**, 108
- [ ] Mulch **dichondra** after seeds fall, 115
- [ ] Avoid problems with **tomatoes**, 118
- [ ] Begin to harvest **potatoes**, as needed, when blossoms show, 119
- [ ] Presprout **hybrid corn** if it won't germinate, 121
- [ ] Harvest **vegetables** while they're young and tender, 143, 191
- [ ] Save branches from pruning to use as pea stakes to support **flowers**, 258

MAY

MAY

The Fast-Growth Month

If you finished your spring planting in March or April, May is the month to watch everything grow. In good years, when seasonal rains have been generous, excess salts have been washed down into the ground and the entire landscape has been well watered. The gardener has helped things along by adding mulch and fertilizer in March, and now as the weather gets warmer all growth systems go full speed ahead. You can almost see some plants expand, especially the trees and bushes put in last fall.

May is also a month for catching up on neglected tasks. If you didn't finish spring planting in March and April, do it now. Heat-loving plants take off even better in May. If you live in an interior valley waste no time getting your final planting done. Interior gardeners can safely expect occasional spells—two or three days long—of scorching heat this month.

While conventional landscape plants, most of which are imported, are beginning a season of fast growth, native plants are in a season of withdrawal. The chaparral is drying up and most wildflowers are going brown and setting seed. Many wild plants pull in their horns and let leaves fall, as nature prepares for a long dry season. Those who live in interior valleys or near a canyon or wild hillside may sense a bit of nostalgia in the air this month similar to that in fall back East.

Deep Watering

From now until November the gardener's main task is to water deeply and appropriately for each plant, whenever available water supplies and local regulations allow it. In drought years, some plants may suffer during the late spring and summer from lack of adequate water. Observe which plants these are and consider replacing them with better choices. If you grow native plants learn which ones can accept summer water and which cannot. All native plants need irrigation to get started. Some, such as mimulus or monkeyflower (*Diplacus aurantiacus*), can be kept blooming longer by gradually replacing rainfall with some summer water. Others, including bush poppy (*Dendromecon rigida*) and woolly blue curls (*Trichostema lanatum*), may succumb to root rot if watered at all. Take the cue from nature and begin to taper off on watering these plants.

Since the price of water continually rises and domestic cutbacks occur whenever there's a drought, wise gardeners are thinking of ways to make the garden less thirsty. If you haven't already installed a drip system to water everything you otherwise would water with the hose, such as container-grown plants, now's a good time to do the job. Also, study your sprinkler system and see whether adjustments can be made to conserve water in the months ahead.

Irises

Bearded irises, those with a hairlike tuft on the falls, or lower petals, bloom this month. Whether or not you're growing them now, enjoy them in bloom, and consider planting some; the rhizomes can be found at nurseries in fall. They're among our best perennials—good in all zones, easy to grow, and not overly thirsty. See displays of them at botanical gardens and nurseries, and watch for newspaper announcements of shows.

Hybridizers have developed many kinds and heights of iris, but the tall bearded ones are the easiest to start with, and they're the most frequently grown. They prefer rich, humusy, well-drained soil but will accept almost any soil as long as they have full sun along the coast, or six hours of sun inland, plus moderate irrigation and protection from snails. If you have some in your garden but they're not blooming chances are they're growing in too much shade or need dividing (p. 155 tells how).

Among other rhizomatous irises to consider growing are Spuria irises, which make tall clumps, bloom in June and July, and need little summer water; and in light shade the native Pacific Coast irises (*Iris douglasiana*), which are drought resistant, low growing, good for naturalizing, and bloom in spring.

Cymbidiums

Now begins the main growing season for cymbidiums, terrestrial orchids that are usually grown in containers. The quality and number of flowers you get next winter partly depends on good summer care.

Although cymbidiums shouldn't be soggy, don't let them dry out. Move those that have finished blooming into less conspicuous places for a season of growth. Through midsummer keep these Asian orchids in semishade, such as under an open tree, then in late summer (see

How to Divide and Repot a Cymbidium

Cymbidiums need dividing when they overcrowd their containers or get too heavy to carry.

· Water plants well before dividing them.

· Use a can cutter or sharp knife to cut off the plastic container. If the plants are in a wooden tub, remove the old container with a hammer, and discard it.

· Use a large kitchen knife kept for gardening to cut between the pseudobulbs (the bulblike structures growing above ground) and down through the roots. Aim for at least three productive pseudobulbs and four or five back bulbs per division. (Back bulbs are fully grown pseudobulbs that once bore leaves and flower spikes but now are bare. They act as storage containers for the remainder of the plant.)

· Trim off all roots that are diseased, damaged, or simply messy. In all, you should remove about one-third of the roots.

· Optionally, soak the divisions in a solution of 1 quart Purex bleach to 10 quarts water for ten minutes to kill any fungus or rot. Air dry them.

· To replant, choose plastic containers that have plenty of holes in the bottom and are the next size larger, or approximately 4 to 6 inches wider than the top of the root ball. (Oversize containers slow growth.)

· Hold the plant so that the bottom of the pseudobulbs is level with the top of the container. Fill around the roots all the way to the top of the container with a commercial soil mix recommended for cymbidiums or a homemade mix, such as 2 gallons pathway bark, 2 gallons ground nitrolized wood shavings, and 1 gallon commercial sterilized potting soil (Super Soil is one such brand). It's important to make sure the roots are completely covered with soil mix but the pseudobulbs are totally above ground. (If the pseudobulbs are buried, they'll rot.)

· Water the cymbidiums thoroughly after planting, keep them in semishade, and wait two or three weeks before starting to fertilize.

p. 229) bring them out into more light. Or keep them year-round under 50 percent shade cloth (35 percent in coastal zones).

As blossoms fade cut off the bloom spikes and start feeding the cymbidiums with a complete fertilizer high in growth ingredients. An easy way to feed them is to place one 21-gram, 20-10-5 slow-release tablet on top of the soil mix of each 5-gallon container. The plant is then fed every time it's watered. Some gardeners prefer to apply liquid fertilizer—30-10-10, for example—once every two to four weeks. For this use a syphon attachment to draw fertilizer solution out of a bucket directly into the hose.

Transplant cymbidiums that have outgrown their containers no later than the end of June, in order not to destroy the next flowering cycle. They can flower well even when crowded, so wait until they're pushing against the sides of the container, then repot them into the next size container. Don't be in a hurry to divide them. A huge plant with twenty bloom spikes can be a showstopper in a home garden. (A half whiskey barrel makes a fine container.) Divide them (see the accompanying box) when plants become too big to handle.

Camellias and Azaleas

Feed, Mulch, and Prune Camellias. Fertilize camellias after they finish blooming. Camellias aren't gluttons; they need only a light application three times a year. The ☞ **Rule of Thumb** is: *Feed camellias for the first time as soon as they've finished blooming, feed them again four to six weeks after that, and finally feed them six weeks later.* Mark these times on your calendar. Use an acid-type, preferably organic commercial fertilizer especially recommended for camellias and

azaleas, or make your own mix of three parts of cottonseed meal to one part chelated iron, such as Tru-Green organic chelate blend. Feed ⅙ cup of this mix to a young plant or ⅓ cup to mature plants per feeding, at the drip line, and water it into the ground.

Never cultivate under camellias. Cover the ground with a fresh layer of mulch, such as fir bark or pine needles, to keep the roots cool and happy.

If you haven't yet pruned your camellias do the job now, to maintain the size you want, improve their shape, and increase bloom. Look closely at the tip of a branch. Notice the bump where last year's growth began and then the growth of the year before that. You can cut back into last year's growth or that of the year before and cause buds farther back on the branch to send out shoots. If this is done right after flowering there'll be no loss of flowers next year; in fact there'll be more. You can even cut way back into smooth gray-barked wood to renew an old plant that's gotten out of hand, but in this case flowering won't resume for a year or two.

Feed, Mulch, and Prune Azaleas. Fertilize azaleas as soon as they've finished blooming. The ☞ **Rule of Thumb** is: *Azaleas need fertilizing only twice a year, once as soon as they've finished blooming and again in late September.* Some people feed them more often—and it's all right to give a lackluster plant a shot of Terr-O-Vite in midsummer—but many an azalea has been killed by overfeeding.

Feed with a dry pelletized or powdered commercial fertilizer especially recommended for camellias and azaleas, and follow package directions. You'll need a yardstick to measure the height of plants as well as your plastic measuring cup marked "Garden." Sprinkle the fertilizer in a wide band under the drip line. You can, if you wish, work it down through the mulch with a gloved hand, but as with camellias don't ever cultivate under an azalea, even with your fingers. Delicate feeder roots lie right under the surface and can easily be damaged.

It's also time to clean up and prune azaleas. Leaves may remain where they fall, but be sure to remove all dead blossoms to prevent blossom blight from getting a foothold. Azaleas take well to pruning, since the dormant buds that will respond to it are hidden under the bark all the way to the ground. Cut out old or ungainly branches and pinch back tips to promote bushiness. The easiest way to get a really professional look is to give azaleas a butch haircut now. Start by watering the plants deeply. Then, using hedge shears, shear off all the tip growth. Next year you'll have a solid blanket of flowers all over the top of the plant.

Roses

Continue to control rose pests and diseases and to water, fertilize, and prune them by picking flowers and disbudding. Follow the guidelines given in March (beginning on p. 76) but, as in April, irrigate twice a week now with up to 1½ inches water per irrigation.

If you're fertilizing with commercial rose food feed your roses with it four weeks after their last feeding. If you're following the Rose-Pro Method of fertilizing switch now from sulfate of ammonia to urea and reduce the frequency of feedings. Now through July, feed 1 level tablespoon of urea (45-0-0) to each plant every other week. (Through the ages, up until the 1920s, the only food most roses ever got was animal manure over their roots plus extra nitrogen from human urine, a natural source of urea. Roses are gluttons for nitrogen and need a lot more of it than most home gardeners realize.) The reason for switching to urea now is that it's less acid than sulfate of ammonia, so by using it you avoid making the soil too acid for roses. Also, since it's based on an organic compound it's more effective after the soil has warmed up. Don't use urea on dry soil, and always irrigate thoroughly after applying it; it's a strong source of nitrogen and could burn roots unless it's well diluted. (Continue to spray with micronutrients, as described on p. 76.)

You can also plant canned roses this month. Prepare planting holes as for bare-root roses (as described on p. 24), but omit building a mound on the bottom of the hole.

Tropicals

Late spring is an excellent time to put in tropicals of all kinds, including citrus and other tropical fruit trees, tropical flowering trees, palms, philodendrons, and flowering vines such as bougainvillea. Tropicals are planted during their active growing season. If you live in a hot interior valley April is an even better month to plant tropicals, because the weather can become scorching by late May and may burn your newly planted specimens.

Many tropicals don't actually have a built-in dormant season. Given a warm climate and a jungle to grow in they grow year-round, sometimes in spurts to coincide with alternating wet-dry seasons that last two or three months in their native habitat. Here in Southern California it's up to the gardener to get tropicals to grow

How to Renew a Hanging Squirrel's Foot or Bear's Foot Fern

- Using a keyhole saw, clippers, and long-handled loppers, saw and cut out the entire center of the root-filled basket.
- Rebuild the sides of the basket with fresh, damp sphagnum moss.
- Fill the cavity you've made with fresh, well-drained potting mix.
- Cut the growing tips from the removed portion of fern, dip them in a rooting powder such as RooTone, knock off the excess, and plant them in the top of the basket. (Use leftover cuttings to start a new basket.)
- Attach a fresh set of wires or chains strong enough to hold up the plant.
- Keep the plant damp and in a shady, protected spot for two or three weeks until it's rooted, then feed it with diluted fish emulsion every week or two to speed its growth until it's well established.

fast during the warm months and rest from growth in winter—even though it's our rainy season. The way to do this is to feed and water your tropicals in spring and summer, but withhold fertilizer in early fall and water less when the weather cools down. Putting tropicals in the ground now in spring gives them a chance to get established all summer long, then slow down and harden off in fall so they can survive light frosts.

Ferns

Start feeding ferns once every two or three weeks now, and continue until fall. Native ferns that sprang to life with the first rain last fall, beneath toyons and on canyon walls, are dying down now and dropping fronds. They need no fertilizer. But most of the ferns we grow in our gardens and houses have awakened from winter torpor and are well into their season of fastest growth.

Ferns are ancient plants with poor plumbing systems. Most require shade, perfect drainage, and acid soil, and they have to be fed with care. Feed most ferns every three or four weeks during spring and summer with a well-diluted, complete, liquid fertilizer. (Feed staghorn ferns less frequently, as discussed below.) High nitrogen often spells "goodbye fern" if the fern is dry before you feed it. The safest food is fish emulsion, mixed according to package directions, because it's nonburning. Or you can choose a complete formula recommended for houseplants or flowering plants, such as Spoonit 18-20-16, and apply it according to package directions, but take care that the soil is thoroughly moist before you fertilize. Ferns appreciate the high phosphorus and potassium plus trace elements that they can get from this or a similar formula. The humus-filled, acid soil mixes in which ferns are grown may contain little or none of these elements.

Now's the best time to transplant ferns that have outgrown their containers. When their roots fill their containers, pot on Dallas and Kimberly Queen ferns to the next sizes, in fast-draining, acid soil mix. Dallas and Kimberly Queen are varieties of Boston fern (*Nephrolepis exaltata* 'Bostoniensis') that can flourish with less light than ordinary Boston ferns, and they grow more vigorously. (Repotting an ordinary Boston fern usually kills it unless it's growing in a greenhouse.)

Footed ferns, such as squirrel's foot fern (*Davallia trichomanoides*) and bear's foot fern (*Humata tyermannii*), are best adapted to growing in hanging baskets. Eventually the baskets become filled and covered with a solid mass of unproductive roots, and the plants begin to look distinctly ratty. Now's the time to renew them. (See the accompanying box.)

Collect Easy-Care Staghorn Ferns. Staghorn ferns (*Platyceriums*) are a group of about seventeen species of strikingly shaped, tropical, epiphytic ferns that are prized by plant collectors. (Certain of them are also called elkhorn, giant staghorn, or moosehorn ferns.) They attach themselves to the bark, branches, or crotches of trees by means of hairlike roots, and they grow two distinctly different kinds of fronds. The sterile fronds, which are at first green but go brown with age, are shaped like shields; they support the plant by accumulating organic matter and by wrapping themselves around the tree or branch on which the plant grows. The fertile fronds are green regardless of age and shaped like antlers; they jut out from the plant and bear *spores* on their undersides. (A spore is a microscopic, spherical, single-celled reproductive unit that's used in place of seeds by some primitive plants, including ferns, fungi, moss, and algae.)

The various common names of platycerium ferns match their striking shapes. The true staghorn fern (*Platycerium bifurcatum*) has fertile fronds shaped like stags' antlers and is the easiest one to grow. (Individual specimens have withstood temperatures as low as 20°F, 7°C, when protected by a shade structure, and the species is widely grown as an ornamental patio plant in both coastal and inland gardens.) Elkhorn ferns (*P. hillii*, *P. veitchii*, and *P. willinkii*) are very similar in appearance to staghorn ferns but generally less hardy. Giant staghorn or moosehorn ferns—*Platycerium grande* is the easiest one of these to grow—are highly decorative and well adapted to coastal gardens. Their 3- or 4-foot-long fertile fronds are shaped like moose's antlers, and they have majestic bright green, sterile fronds that often grow 4 or 5 feet wide. Moosehorn ferns are usually raised in greenhouses and adapt to gardens best when purchased and put outdoors now.

Keep all staghorns in bright, indirect light or in filtered sunshine. Protect them from hot sun, winds, and cold weather. When you water them drench them thoroughly, but then allow the moss (or soil) to dry out before you water again. Platyceriums are much more drought resistant than their lush tropical appearance might lead you to think. In dry interior zones water staghorns thoroughly about twice a week during the summer and once a week in winter. Along the coast water them once a week in summer and once every two weeks in winter.

How to Sterilize Potting Soil or Peat Moss.
Thoroughly moisten 1 gallon of potting soil or peat moss. (Moisten peat moss by mixing it with 1 to 3 cups of boiling water.) Spoon the soil or peat moss into a plastic cooking bag; make a hole in the top of the bag, and place it in a baking pan. When using a conventional oven bake at 350°F for fifteen minutes. When using a microwave oven cook on high for three minutes per quart of soil. (Cooking times may vary depending on your oven, so watch over this process closely. When the soil or peat moss is steaming hot throughout, it's done.) Place the bag outdoors and allow the contents to cool to 70°F (22°C) before you use it.

(In any zone, a heat wave or a Santa Ana might make more frequent watering necessary, but feel with your finger to make sure. It's important not to overwater your staghorn ferns or they'll rot.)

Staghorns are easy-care plants. They need to be fed only once every two or three months, beginning in spring. Don't feed them during winter. The easiest way to fertilize staghorns is to drench them with a complete liquid fertilizer such as 18-20-16, mixed according to package directions.

Moosehorn ferns aren't easy to propagate, but you can do so with a combination of luck and patience. First, wait until one of the brown spore patches under the fertile fronds flakes off easily when you lightly rub it. This means those spores are ripe. Sterilize a clear plastic shoe box by washing it in a solution of 1 quart of water and 2 tablespoons of bleach. Allow the shoe box to air dry, and then fill it with a 3-inch-deep layer of damp, sterilized peat moss. Hold the prepared shoe box directly under the spore patch, and with clean hands sprinkle some of the ripe spores—they're like fine, brown dust—onto the surface of the damp peat moss. Close up the box and keep it in bright light but out of direct sun and in a warm place (daytime temperatures of 72° to 80°F, 24° to 27°C, and nighttime temperatures about 10 degrees cooler). Use distilled water to keep the contents damp, but never soggy, and in six months to a year you may be lucky enough to have some tiny 1-inch-wide platycerium ferns, big enough to plant in paper cups filled with light acid soil mix. Keep them warm and in filtered light, feed them lightly, and pot them on occasionally as they grow. Eventually you can mount them on boards as described in the

How to Separate and Mount the Pups of Staghorn Ferns

Once the pups (offsets) of staghorn ferns have sprouted and grown to be at least 4 inches long, you can separate them from the parent plant to make new specimens.

· Soak some green sphagnum moss in a bucket of water while you prepare the planting base. To the back of an appropriately sized piece of wood or plywood (flat cork bark or a fern trunk can also be used) attach a plastic-covered wire for hanging. (Use screws or nails to fix it firmly in place.)

· Cover the front of this base with a 1- or 2-inch-deep layer of premoistened sphagnum moss, and hold it in place by winding nylon fishing twine around it or, alternatively, cover the entire face of the sphagnum moss with a piece of Ross Garden Netting. (Secure the netting by stapling the edges to the back of the base.) Turn the base over and cut a horizontal slit 1 or 2 inches long in the center of the netting.

· With your fingers, carefully pull off a clump of pups from the mother plant. For each new plant, take between one and four pups; each one must have a sterile frond as well as at least one fertile frond. (If possible, remove a small portion of the sterile frond of the mother plant to help hold the new plant together.)

· Wrap the roots of the pup (or pups) in damp sphagnum moss, and seat them in the center of the base you have made. Tie them in place with fishing twine, being careful to wrap the twine under but not over the face of the sterile fronds.

· Hang the new plant in a shady protected spot in bright light and keep it moist for two or three weeks until it's rooted. Then begin to feed it once every two weeks with diluted fish emulsion until it's well established.

· For even faster growth mist your young staghorn with water once or twice a week. Occasionally add diluted fish emulsion to the water you use for misting.

accompanying box for the more common variety of staghorn fern.

Many staghorn and elkhorn ferns not only have spores but also make a great many offsets, called pups. You can propagate these very easily by dividing them off any time in spring after they reach the proper size. (See the accompanying box.)

Volunteers

Look around the garden now for plants that have seeded themselves in the wrong places, and weed them out. Admittedly some plants are weedier by nature than others, but any plant can be a weed if it's growing where you don't want it. Even a native Torrey pine, live oak, or Washingtonia palm can be a weed if it seeds itself between the sun and your vegetable garden.

Develop the eye of an artist in regard to what to keep and what must go. If shade draws your sensibilities and your need is a forest retreat you can achieve it easily by planting well-chosen trees, but don't let it happen by accident. If there's something you really don't want grit your teeth and pull it up now, or you'll find yourself in a few years chopping it down at great expense to pocketbook and conscience.

Control of Mildew

Moderate temperatures combined with damp oceanic air make May the worst time for mildew. If you're still growing peas and you don't want to pull them out yet try dusting the plants with sulfur at intervals of one week. Roses and tuberous begonias are particularly sensitive to mildew. Control it on them with a fungicide

such as benomyl mixed with a spreader-sticker, like Spraymate, to make it more effective. Or try using an antitranspirant such as Wilt-Pruf. This is a biodegradable, organic, film-forming chemical especially made to protect plants from loss, injury, or shock caused by excessive water loss through leaves, stems, and branches. Some gardeners find that it has the additional benefit of protection from mildew, though the product isn't labeled for this use. Antitranspirants may help plants withstand drought and also air pollution, especially from excessive levels of ozone.

Pruning

Prune winter- and spring-flowering vines, bushes, trees, and ground covers after they finish blooming. A ☛ **Rule of Thumb** that applies in almost all cases is: *Prune flowering plants that bloom once a year after they bloom, not before they bloom, or you'll prevent them from flowering.* Refer to a pruning manual for additional directions by plant type; I especially recommend the *Sunset Pruning Handbook*, listed in the bibliography. Here are a few examples of plants to be pruned now.

• **Polyanthum Jasmine (*Jasminum polyanthum*).** Lightly cut back this fragrant, winter-blooming vine after bloom, to remove unsightly dead blossoms and produce a second wave of bloom. Then cut it back hard—almost to bare wood—to clean up the plant, prevent it from building up a tangled interior, and produce new wood to bloom next year.

• **Lady Banks' Rose (*Rosa banksiae*).** Cut this rose back hard after bloom to keep it in bounds, produce a second, lighter wave of bloom, and produce new wood to bloom next year.

- **New Zealand Tea Trees (*Leptospermum scoparium*).** Shape these during bloom by cutting sprays for cut flowers. After bloom you can further shape them by cutting out whole unwanted branches and by heading back tips of selected branches to increase bushiness and develop a natural billowy shape. Don't ever shear leptospermum shrubs or trees like a ball—this practice ruins their growth habit and prevents proper flowering.

- **Wisteria.** Train young plants onto a strong support. Prevent long streamers from twining around each other, and tie them lightly where you want them. Once a vine has reached the size and shape you desire, begin in May to cut back all unwanted new growth to two or three buds from the main branch, to create bloom spurs that will flower for many years. (This will stimulate sporadic summer bloom.)

- **Trailing African Daisy (*Osteospermum fruticosum*).** Give osteospermum a yearly haircut in early May after bloom to prevent the buildup of thatch, which could lead to death from summer fungus. Clean up the ground; remove clippings and dead leaves. Mulch with nitrolized wood shavings, and follow up with fertilizer. You'll get another show of bloom.

- **Geraldton Waxflower (*Chamelaucium uncinatum*).** One of our loveliest drought-resistant plants, this one responds well to heavy pruning after bloom. Cut back whole sprays—not all the way down to the ground but into the body of the plant and back to the trunk. If you have room, let it grow big

like a small shaggy-barked tree, but if it's outgrown its space it can be chopped back to 2 feet high now. Fresh shoots will spring from apparently dry wood below the cuts, and you'll have a whole new plant by fall. (Don't ever give this plant manure. It hates the stuff.)

Bulbs

Plant Tuberoses. If you're especially fond of fragrant plants, try planting tuberoses (*Polianthes tuberosa*)—known in Hawaii as lei flowers—in early May. Choose tubers with a green growth tip, and place them so that the tips are level with the soil surface, 6 inches apart, in acid, well-drained soil in pots or the ground. Choose a warm spot; in full sun along the coast, or slightly shaded but with reflected heat inland. Water them and wait for a sprout to appear, then water often and well. Feed them monthly with an acid fertilizer for bloom and growth.

The heavily scented white flowers will appear in August or September. After the plants die down, you can leave the tubers in the ground, though if you do sometimes they'll skip a year before repeating bloom. For surer results, lift them and store in perlite until next May.

Care for Spring-Flowering Bulbs as the Bloom Season Ends. Continue to keep spring-flowering bulbs well watered during and after bloom. If you grew some in pots and want to reuse the containers, slip the bulbs out carefully and plant them as clumps in a sheltered spot.

A shot of complete liquid fertilizer after bloom will help your bulbs store up strength for next year. Don't cut off leaves before they go brown.

Flower Beds and Containers

Clean Up and Replant Flower Beds as They Finish Blooming. In Southern California we grow annual flowers year-round by planting with the seasons, twice a year. Beginning in September, but mainly in October, we plant cool-season annuals that bloom all winter and peak in April. This makes May the logical time to replace them with warm-season annuals for blooms all summer long. (If you planted ahead from seeds in flats, as suggested in March, you'll have plenty of home-grown transplants all ready to go in the ground.) So now's the time to pull out all cool-season annuals that have finished blooming, such as cineraria, calendulas, Iceland poppies, malacoides primroses, snapdragons, and stock. As you clear the beds also clean them up, add some mulch and fertilizer, and replant the bare spaces with summer annuals, including marigolds, zinnias, cosmos, gomphrena, and petunias in full sun and lobelia, impatiens, and begonias in partial shade. (Semperflorens and richmondensis begonias can be planted in sun or shade in coastal zones.) Plant scarlet salvia in partial shade inland, full sun along the coast. (For more, see the April flowerbed section beginning on p. 114.)

Keep Plants That Are Still Going Strong. May border planting isn't like October's, when every summer annual can be pulled up by the roots to make way for cool-season flowers. Some of the seeds and transplants we put in during fall or early in spring, such as Shasta daisies, cosmos, and new heat-resistant pansies and violas, will continue to bloom all summer long in most coastal and some inland zones. Lavatera, lark-spur, clarkia, and many annual and perennial wildflowers will bloom through June, and perhaps into July. Take care not to pull them up by mistake. Do clean up spring-blooming perennials such as perennial candytuft (*Iberis sempervirens*). Shear it all over after bloom to remove the seed pods, leaving a neat evergreen plant—excellent for edging summer beds.

Plant the Heat-Lovers from Seed. At last it's time to plant heat-loving annuals, such as zinnias, from seeds. Modern hybrid zinnias bounce back quicker after transplanting than old varieties, but as a rule zinnias do best when planted from seeds right where you want them to grow. This also allows you to choose varieties not usually found in nursery packs. If you've never grown anything from seeds and would like to try, zinnias are a good choice to start with. (See the accompanying box.) Other flowers you can plant now from seeds include sweet alyssum, calliopsis, celosia, marigold, portulaca, nicotiana, scarlet sage, sunflower, vinca rosea, verbena, and morning glory.

Use Nursery Transplants for Instant Color. Pony packs of many summer annuals can be planted now; they'll soon fill out in size. Or, for instant flowerbeds and patio pots chock full of plants, use the more expensive but larger-rooted "color packs." Arrange them in your shopping cart to see which color combinations look good together.

Years ago it was preferable to purchase flowers before they bloomed, but new varieties are made to bloom in the pack—even in tiny pony packs—and continue to perform spectac-

A Foolproof Way to Plant and Grow Zinnias from Seed

· Choose a spot in full sun that is not hit by overhead sprinklers.

· Dig the ground deeply and mix in a generous layer of organic soil amendment. Add a complete fertilizer recommended for annual flowers according to package directions, and mix it into the top 6 inches of soil.

· Use the garden hoe to make a dike of soil 3 or 4 inches high all the way around the seedbed; it will hold the water in when you irrigate. Rake the seedbed level inside this dike. Or first rake the seedbed level and then install a drip system that will water the bed at ground level. (Drip systems make water basins unnecessary.)

· Pour some seeds into the palm of your hand. Grasping them one by one place each seed right where you want it to grow, in a continuous diamond pattern all over the bed or drift. (As for all bedding plants and ground covers, alternate the rows when planting so that the plants grow all over, evenly, rather than standing like soldiers in foursquare rows.) Follow the directions on the package as to spacing. (Large varieties should be spaced about 12 inches apart, small varieties about 6 inches.)

· Cover the seeds very lightly with about ¼ inch of soil—zinnias need light in order to germinate—and pat it down gently. (If you're planting in clay soil, cover the seeds with potting mix rather than soil so they won't have to break through a hard crust.)

· Mist the seedbed thoroughly after planting. Continue to mist it twice daily (even more in interior zones) until the seeds germinate. (Covering the bed with a floating row cover, such as Reemay, can help keep seeds damp and speed germination in hot interior valleys. After seeds have germinated, take the row cover off.)

· Sprinkle the ground with granulated cutworm bait containing Sevin or diazinon. (If using a row cover, sprinkle on the bait before covering the bed.) Bait again a week or two later.

· Once the zinnias are up and firmly rooted, stop misting and start irrigating with the drip system or by putting the hose on the ground inside the dike. (Aim the hose into a sideways flower pot to break the force of the water.) The ☞ **Rule of Thumb** for zinnias is: *Always water zinnias on the ground, never overhead, or you'll ruin the foliage.*

· When the plants are 3 or 4 inches high, start watering them more infrequently and deeply until you're applying 1 to 2 inches of water per week, depending on your soil and climate zone.

· To encourage branching, pinch out the first flower bud on each plant or pinch above the third set of leaves.

· Pick and deadhead zinnias throughout the summer.

◄
Quick Tip

How to Scarify Seed.
Some seeds with hard coats, like morning glory
(Ipomoea tricolor) and lupine, have to be
scarified (nicked) prior to planting or they won't
sprout under garden conditions. To scarify a
seed easily, grasp it with pliers and use a small
three-cornered file to carefully file through
the edge of the seed at any spot other than the
"eye" from which it will sprout. Soak scarified
morning glory seeds overnight in warm water
before planting.

ularly in the garden. The one thing the gardener must remember is to loosen up those roots when you plant, or they'll just sit there for months thinking they're still in the container.

Lawn Care

Plant Warm-Season Lawns and Tall Fescue. St. Augustine, Bermuda, and dichondra get off to a fast start when planted in May. (Hold off until June to plant zoysia, see p. 161.) Salt-tolerant Adalayd grass (*Paspalum vaginatum*), which is from Australia and is called Excalibre when it's sold as sod, can also be planted this month. It's too late to plant most cool-season grasses from seed, but tall fescues—for example, Water Saver, an attractive blend of drought- and disease-resistant varieties—can be planted from sod. (Despite this trade name, tall fescues use much more water than Bermuda or zoysia.)

Lawns can be planted in several ways: sown from seeds, plugged in from flats, or rolled out from sod like an instant carpet. Bermuda, zoysia, and Adalayd can also be planted from stolons. Whichever method you use, be sure to prepare the ground properly. Before beginning, decide whether to plant a warm- or cool-season lawn (as discussed on p. 87) and choose a variety appropriate for your area and needs.

Select the Best Variety for You. When you research grass types be sure to consult with successful local gardeners and the nearest University of California Cooperative Extension Office. Consider these factors: St. Augustine is better adapted to shade than other lawn grasses but needs a lot of water. Dichondra is best used as a design element in small areas only. If you live close to a Bermuda golf course it will seed itself eventually into any cool-season lawn, making it look ratty. To minimize this, plant a hybrid or selected strain of Bermuda for your own lawn in the first place. You might use Santa Ana, Tifblue, or Tifgreen; all three are vigorous hybrids that make such a dense, fine-textured turf that common Bermuda usually cannot invade them. Another possibility is a newer variety with improved early spring color, such as NuMex Sahara; it's actually not a hybrid but a seed selection from common Bermuda. (You'll need a reel mower, not a rotary one, for cutting Bermuda.) As mentioned before, don't plant such troublemakers as bentgrass or Kentucky bluegrass—they'll die in the first drought. Common Bermuda and Santa Ana hybrid Bermuda grass are the two most drought-resistant choices.

Fertilize Lawns. Continue to feed warm-season grasses this month, and in coastal zones apply fertilizer to cool-season lawns once more this month at the same rate as you have used during the winter. But in interior zones stop feeding cool-season lawns now, other than an occasional light application (one-fourth to one-half the normal dosage) applied only when necessary to maintain a healthy green color. Tests done by the University of California Division of Agriculture show that heavy feeding of cool-season grasses such as ryegrass, bluegrass, and fescue during the warm season of the year subjects them to unnecessary stress.

Check Dichondra for Flea Beetles. Control flea beetles before they damage dichondra. These tiny black, $\frac{1}{25}$-inch-long insects skeletonize leaves and cause brown areas that often are confused with dry spots or fertilizer burn. To look for the culprits get down on your hands and knees, put a white piece of paper on the lawn, and tap it. The beetles will jump on top. Control them with a pesticide-containing fertilizer or spray with a product containing diazinon or chlorpyrifos.

Vegetable Gardening

Irrigate and Fertilize Summer Crops. Summer vegetables grow fast this month, and watering is the most important task. Vegetables aren't drought resistant—they need plenty of water—but you can cut down on the water you use by installing drip irrigation. Plan the system now and switch to it prior to fall planting.

If any crop shows signs of slowing down side-dress the row with vegetable fertilizer following package directions. But don't overfertilize beans or tomatoes with nitrogen, or you'll risk encouraging leafy growth at the expense of harvest. (If you've already done that by mistake, soak the ground with 0-10-10 to stimulate flowering.)

Continue to Plant. For continuous crops of vegetables keep planting summer crops in whatever spaces you may have. By staggering plantings you'll get longer harvests and more manageable quantities. All the vegetables for summer plus the ones that can be planted year-round can be put in now, including corn, green beans, lima beans, beets, carrots, chayote, cucumbers, eggplant, melons, New Zealand spinach, peppers, pumpkins, radishes, leaf lettuce, summer squash, winter squash, Swiss chard, turnips, and tomatoes, as well as many herbs.

How to Grow a Cantaloupe in a Tire

Gardeners in cool coastal areas often have problems growing cantaloupes. Here's a heat-increasing method that brings success.

- In early May plant a cantaloupe variety that will ripen at relatively cool temperatures, such as Ambrosia.

- Dig a hole 2 feet wide and 1 foot deep in full sun. Mix together aged manure, compost, organic soil amendment and some of the native soil from the hole to make a richly organic soil. Into this, mix 3 tablespoons 6-12-6, or similar vegetable fertilizer, and refill the hole.

- Lay an old auto tire over the hole, pack native soil into the sides of the tire with your hands, and fill the center up to the inside edge of the tire with more manure, compost, soil, and 2 tablespoons fertilizer. Finish with a layer of potting soil and water deeply. (The bulging tire makes a perfect watering basin.)

- Plant five or six seeds, 1 inch deep; space them evenly around the top.

- Water deeply and daily until the seeds sprout. When the seedlings are up 4 inches, choose the strongest two. Clip off or pull out the others. For continued harvests plant other tires. Separate them from the first by 3 or 4 feet.

- Cover the ground all around the tires with a layer of black plastic mulch to raise the temperature of the melon patch. (Peg it down.) The vines will grow out over the plastic and it will keep the fruit clean.

- Once the plants are established water deeply; lay the hose in the tire and let water soak in slowly. Do this twice a week when the plants are young, once a week when they're full grown. (If plants wilt, water them right away.)

- Water less as the fruit nears maturity. (Too much water then makes fruit less sweet.)

- Pick at *full slip*, meaning there's a crack around the vine so that the melon slips off easily when it's lifted. Enjoy the sweetness and flavor.

Harvest Regularly. Once beans and squash begin to bear, pick them daily to keep them coming. Picking vegetables is a type of pruning, like deadheading flowers to keep them blooming. Most crops, including root vegetables, should be harvested when young and tender. Hunt for zucchinis daily or you'll be tripping over giants as big as blimps. Eat the little ones flowers and all. Some oversized zucchini are good for nothing but laughs, but if you catch them in time they're delicious sliced, breaded, and fried, or in zucchini soup.

Pick herbs to keep them in bounds, and plant more to discourage pests. (There's little reliable research on the value of herbs as pest traps or pest repellents, but many home gardeners find that planting herbs among their vegetables provides a more pest-free garden.) Among herbs to plant or replace now is parsley. If you planted a row last year, it will probably go to seed now because it's biennial. Pull it up (don't throw away the roots, cook them in soup) and plant a new row in another spot.

Care for Tomatoes. Continue to tie up tomatoes growing on stakes and trellises (as described on p. 95). Except on cage-grown plants pinch out the suckers to maintain one or two main trunks per plant, according to your preference. After indeterminate tomatoes (the ones that keep growing and bearing until they're cut down by cold weather) reach the top of 8-foot stakes, stop pinching out the suckers and tie bamboo or wooden stakes horizontally overhead between the vertical stakes, to hold up flopping vines. (Determinate varieties usually don't grow this tall because they're genetically programmed to grow only to a certain height, which differs according to variety.)

Quick Tip

Enlist the Help of Scrub Jays.
Nail an empty tuna can on top of a tomato stake. Stock it with a few unshelled peanuts, to attract scrub jays. They'll take the peanuts, notice the caterpillars, and come back for them.

Keep the soil evenly moist in order to avoid blossom-end rot. If you want plenty of evenly shaped, big tomatoes with many seeds in them, continue to hit tomato stakes and cages with a hammer at midday, or vibrate the individual flower clusters, to increase pollination. If you prefer meaty fruit with few seeds you can stop this practice now, because warm temperatures, breezes, and insect activity will give you ample fruit anyway; if the fruit is not well pollinated it may be somewhat strangely shaped, but it will contain fewer seeds. For best flavor pick tomatoes when they're red and ripe.

Control Pests and Diseases. Continue to use organic methods to control pests and diseases on vegetables. Interplant with herbs to confuse the bugs. (A diverse collection of plants helps to prevent pests from specializing, as they can do when only one crop is grown.) Introduce lady bugs, green lacewings, and other beneficials. Handpick bugs and caterpillars, catch slugs and snails with raised boards (described on p. 73), and go out at night with a flashlight and gather snails. (Just be sure to sing out a warning to any grub-digging skunks you might accidentally surprise.) If you feel you must spray stick to a biodegradable insecticidal soap, such as Safer, and use BT against caterpillars.

Since many disease problems can be controlled by keeping the garden clean, cut off diseased lower leaves on tomato plants. (Dip the clippers in alcohol between cuts to disinfect them.) Don't pick beans when the dew is on them, in order not to spread rust. And always rotate your crops; when you harvest a row, plant something different in its place.

How to Grow a Giant Pumpkin

There's time to grow a giant pumpkin for Halloween if you plant now.

- Choose a giant variety, such as Big Max. (It's actually a squash.)

- Dig a hole in full sun. Add the organic matter and fertilizer prescribed for cantaloupes in the accompanying box. Include horse manure if it's available.

- Build a hill of amended soil that's 18 inches wide at the base and 4 or 6 inches high. Make a small watering basin on top for starting the seeds; also make a large watering basin in amended soil on the north side for watering the mature plant. (Later arrange the vines so they grow away from the basin.)

- Plant 4 to 6 seeds 1 inch deep on the top of the mound. Water them daily until sprouted. When the plants are up 4 inches choose the best one, and clip off the others. Start watering deeply in the basin.

- Allow many fruits to reach grapefruit size. Then choose the best one—the one closest to the roots and with the thickest stem and best color, size, and shape. Clip off all the others.

- Feed the pumpkin monthly with a high-nitrogen fertilizer. Fill the watering basin regularly so that total water is equal to an inch of rain per day.

- While you can still lift your pumpkin slip a piece of plywood under it to keep the bottom dry and protect it from rot and pests.

- Here's an optional step, for even larger growth and contest-size fruit. Force-feed the pumpkin with a woolen wick that you enclose in a plastic tube. Insert one end into a gallon of milk, the other into the stem of the pumpkin. Replace milk bottles as necessary until the pumpkin stops growing (or perhaps until you hear a giant burp?).

Purchase / Plant

- [ ] Plant **irises**, 128
- [ ] Plant canned **roses**, 131
- [ ] Plant **tropicals**, 131
- [ ] Plant **tuberoses**, 137
- [ ] Transplant potted **bulbs** into the ground, 137
- [ ] Replace **cool-season bedding flowers** with flowers to bloom in summer, 138
- [ ] Plant **zinnias** and other heat-loving flowers, 138
- [ ] Plant **morning glories**, 138
- [ ] Plant **warm-season lawns**, 140
- [ ] Continue to plant **summer vegetables**, 141
- [ ] Plant **melons**, 142
- [ ] Replace **parsley**, if you haven't already done so, 143
- [ ] Plant a **giant pumpkin** for Halloween, 145
- [ ] Start **perennials** from seed in interior zones, 158
- [ ] Purchase, plant, and transplant **succulents**, including **cacti** and **euphorbias**, 185

Trim, Prune, Mow, Divide

- [ ] Stop pinching **fuchsias** if you did not do so last month, 55, 82
- [ ] Mow all **grass lawns**, 86
- [ ] Thin out fruit on **deciduous fruit trees**, 105
- [ ] Pinch **dahlias** back when the plant has three sets of leaves; tie the plants up as they grow, 106
- [ ] Continue to pick and deadhead **roses**. Disbud them if desired, 107
- [ ] Divide and repot **cymbidiums** that have outgrown their containers, 130
- [ ] Cut off bloom spikes from **cymbidiums** after flowers fade, 130
- [ ] Prune **camellias** if you have not already done so, 130
- [ ] Clean up and prune **azaleas**, 130
- [ ] Divide and mount **staghorn ferns**, 135
- [ ] Prune **winter-** and **spring-flowering vines, shrubs, trees,** and **ground covers** after they finish blooming, 136
- [ ] Continue to tie up and sucker **tomatoes**, 143
- [ ] Remove berries (seed pods) from **fuchsias** after flowers fall, 154
- [ ] Pinch back **petunias** when you plant them, 178
- [ ] Continue to prune and train **espaliers**, 203
- [ ] Propagate **daylilies** by planting their proliferates; cut off spent bloom stems, 206
- [ ] Remove the seed pods from **white fortnight lilies,** but leave the bloom stalks on the plant, 206

Fertilize

- [ ] Feed **citrus trees**, 30
- [ ] Feed **avocado trees**, 48
- [ ] Feed **fuchsias**, 55
- [ ] Feed **tuberous begonias**, 78
- [ ] Feed **water lilies**, 110
- [ ] Fertilize **corn**, 117
- [ ] Feed **cymbidiums** that have finished blooming, for growth, 130
- [ ] Fertilize **camellias** after bloom, 130
- [ ] Feed **azaleas** after bloom, 130
- [ ] Feed **roses**, 131
- [ ] Feed **ferns**, 132
- [ ] Feed **flower beds**, 138
- [ ] Fertilize **lawns**, 141
- [ ] Side-dress **vegetable** rows with fertilizer, 141
- [ ] Feed all container-grown **succulents** with a well-diluted complete liquid fertilizer, 186
- [ ] Fertilize **peppers** when flowers first show, 191
- [ ] Feed and water **cycads**, 213

Water

- [ ] As the weather becomes drier water **all garden plants** regularly, 128
- [ ] Taper off watering those **California native plants** that do not accept summer water, 128
- [ ] Water **cymbidiums,** 128
- [ ] Water **roses,** 131
- [ ] Water **vegetables,** 141
- [ ] Do not water **succulents,** 186

Control Pests, Diseases, and Weeds

- [ ] Control **rose** pests and diseases, 106
- [ ] Spray **junipers** and **Italian cypress** for juniper moths, 110
- [ ] Control **mildew,** 136
- [ ] Control **flea beetles** on dichondra, 141
- [ ] Control pests on **vegetables,** 144
- [ ] Control weeds among **permanent plants** by mulching or cultivating, 170
- [ ] Control weeds among **vegetables** and **flowers** by hand pulling, 170
- [ ] Trap gophers, or control them prior to planting **lawns,** 263, 287

Also This Month

- [ ] Keep **bamboo** from running into your neighbor's garden, 84
- [ ] Keep **cymbidiums** in semishade, but where they will get some sun, 128
- [ ] Mulch **camellias** and **azaleas,** 130
- [ ] Renew overgrown **fern** baskets, 132
- [ ] Remove **volunteers** that are growing where they aren't wanted, 136
- [ ] Pull out **cool-season annuals** that have finished blooming, 138
- [ ] Harvest **vegetables** regularly, 143
- [ ] Harvest **bananas** whenever they are ready, according to type, 211
- [ ] Begin to harvest **short-day onions** to slice and eat raw, 290

JUNE

JUNE

The Easy-Going Month

June is the month when we're usually most aware of our proximity to the ocean. As the continental air mass warms, in early summer, it has a tendency to rise and pull cool oceanic air inland. There's always a chance that the year may be different, but if the weather behaves in a normal manner damp ocean air now often extends inland beyond the first range of hills, well into Zones 21 and 20. The weather man's familiar "night and morning fog along the coast" often lasts all day, and even gardeners in the interior may experience some overcast.

It's an easy-going month in the garden. Most of the spring planting should be done by now, and the hot, dry days of summer haven't yet arrived. Gardeners in interior valleys face the onset of scorching heat by month's end, but early in June, except for an occasional hot spell

of two or three days in the hundreds, it's still pleasant enough to garden in the middle of the day.

June Bloom

It's possible here to have color year-round from permanent plants. If your garden lacks color now notice what's in bloom in local gardens, and visit botanical gardens and nurseries to see what's flowering. Consider adding one or two of the following plants that bloom during June.

- **Jacaranda with Agapanthus.** Jacaranda is a spectacular tree. Try planting white agapanthus, also in bloom now, at its feet. Or use blue agapanthus for a mirror effect—blue on the tree and on the ground as well.

- **Chinese Fringe Tree (*Chionanthus retusus*).** White flowers shaped rather like lilac blossoms cover the entire tree in June.

- **Puya.** This spiky accent plant, drought resistant once established, has flower stalks like huge asparagus, 3 to 6 feet tall, that open to red, lavender, turquoise, and white flowers. Use them to complement areas of cacti and succulents, in a spot where they can get slightly more water.

- **Fuchsia, Hydrangea, and Lantana.** All these are at the height of bloom in June. Fuchsias need regular water but adapt well to drip systems. Hydrangeas also need plenty of water, but they make good container plants or choices for moist canyons with damp but well-drained soil. Lantana is one of the easiest full-sun, drought-resistant plants to grow and is a great bank cover.

- **Bottlebrush (*Callistemon citrinus*).** Among our finest drought-resistant small trees or shrubs, bottlebrush grows slowly to 25 feet. Named cultivars have the best color, and largest flowers.

- **Vines.** All of the following bloom in summer and can be purchased and planted now.
  - Orchid trumpet vine (*Clytostoma callistegioides*) is easy, disease resistant, and gorgeous in its late spring, early summer bloom.
  - Royal trumpet vine (*Distictis* 'Rivers') is a strong grower, disease resistant, with flowers ranging from mauve to royal purple.

- Bower vine (*Pandorea jasminoides*) is pink (Rosea) or white (Alba). Protect it from wind.

- Red trumpet vine (*Distictis buccinatoria*) does best near the sea, but can be grown in the interior, though it will suffer frost damage.

- Vanilla-scented trumpet vine (*Distictis laxiflora*) is violet fading through lavender to white.

- Mandevilla (*Mandevilla splendens* 'Alice du Pont') is bright pink and a good choice to espalier on an east wall.

Tropicals and Subtropicals

Fertilize tropical and subtropical plants, according to their individual needs, during summer while they're growing. Continue to plant them except in interior valleys, where scorching days may burn their foliage if they're planted this late. Tropicals and subtropicals give us our distinctively Southern California atmosphere, and not all are great water users—some are drought resistant.

Among the numerous tropical and subtropical plants that like to be planted in June (in all but the hottest interior zones) are bougainvillea, Natal plum, hibiscus, gardenia, ginger, palms, tree ferns, and many flowering trees, such as golden trumpet tree (*Tabebuia chrysotricha*), floss silk tree (*Chorisia speciosa*), orchid trees (*Bauhinias*), crape myrtle (*Lagerstroemia indica*), cassias, and coral trees.

Also plant blue hibiscus (*Alyogyne huegelii*), a splendid dry-climate shrub from Australia with eye-catching bright blue flowers that bloom on and off year-round in full sun. It's widely

* ❋ *

How to Plant a Bougainvillea and Get It Growing

Bougainvilleas are drought resistant, free from pests and disease, romantic, glowingly colorful, and easy to grow—but not easy to plant or get started. Use them as large ground covers on banks and have them pouring over walls, roofs, fences, and arbors. Here's how to plant them.

- Choose plants with the color, eventual size, and growth habit you desire in mind. Some are vines and some shrubs. Some are more vigorous than others. Five-gallon sizes make a faster start in the ground than 1-gallon sizes do.

- Choose a spot in full sun, preferably where the *root run*—the area where the roots grow— is also hit by full sun. (In the desert and hot interior valleys bougainvilleas will bloom in light shade.)

- Dig a hole twice as wide as the container and the same depth as the container. Loosen the soil in the bottom of the hole, and work in 2 or 3 cupfuls of bone meal. (If the soil is heavy clay also work in gypsum.) Cover this with enough soil that, when you set in the plant, the top of the root ball will be level with the surrounding ground. Add slow-release fertilizer tablets, according to package directions, around the bottom of the hole.

- Bougainvilleas are fragile when young and often killed when they're planted because their roots and crown are broken. Turn the plant on its side. With sharp pruning shears, cut around the bottom of the container and look to see whether it's well rooted. If it is, slip the plant out sideways by pushing from the bottom. Lower it carefully into the hole while supporting the roots with your hands. Backfill with native soil.

- If the plant is not well rooted, slit the sides of the container from the bottom up in several places, then tape it back together with masking tape. Lower the plant into the hole with the taped container holding the roots in place. Loosen the tape and slide the bottom out. Slip out the cut pieces from the sides as you backfill the hole with native soil.

- Press the soil down around the plant with your hands. The top of the root ball should be even with the surrounding ground.

- Make a watering basin, and water deeply right away. Then, in fast-draining soils, for three days water once a day; for the next two weeks water three times a week; and for the following month water twice a week. Thereafter, for the first three years, water once a week. In clay soils you should water enough to keep the root ball damp but not soggy for the first three weeks to a month. Thereafter water deeply after the ground dries out. Bougainvilleas are drought resistant not because they don't need water but because their roots go deeply into the ground until they find an underground water source. When young they take all the water they can get, as long as drainage is adequate. Feed them once a month each year between April and August.

- After three to five years you can stop fertilizing in summer, stop watering in winter, and reduce the frequency of summer watering to once a month or every six weeks—or perhaps never, depending on placement and variety. (Container-grown vines will always need regular fertilizer and water.)

❋ ❋ ❋

available either in its natural shrub form or as a standard, with a 3- to 4-foot trunk. The only fault of blue hibiscus is that it's rangy and open, and doesn't branch freely. You can remedy this and also keep the plant blooming if once a month from spring to fall you cut back two or three of its longest branches by half or two-thirds their length.

Other choices to plant now include tropical fruit trees, such as avocado, banana, citrus, pineapple guava, sapote, and cherimoya. (As mentioned under other months some of these species can be planted happily at other times as well.) In most areas—other than the warmest interior valleys—the early summer weather stimulates growth but isn't yet hot enough to dry them out. Keep them well watered until established.

Morning Glories

Perennial morning glories (*Ipomoea acuminata*) get started rapidly when planted now. Grow them from seeds or plants in full sun and in ordinary or poor soil, with no nitrogen fertilizer added. Scarify the seeds (as described in the box on p. 140) and soak them overnight in warm water before planting. (Keep the seeds away from children—they're poisonous.) Water them regularly to get them going and occasionally thereafter.

These vines are invasive, drought resistant, and permanent once established. Use morning glories for an old-fashioned, colorful, countrified look and to camouflage chain link fences. They're not for formal gardens but can be an eyecatching ornament in the right spot and in old neighborhoods, sometimes clambering into trees and covering neglected hedges.

Bearded Irises

If your irises don't bloom they're either growing in too much shade or they need dividing. (They need full sun along the coast and six hours of sun daily in the interior.) After bearded irises have been in the ground for three or four years, they become crowded. Their roots intertwine, the clumps rise ever higher out of the ground, and if they're not divided they'll stop blooming. In coastal zones divide irises as soon as flowering is finished, in June. If you don't finish the job in June, you can continue into July in most areas. In the hottest interior valleys wait until October. Sometimes, in old gardens, irises have been neglected for years and it's a big job to divide them.

Fuchsias

Fuchsias should be covered with a blanket of bloom this month. Feed them often with a balanced fertilizer that's high in nitrogen as well as bloom ingredients. When the individual flowers of most fuchsia varieties fade they fall off the plant, but they leave their seed pods still attached to the branch. Pinch off these seed pods—or berries as they're often called—daily if possible, after the flowers fall. This keeps the plants blooming. If you don't have time for removing seed pods, grow single varieties such as Red Spider, Orange Drops, Display, Nonpareil, or Gartenmeister Bonstedt, rather than double varieties. (The top four, often upward curving, petallike parts of fuchsias are called the *sepals*. The true petals hang down in the center and are called the *corolla*. Varieties with five or six petals in the corolla are considered single. Flowers with big, fluffy, many-petalled corollas are double.)

How to Divide Irises

- With a garden fork dig up an entire clump, shake off excess soil from the roots, then squirt it with the hose to wash all soil from the *rhizomes*. (A rhizome is a thickened stem that grows horizontally underground or on the surface of the ground.)

- Working with a sharp knife from the outside of the clump cut vigorous, healthy divisions. Each division for planting should have one fan of leaves, a section of young, healthy rhizome approximately 2 to 6 inches long, and some roots coming out the bottom. It may also have one or two new growth buds, or eyes, bulging out on the sides.

- Discard the following: the old, woody center of the clump that has no leaves; anything that is diseased, rotted, or has been attacked by pests; any thin or spindly growth, and all immature rhizomes with no leaves.

- Cut off the tops of the fans at a neat right angle, with the center point 4 inches higher and the sides 2 to 3 inches higher than the rhizome.

- Cut back the roots by about one-third, dip the cut ends of the rhizomes in a fungicide, such as captan, and allow them to dry in the sun for two or three hours.

- Dig up the bed or prepare individual planting areas, in full sun along the coast or where there's six hours of sun inland. Work in compost and bone meal.

- Replant the rhizomes on the same day, three to a clump, with the leaves pointing out from the center. Irises keep growing in the direction of each fan of leaves. On hillsides plant them with the bare rhizomes pointing downhill and the part with the leaves pointing uphill.

- For each rhizome use a trowel or a small spade to dig a hole approximately 4 inches deep and 8 inches wide. Make an elongated mound in the planting hole. Arrange the roots over the mound with the rhizome resting on top so that the top of the rhizome is level with the surrounding soil. If the roots bend on the bottom dig the hole deeper. Cover the roots with soil and press it down firmly with your hands. When you're finished the top of the rhizome should still be level with the surface of the soil.

- Water the bed thoroughly after planting and keep it damp, but not soggy, until the plants are rooted.

Water fuchsias regularly to prevent them from drying out, but don't overwater. Soggy soil can lead to root rot, fuchsias' worst bugaboo. Be on the lookout for pests, and spray if necessary with BT for cabbage loopers, with a miticide for spider mites, with Sevin for rust mites, and with Science Garden Insect Spray for whiteflies (as discussed in detail on p. 160). Or you could use Orthene to control both spider mites and cabbage loopers. Continue to introduce beneficial insects and encourage garden spiders. If these seem to be controlling most problems, don't spray. (Always use broad-spectrum insecticides like Sevin, Orthene, or Science Garden Insect Spray with restraint because they can kill beneficials.)

Visit nurseries to pick out new fuchsia varieties this month and you'll have a whole summer and fall to enjoy them. Choose them according to the environment you'll provide. White and pastel colors usually need more shade. Reds, purples, and small single varieties usually can take more sun. No fuchsia can bloom in solid shade; all need partial sun, such as under lath, shade cloth, or an open tree. In interior zones concentrate on growing heat-resistant varieties such as California, Carnival, Checkerboard, Papoose, Display, Swingtime, and Bonanza. Such upright varieties as Gartenmeister Bonstedt are best in the ground or tubs. Trailers, such as Pink Galore and Lisa, are best in hanging baskets. Some, like Swingtime, one of the easiest fuchsias to grow, can go either way.

Epiphyllums

Some epiphyllums are still in bloom, so it's not too late to choose these undemanding and dramatic plants at nurseries. After they finish blooming prune off diseased and dessicated branches and feed them occasionally with a weak balanced formula, such as 8-8-8 or fish emulsion. Keep them in semishade.

Prune off ungainly branches and root them to make new plants. (See directions in the box on p. 104.) For a faster start root four cuttings of the same variety in one 6-inch plastic container. (Never mix two varieties in the same container. The more vigorous one will soon crowd out the other, and you'll lose a prized color.) Pruning stimulates growth more than fertilizer alone, so

if you desire to hasten growth of a sluggish variety cut off all unsightly branches and feed it often. If you want to keep plants the same size, however, don't prune them too much and never overfeed with nitrogen.

Gardenias

Gardenias are among our most grown and least understood plants. They're often put in the wrong spots, such as small, shady patios where they invariably get whiteflies. Wrong locations can also cause bud drop, especially in warm coastal zones. Gardenias need acid soil, good drainage, adequate moisture, full sun along the coast or part shade inland, protection from thrips, and also regular fertilizing for growth and flowers with an acid-type product that contains trace elements, to prevent chlorosis. However, you can meet all these requirements and still have gardenias that drop buds instead of blooming. The reason is that if night temperatures get over 60° to 62°F (15° to 16°C) the buds won't develop. They'll stay on the plant but they won't grow. Then if suddenly a few cool nights occur, they'll all drop off. So don't grow gardenias where they'll be subjected to warm night temperatures—for example, in patios, on porches, or close to house walls. Put them where temperatures are colder at night— away from the house and out under the open sky; with the daily temperature spread they'll bloom.

Deciduous Fruit Trees

Do the last thinning on deciduous fruit trees after *June drop* has occurred. June drop is nature's way of getting rid of an overload of fruit. It may occur any time between early May and July but is most likely to happen around the first of June. One day you visit your apple, peach, or apricot tree and find a circle of immature fruit lying on the ground under the branches. These trees often set more than double the amount of fruit they could possibly ripen properly, so they simply drop off part of it.

If you followed the advice for April and thinned out the fruit on your trees then and again four to six weeks later, you enabled the remaining fruit to grow larger and thus less fruit will drop off now. Nevertheless, you may need to remove even more fruit than naturally drops in order to space your crop evenly down the branches. Inspect other deciduous fruit trees that are less subject to June drop—plums, for instance—and thin out their fruits also.

Clean up the fallen fruit under the tree before it has time to rot and spread disease. If it's healthy, chop it and add it to the compost pile (cover it with earth against flies and rodents). Also water deciduous fruit trees well in June and July.

Yellow Shrub Daisies

Marguerites, native to the Canary Islands, and gamolepis and euryops, from South Africa, are all members of the daisy family that grow in shrubby form and bear single yellow flowers. (Marguerites also come in pink and white and in doubles.) Despite their apparent similarities they have different characteristics and needs.

Marguerites. Use marguerites (*Chrysanthemum frutescens*) inland for winter and spring bloom in semishade. In coastal zones marguerites can be treated as a short-lived perennial for full sun or partial shade; they last three years. In interior zones they're best grown as a cool-season annual. They're not drought resistant; water them regularly or they'll wilt. Deadhead marguerites regularly and keep them well fed.

Eventually—usually in June—the flowers begin to get smaller, then all die at once. In hot interior valleys it's then time to replace the plants with something else. Along the coast its the cue to give your marguerite a butch haircut; using hedge shears chop away the outer edges of the plant all over the top and sides. Remove all flowers, dead or alive, some green tips (not too much) and, unavoidably, a few buds. Follow up with fertilizer and water. In a week or two flowers will return with a new burst of energy. The ☞ **Rule of Thumb** is: *Never cut marguerites back into old wood, or you'll kill the plant.* (There are no buds down there to sprout.)

Gamolepis. Gamolepis (*Gamolepis chrysanthemoides*) are different from marguerites; they have dormant buds hidden under the bark all the way down their height. You can cut them to the ground or to any level and they'll come back. Follow up with water and fertilizer. With reasonable care gamolepis are long-lived landscape plants, much more drought resistant than marguerites, and larger—to 6 feet if you allow them—and rangier. They're tolerant of heat and frost and bloom year-round without deadheading. Prune them frequently to keep them neat. They can be grown as a hedge but look best when cut in rounded and mounded shapes (wider below than above), rather than square cut.

Euryops. Two euryops cultivars are widely grown in Southern California. One has gray foliage and bright lemon-yellow flowers with narrow petals (*Euryops pectinatus*), and it blooms mainly in fall, winter, and spring. Cut this type back in June after bloom. Shear the plants all over with hedge shears. Remove dead flowers and 3 or 4 inches of tip growth to shape and renew the plant.

The other most commonly grown cultivar is Green Gold euryops (*Euryops pectinatus* 'Viridis'). This has golden yellow flowers, wider petals, and dark green foliage. It blooms year-round but a little less in summer than in the cooler months. It can be pruned, if necessary, at any time of year, but now's the best time to shear and shape it.

Euryops are a little less drought tolerant than gamolepis but are nevertheless valuable drought-resistant plants.

Flower Beds and Containers

Annuals. It's a little late for planting seed for summer annuals, but there's no rule against it. You'll simply get a shorter season of color than if you'd planted earlier. Seeds will sprout fast now. So if you've just moved into a new home with oceans of bedding space to fill but no money for transplants, planting from seeds is the way to go. Just don't skimp on soil prep.

Annuals that can be planted from seeds now include anchusa, sweet alyssum, cosmos, marigold, portulaca, sunflower, coleus, lobelia, and zinnia. For the fastest and easiest results choose zinnias and marigolds, perhaps with an edging of alyssum. Dwarf sunflowers are equally easy and even faster to grow, though the splash of color they give you is soon gone. They're worth growing simply because people find them so amusing. (Pull the plants out after their flowers fade or they'll ruin the look of your border.)

In semishade, sprinkle seeds of impatiens onto well-prepared ground and blue lobelia along the edge.

For quicker results and to fill empty spots in existing beds purchase nursery transplants. Madagascar periwinkle (*Catharanthus roseus*) is a good choice for filling bare spaces in the hottest spots in full sun. It's easy to grow and mixes well with other flowers. Cosmos is good for the backs of beds. It blooms into fall and, in coastal zones, often seeds itself so new plants bloom through winter.

Deadhead and pick summer annuals to keep them going. Keep an eye out for stem borers on zinnias. These worms enter the stem and cause the top of the plant to die and sometimes fall over. Open the stem and find and squash the worm. If the plant is high enough, it will branch and continue to bloom.

Perennials. Be on the alert for interesting summer-blooming perennials at your nursery. More are for sale in June than at almost any other time of year because many perennials bloom in June. Some of the best are sold only when flowers are on the plant, so now's your chance to find some treasures. In recent years there's been an increasing interest in perennials among knowledgeable gardeners, but many of the ones grown in cool climates, such as the Pacific Northwest and England, aren't easy to grow here. The roots tend to rot in our hot, dry summers. Concentrate on growing the ones that do well here, such as daylilies, and fill in around them with annuals.

June is the best month to start perennials from seeds in coastal zones. (Gardeners in the interior can start a month or two earlier.) Warmer temperatures help seeds sprout faster.

This is an enthralling undertaking that can save money and give your green thumb the acid test, but it takes perseverance—almost a whole year of it.

First choose and purchase seeds, taking care to select plants that are recommended for your climate zone. Fill flats or peat pots with sterilized soil and plant the seeds according to package directions. (Some are easy to germinate, others not.) Mist the flats to moisten them, cover them with glass or plastic, and keep them in semishade. As soon as seeds sprout remove the cover and replace it with bird netting, to protect the seedlings from birds and cats. Water regularly, and after the plants form two true leaves start fertilizing with a weak solution of complete fertilizer or fish emulsion. As the seedlings grow move them gradually into more light, protect them from pests and disease, transplant them into 4-inch individual containers, and pot them on throughout the year. If all goes well by next spring or summer you'll have sturdy, gallon-size plants to go into the ground.

Pest Control

Many pests are active in June. Spider mites, caterpillars, slugs, and snails are just a few of the pests discussed in other chapters of this book that you may also be trying to control now. But among the pests that seem to rear their ugly heads most avariciously this month are thrips and whiteflies. If your garden suffers from an infestation of whiteflies you probably know it already because they're highly visible, but if it's inhabited by a large population of thrips you may be aware of the damage they're causing but not know which culprit you should blame.

Thrips. Thrips are small, slender, black, rasping insects that often step up activities in June. They're difficult to see, so be on the alert for signs of damage by thrips—distorted flowers on marguerites, roses, and gardenias and scratched stems and leaves on gladioli and beans.

If you feel you must use a chemical control use systemics in the ground, but only on ornamentals. (Spray with systemics only as a last resort.) In the vegetable garden diazinon and carbaryl sprays can be used. The best solution is to use organic controls that don't upset the balance of nature. These include insecticidal soaps, silicone-based powders such as Earth Guard, and diatomaceous earth, as well as keeping a clean garden, destroying weeds, growing resistant plants, and rotating crops. Continue to introduce beneficial insects to your garden and neighborhood to control pests.

Whiteflies. Of all the pests that plague gardeners, greenhouse whiteflies (*Trialeurodes vaporariorum*) seem the most maddening. These tiny—$\frac{1}{16}$ inch—winged insects skulk under the leaves of favored plants and fly out in an embarrassing cloud every time someone brushes past the foliage. Lift a leaf gently and you can see them hiding underneath. It's actually not the flying insect but microscopic larvae that do the damage, sucking plant juices, weakening plants, and excreting a sticky honeydew that's attractive to ants. Some of whiteflies' favorite plants are tomatoes, cucumbers, mint, fuchsias, and neglected patio plants such as ferns and gardenias that grow in too much shade.

Whiteflies are difficult to get rid of because they multiply rapidly and quickly develop new generations with resistance to pesticides. That's what happened with common, generic

Pest Management in New Gardens

Gardens on freshly bulldozed land usually have few problems during the first year other than with soil type, drainage, and possibly wire-worms (clickbeetles) left over from chaparral. The ground hasn't yet built up a resident population of pests and diseases.

Get rid of wireworms with diazinon granules. Be careful not to import pests. Inspect gift and nursery plants carefully. Introduce beneficial insects, and try to interest your neighbors in integrated pest management. Develop a healthy garden from the beginning with a well-balanced population of pests and beneficials.

Quick Tip

Control Whiteflies with Ladybugs and Spiders.
In the evening, put small teaspoonfuls of ladybugs on premoistened foliage. (Adults may fly away but leave eggs to hatch into beneficial larvae that eat the larvae of whiteflies.) Catch house spiders without harming them. Either use a commercial spider-catching device or drop a damp facial tissue over each spider and close the tissue gently under it. (Spiders escape from dry tissues but climb up inside wet ones.) Place your captured spiders outdoors on such plants as hanging-basket fuchsias.

malathion, which once was an effective control. Also, whiteflies go through five different stages of growth between egg and adult, each of which is susceptible to a different pesticide or to none at all. Thus, if you spray with a pesticide and are successful in killing those in one stage, those in other stages remain to proliferate. Only repeated spraying works.

The best defense against whiteflies is keeping a clean garden of healthy, well-fed plants that's well stocked with beneficial insects, tree frogs, and spiders and is free from ants. (In my garden I don't spray against whiteflies, preferring to control them by the method described in the accompanying box.) *Encarsia formosa* is a tiny insect that specializes in killing whiteflies and can be purchased in quantity from some garden supply houses. Ladybugs and spiders can be effective when placed on plants early in the season. Sticky yellow traps are effective in greenhouses and enclosed spaces such as patios. Whiteflies are attracted to the bright yellow color, which they interpret as young foliage, and they stick tight. Purchase these traps ready made, from nurseries, or make your own. (To make your own first spray bright yellow paint—the same shade as that on a container of Prestone Antifreeze—on strips of cardboard or on empty food cans. Then cover the painted surfaces with a sticky substance such as Vaseline or Stickem, and hang the traps among infested plants.)

If you must spray use insecticidal soaps. The best chemical control at the time this is written is Science Garden Insect Spray, a specific brand of malathion that has an attractive perfume added. Since it kills beneficials along with pests I don't recommend its use except in badly infested small patios and condo gardens where all else has failed. You'll need to spray twice or three times, at intervals of four to six days. This pesticide can also be used with minimal side effects during winter when large numbers of whiteflies migrate onto myoporum, iceplant, and eugenia, especially in coastal zones. When you find them congregating on these "trap" plants, get rid of them by spraying.

Lawn Care

Cool-Season Grasses. It's time to reset the cutting height of your lawn mower. Cool-season lawns such as ryegrass, bluegrass, bentgrass, fescue, or a mix of cool-season grasses should be allowed to grow longer during the summer. Longer leaves give them more resistance to hot weather. So set the blades of your lawn mower to 2 inches. If your lawn is one of the improved drought- and disease-resistant tall fescues, such as Marathon or the Water Saver blend, set the mower to its top setting of between 2 and 3 inches and be sure to keep the blades sharp. The ☛ **Rule of Thumb** is: *Never cut off more than one-third of your lawn's height at one time.* (This rule applies to all lawns, but it's particularly important for tall fescue.)

Keep cool-season lawns well watered according to the needs of each type. From now until fall feed them lightly at the rate of ½ pound of nitrogen per 1,000 square feet, when and if needed, to maintain color.

Warm-Season Grasses. If your lawn is warm-season grass, such as Bermuda, zoysia, or St. Augustine, start now to mow it as short as possible. Set the mower blades lower in order to cut common Bermuda to 1 inch. Hybrid Bermudas like Tifway and Santa Ana can be cut

even shorter, to ½ or ¾ inches. (Tifgreen, more often used for golf greens than home lawns, can be cut as short as ⅛ inch.) Cut zoysia and St. Augustine to between ¾ inch and 1 inch, and cut kikuyu to ½ inch. Feed all warm-season grasses regularly during their growing season except for Adalayd grass (*Paspalum vaginatum*; as sod, called Excalibre), which can be fed in June and July but, during the heat of August and early September, only lightly if at all. Kikuyu grass is another exception; because of its invasive qualities, don't feed it unless you notice poor color or stunted growth. Continue to water warm-season lawns deeply and as infrequently as possible while still maintaining good appearance.

Dichondra. Mow dichondra or not—it's up to you. Feed it lightly every three weeks to keep it thick and healthy. Regular fertilizing is extremely important and should include pest and disease control if you've ever had problems. Use a regular lawn food half-strength, or choose a fertilizer especially formulated for dichondra. (For more about dichondra see the UC publication *Dichondra, Establishment and Maintenance*, Leaflet 2983.)

Dichondra is more drought resistant than we give it credit for. You can tell whether it needs watering by walking on it. If you leave footprints it's time to water. If not it can go longer.

Zoysia. Late spring or early summer is the best time to plant zoysia in Southern California. Tests done by the University of California have shown that when you plant from stolons or plugs in June, zoysia grass will take off faster and have less competition from weeds then when planted at any other time of year. (For fast coverage, when planting from stolons use the rate of 12 bushels per 1,000 square feet, double the commercial rate. When planting from plugs space them on 9-inch centers.)

Zoysia makes a tough, good-looking turf that's tolerant of drought, heat, salinity, and heavy foot traffic. It has few, if any, pest problems and is largely disease free, especially when grown in hot, dry interior zones. Once established it's practically immune to weeds. Despite these virtues it hasn't been much grown, because of its slow rate of establishment, tendency to produce thatch, and long dormant period. A new variety called El Toro developed by the University of California has a much faster rate of coverage, a nice springy texture underfoot without building up thatch, and best of all it has a tendency to green-up much faster in spring.

As zoysia fills in, water it regularly for fast growth, and keep weeds pulled. Feed mature zoysia grass at the rate of 2 to 3 pounds of nitrogen (37-0-0) per 1,000 square feet at intervals of 6 to 8 weeks. (What you want is a deep green color. Feed it when its color declines.) Water well after fertilizing. Mow zoysia regularly to a height of ⅝ inch with a reel mower.

Vegetable Gardening

By now the summer vegetable garden should be in full swing. Harvest root and leaf crops regularly, while they're still young and tender. Pick the outside leaves of lettuce as needed. Pick beans and summer squash daily while they're still small, but pick tomatoes when fully ripe.

As crops reach the midpoint in their growing seasons, if you didn't do the job last month,

side-dress the rows with fertilizer to keep them going. Most crops need additional nitrogen at some point during the growing season. Beans are an exception; don't fertilize them unless they show signs of nitrogen deficiency (slow or stunted growth), because too much nitrogen can prevent them from bearing. Beans that were inoculated at planting time need no fertilizer. Corn needs additional nitrogen and plenty of water when it starts to tassel out. The best time to side-dress tomatoes with additional nitrogen is when they start to bloom.

Water regularly and deeply. Overhead watering is all right inland but must be done early in the day. Ground-level soaking or, even better, subterranean irrigation with a drip system is best in all areas. Most vegetables require the equivalent of 1 inch of rain per week. It's especially important not to let cucumbers or tomatoes dry out. Thirsty cucumbers turn bitter. Watering tomatoes unevenly can cause *blossom-end rot,* a black discoloration on the bottom of fruits. Overwatering tomatoes can cause root rot and wet, rotting fruit.

It's not too late to put in seeds, either to fill in for continued harvests or to plant a whole garden. As with annual flowers you'll simply get later results. Seeds that can be planted now run the gamut of summer vegetables, including corn, lima beans, green beans, winter squash, summer squash, okra, peppers, pumpkins, leaf lettuce, cucumbers, New Zealand spinach, and melons, and also the vegetables we plant year-round, such as carrots, beets, Swiss chard, turnips, and radishes. Heat lovers such as eggplant and peppers do well and grow rapidly when put in from transplants this month. For a fall crop of tomatoes, plant seeds now or put in transplants next month.

Rotate Crops. Crop rotation is important not only because it prevents soil depletion but because it cuts down on pest damage. If you plant the same thing in the same place time after time, pests and fungus organisms and other diseases build up in the soil. Wireworms (the larvae of clickbeetles), for example, like onions and carrots, and they'll settle down and multiply in rows where these crops are repeatedly planted. If you clear out two rows at the same time crop rotation is easy; just switch when you replant. When you clear only one row look for the next item that's likely to be harvested and replant with that, or with something totally new and different. Branch out and try exotic vegetables you haven't tried before.

Control Vegetable Pests and Diseases. As in the ornamental garden, concentrate on keeping the garden clean and keeping an eye out for pests and disease. Also continue to introduce beneficial insects and arachnids (spiders and beneficial mites), still our best and most enlightened defense against pests. Resist the temptation to spray, which can upset the balance of nature.

If you live along the coast cut off brown leaves on the bottoms of tomato and bean plants. They provide hiding places for slugs, snails, and sowbugs. Inland, leave them on, because they provide extra shade. Don't pick beans early in the day when plants are wet with dew. This can spread rust and mildew. Wait until midday or late afternoon when the vines are dry. Wash off aphids with soapy water. Handpick large bugs and beetles. If caterpillars are a problem spray with BT or introduce beneficial wasps. Mint, basil, and dill are said to protect tomatoes from hornworm. (Confine mint to 5-gallon cans; don't let it loose in the garden. Like horseradish it will take over.) Attract scrub jays. (See the tip on p. 143.)

Leafhoppers on tomatoes, beans, and cucumbers spread mosaic virus diseases. Spray with insecticidal soaps or homemade sprays of onion or garlic, or try diatomaceous earth or silicone dusts such as Earth Guard. But remember, these dusts can kill some beneficials too. Personally I never spray with chemicals in the vegetable garden and seldom, if ever, in the ornamental garden, but if you feel you must go this route diazinon, carbaryl, or malathion will control leafhoppers. (Always follow package directions to the letter and only spray affected plants, or you risk killing more beneficials than necessary.)

Mix vegetables as much as possible and interplant them with herbs and marigolds to muddle and confuse insects. Remember that solid plantings of anything, whether ornamental or vegetable, always get hit more severely by pest and disease problems than plants grown in a mixed landscape.

Help Strawberries Bear More Fruit. Strawberries tend to grow vegetatively in June, by sending out runners instead of blooming and bearing fruit. Clip off the runners as they occur. A shot of 0-10-10 fertilizer now will help elongate the harvest.

Unless you're growing strawberries on plastic keep the ground deeply mulched with pine needles or straw. Sprinkle bait underneath organic and plastic mulches against sowbugs, snails, and slugs. Don't let the plants go dry now, or fruiting will stop.

Purchase / Plant	*Trim, Prune, Mow, Divide*	*Fertilize*
☐ Continue to plant **drought-resistant plants,** 15, 72	☐ Continue to pick and deadhead **roses,** 77, 107	☐ Feed **citrus trees,** 30
☐ Continue to plant **melons,** 142	☐ Pinch back **chrysanthemums** to make them bushy, 79	☐ Look for yellow leaves and green veins indicating chlorosis in **citrus, gardenias, azaleas,** and others; treat it with chelated iron, 31
☐ Plant **tropical** and **subtropical plants,** 152	☐ Divide and repot **cymbidiums** that have outgrown their containers, 129	☐ Feed **avocado trees,** 48
☐ Plant **bougainvilleas,** 153	☐ Remove berries (seed pods) from **fuchsias** after flowers fall, 154	☐ Feed **fuchsias,** 55
☐ Plant **perennial morning glories,** 154	☐ Divide **bearded irises** if necessary. (In hot interior valleys wait until October.) 155	☐ Feed **tuberous begonias,** 78
☐ Purchase **fuchsias,** 154	☐ Prune **epiphyllums,** 156	☐ Feed **bamboo** with a slow-release fertilizer, 86
☐ Continue to purchase **epiphyllums,** 156	☐ Thin out **deciduous fruit trees** after June drop, 156	☐ Feed **water lilies,** 110
☐ Plant seeds of **heat-loving annuals,** 158	☐ Give **marguerites** a "butch" haircut, 157	☐ Fertilize **corn,** 117
☐ Use **bedding plants** for quick color, 158	☐ Cut back **gamolepis** and **euryops,** 157	☐ Fertilize **cymbidiums** with high nitrogen for growth, 130
☐ Purchase **perennials** in bloom now at nurseries, 158	☐ Deadhead and pick **summer flowers** to keep them going, 158	☐ Give **camellias** their second feeding for the year, 130
☐ Start **perennials** from seeds in coastal zones, 158	☐ Mow **cool-season lawns** longer, 160	☐ Fertilize **roses,** 131
☐ Plant **zoysia** grass, 161	☐ Mow **warm-season grasses** short, 160	☐ Feed **ferns,** 132
☐ Continue to plant **summer vegetables,** 162	☐ Clip runners off **strawberries,** 163	☐ Fertilize **tropicals,** 152
☐ Plant **exotic vegetables,** 163	☐ Prune **climbing roses** that bloom once a year in spring, but wait until flowers fade, 172	☐ Feed **epiphyllums,** 156
☐ Purchase, plant, and transplant **succulents,** including **cacti** and **euphorbias,** 185	☐ Divide **English primroses** after bloom, or wait until September, 182	☐ Fertilize **marguerites** after pruning, 157
☐ Purchase **alstroemerias** throughout summer while they are in bloom, 207	☐ Continue to prune and train **espaliers,** 203	☐ Feed container-grown **annuals** and **perennials** with a complete fertilizer, 158
☐ Plant **papayas** and **bananas,** 210	☐ Continue to remove spent bloom stems from **daylilies** and to propagate the types that make proliferates, 206	☐ Fertilize **cool-season lawns** lightly, 161
☐ Plant and transplant **palms,** 212	☐ Deadhead **alstroemerias** often by pulling off the stalks with a sharp tug, 207	☐ Fertilize **warm-season lawns,** according to type, 161
		☐ Fertilize **dichondra,** 161
		☐ Side-dress **vegetable** rows if you didn't do it last month, 162
		☐ Give **strawberries** a shot of 0-10-10 to elongate the harvest, 163
		☐ Feed all **succulents** growing in containers with a well-diluted complete liquid fertilizer, 186
		☐ If **peppers** look yellow despite adequate nitrogen, spray them with Epsom salts, 191
		☐ Feed **cycads,** 213

Water

- ☐ Water **all plants** except some well-established drought-resistant plants and some native plants, 128
- ☐ Water **cool-season lawns** more often and shallowly, 161
- ☐ Water **warm-season lawns** deeply and infrequently, 161
- ☐ Water **corn** well as it tassels out, 162
- ☐ Water **vegetables**, 162
- ☐ Don't let **strawberries** dry out, 163
- ☐ Water **cyclamen** occasionally, though they are semidormant now, 184
- ☐ Most **succulents** growing in the ground need no water this month, 186

Control Pests, Diseases, and Weeds

- ☐ Control **slugs** and **snails**, 73
- ☐ Watch **chrysanthemums** for pests, 79
- ☐ Control **rose** pests and diseases, 106
- ☐ Control pests on **fuchsias**, 154
- ☐ Watch for stem borers on **zinnias**, 158
- ☐ Control **thrips** and **whiteflies**, 159
- ☐ Manage pests in **new gardens**, 160
- ☐ Control pests and diseases on **vegetables**, 163
- ☐ Protect **strawberries** from slugs and snails, 163
- ☐ Control weeds in the **vegetable garden** and **flower beds** by hand pulling, 170
- ☐ Control weeds among **permanent plants** by mulching or cultivating, 170
- ☐ Spray **tuberous begonias** against mildew, 177
- ☐ Protect **English primroses** from caterpillars and slugs and snails, 184
- ☐ Control **corn** earworm if you can't live with it, 215

Also This Month

- ☐ Hand pollinate **corn** growing in small plots, 117
- ☐ Prevent bud drop from **gardenias**, 156
- ☐ Reset mower blades for **cool-season lawns**, 160
- ☐ Harvest **vegetables** regularly, 162
- ☐ Practice **crop rotation**, 163
- ☐ Put bloomed-out **cyclamen** and **English primroses** in a shady spot for the summer, 182
- ☐ When the tops of **globe onions** fall over stop watering them; allow them to cure, then harvest, eat, and store them, 290

JULY

JULY

The First Real Summer Month

In July the weather starts getting hot even along the coast, and we like to spend as much time as possible outdoors. In hot interior valleys the early morning and evening hours are the best ones for sitting, playing, or working outdoors, but in coastal areas outdoor living is comfortable all day long if we've taken steps to make it so. Since we're in the open air so much this month, it's a good time to notice whether our landscape is as attractive and useful as we want it to be. We may find garden improvements taking root in our minds. July is not a particularly good month to do the planting—spring and fall are much better for that—but it's a great time for planning ahead. Do you need to plant another shade tree? Except in the hottest areas, tropical and subtropical plants can still be planted early this month, as well as in June. Perhaps you have space for a romantic vine-covered arbor or pergola, or an additional patio. Think about these options now when you can see just where shade and comfort are most needed. (For detailed advice on shade planting consult this chapter's section on shade plants.)

Hot, dry weather makes regular watering the most important task now through September. And since there are right and wrong ways to water summer is a good time to plan as well for water conservation. It's the prime time of year to benefit from a basic landscape of drought-resistant plants that's irrigated by a drip system. Plants that are heavy water users can be limited to small areas close to the house and to containers that can be phased out in times of drought.

Watering

Except for some California native plants and a few well-established drought-resistant plants from other parts of the world, all plants need regular watering now. Water large trees deeply but infrequently, to encourage deep but healthy roots. Allow the soil to dry out somewhat between irrigations, to permit air to enter the soil pores and provide the oxygen that roots need. When drought is inevitable, trees with deep, healthy root systems are better able to survive it. The best, most water-saving time to do regular watering is early in the day.

Mist systems that pulse on briefly throughout the day in shady areas enhance the environment for some plants. Many shade plants, including bromeliads, orchids, ferns, epiphyllums, and fuchsias, either absorb water through their foliage or appreciate the cooling evaporation of a fine spray of water.

Care of Bare Ground

Two entirely different garden techniques can help you save water, reduce weed problems, and keep the surface of the ground from baking to a hard crust. One of these techniques is to shallowly cultivate and the other is to apply mulch. In most cases mulch, as discussed below, is by far the best method to use, but in some cases young annuals and vegetables can profit from having the ground around them carefully cultivated.

Cultivate Areas That Need It. To shallowly cultivate, or break up the surface of the soil around plants with a tool designed for the purpose, can destroy weeds and let air reach roots, increasing the speed of plant growth. It can also reduce the need for water. Cultivation saves water because it aids penetration, then prevents capillary action from drawing water through compacted soil to the surface, where it would be released as vapor. When you cultivate, in a sense you're making the top 2 or 3 inches of soil into a built-in mulch. It's something people have been doing ever since some resourceful human attached a clamshell to a stick and invented the first hoe. Today there are dozens of hoelike tools; trial and error is the only way to find an eventual favorite.

In heavy clay soils where young plants— annuals and vegetables, for example—have not yet shaded the ground, you can cultivate the soil surface around plants at weekly intervals to break up the hard crust. In light or sandy soils that don't form a crust, cultivate whenever necessary to destroy young weeds before they've gone to seed. Don't cultivate ground immediately after it's been watered; this compacts the soil. The ☞ **Rule of Thumb** is: *Cultivate 1 to 3 days after watering when the soil is still moist and crumbly but not soggy wet.* (Clay soil dries out slowly.) Take care not to damage surface roots. You need to loosen only the top 2 or 3 inches of soil. Don't cultivate around tomatoes except to destroy weeds, and never cultivate close to corn. In many cases hand pulling down on your hands and knees is not only the most thorough way of getting rid of weeds but the safest for surrounding plants. Once plants have completely shaded the surface of the soil, cultivation isn't necessary.

Although cultivation can be good for annuals and vegetables don't dash around the garden cultivating everything in sight. Many ornamental plants, including azaleas, camellias, and roses, have shallow surface roots that can be seriously damaged by cultivation. These and many other garden plants, such as most trees and shrubs, are better adapted to mulch.

Spread Mulch. If you don't have time to cultivate, a layer of mulch can do the job for you. It's always a longer-lasting solution and often a better one. Organic mulch keeps the ground cool, conserves water, keeps many weeds from growing, and adds valuable organic matter to the soil.

Unfortunately, many experienced gardeners find that mulching the ground around vegetables and annual flowers in Southern California can itself lead to problems, such as stem rot and pest buildup. Rough-textured mulches make ideal hiding places for slugs, snails, and sow-bugs. Organic mulch works best on woody plants and should be widely used on them. Because of the problems with organic mulches many gardeners use black plastic mulch on heat-loving vegetables.

Citrus and Avocado Trees

Don't let citrus and avocados dry out in July or August or a great deal of fruit may fall off. This doesn't mean to keep the trees in a boggy condition. They don't like that either. Established trees in most soils need watering deeply every two or three weeks depending on soil type and weather conditions. Newly planted trees usually need deep watering once a week. (The best way to know when trees need water is to use a soil auger or a tensiometer.)

Citrus need water in a broad band starting one-third of the distance from the trunk to the drip line and extending an equal distance beyond the drip line. This is where their feeder roots are, not next to the trunk. Put the hose on the ground and let it run slowly, filling a well-placed watering basin. The bark of citrus trees must be kept dry to prevent the fungus disease gummosis, which can infect their trunks.

Avocados need water all over the ground under the branches, up to a foot or two from the trunk. The best way to water them is slowly, with a sprinkler. Avocados are highly prone to phytophthora root rot (a fungus disease that's spread by infected plants and favored by wet or poorly drained soil), but they're not susceptible to gummosis.

Cymbidiums

This is the time of year when cymbidiums are growing new leaves and pseudobulbs. Continue to feed for growth with a product such as 30-10-10 liquid or 20-10-5 slow-release tablets. Keep them in filtered shade for the summer, and don't let the roots dry out. In interior gardens a drip system is ideal. Misting the foliage can be beneficial in the dry interior, but it's not necessary in coastal regions. Along the coast watering once or twice a week suffices. Overhead sprinklers are fine, but beware of allowing them to run for a long time—and of overwatering in general—since these practices can cause fungus problems, especially when the irrigation is done late in the day.

Sometimes cymbidiums are kept in too much shade, such as under a dense tree—a frequent mistake in home gardens. Black marks on the leaves and pseudobulbs are signs of fungus problems. The plants don't die, but they won't bloom as well. It's probably best to get rid of stricken plants so they don't spread the disease to healthy specimens. Some varieties seem more resistant to disease than others. Stick with those, and grow plants in a coarse, fibrous potting soil that drains well and in appropriately sized plastic containers. Don't put a cymbidium in a container that's too large for its roots or you'll drown it with soggy soil.

Roses

Continue to control rose pests and diseases and to water, fertilize, and prune the plants by picking the flowers, but stop disbudding them now. Follow the basic guidelines given in March (p. 76) and expanded in May (p. 131). In hot interior zones step up the frequency of irrigations now to three times per week at the rate of 1½ inches of water per irrigation. (In coastal zones, twice a week may be sufficient.) Keep the ground around the plants well mulched.

Prune Climbing Roses That Bloom Only Once a Year. Most modern climbing roses bloom continuously from April to January. These should be pruned along with your other roses in January. But there are some types of rose still grown in Southern California that bloom only once in spring. The ☞ **Rule of Thumb** is: *Established climbing roses, over three years old, that bloom only in spring or early summer should be pruned after bloom.* They bear their flowers on wood that grew during the previous year. If you wait until winter you risk cutting off new canes that will bear next year. There are several kinds of spring-blooming climbers, among which are the following.

• **Ramblers.** Rambling roses have thin, bendy canes and massive clusters of small, flattish flowers, no bigger than 2 inches in diameter. Older types bloom magnificently but only once, in spring or early summer. Newer types bloom several times during the year. Where there's room, ramblers can be allowed to sprawl over the support of mature trees, large shrubs, or house or shed roofs, and they'll continue to grow larger and bloom massively without ever being pruned. (If they've been allowed to mound and climb for many years, clean out as much as possible of the dead interior after bloom.)

If you want to control the size of old-fashioned rambling roses, prune them immediately after their bloom finishes by cutting out old (gray) wood and canes that have bloomed this year. But don't cut out any fresh green canes. You have a choice of options; you can cut all the way to the ground, or you can keep a structure of main canes over a support and cut back the laterals that have bloomed to two buds, or eyes.

New growth starts now, in summer. Tie up the abundant new canes as they grow, but cut off weak, twiggy ones at ground level. All new canes will bloom the following year.

• **Spring-Blooming, Large-Flowered Climbers.** Large-flowered climbers have thicker canes than ramblers and larger flowers, with fewer per cluster. Some old types bloom once in spring; many repeat the bloom once again in summer. Several, such as America, Don Juan, and Handel, three of the best, bloom continuously from April through December.

Don't prune young plants. Prune established plants that bloom only once, right after the bloom finishes, by cutting out old woody canes more than three years old but leaving all younger canes and as many succulent ones that grew this year as you have room for. (Two- and three-year-old canes bloom best.) Cut back laterals on canes that have flowered to two or three buds each. These will bloom next year. Rearrange them and retie them onto their supports. Remove any suckers that sprout from below the bud union.

- **Spring-Blooming Species Roses.** These old-fashioned roses were originally found in the wild, though some selections, such as the Chinese species known as Lady Banks' rose (*Rosa banksiae*), have been cultivated for centuries. In some areas Lady Banks' rose continues to bloom through June. In early July, or as soon as blooming stops, cut back the outsides of established plants hard, to shape and control them, and to encourage lots of new growth that will bloom next year. Follow up with a balanced fertilizer, and water deeply.

Shade Plants

How to Garden in Shade. Every garden is bound to include a certain amount of shade, and now's a good time to study these areas while their relative coolness is most appreciated. Well-designed and properly planted shade gardens are the most refreshing parts of any landscape, but you can't plant them properly unless you understand the characteristics of shade.

How Shade Occurs. Many homeowners start out with mostly full sun, but then either plant too many trees or let volunteers grow wherever they plant themselves. After a few years on this course a sunny garden can become a shady or even gloomy one. It takes real courage to cut down mature trees, but sometimes this is the only way to reclaim the sun. In some cases you can lace trees out to let adequate light through. The best shade is that which you create yourself, either by building a shade structure or by planting an appropriate number of well-chosen trees in the right places. The most difficult shade is that which you can't control—solid shadows of buildings or walls, sometimes alternating with an hour or two of burning hot sun.

How Shade Moves and Differs in Degree. Shadows don't stand still; every day they move from west to east as the sun moves across the sky from east to west. They also lengthen northward as the sun moves south during fall and winter, and then they gradually shorten again as the sun moves north in winter and spring. These factors make gardening in the shade a lot trickier than gardening in full sun. So if you're interested in shade gardening, begin by observing and understanding the shadows in your own garden; notice where they occur, how dense they are, and their duration.

Not all semishade or even dense shade is alike. It differs widely according to what causes it and its exposure (the direction it faces). It's important to learn how to distinguish between these various degrees and exposures of shade and to learn which plants are most likely to succeed in each of them. Shade plants vary greatly in shade tolerance. Most shade plants, particularly flowering ones, need semishade, which by definition means part sun. Only a

✳ ✳ ✳

The Kinds of Shade and Some Plants to Grow in Them

Some shade plants are adapted to several of the areas described below, others to only one or two. So use the following list as a starting point rather than as a set of immutable rules. You can learn more by experimenting with the shade in your own garden.

Full Shade. This occurs under thick evergreen trees and north-facing overhangs and in some patios, atriums, and covered porches.

- **Characteristics.** Virtually no sunshine hits full shade, at any time of year. This is the most difficult kind of shade to cope with, since few plants survive in dark places. (If these areas get some reflected light they're easier to plant.) The ground in full shade is cold and often poorly prepared. When it gets wet it stays wet, unless it contains tree roots. Yet if it's under an overhang it's often neglected, and in that case it's watered too seldom.

- **Special Tips.** Prepare the soil by first removing some of it. Then dig up the ground deeply and replace the removed soil with large quantities of acid soil amendments (most shade plants are acid loving). Check the soil often to make sure it's moist but not soggy. Cover bare ground with a smooth-textured mulch or cloak it with a ground cover. Accent gloomy areas by digging holes in the mulch or ground cover and slipping in potted, seasonal plants already in color or bloom, including caladiums, chrysanthemums, calceolarias, cymbidiums, cineraria, and cyclamen. Rely heavily on design elements, like bromeliads mounted on driftwood, stepping-stones, and fountains. Illuminate at night with soft light.

- **Plants That Grow in Full Shade.** Kentia palm (*Howea fosterana*); Japanese aralia (*Fatsia japonica*);

fatshera (*Fatshedera lizei*); Japanese aucuba (*Aucuba japonica*), including gold-dust plant; monstera; many houseplants, including philodendron, corn plant (*Dracaena marginata*), and aspidistra (one of the best for difficult, dark shade, including windy exposures); ferns, including leather-leaf fern (*Rumohra adiantiformis*), Dallas and Kimberly Queen ferns (*Nephrolepis exaltata*), sword fern (*Polystichum munitum*) and asparagus ferns; liriopes and ophiopogons, including mondo grass; baby tears (*Soleirolia soleirolii*); small-leaved ivy, including Needlepoint; cryptanthus; and—where there's plenty of reflected light—clivia.

Filtered Shade. This occurs—though rarely—as dappled shade under an open-branched tree. More often it's found inside a structure built especially for shade plants and covered with wooden lath or shade cloth.

- **Characteristics.** From morning to night at all times of year small shadows move from west to east over the plants. This is the ideal situation for most shade plants because it cuts the intensity of the sun, which otherwise could burn leaves or flowers. Plants stay cool and comfortable, but they get plenty of sunshine for growth and bloom.

- **Special Tips.** Shade houses are best built in areas that were originally in full sun. When using wooden lath always arrange it so the individual slats run north and south. When using shade cloth choose its degree of shade according to your climate zone and the plants you wish to grow under it. In general, use cloth that casts 25- to 50-percent shade in coastal zones and 50- to 75-percent shade inland.

- **Plants That Grow in Filtered Shade.** All shade plants without exception. Some plants that are especially well adapted to filtered shade include camellias; azaleas; bromeliads; all ferns, including staghorn ferns; fuchsias; epiphyllums; all orchids that can grow outdoors in your climate zone; tuberous begonias; and shade-loving annuals, particularly coleus.

East-Facing Partial Shade. This occurs on an east-facing porch, under an east-facing overhang, or to the east of a house, wall, or tree.

- **Characteristics.** This is one of the finest kinds of shade to plant in. Cool morning sun shines into these areas, but they're protected from the burning hot sun of midday and afternoon hours.

- **Special Tips.** Grow plants that must have sunlight in order to bloom but can't stand the burning rays of hot midday or afternoon sun. Plants that need partial shade inland but full sun along the coast will usually do well in eastern exposures. Hanging-basket plants such as fuchsias will be one-sided. Don't attempt to turn them, since that would deprive them of necessary light.

- **Plants That Grow in East-Facing Partial Shade.** Tree ferns; mahonia (*Mahonia bealei* and *M. lomariifolia*); dwarf pittosporum (*Pittosporum tobira* 'Wheeler's Dwarf'); Japanese privet (*Ligustrum japonicum*); euonymus; acanthus; daylilies; agapanthus; breynia; bergenia; fuchsia; impatiens; cymbidiums; epiphyllums; begonias, including tuberous begonias; coleus; geraniums; calla lilies; hydrangeas; so-called sun azaleas; and all shade-loving annuals.

West-Facing Partial Shade. This occurs to the west of a house, wall, or tree or under a west-facing overhang.

- **Characteristics.** Plants are totally shaded throughout the morning and hot noonday sun, and then suddenly in the afternoon the sun

strikes them in all its fury. When this condition is combined with a heat wave or Santa Ana all west-facing plants get fried. (The problem is at its worst in inland areas.)

- **Special Tips.** Unless you live near the coast, don't even try to grow shade plants in unprotected western exposures. Instead choose plants that are capable of growing either in sun or shade. Cut the force of the afternoon sun by planting open trees and shrubs or by building a patio overhang, view garden, or shade structure that will allow you to grow a wider selection of plants.

- **Plants That Grow in West-Facing Partial Shade.** Pittosporum; rhapiolepis; nandina; daylilies; gamolepis; fortnight lilies (*Dietes*); agapanthus; geraniums; richmondensis begonias; semperflorens begonias; Gartenmeister Bonstedt fuchsia; and any plant that's described in the *Sunset Western Garden Book* as being suitable for planting either in sun or shade in your climate zone.

North-Facing Partial Shade. This occurs to the north of a house, wall, or tree but not directly beneath a north-facing overhang, porch cover, or tree. (These areas are in full shade.)

- **Characteristics.** North-facing shade changes with the seasons. In winter such areas enjoy full bright shade under the open sky, sometimes called "skyshine." Unless shaded from the side, they get full sun for a month or two in late spring and early summer when the sun reaches its northernmost position. The shadows to the north of houses and trees will be shortest at the summer solstice (June 21 or 22).

- **Special Tips.** Make sure these areas get adequate water in summer while they're exposed to more sunshine. If shade plants get burned by summer sun install removable panels of lath or shade cloth. Provide more shade in summer for a north-facing backyard by building a freestanding shade structure or pergola, and growing a deciduous vine, such as wisteria, over it.

Annual flowers and vegetables can be grown in north-facing flower beds that are shaded in winter but sunny in summer. In fall plant them with winter-blooming flowers for shade. In summer switch them to sun-loving flowers or vegetables, like zinnias or tomatoes. You can also plant bulbs, if you plant them where sun will hit them when it's time for them to bloom. Raised beds can increase the speed of the returning sun by lifting plants above the shadow of the house.

· **Plants That Grow in North-Facing Partial Shade.** Camellias; azaleas; clivia; many ferns, especially tree ferns; Japanese maple (*Acer palmatum*); leopard plant (*Ligularia tussilaginea*); billbergia; bergenia; cineraria (plant in October for late-winter bloom); bulbs, including daffodils and prechilled hyacinths and tulips (also for fall planting); and annual flowers and vegetables as described above.

South-Facing Partial Shade. This occurs under a deep, south-facing overhang, under a south-facing porch cover, or under the branches of a south-facing tree. (Areas to the south of a wall, a tree, or your house that are open to the sky or under a very narrow overhang—1 to 3 feet—are in full sun.)

· **Characteristics.** South-facing shade exists in summer but not in winter. In winter the area under the branches of a large, dense, south-facing tree or under a deep south-facing overhang, solid-roofed patio, or porch will be flooded with sun in the middle of the day. In summer these same areas will be in total shade in the middle of the day. Thus the comfort level for people in south-facing shade is first-rate, but plant choice is difficult.

· **Special Tips.** In general, south-facing shade is a prime place for a patio or porch. Pave these areas wherever possible and you'll have an ideal spot for sitting comfortably outdoors in both winter and summer. Decorate south-facing covered patios and porches with containers that can be moved or replanted according to the seasons.

· **Plants for South-Facing Shade.** Winter-blooming annuals for full sun or part shade, including primroses, violas, pansies, and snapdragons, can be switched in summer to such house plants as creeping Charlie and African violets—those that like extremely bright light but no direct sun. Or grow succulents year-round. They like sun in winter and don't mind shade in summer, and many, such as *Kalanchoe blossfeldiana*, have the added attraction of winter or spring bloom.

✳ ✳ ✳

small number of plants will grow with no sun at all, yet many gardeners have to contend with total unmitigated shade in some areas. (See the accompanying box for a list of the main types and exposures.)

How to Create a Restful Atmosphere. A peaceful shade garden can remind you of a cool forest glade even if you've housed it in lath or covered it with man-made shade cloth. So when you design your shade garden work for a natural and informal feeling. Accent your plantings with rocks, driftwood, and stepping-stones—perhaps surrounded by moss or baby tears. Pools and waterfalls lend a cooling atmosphere, and in some cases they use less water than heavily irrigated plants. The sight and sound of a splashing fountain can make a hot day seem cooler. Create charm and interest by adding rustic seats and wandering paths, and use pastels and color tones from the cool half of the spectrum; they're more restful than bright colors.

Tuberous Begonias. If you planted tuberous begonias in March they'll be in full bloom now. They're heavy feeders, so feed them regularly with balanced liquid fertilizer, such as 8-8-8, every week, or use slow-release 14-14-14. Don't overwater. Let them dry out between waterings. Always remove spent blossoms but leave the stems on the plant. They'll fall off in a few days and can then be removed.

Control mildew with a chemical product, for example Bayleton or Benlate (benomyl), or try an organic control such as an antitranspirant, including Wilt-Pruf or Cloud Cover. (These products often clean up mildew as a byproduct of their labeled uses.) Also, dot the ground

Quick Tip

Instant Shade for a Hanging Basket.
Fuchsias, begonias, and other shade plants are often burned by afternoon sun when hung from west-facing shade structures or porches. For these, spray a Japanese parasol with clear plastic, to weatherize it, and shove the handle into the soil at a low angle to provide shade.

≺

Quick Tip

Keep New Guinea Impatiens from Wilting in Hot Weather.
Place shallow saucers under 8- and 10-inch plastic containers of New Guinea impatiens. Water the plants daily with enough water to flow out the drainage hole and fill the saucer to overflowing. During the day, roots will take an extra drink as needed, and the saucer will be dry by nightfall. (Don't try this on other plants— they'd die from root rot.)

≺

Quick Tip

Keep Impatiens from Getting Leggy by Progressive Pruning.
Each time you feed impatiens, select the two longest shoots on opposite sides of the plant. Cut off two-thirds of their length. The plants will remain full, well branched, and bushy at all times.

≺

Quick Tip

How to Revive a Wilted Impatiens.
When an impatiens wilts from too much heat, sun, or dryness don't despair. Plunge the entire container up to the stems of the plant in a bucket of water. Come back in half an hour; the plant will have recovered.

around the base of your tuberous begonias with Deadline to protect them from snails and slugs. If you didn't raise these flamboyant flowers yourself you can find them in bloom now at some specialty and dig-your-own nurseries.

Impatiens. Impatiens fill dappled shade with color faster than any other flower. For the most color and easiest care choose the regular single variety. New Guinea impatiens have colorful leaves as well as flowers. They need more light than other types, and plenty of water. Miniatures developed in Hawaii and doubles, with flowers that look like tiny roses, make good accent plants in coastal zones but are difficult to grow inland.

Water impatiens daily now, especially when growing them in containers. They like loose acid soil but aren't as fussy about drainage as other plants. You can buy small bedding sizes of impatiens to transplant into tubs or the ground, or purchase them in hanging baskets and keep them in the containers they came in. The New Guinea impatiens is an exception to most plants in that you can pot a rootbound 8-inch size straight into an 18-inch tub, which should be filled with fast-draining potting soil. The roots will soon fill the tub, and you'll have a plant 3 feet wide. Feed impatiens every two or three weeks with a complete fertilizer, such as 15-30-15, mixed half-strength.

Flower Beds and Containers

Plant Annuals. You can still plant annuals this month, especially in coastal zones. You'll just get a shorter season of bloom. The best choices are the heat lovers, such as vinca (*Catharanthus roseus*), marigolds, zinnias, portulaca, and, early in the month, celosias. (If you plant the last too late it won't make a proper head.)

Prune Petunias. Our garden petunias—there are dozens of named varieties—are complicated hybrids of annual and perennial species native to Argentina. Technically these hybrid petunias are perennial plants, so you could actually propagate them from cuttings and carry them over from year to year. This isn't practical, however, because petunias are subject to virus diseases. For this reason they're always grown from seeds and treated as annual plants.

Petunias are *thermophotoperiodic*, which means that their flowering and growth habit depends on the temperature combined with the length of the days. As long as the daytime temperature is in the low 60s and nights are about ten degrees cooler they'll always be bushy and bear lots of flowers. When the weather gets a little warmer, 63° to 75°F (17° to 24°C) by day, they get leggy and have only one bloom per stalk unless they get 12 hours or more of daylight, which is what usually happens here in late spring. But once the temperature exceeds 75°F in the daytime, day length doesn't matter; petunias just naturally get leggy and have few flowers. So if by mid-July your petunias are looking leggy and not as colorful as you'd like, it's time to cut them back.

Begin by dipping your pruning shears in Lysol, bleach, or alcohol so you won't infect the plants with virus diseases. (Wash your hands if you're a smoker so you won't risk giving the plants tobacco virus.) Then cut back the plants to 4 inches above ground, except in the case of Cascade varieties, which should be cut back lightly. Ideally petunias should be cut back four times: once at planting time, again in mid-July,

next in mid-August, and finally in late September. After pruning clean up the ground and plants, remove the seed capsules, fertilize with a complete liquid fertilizer, and they'll bounce back into bloom in two weeks.

Care for Coleus. Coleus is grown for its colorful leaves rather than for it's flowers. In Hawaii it's a permanent shrub; here we grow it as a warm-season annual. Coleus is eye-catching in nurseries, but it often looks unkempt in home gardens because it's misunderstood. You can have success with this potentially fine plant if you give it what it needs.

Coleus sickens in full shade and burns in too much sun, so grow it in filtered sunshine. Plant it in porous, slightly acidic soil, either in containers or in beds, away from the roots of invasive trees and protected from snails. Keep the soil damp but not soggy or coleus' leaves will drop off. When the flowers appear pinch them off, since they sap the strength of the plant. Feed coleus lightly with fish emulsion or a complete fertilizer mixed half-strength. (Don't overfeed it or you'll get all stalk instead of leaves.) Coleus is almost always sold in mixed packs, but it looks especially attractive when, instead of mixed colors, only one color is grown solidly in a drift among other shade plants of contrasting colors.

Start Biennials. Now's the time to start biennials from seed. These are plants that take two years to bloom, such as foxgloves, sweet William, and Canterbury bells. Foxgloves are well worth growing from seed because tall varieties aren't always available in nurseries, especially in fall when you most want to plant them. (Dwarf varieties, such as Foxy, bloom soon after fall

≺

Quick Tip

**A Timesaving Way to Grow Foxgloves
from Seed.**
*Sprinkle seeds on any warm, semishaded section
of bare ground kept continually moist by a
drip system, such as the top of a hanging basket
under a mister or a vegetable row between
stalks of a tall crop, like tomatoes. Dig up and
transplant the resulting seedlings in late summer
or early fall.*

planting instead of waiting until spring, and the bloom usually doesn't last long.) Tall varieties take up no more space than short ones, and give you a bigger display for the same amount of effort. Take these steps to grow them from seed.

· Provide rich, fertile, well-dug soil. Alternatively, use a flat filled with damp, sterilized potting soil that contains a high percentage of milled peat moss.

· The seeds are tiny, so mix them with a little sand and sprinkle them on the surface of the soil. Press them gently into the soil surface with a flat piece of wood. Don't cover them with soil; they need light to germinate. Mist them with water.

· Put flats in a warm shady spot. Cover them with a plastic sheet to keep them moist until the seed germinates. Once they sprout remove the cover.

· After the plants have developed two real leaves start feeding them with a well-diluted solution of fish emulsion. Transplant them to the garden in late August or September.

Control of Bark Beetles on Conifers

Most vigorous and healthy conifers, such as cypress and pine trees, can withstand numerous attacks from bark beetles. If the trees are already stressed from lack of care, however, now in summer whole trees or portions of trees such as Monterey cypress and Monterey pine may suddenly die. If a tree's looking sick inspect the trunk. Look for drill holes, *frass* (boring dust), or "pitch tubes" of frass and sap mixed together. Peel back the bark around a drill hole and you may see galleries excavated by beetles right under the bark, where they live and reproduce.

(Also refer to the *Ortho Problem Solver*, edited by Michael D. Smith.) Once damage has girdled the trunk the tree will die. Preventions and solutions include the following.

- Maintain healthy trees: don't plant pines and other conifers in wet, poorly drained areas; do fertilize with nitrogen; and irrigate the trees adequately and deeply from early spring to late fall, particularly in hot dry weather.

- Once beetle damage is noticeable don't expect sprays to cure the problem, especially in a weakened tree. However, professional spraying with the appropriate product may help protect a healthy tree.

- Remove badly infested or dying trees promptly. Don't pile the wood or tree trimmings near conifers, or the beetles may spread to healthy specimens. (If you want to save the wood for your fireplace, remove its bark so it will dry quickly; this will prevent the larvae from maturing.)

- Valuable trees may be worth spraying for protection from attack. Call your University of California Cooperative Extension Office and ask for pamphlets on the control of bark beetles.

- Wait until cool weather (November through February) to prune conifers. Warm-weather pruning increases beetle activity and stresses the trees.

Don't Kill All the Butterflies

Caterpillars, loopers, and worms—especially green loopers, tomato hornworms, and cabbage worms—are the bane of many gardeners. If necessary, control them with BT. But butterflies, with the possible exception of white cabbage butterflies, are the floating flowers of the garden. So why kill them all? In fact, why not encourage them? Gardeners who plant meadows filled with wildflowers often provide perfect habitats and never notice the depredations of the attendant caterpillars, a necessary stage before you get butterflies.

If you like swallowtail butterflies grow parsley and sweet fennel (*Foeniculum vulgare*)—plenty of it, for both you and them. The caterpillars are attractively striped and not overly voracious. They do, however, like willow trees, poplars, and sycamores. If you grow these trees you're likely to have a resident population already.

Monarch butterflies can be attracted by growing butterfly weed (*Asclepius tuberosa*, available from Park Seeds, Greenwood, N.C. 29647). Large-flowered passion vine will attract Gulf fritillary, a red-orange butterfly with black-to-brown markings and silver spots under the wings. The fuzzy black caterpillars will decimate leaves of passion vine but not touch much else in the garden. The mourning cloak butterfly is attracted to newly mown lawns, and is often fearless enough to sit on a gardener's moist outstretched palm. For more about attracting butterflies see Mathew Tekulsky's *The Butterfly Garden*.

Hydrangeas

Once hydrangea flowers have faded to brown or green cut back each stalk that has bloomed, leaving only two buds or leaf scars, from which new wood will spring to bloom next year. (Cut back young plants lightly.) Don't cut off green stems that haven't yet bloomed because

**How to Make Cut Hibiscus Flowers
Stay Open at Night**

Most hibiscus flowers close up at night. You
can keep them open this way.

· Pick blossoms just as they're barely open at
9 or 10 A.M., and slip each one into an
empty Sno-Cone cup to protect it. (Pick
them right under the flower rather than at
the base of the stem in order not to tear
the bark.)

· Put the Sno-Cone cups containing the
flowers in a plastic bag and place them in
the refrigerator for the day.

· Take the flowers out in the evening. They'll
stay open all night without water. (Some
new varieties will stay open for three days.)

· Since water isn't needed you can use these
methods to arrange them. Spear the
blossoms on toothpicks, and stick the
toothpicks into arrangements. Or, to use
the flowers in vases, spear them on long
bamboo barbecue skewers and arrange the
skewers. Or instead of the stiff bamboo
skewers substitute the center veins of
fronds cut from a pigmy date palm (*Phoenix
roebelenii*). Cut off the individual leaflets
from each vein so it becomes a bare stem
before spearing a flower with its sharp tip.
Your hibiscus will be transformed into
cut flowers with long, graceful, arching
stems.

they'll bear flowers next year—or later this year
if the plant has a north-facing exposure.
(Hydrangeas perform best facing east.) Feed for
growth.

Hibiscus

Continue to prune, water, and fertilize hibiscus.
Now's a good time to plant these showy garden
shrubs. There are about thirty varieties available,
including a wide range of shapes, sizes, and
vibrant colors. Fancy-flowered varieties are less
vigorous, lankier in growth, and need more
protection from frost than common garden
varieties. Grow them for their flowers, prune
them lightly, train them as espaliers, or grow
them as large perennials at the backs of beds.

Camellias and Azaleas

Feed camellias for the third and last time
approximately one month or six weeks after
their last feeding. (Feeding is discussed on p.
130.) Use an acid fertilizer that's recommended
for camellias and azaleas, and follow package
directions exactly. Avoid overfeeding camellias;
neither they nor azaleas are heavy eaters. Keep
the roots damp but not soggy. Check to see that
soil is not collecting around the trunk.

Give azaleas that bloomed through June their
first feeding of the year immediately after
blooming stops. Don't feed them again until late
September unless one or two fail to respond. If
this should occur treat these sluggish growers
once or twice with Terr-O-Vite.

Check all your camellias and azaleas for signs
of chlorosis (yellow leaves with dark green veins,
showing a lack of iron). Treat the soil around
chlorotic plants with a chelating product that

✳ PREVIOUS PAGE: *This drought-resistant perennial border in an interior climate zone features a bulb display in spring. Clockwise from left background:* Lantana montevidensis, Malva maritima, *Tulip 'New Design' with a bulb cover of nemesia 'Blue Gem,' mayten tree* (Maytenus boaria), Westringia rosmariniformis, *Flowering kale 'Peacock,' Tulip 'Ballade,' Wallflower 'Bowles Mauve,' and Alyogyne 'UCSC Blue.' (Design by the late Charles Cozzens.)* ✳ TOP: *Acacias, such as Bailey's acacia* (Acacia baileyana), *often survive with little or no irrigation other than what they scrounge for themselves underground.* ✳ BOTTOM: *Cymbidiums are one of the easiest plants to grow once you understand how to grow them. I count on them to provide a long season of winter color on my patio, starting at Thanksgiving and lasting until June. Yours will bloom like this too if you follow the instructions given in the month-by-month chapters, including pages 128 and 228.* ✳ RIGHT: *Fronting Bill Gunther's unique garden is a giant plant that passers-by think is some kind of cactus, but it's not even related to cactus; it's* Euphorbia ingens, *a native of Africa (as discussed on p. 184), where it spreads by getting top heavy, falling down, then rerooting. Bill frustrates this action by securing his euphorbia to his house eaves to prevent it from crashing down.*

LEFT: *Young spur wood on an immature espaliered apple tree in my garden. Flowers are about to emerge from each cluster of leaves. On the right, an unwanted whip of growth has been cut back to two buds (as described on p. 204) so that a new flowering spur will form.* **RIGHT:** *Anna apples in summer, including a bright red one that's ready to pick and eat, on a young espaliered tree on a south-facing fence in my garden. (An east-facing fence or wall is better in interior zones.) Espaliered fruit trees are attractive, space saving, and practical; branches trained horizontally produce more fruiting spurs. Anna often provides two crops per year and performs best with a pollinator (as discussed on p. 20).* **BACKGROUND:** *I plant my peas in two rows providing them with a stout support of metal posts and wire hardware cloth and protecting them on each side of the row with an A-frame house of bird netting (as described on p. 237). On the right is Mammoth Melting Sugar Pod, a Chinese-type pea, and on the left is Snappy and a mildew-resistant snap pea that you eat, pod and all, when the peas inside the pod are plump. The lettuce in the center row is large enough now to begin harvesting the outer leaves or taking whole heads if desired.*

✸**LEFT:** *Gray tones of dusty miller (in foreground) and Turner's Variegated Dwarf pittosporum provide a pleasing contrast to the long-lasting, pinkish lavender blooms of the spectacular drought-resistant vine* Hardenbergia violacea, *'Happy Wanderer.' It blooms in late winter and early spring, performs best in dry years and, once established, needs only occasional deep watering in summer.* ✸**TOP:** *Peruvian bell flower or datura (*Brugmansia versicolor *'Charles Grimaldi'), at the bottom of my garden, blooms in cycles year-round when sufficient water reaches its adventuresome roots, but it can pull in its horns and survive a drought. In spring I cut this plant back severely to maintain a shrub shape with many trunks, but you can also remove the suckers and grow it as a small tree. (In cold areas datura dies to the ground in winter but returns in spring.) Foreground: gray foliage is butterfly bush (*Buddleia davidii), *a drought-resistant shrub that blooms with blue lilac-shaped flowers in summer; 'Gartenmeister Bonstedt' fuchsia and an old unnamed red zonal geranium with small double flowers and an iron constitution; and the straplike leaves of drought-resistant watsonias.*
✸**BOTTOM:** *The introduction of* Osteospermum fruticosum, *'Whirlgig,' gave that old standby—the freeway daisy—an excitingly new and different personality.*

ABOVE: *I believe in wearing protective clothing, including mask, goggles, boots, rubber gloves, and a shower cap when applying a chemical spray—in this case I'm using dormant oil spray after pruning a fruit tree for my daughter and her family.*

BACKGROUND: *Azalea 'Phoenicia' has smaller leaves and a more rounded growth habit than Formosa, though the two plants are similar and often mislabelled.*

✳ TOP: *Tulips are grown as a spring accent in an otherwise drought-resistant landscape: Counterclockwise from left foreground:* Echium vulgare, *Tulip 'Queen Wilhelmina,' Lady Banks rose (in distant background), ixia 'Venus.' (Design by the late Charles Cozzens.)* ✳ BOTTOM: *After our children grew up we bricked in the lawn to make a patio surrounded by non-thirsty shrubs and trees. Now in years when water can be spared for them I enjoy growing bright yellow King Alfred daffodils. These were planted in half-whiskey barrels in November. (See p. 282 for how to grow them in pots.) Blue hyacinths get potted up in December or January (pages 252 and 300 tell you how). I planted cineraria (foreground) in 8-inch plastic pots in October, then slipped them pot and all into empty terracotta pots for display. Double-potting (as described on p. 203) helps to keep roots moist and cool. In March everything is in full bloom.* ✳ RIGHT: *Fuchsia Non Pareil is protected from strong afternoon sun by a parasol (as described on p. 177) and irrigated by means of a drip line concealed above patio overhang (note small spray head above basket next to support wires). Fuchsias are easily grown from cuttings and bloom best when they're two years old. Toss out your old ones in time of drought; you can quickly grow new ones when good rains return.*

❋**ABOVE:** *Wisteria grows many long, unwanted twiners throughout the summer, and I cut them back to one or two buds as they occur. In winter after the leaves fall I can see the results—many spurs bearing flower buds are growing on short branches that protrude from the main framework of the vine. A straight, smooth twiner that bears no flower buds (lower right diagonally to left) can be cut back now to two buds so that next year it will grow flowering spurs like the others.*

❋**BACKGROUND:** *About five years ago I planted Chinese wisterias (Wisteria sinensis) to cover our entryway pergola with greenery in summer and flowers in spring. If you water wisterias deeply and infrequently once they're established they'll develop deep roots. When the roots are deep in the ground these spectacular vines can survive without any summer irrigation if necessary.*

✳**LEFT**: *William and Linda Teague's garden is influenced by, but not imitative of, Japanese gardens. Linda is a flower arranger so the garden contains many plants prized by arrangers, such as kangaroo paws and bulbs of many kinds, especially South African bulbs; also included are dwarf daylilies, California irises* (Iris douglasiana), *redbud* (Cercis occidentalis), *and Bill's bamboo collection. Plants shown: Orange and white harlequin flower* (Sparaxis tricolor), *purple and white baboon flower* (Babiana stricta), Homeria breyniana, *'Aurantiaca,' and Korean cherry* (Prunus jacquemontii).

✳**TOP**: *Flame vine* (Pyrostegia venusta), *a native of Brazil that blooms in winter, is reputed to be at its spectacular best in full sun and in the hottest spots, but its sheets of orange flowers here provide a magnificent ornament a few blocks from the sea. Inland it needs an average amount of summer water, but along the coast very old and deeply rooted vines have been known to survive on groundwater alone.*

✳**BOTTOM**: *Annual African daisies* (Dimorphotheca sinuata) *planted in the fall from seeds on bare, bulldozed banks sprout after the first rains and need nothing more than full sun and natural rainfall to produce sheets of bloom in winter through spring. The flowers close on cloudy days.*

❋TOP LEFT: *I plant wildflowers (described p. 259) every year in September or October in this raised island bed. First I spade the ground deeply, add soil amendment and work it in. Then I rake the surface level, and arrange drip lines on top of the bed. Since this bed is too wide to reach across and doesn't lend itself to a central path I distribute stepping stones across it to enable me to reach all parts of it without ever walking on the soil once it's been spaded.* **❋TOP RIGHT:** *After I've buried the drip lines and planted the seeds I cover the bed with pea stakes (as described on p. 258) which hold up bird netting and later support the plants through winds and rain. (If you plant less thickly than I do you don't need the pea stakes.) I read somewhere that Monet's gardener complained because the painter allowed his plants to grow too close together. I have the same failing, but I get a great effect.*
❋BOTTOM LEFT: *Wildflowers grow up inside bird netting supported by pea stakes. When they're this high it's time to remove the netting.* **❋BOTTOM RIGHT:** *By mid-December linaria and tall calendulas have already begun to bloom and the pea stakes are almost totally hidden (bottom). Picking the flowers and cutting them back occasionally, especially before a heavy rain, keeps linaria blooming for two or three months until the later flowers take over. Calendulas bloom throughout winter and spring.*
❋BACKGROUND: *By April most of the linaria has faded and I've either picked the flowers, pulled the plants out by the roots, or cut them to the ground. Now scarlet flax (Linum rubrum) and orange California poppies dominate the scene, changing the color scheme from the soft pastels of linaria to vibrant sun colors. White paludosum daisies, pink and white Shirley poppies, and red Flander's Field poppies were planted only once, but all three have naturalized in my garden, and come back every year. Yellow flowers next to the king palm in the background are on Green-Gold euryops (Euryops pectinatus 'Viridis'), one of California's most useful and water-thrifty shrub daisies (as discussed on pages 78 and 157).*

✳TOP: *Matilija poppy* (Romneya coulteri), *one of the loveliest of California native plants, blooms longer in summer if given some water but can survive with none. Plant in fall (as described on p. 275).* ✳BOTTOM: *I've never planted a rose garden because I prefer to grow just a few roses and use them as landscape plants mixed in with other flowers. Here the climbing rose, Joseph's Coat, backs a flower bed filled with wildflowers and bulbs. Climbing roses and many old-fashioned roses are deeply rooted and survive drought much better than most Hybrid Tea roses.* ✳RIGHT: *Year-round, non-thirsty color: yellow gazaneas, gray-colored blue fescue (*Festuca ovina glauca)*, and red bougainvillea 'San Diego.'*

❋**ABOVE:** *The lath covering a portion of our patio runs north to south (for the reason given on p. 174). Removeable lath panels next to the house can be taken off and stored on a flat roof in fall to provide more light in the living room during the winter. I'm replacing a panel in spring to shade the cymbidiums in the patio below so their blooms will last longer.* ❋**BACKGROUND:** *Hanging baskets of impatiens and brunfelsia (not yet in bloom) ornament a shady view-garden outside my kitchen window. The impatiens baskets have snap-on saucers that hold extra water to keep impatiens, which need a lot of water, from drying out between irrigations. To save water these baskets are watered by a drip system (the header runs along the fence behind the baskets and the microtubes are aesthetically hidden behind the baskets). When drought is severe, impatiens can be tossed out without a qualm. An undemanding permanent landscape of Algerian ivy (drought-tolerant when grown in shade in coastal zones), Australian tea trees, and clivias can survive with little or no irrigation until the rains return.*

✳**ABOVE:** *One of the most important lessons a gardener can learn is to spade the ground deeply and add organic soil amendment before planting vegetables or flowers. Above the dry wall, arugula (rocket) is flowering. I allow it to go to seed in order to have a plentiful supply of new plants coming up among the other vegetables. The flowers also taste good in salads.*

✳**BACKGROUND:** *Like all lantanas, 'Radiation' gives us cheerful color (year-round in mild climates) in return for little care and water. Use lantanas to cover dry banks (as discussed on p. 279). Standard lantanas (those grown in tree form) make handsome ornaments for patios.*

✳ **LEFT**: *Azaleas Alaska and Redwing, several camellias, and an Australian tree fern grow on a north-facing bank flanking our driveway and are watered by means of a drip system. I keep the ground around azaleas and camellias deeply mulched with pine needles, my favorite mulch for acid-loving plants—much too valuable to send to the dump. I also use pine needles for covering informal pathways all over the garden (as discussed on p. 271). When the sun shines on them they give off an aroma that reminds me of childhood summers in Maine.* ✳**TOP**: *This unnamed yellow daylily blooms almost year-round in my garden but it's especially colorful in summer. Fertilize daylilies in spring, irrigate them regularly, and divide them occasionally (as described on p. 248). In time of drought they can pull in their horns—they may not bloom as much but their thick, fleshy roots help them store enough moisture to keep them alive.* ✳**BOTTOM**: *Heat-resistant, single-flowered, Fischer 'Cascade' geraniums are shown here with Aeonium arboreum 'Atropurpureum.' Cascade and Balcon geraniums are the types seen spilling out of window boxes in Europe. They may not look like much in a nursery container, but in pots or the ground they make a huge display of color with sparse irrigation. (Designed by Jody Honnen.)*

✱ABOVE: *A young Grandiflora rose after pruning. I've cut out all diseased, twiggy, unwanted, or crossing growth, but I've left the plant tall (as described on p. 27). In Southern California there's no point in cutting your roses down short.* **✱BACKGROUND:** *At pruning time in January I arranged the canes of these two climbing roses, Joseph's Coat (foreground) and Butterscotch, in fountain form by bending the tips of the canes to the ground and pegging them down (as described on p. 28). The subtle color of Butterscotch, the first brown rose, never fails to cause comment; it's vigorous, disease resistant, and easy to grow.*

❋**ABOVE LEFT:** *A ball of malacoides primroses (as described on p. 255) immediately after planting in September or October.* ❋**ABOVE RIGHT:** *Blooms open prior to Christmas; water as necessary, feed and deadhead occasionally, and flowers will continue throughout winter and spring.*
❋**BACKGROUND:** *This handsome bank needs only occasional irrigation in summer and gives streetside color over a long summer and fall season. On the left, Mexican bush sage (Salvia leucantha)—like many drought-tolerant plants it doesn't look like much in the nursery, but here's what it can do in the ground. On the right, red fountain grass (Pennisetum setaceum, 'Cuprium') won't come up as a weed in your garden because it doesn't set seeds. Cut ornamental grasses to the ground in late winter; they spring back with fresh growth in spring.*

✸**ABOVE:** *Every year in fall I purchase paper white bulbs or other Tazetta narcissuses and force them in water and pebbles to bloom at Christmas (as described on p. 280).* ✸**BACKGROUND:** *Salmon-colored seed pods of Chinese flame tree (Koelreuteria bipinnata or K elegans [K formosa, K henryi]) make a striking fall display on a trouble-free, drought-resistant tree with many virtues; it's briefly deciduous and neither messy nor invasive.* ✸**FOLLOWING PAGE:** *A shady path invites exploration of a unique coastal garden. What was once a steep, clay cliff was gradually terraced with a network of wandering paths leading between rock-walled terraces that are filled with mushroom compost and planted with many species of palm. (Designed by Bill Gunther and friends.)*

Layer Camellias and Azaleas to Make New Plants

Treasured varieties of camellia and azalea that you cannot find commercially, plus many other woody ornamental plants, can be propagated now. To *layer* them (to bury an attached branch in the ground and allow it to root, so it can be cut off as a plant in its own right) follow these steps.

· Choose a low-lying branch. (If none is low enough to bend to ground level place a pot filled with damp potting soil under a suitable branch.)

· With a sharp knife carefully cut halfway through the chosen branch, making your cut several joints from the tip of the branch.

· Brush the cut with a powdered rooting compound, such as RooTone.

· Insert a sliver of wood or a small pebble into the cut section to hold it open.

· Bury the cut section in damp soil. Peg the branch down firmly on both sides—"elbows" cut from coat hangers work well—and place a brick on the ground over the cut section to hold it down. Keep the soil damp throughout the summer.

· Check the branch in fall. When it's thoroughly rooted sever the new plant from the parent branch, dig it up, and plant it in a suitably sized container (unless you already rooted it in a container of the right size).

Note: *Air-layering* is a method of propagation similar to layering, but it's done above ground. For this method first wrap a section cut as above in damp sphagnum moss. Then cover the moss with plastic sheeting, and wind tape around the plastic and the branch both above and below the cut section to keep the moss damp. In a few weeks, after roots grow, sever the branch below the cut. This system is very easy to use on some houseplants, especially corn plant (*Dracaena fragrans*).

contains iron, manganese, and zinc. Liquid formulas can also be sprayed on leaves. (Terr-O-Vite contains trace elements, so when you treat sluggish growers with it you also correct chlorosis, especially when you spray it on the foliage as well as pour it around the roots.) To start new plants, layer camellias and azaleas (see the accompanying box).

Primroses and Cyclamen

Cyclamen and certain primroses, including English or polyanthus primroses (*Primula polyantha*), are perennials often grown as cool-season annuals. When they've finished flowering at the end of June you can, if you wish, just toss them out. But many gardeners, especially in coastal zones, keep them from year to year (reviving them in September—pp. 224, 234). After polyanthus primroses stop blooming leave them in their pots or, if they're in conspicuous beds, dig them up, divide the plants, throw out the woody centers, and plant healthy offshoots in 6-inch plastic pots. Put them in a shady, out-of-the-way spot for the summer. Water the primroses about once a week to keep them damp, feed them occasionally with fish emulsion, and protect them from slugs, snails, mites, and caterpillars.

Cyclamen can be summered-over in one of two ways. One way is to allow a plant to become completely dormant by removing it from the pot and drying the entire root mass in the sun. Once dry, slip the root and tuber back into the pot and store it on its side in a cool, dry place. This way is best for gardeners in hot, dry interior regions, although a few tubers may be lost to rot during the summer.

Coastal gardeners will have more luck allowing cyclamen to go into semidormancy. Put the plants in a shady, out-of-the-way spot—in a hanging basket under a tree is ideal. Keep them on the dry side, watering occasionally. Most leaves will fall off but a few will be retained. Don't fertilize. You can keep cyclamen flowering, especially plants with small blooms, by fertilizing them for growth and bloom year-round in cool gardens. But forcing semidormancy, as described here, will give you a better winter display.

Succulents and Cacti

Succulents and cacti are such a basic part of the Southern California landscape that almost all gardens contain at least one or two. But despite our familiarity with them, many people don't know the difference between a succulent and a cactus. The difference is simple: all plants that store water in their leaves or stems are called "succulents," while "cactus" actually is the name of just one large family of plants within the succulent group. All cacti have spine cushions, called areoles, out of which arise the spines, but many succulents—crassulas from Africa and echeverias from the Americas, for example—have no spines at all.

Euphorbias are another large group of mostly succulent plants that are often confused with cacti because, at first glance, there's considerable resemblance. But whereas many euphorbias have spines none of them have spine cushions. Other differences are that cacti are nonpoisonous and their sap is clear, while euphorbias are usually poisonous and their sap is white and cloudy. Also, all but a few cacti are native to the Americas, and most euphorbias are from Africa or Madagascar. Many of the vast number of tender succulents we're fortunate to be able to grow outdoors are houseplants in the rest of the country.

Choose Succulents for Widely Varying Conditions.

Succulents have playful shapes, lovely flowers, undemanding, drought-tolerant natures, plenty of variety to keep one interested, and the ability to draw enthusiastic comments from anyone who sees them. If you live in a place where it's difficult to garden they're ideal plants. They're also perfect for collecting—they make good hobby plants. One plus to growing succulents in containers is their portability. If you move take them with you. Or for the easiest care grow them in the ground.

Your garden needn't look like a desert scene for succulents to fit in. Many have a lush, green look, some make good accent plants, and others can be used as ground covers. They're good choices for rock gardens, and they mix well with other drought-resistant plants.

Clean Up, Feed, and Water Succulents.

Choose and plant succulents year-round. Some take full sun, others need semishade. Most container-grown specimens do best in partial shade. They're perfect for dressing up a balcony or a condo patio where hot sun alternating with solid shade makes survival difficult or impossible for most other plants.

The colorful blooms of succulents occur mostly in winter and spring. After plants have finished flowering, if the spent blooms and seed pods are unsightly cut them off. This applies also to cactus—epiphyllums, for example— unless you wish to propagate the seeds or eat the fruit. (The fruit of some cacti and both the

A Good Soil Mix for Succulents and Cacti

Choose a commercial mix especially formulated for succulents and cacti, or make your own by combining these ingredients.

- Six to seven parts pumice
- Two parts commercial potting soil (such as Unigrow)
- One part sterilized oak leaf mold

Quick Tip

How to Remove Cactus Spines from Your Skin.
Some cactus spines are easy to see and remove with tweezers. But fine, almost invisible, hairlike spines called glochids *have hooks on their tips and are painfully irritating when imbedded in human flesh. To remove them glob on rubber cement. Let it dry. Then rub it off, spines and all.*

* ✳ *

How to Transplant Cacti and Spiny Euphorbias

Most spiny succulents can be safely handled with leather gloves, but all cacti and a few euphorbias have spines that are either sharp enough to penetrate leather or, in the case of some cacti, are barbed so they can permanently attach themselves to it. To avoid ensnarement, try this method.

· Hold tiny plants gently with barbecue tongs. To grasp small plants roll a sheet of newspaper in the shape of a tube; flatten it, and wrap it around a cactus. Grasp large plants with rolled burlap. Use these handles to securely hold and support the plant as you dig up its roots and lift it out of the ground or container. (More than one handle may be necessary for large specimens.)

· Transplant the cactus into loose, well-drained soil mix appropriate for cactus and other succulents. Use a chopstick to work the soil mix down around the roots.

· Cover the roots completely with soil mix up to the original soil level. Tamp gently but firmly with a blunt stick. Stake and tie tall specimens.

· Cover the soil mix with a layer of ornamental gravel or volcanic rock. Water thoroughly. Keep potted plants in semishade for a month.

* ✳ *

young leaves and fruit of prickly pear cactus [*Opuntia ficus indica*] are edible, but remember, all parts of African euphorbias are poisonous.) Clean up all succulents by pruning off diseased or desiccated portions.

Feed all cacti and euphorbias in July with a complete product such as Watch-Us-Grow 8-8-8 or Liquinox Grow 10-10-5. Mix it in a watering can according to package directions and pour it around their roots. If you grow succulents of any type in containers, feed them at the rate of 1 tablespoon per gallon once a month during the growing season or, alternatively, ⅓ tablespoon per gallon every time you water, or three times out of four. (Many succulents, other than cacti and euphorbias, need little or no fertilizer when they grow in the ground.)

Most succulents growing in the ground need no irrigation during the winter. Those in containers need water only during dry spells. The ☞ **Rule of Thumb** for watering container-grown succulents, including cacti and euphorbias, is: *If the soil is dry 1 inch below the surface it's time to water.* But all begin to need irrigation this month. Depending on the weather and your climate zone water them every one to three weeks throughout summer and fall. Allow plants to dry out slightly between waterings. Good drainage is important.

Bromeliads

Like cacti, bromeliads are all native to the Western Hemisphere, except for a lone adventurer found in Africa. The bromeliad family includes such widely differing plants as the pineapple and Spanish moss, but most family members share the basic shape of a rosette of leathery leaves, sometimes plain and at other

How to Pot On Fragile Donkey Tails

When donkey tails (*Sedum morganianum*) outgrow their small hanging pots, pot them on into large baskets. When grown this way the plants can attain stunning beauty and spectacular size—often growing to 5 feet or more in length.

- Paint an 18-inch wire basket with rust-resistant gutter paint. Allow it to dry. Attach chains strong enough to support approximately 75 pounds. Hang the basket briefly to test the chains' length and make sure it hangs level.

- Presoak sphagnum moss. Wearing gloves shove moss tightly between the two top wires of the basket. Trim this with grass shears into a neat circle to make a finished lip all around. (Shape it like the fat inner tube of a child's bicycle.)

- Line the basket with a thick layer of premoistened sphagnum moss.

- Fill the lined basket with loose, fast-draining potting soil. Make a hole in the middle.

- Gently place the plant, pot and all, into the hole, carefully spreading the long stems over the edge of the basket. (This may take two or three people.)

- Carefully break the pot in several places with a hammer. Pull out the shards. (If the pot is plastic reach between the stems and cut it apart with strong clippers. Then remove it.) Fill in the gaps with more soil.

- Dip the ends of broken branches in Roo-Tone and plant these too. Hang the basket on a stout hook in semishade. Protect it from wind and birds. Keep it moist, and feed occasionally.

times strikingly variegated. They can be brilliantly colored, striped, or mottled. Often these leaves are arranged in a cone that forms a natural reservoir to collect rainwater and see the plant through drought. Flowers either are hidden in the cone or arise from it on straight or cascading stems. Often the inflorescences are bizarre, exciting, and spectacularly colored.

Queen's tears (*Billbergia nutans*) was the first bromeliad to be widely grown in California gardens; it thrives on neglect. In recent years silver vase plant (*Aechmea fasciata*) has taken its place as the most popular bromeliad. Most bromeliads are experts at survival, and they thrive outdoors in Southern California, even naturalizing in some gardens.

Propagate Bromeliads. All bromeliads except one are monocarpic—they bloom but once, then die. But in the process they leave many progeny in the form of seeds and offshoots called pups, which sprout from the mother's stalk. Once you buy a variety, with proper care you'll have it for life. Now's a good time to propagate bromeliads

* ✳ *

How to Divide and Multiply Bromeliads

When you propagate bromeliads remember that spines from prickly varieties can enter your flesh and fester; wear leather gloves when handling them. (If you get a spine in your flesh, see p. 185.) You can divide a plant when the pup is at least a third or half the size of the mother or has formed roots of its own. Here are two methods.

- Depending on what will work with the size and type of plant you're propagating, stick a serrated knife, keyhole saw, sharp hunting knife, or blade-type pruning shears down into the soil and cut off the pup as close to the mother plant as possible. Continue with the directions for pot planting that follow immediately, or skip to the last item.

- Place one 5-gram tablet of slow-release fertilizer, such as 14-4-6, in the bottom of a 4- or 6-inch plastic container, and fill it with premoistened fast-draining potting soil.

- Dip the cut section of the bromeliad pup in a rooting hormone, such as RooTone, and knock off the excess. Make a hole in the planter mix. Insert the plant and press the damp soil mix around it.

- Water the bromeliad occasionally, and keep it in semishade.

- Most tillandsias are grown on a piece of wood or bark, with no soil at all. Vase-type bromeliads can also be grown without soil. To mount them this way, first cover the base of the bromeliad with a handful of damp sphagnum moss. Then place the plant upright on a branch or in the crotch of a tree or on a large piece of driftwood, and attach it firmly in place by winding clear fishing twine around the branch or driftwood, the moss, and the plant base. The bromeliads will soon develop aerial roots. (Mature Australian tea trees (*Leptospermum laevigatum*) make particularly attractive settings for bromeliads because their branches are often at eye level and they have interesting, twisted shapes.)

* ✳ *

by separating the pups from their parents to make new plants (see the accompanying box).

Give Them Proper Care. Bromeliads need good air circulation, fast-draining acid soil mix, and occasional watering. In interior zones hook up a mist system to mist them in hot, dry weather. It's not necessary along the coast. Most bromeliads need bright light—up to 50 percent sunshine in coastal zones, 25 percent inland. Once in a while let their center cups go dry.

Flush them out occasionally to prevent mosquitoes from setting up housekeeping. But if tree frogs live in them, as they do in mine, you'll have no mosquitoes.

Feed and Flush Bromeliads. Feed bromeliads lightly with a close-to-equally-balanced fertilizer, such as 20-20-20, mixed one-third to half-strength. (Spoonit, Miracle Gro, Hyponex, Peters, Watch-Us-Grow, and Liquinox Gro are a few of the fertilizers that have been found to work well. For bromeliads, dilute any one of these so it becomes one-third or half the strength of the recommended solution for most other plants.) Some hobbyists feed their bromeliads only three or four times a year, with fine results. Others fertilize once every two or three weeks in the summer months, which brings even better results. Pour some of the diluted fertilizer around the roots and a little into the cup. Mist tillandsias—air-plant bromeliads—with the solution. (Foliar feeding benefits all bromeliads regardless of type.)

Lawn Care

Cool-Season Grasses. As in June, cool-season lawns such as perennial ryegrass, bluegrass, and fescue are growing slowly now, so don't mow them short. Cut ryegrass and bluegrass 2 inches high now. Tall fescues should be left even taller—between 2 and 3 inches after cutting. (Use the top setting of your mower.) Mow tall fescues often, never cut off more than one-third of their total height, and always use a sharp mower.

Extend the time between irrigations of tall fescue now, and water it deeply to encourage deep roots. Most other cool-season grasses need shallower and more frequent watering than do warm-season grasses. In hot weather most cool-season grasses need to be watered twice or three times a week in interior zones, and at least once a week along the coast. Early morning—any time between midnight and dawn—is the best time to irrigate both for water conservation and for lawn health except in the desert, where evenings are acceptable.

Don't fertilize cool-season grasses now in interior zones. Along the coast fertilize very lightly—one-half the normal amount.

The Apple Trick to Make a Bromeliad Bloom

Some years ago smoke from a wood-burning heater accidentally escaped overnight into a greenhouse filled with bromeliads, including some species that had been there for years without blooming. Within six weeks to two months most of the plants—including those that had never bloomed—suddenly sprouted inflorescences. The smoke was analyzed and found to contain ethylene gas. This discovery enabled growers to make pineapples bear fruit year-round.

In our climate most well-grown bromeliads will cycle into bloom naturally at the right time of year for each species. But if desired, mature plants, particularly any recalcitrant ones that have never bloomed, can often be "gassed" to stimulate bloom on demand. One way to do so is to place a full-grown plant into a large plastic bag and drop in a whole Red Delicious apple (a better source of ethylene gas than Yellow Delicious). Tie the bag closed and keep it in cool solid shade for one week. Then take the bromeliad out and care for it as usual. Another method is to spray the plant and the interior of the cup with Florel, which produces ethylene gas, or pour into the bromeliad's center cup a solution of ¼ ounce calcium carbide in 1 quart water.

Warm-Season Grasses. Warm-season lawns such as Bermuda, zoysia, kikuyu, Adalayd grass, dichondra, and St. Augustine thrive in summer and are growing at their fastest now. As in June, cut common Bermuda short, to 1 inch, and cut improved Bermuda even shorter, to ½ or ¾ inches. Cut zoysia to between ¾ inch and 1 inch and kikuyu as short as ½ inch, to keep it in bounds. (Slice down through and pull out escaped kikuyu stolons often, to thwart their tendency to creep into flower beds.) Dichondra should look billowy and lush now. Cut it high or not at all. St. Augustine grows fast, so cut it often to ¾ or 1 inch—at least once a week.

All warm-season grasses should be watered deeply and infrequently, to encourage deep rooting, rather than shallowly and often. St. Augustine needs the most water; it can die if allowed to go dry. Water it at least once a week—more often in sandy soils. Bermuda, zoysia, and kikuyu can often go as long as two weeks between waterings, depending on the weather and your climate zone. Water deeply, and extend the time between irrigations as much as possible while still maintaining good appearance.

Feed most warm-season grasses every four to six weeks during the growing season. Feed Adalayd half-strength, early in the month. (Too much fertilizer in hot weather can stress it.) If kikuyu is growing well don't feed it at all. Too much fertilizer can turn it into a monster. If you want to get rid of kikuyu or Bermuda as weeds, kill them now, with glyphosate, and pull them out by the roots, but be aware that they may come back from seeds.

Lippia as Lawn. Lippia repens (*Phyla nodiflora*) is a useful and attractive lawn substitute for interior and desert regions. It's tough, evergreen, drought tolerant, and once established it withstands foot traffic. It creates a thick mat that blooms in early summer and fall with pink flowers that are pretty to look at and attractive to bees. To protect children and dogs from bee stings, mow the flowers off now. Follow up with lawn fertilizer and deep water.

Vegetable Gardening

As early summer vegetables are harvested clean up the rows, add soil amendment and fertilizer, then plant more crops. All summer vegetables can be planted now, but they'll have a shorter growing season. If you need the space in September for winter vegetables don't plant crops now that won't bear until fall. (Read the seed packages and count the days to harvest.)

Crops You Can Still Plant. The best things to plant now are the heat lovers, such as summer squash, eggplant, peppers (in coastal zones only; see the accompanying box), cucumbers, and corn. Tomatoes and chard can also be planted. Continue to put in carrots, beets, and radishes in small quantities for successive crops. Green beans can be planted now but will be less vigorous and have more insect problems than those planted in March. It's too late to plant melons along the coast. Inland you can plant cantaloupe, pumpkins, and cranshaw and honeydew melons early in the month, if you know from experience there'll be enough hot weather to ripen them in October. (Planting this late is much riskier than planting in May or June.) It's too late to put in winter squash and be sure of a harvest. For all these crops keep the seed rows damp. It's often necessary to mist them more than once daily (see accompanying quick tip).

Fending Off Problems. Watering and either cultivating or mulching (as well as harvesting) are the most important tasks in the July vegetable garden. There's no use in kidding ourselves—vegetables aren't drought resistant; they need a steady supply of water. If a cucumber plant goes dry the cucumbers will be bitter. If tomatoes go dry they'll drop flowers or get blossom-end rot. (Tomatoes growing in heavy soil can go a long time between waterings if their roots are deep in the ground but not if they're shallow rooted, in very sandy soil, or in containers.) If drought forces the shutdown of your vegetable garden, or part of it, don't be discouraged. Work for solutions to our water problems, keep up your hopes, and plant again in fall. Drip irrigation is the most water-wise method for keeping row crops happy.

Continue to side-dress rows with fertilizer halfway in vegetables' growing seasons. If you're an organic gardener use cottonseed meal and blood meal to provide extra nitrogen if crops show signs of nitrogen deficiency, such as yellowing foliage or a slowdown in growth. Excellent vegetables can be grown without the addition of commercial fertilizer if the soil has been deeply dug up and turned and is rich in organic matter, and if the plants have plenty of sunlight and water.

All gardeners need to watch for pest problems now. Handpick caterpillars, get birds to help, or use BT. Continue to release beneficials.

When and How to Harvest Summer Vegetables. Pick summer vegetables when they're young

Quick Tip

How to Keep Seed Rows from Drying Out in Hot Weather.
Cover a seeded row with a 4-inch-wide strip of burlap. Sprinkle it thoroughly to soak the row every morning. Pick up the edge of the burlap daily to check progress; remove it as soon as the seeds sprout.

How to Have Success with Peppers

Peppers are classed as hot-weather vegetables, but they perform best within a precise range of temperatures. The fruit sets best when night temperatures are between 60° and 75°F (16° to 24°C). Daytime temperatures near 75°F are best—when they top 90°F (32°C) they can cause blossom drop.

Feed peppers lightly with a balanced liquid fertilizer as soon as you see the first blossoms open, and keep the ground evenly moist. A lack of dark green leaf color despite adequate nitrogen may come from lack of magnesium. In this case spray the leaves with a solution of 1 teaspoon Epsom salts to a pint of lukewarm water.

and tender—it's half the fun of growing your own. They grow so fast that many crops need checking daily. Whenever possible eat them the day you pick them.

- **Green Beans.** Pick often and pick young—as soon as immature seeds fill the pod but before the pods get bumpy, and while the outside's still slightly velvety. Wait until the leaves are dry before walking among the plants to pick beans. (Picking when the leaves are wet from dew can spread rust.)

- **Summer Squash.** Pick while the skin can be easily pierced with your thumb nail. Try picking tiny ones with the blossom still on the plant and cooking them blossom and all. If crops get too overwhelming, slow them down by picking both male and female blossoms to batter-fry or add to ratatouille.

- **Corn.** When the tips of the silks go crispy brown and the ears are filled out, pierce a kernel with your thumbnail. If the juice is milky it's just right; if clear it's not yet ready; if dry or pasty you've waited too long.

- **Cantaloupe.** Pick at *full slip*, when a crack forms around the stem next to the fruit and the fruit falls off in your hand with no pulling.

- **Watermelon.** Harvest when the skin under the melon turns from pure white to a creamy color and the tendril on the stem starts to dry up. Thumping doesn't help. (When the sound changes from a sharp tap to a dull thud the melon is usually overripe.) Also count the days since planting. Small varieties may ripen in late July; large varieties, maybe not until August.

* ✺ *

Beware of Sleepy Bumblebees

Pole beans, dahlias, and zinnias are bedrooms for bumblebees. Watch for them when picking flowers and vegetables in the late afternoon or evening. These gentle creatures don't want to sting you, but they will if you grab them.

* ✺ *

- **Peppers.** Pick as soon as the fruit are well formed and full sized, with crisp, thick skins and seeds that are almost mature. Leave a few fruits on the plant to go red if desired, but not all, because the plants have a built-in fruit load. Once they reach their limit they'll stop blooming unless you pick some.

- **Tomatoes.** For the best flavor leave these on the vine until they're fully red and ripe, unless birds, animals, or caterpillars are getting them first.

- **Carrots.** Ready to eat when finger sized. In sandy soils pull them up by the leafy crown. In clay soils loosen them first with a garden fork or trowel. (Be careful not to disturb others left in the ground.)

- **Beets.** Harvest at any size, but they're best between tiny and golf ball size.

- **Radishes.** Plant often and pull daily in small quantities, as soon as they mature but before they split. (These tend to get very hot to the taste during summer.)

- **Eggplant.** The fruit should be glossy, filled out, and big enough to eat. The flesh should not spring back when you press it with your thumb. If the seeds or skin go brown the eggplant's gone too far. Pick often; the more you pick the more you get.

- **Lima Beans.** Don't pick these too soon. Leave the full-grown pod on the plant until it fills with beans and you can clearly feel them inside.

- **Cucumbers.** Harvest at any size, but mature fruit with small seeds, dark green skin, and crisp texture taste best. Harvest often to keep the vines bearing.

Stop Removing Runners from Strawberries.
Summer heat shuts down fruit production, so stop pinching off runners early in July. In fall you'll be able to use the runners that have grown to make new plants. Fertilize them to encourage growth. If you're growing strawberries on plastic mulch, remove it now so runners can root in the soil.

Purchase / Plant

- [ ] Continue to plant **tropicals** in coastal zones, 152
- [ ] Purchase **tuberous begonias** already in bloom, 178
- [ ] Transplant large **New Guinea impatiens** plants into large tubs, 178
- [ ] Continue to plant **summer annuals**, 178
- [ ] Start **biennials** from seeds, 179
- [ ] Choose and plant **hibiscus**, 182
- [ ] Choose and plant **succulents**, 185
- [ ] Transplant **succulents**, including **cacti** and **euphorbias**, 186
- [ ] Continue to fill in **vegetable** rows with **summer crops**, 190
- [ ] Continue to plant **papayas**, **bananas**, and **palms**, 210
- [ ] Transplant **palms**, 212

Trim, Prune, Mow, Divide

- [ ] Continue to pinch back **chrysanthemums**, 79
- [ ] Continue to pick and deadhead **roses**, but stop disbudding them now, 107, 172
- [ ] Remove berries (seed pods) from **fuchsias**, 154
- [ ] Deadhead **flowers**, 158
- [ ] Prune **climbing roses** that bloom only once a year, 172
- [ ] Prune **impatiens** progressively, 178
- [ ] Prune **petunias** by cutting them back to 4 inches. (Cut back cascading types lightly.) 178
- [ ] Pinch flowers off **coleus**, 179
- [ ] Cut back **hydrangeas**, 181
- [ ] Pick **hibiscus** blossoms to use as cut flowers, 182
- [ ] Divide **English primroses**, or wait until fall, 182
- [ ] Clean up **succulents** by pruning off diseased and dessicated portions and removing unsightly spent blooms and seed pods, 186
- [ ] Propagate **bromeliads** by dividing the offshoots from parent plants, 187
- [ ] Mow **cool-season lawns** long, 189
- [ ] Mow **warm-season lawns** short, 190
- [ ] Mow off the flowers from **lippia lawns** to protect children and dogs from bee stings, 190
- [ ] Stop removing runners from **strawberries;** let them grow and root in the ground, 193
- [ ] Continue to prune and train **espaliers**, 203
- [ ] Continue to propagate and clean up **daylilies**, 206
- [ ] When **Martha Washington geraniums** stop blooming clip off their faded flowers and begin to cut them back progressively, 250

Fertilize

- [ ] Feed **fuchsias**, 55
- [ ] Feed **water lilies**, 110
- [ ] Feed **cymbidiums** with a high nitrogen fertilizer for growth, 130
- [ ] Fertilize **roses**, 131
- [ ] Feed **ferns**, 132
- [ ] Fertilize **tropicals** according to need during the summer months, 152
- [ ] Feed **tuberous begonias**, 177
- [ ] Fertilize **impatiens**, 178
- [ ] Feed **coleus** lightly, 179
- [ ] Fertilize **azaleas** that bloomed through June, 182
- [ ] Check **camellias** and **azaleas** for chlorosis; treat if necessary, 182
- [ ] Give **camellias** their third and final feeding for the year, 182
- [ ] If an **azalea** fails to respond to spring feeding by month's end, treat it with Terr-O-Vite, 182
- [ ] Fertilize **cacti** and **euphorbias** that are growing in the ground, 186
- [ ] Fertilize **bromeliads**, 188
- [ ] Fertilize **cool-season lawns** lightly along the coast; do not fertilize them inland, 189
- [ ] Feed **warm-season lawns** according to type, 190
- [ ] Feed and water **lippia** after mowing, 190
- [ ] Continue to side-dress **vegetable** rows with additional fertilizer according to need, 191
- [ ] Treat **pepper plants** that lack good green leaves with Epsom salts, 191
- [ ] Feed and water **cycads**, 213

Water

- [ ] Water all **bougainvilleas** that are under three years old, paying particular attention to newly planted ones, 153
- [ ] With the exception of certain **California natives,** water **all garden plants** according to their individual needs. Don't neglect to water young **drought-resistant plants,** 170
- [ ] Water **citrus** and **avocado trees,** 171
- [ ] Water **cymbidiums,** 171
- [ ] Increase water for **roses** to as much as 1½ inches three times a week in fast-draining soils, 172
- [ ] Give **plants in north-facing shade** extra water now while sun hits them, 175
- [ ] Water **impatiens** daily, 178
- [ ] Begin to water **succulents** that are growing in the ground, once every two or three weeks, 186
- [ ] Water **lawns** according to their specific requirements, 189
- [ ] Keep newly planted **seed rows** damp, 190
- [ ] Continue to water **vegetables** regularly; don't let **tomatoes** or **cucumbers** run dry, 191
- [ ] Keep transplanted **palms** well watered, 212

Control Pests, Diseases, and Weeds

- [ ] Control **weeds** by cultivating, mulching, or hand pulling, 170
- [ ] Continue to control **rose** pests and diseases, 172
- [ ] Control mildew and slugs and snails on **tuberous begonias,** 177
- [ ] Control bark beetles on **conifers,** 180
- [ ] Don't kill all the **butterflies,** 181
- [ ] Kill unwanted **kikuyu** or **Bermuda grass** with glyphosate, 190
- [ ] Continue to control pests on **vegetables,** 191
- [ ] Control **corn** earworm if desired, 215

Also This Month

- [ ] Spread mulch to cool the ground and conserve moisture, 171
- [ ] Study the **shady areas** in your garden with an eye to improving them, 173
- [ ] Create additional **shade** where it's needed, 173
- [ ] Replace **plants** that are dying or doing badly in full shade with better choices for dark places, 174
- [ ] Replace **plants in west-facing shade** with better choices if they are being burned by sun or wilting in the afternoon, 175
- [ ] Protect **fuchsias** from burning rays of sun, 177
- [ ] Propagate **camellias, azaleas,** and other **woody plants** by layering, 183
- [ ] Move **cyclamen** and **English primroses** to a shady spot for the summer, 184
- [ ] Repot **donkey tails** (*sedum morganianum*), 187
- [ ] Flush out **bromeliads** occasionally to prevent mosquitos from breeding, and allow the cups to dry out from time to time, 188
- [ ] Harvest **summer vegetables** according to special techniques for each, 191
- [ ] Beware of bumblebees as you harvest **vegetables** and pick **summer flowers,** 192

AUGUST

The Height-of-Summer Month

August may not always be the hottest and driest month of the year, since September sometimes shoves the thermometer higher, but August usually attacks the job with more persistence. Along the coast the weather's almost always sunny this month, with oceanic breezes to keep temperatures cool and comfortable, albeit drier than in early summer. Every few years, however, if you live along the coast you can experience a disappointing August—either overcast skies or a blanket of fog. Thirty or forty years ago in interior zones there was seldom if ever a cool or moist August day and almost never a cloud in the sky. In recent years, however, there have been a reliable number of tropical storms that wheel up from the South Pacific and hit various portions of Southern California. Sometimes these storms bring humid weather; at other times they simply bring clouds that have a cooling effect. Usually they don't bring a measurable amount of rain, so watering is still the major task in the garden, and pest control comes next.

Other than in coastal zones it's too hot to plant most permanent additions to the landscape, but it's a good time to start seeds. In the vegetable garden harvesting is important. For the most part August is a time to enjoy life, take it easy, and maintain what you've got. Go to the beach. And if you want, bring home a bag of seaweed to add to the compost pile or work directly into garden soil.

Watering

When the weather's hot and dry and there's no measurable rain, even the most inept gardeners are aware that most plants won't survive without regular irrigation. Unfortunately, one response is to stand with hose in hand and squirt water on the plants or on the surface of the ground around them. This doesn't do much but dig up the soil. Wise gardeners give their plants the amount of water each one needs in ways that save time, effort, and water.

Use the Right Equipment. Much water can be saved in summer by watering each part of the garden by a method appropriately suited to it. Briefly, hand sprinkling is fine for sprouting seeds, but all other watering should be done with conventional irrigation systems or drip systems. In general, conventional irrigation systems work best for most of the basic landscape, including lawns, while drip systems work best for plants in containers and vegetable gardens. Reserve watering by hose for filling furrows and basins around trees and bushes, when these are not equipped with bubblers. (When you water this way, put the hose right down on the ground, and let the water sink in slowly.)

How Often Should You Water Now? For most plants it's best to irrigate deeply once a week or every ten days—even less for many plants,

depending on your climate zone and soil. Lawns—with the exception of Bermuda and zoysia—and vegetables, certain annual flowers, and some perennial shade flowers are the thirstiest plants in the garden. Water these as frequently as necessary to prevent wilting. Some plants, such as fuchsias and impatiens, need water daily when growing in containers. Some drought-resistant native and exotic plants need little summer water or none at all. (In general, native plants that are summer deciduous should never be watered during the hot summer months or they'll die from root rot. Some native plants that don't drop their leaves in summer, including flannel bush [*Fremontodendron*], should be watered only if they show severe wilting and, even then, sparingly if in clay soils.)

Other plants recommended for their resistance to drought—Mexican fan palms (*Washingtonia robusta*), Torrey pines, and Aleppo pines are good examples—will look better if watered deeply at least once during August. Water all pine trees deeply as needed—usually once every three weeks—to prevent stress in hot weather, which invites attack from bark beetles. Subtropical trees—including coral trees and floss silk trees (*Chorisia speciosa*)—should be watered deeply, early in the month. Allowing chorisia to go on the dry side in late August often contributes to more spectacular fall bloom.

Remember to look for signs of stress and think of each plant as an individual; water accordingly. With deep, infrequent waterings teach them to send their roots far into the ground, so when there's a drought they'll survive.

Check for Malfunctioning Sprinklers and Drip Emitters. The easiest way to supply plants with the water they need is by an automatic system controlled by a clock, but once it's installed don't just walk away and forget it. Automatic irrigation isn't entirely trouble free; when it goes wrong it can cause havoc. Broken sprinklers and buried drip hoses with holes in them waste water. Clogged sprinklers and drip emitters can kill plants. If you go away on a trip be sure to ask a responsible person to watch your garden, and leave the phone number of an irrigation repair person in case something goes wrong.

Now's a good time to check out your irrigation system. Begin by installing a new backup battery in your time clock. Then flush the filters and the header lines of drip systems. Also, check all the drip emitters and clean out or replace those that are either flooding plants or failing to give them adequate water.

Run each section of your conventional sprinkler system on the manual setting; look for broken or clogged sprinklers or bubblers, and replace or repair the culprits. If your sprinklers don't adequately reach all parts of the lawn you may get brown spots, especially after fertilizing. Sometimes gardeners don't realize how little water is actually penetrating the top layer of soil. In lawns, insufficient penetration may be caused by thatch (discussed on p. 61). Or the problem may be that sprinkling is done too often and not long enough at one time. Set out empty juice cans to see how much water your sprinklers deliver in the amount of time you let them run. Adjust the timer to deliver water sufficient to sink deeply into the ground.

Another possible problem is that the soil has gotten so dry it won't absorb water. (Dry sandy soils often shed water.) Check now by digging down to take a look. If this is the

How to Keep Water from Pouring Off a Bank

When sloping ground is irrigated water often runs off and pours down the street. It may run off because the ground is hard and dry or simply because insufficient time is allowed for it to sink in. Here are some solutions.

· Apply a layer of mulch over the roots of plants growing on the slope to catch and hold moisture and increase water penetration. (Be sure to irrigate enough that water enters the ground as well as the mulch.)

· Install a time-lapse control clock that pulses water onto the area in brief bursts; the water sinks into the ground during the shut-off periods. (Check the instructions for your existing timer; it may already have this option.)

· Install low-volume sprinklers and set them to run for a longer time.

· If the slope is planted with lawn aerate it in fall and follow up with mulch.

· If all else fails, terrace the area by installing retaining walls or Gardenblock mortarless garden wall (a patented concrete block used to create miniature terraces in which to grow plants on a bank).

problem treat the soil with a surfactant to increase water penetration.

A new technology for keeping the soil in containers from drying out is to work into the soil or soil mix a water-saving polymer, such as Broadleaf P4 (a nontoxic chemical product designed to reduce plant watering frequency). Polymer crystals can aid aeration as they expand and contract. They catch and store up to two hundred times their weight in water and release 95 percent of it to plants as they need it. The crystals remain effective for more than two years. Polymer crystals can also be worked into the ground of flower beds or vegetable gardens where the soil is dry or drains too rapidly, but some cautions must be heeded. Never use them in clay soils, since they could restrict drainage; use them only for shallow-rooted plants, such as annuals and some vegetables; and don't use them in areas where deep-rooted plants like shrubs, trees, or vines are growing, because polymers need to be in contact with roots to be helpful. (Also, a thin layer of damp soil on the surface would harm rather than help such plants by encouraging the growth of shallow roots.) Polymers work best when you place them under the roots of plants at planting time; mix a few granules into the soil in the bottom of each planting hole.

Renew Watering Basins and Terraces.
Creating a basin of soil to hold water around the roots of bushes and trees is a typical way to handle irrigation in the Southwest, particularly on sloping ground, and the basin can be made into a decorative feature. Loose rocks can be used to hold the mounded soil in place. (Early Californians used abalone shells.) In some gardens a permanent system of wooden, concrete, or rock walls can convert steep slopes into usable garden space.

If no rock or cement is used to hold the soil, eventually it will erode away. Now's a good time to check watering basins and rebuild them if necessary. (Get the children involved. Shaping the walls of the basins can be fun, especially if it's wet and muddy.) Sometimes it's best to haul in unwanted clay soil from somewhere else in the garden, if you have some, instead of digging into the soil on a slope and creating more erosion.

Be sure to make tree basins big enough. Water standing around the trunk can cause crown rot and will never reach the roots, which aren't near the trunk but out farther, under the drip line. If the walls of the basin are made high enough the center can be filled with mulch to hold moisture and improve the soil.

Give Special Care to Plants in Containers.
Plants in containers often suffer at this time of year. Water them frequently. (A drip system can save time plus all the water that's wasted when you go from plant to plant with a hose.) In interior zones containers often dry out as soon as they're watered. It's not only the heat; dry air literally pulls moisture out of the soil right through the sides of terra-cotta pots.

Terra-cotta containers add charm to gardens and patios, but unfortunately for aesthetics most plants actually grow better in plastic. The idea that plants are helped by a pot that "breathes" is a mistaken one. The soil mix itself should breathe. It should be light and airy, which can be accomplished by adding perlite or sponge rock. In containers that breathe, roots follow the water as it escapes through the sides of the pot. They form a solid mat that clings to the inside of the pot, drying out daily and causing the plant to wilt. When plants are grown in plastic roots tend to form more evenly throughout the mix. (Eventually they congregate at the bottom and wind around the sides, but then it's time to pot them on to the next size.) Before planting in porous containers seal the insides with a double coat of black waterproofing tar, to help prevent escape of moisture.

Deciduous Fruit Trees

Don't feed deciduous fruit trees now even if you happen to read a newspaper column advocating this practice. Such columns are syndicated for the country at large and the advice doesn't apply here. It's difficult enough for us to get our fruit trees into dormancy in this area without stimulating growth so late in the season.

Prune Unwanted Sprouts. *Water sprouts* are tall shoots that grow in summer straight up from the trunk and branches in the centers of mature deciduous fruit trees. Their growth is so sudden and rapid they soon look like buggy whips. Spot this growth as it begins and cut it out flush with the bark. A tree in which water sprouts have been allowed to persist and take over is a sorry mess. They eventually thicken and bear branches just like miniature trees within a tree, taking energy from the parent and ruining it's shape. Some deciduous fruit trees also send up suckers from the base of the trunk and from roots. Cut these off now too, so they don't sap the strength of the tree.

Water These Trees Infrequently. Water deeply and infrequently to encourage deep rooting, but don't subject your trees to absolute drought unless it's unavoidable. The **Rule of Thumb** is:

Double-Potting Beats the Heat

Hot sun hitting dark-colored containers can burn roots and damage or kill plants. Use double-potting to grow plants in plastic containers, enjoy the artistic look of terra-cotta pots, and keep plant roots cool.

- Plant any item you wish to grow in an appropriately sized plastic container or, when roots aren't crowded, leave it right in the nursery can.

- Sink the planted container into a terra-cotta pot large enough to hide it. (Round Mexican pots are ideal; they hide planted containers best.)

- Fill the outer pot with an insulating layer of damp sphagnum moss, or any lightweight mulch or soil that absorbs water.

- When you water the plant container also water the outer insulating layer. As water evaporates from the mulch it will help cool the inner pot.

- Try covering the soil mix in the plant container with a loose ring of black plastic covered with organic mulch. (Make some holes in the plastic so water can penetrate.) This will help the inner pot to dry out less quickly.

- Spraying the foliage with an antitranspirant, such as Wilt-Pruf or Cloud Cover, can cut down the amount of water that evaporates from leaves and reduce wilting.

Mature deciduous fruit trees growing in hot interior valleys need two or three deep irrigations per month throughout the growing season in order to grow well and bear good fruit. Full-grown trees along the coast should be watered deeply once or twice a month. Trees in sandy soil need more water. Young trees require more frequent water to get established.

Train Fruit Tree Espaliers. Throughout the growing season train the whippy new growth that you want to save into the shape you want, while it's still soft and pliable. Tie it gently but firmly into place. (Refer to pruning manuals such as *Hedges, Screens and Espaliers* by Susan Chamberlain for detailed instructions.) While the branches are still flexible try tying bamboo poles onto them to train them in straight lines. This system can be especially helpful if you're training your espalier onto a wire framework, because wire bends but bamboo is rigid. Remove the poles when the wood has hardened. Cut off unwanted water sprouts, flush with the bark, from espaliered trees too, now.

On trees that bear on spurs, such as apples, apricots, and pears, cut new growth back to two or three buds to stimulate production of fruiting spurs. (Apricots aren't ideal to espalier. After several years, when their old wood no longer bears as well as formerly, retain some well-placed fresh growth to replace it. Then during winter dormancy cut out the old wood; start training the new growth to take its place.)

Pool Planting

Replace or trim drippy vines and trees growing near swimming pools. Tidy vines such as stephanotis, Carolina jessamine (*Gelsemium sempervi-*

rens), and star jasmine (*Trachelospermum jasminoides*) do well in the special microclimate near pools, and they add fragrance. If a tall accent is needed choose a tree that has a tendency to hang onto its foliage until trimmed, such as carrot wood (*Cupaniopsis anacardioides*), many palms, Spanish dagger (*Yucca gloriosa*), giant bird of paradise (*Strelitzia nicolai*), or Australian firewheel tree (*Stenocarpus sinuatus*). For color try epidendrum, succulents, hibiscus, canna lilies, moraea, gazanea, and verbena. These plants aren't messy, and they can stand the refected glare at poolside. Kahili ginger does well if given rich soil, plenty of water, and protection from burning hot sun.

Fuchsias

Most fuchsias look bedraggled and bloomed out in August. Cut them back lightly, pinch the tips for a week or two, and you'll have a second flush of bloom that will last until cold weather. Continue to feed them regularly and remove berries (seed pods).

Cuttings root quickly now. (Use the method described on p. 83.) Take your cuttings from the fresh, succulent growth that results from pruning. Root them in small pots filled with the same potting soil that you grow your fuchsias in, and the plants won't suffer root shock when they're potted on.

Watch for pest problems. If possible avoid spraying other than with a soap spray, like Safer soap, in order to preserve beneficials. Well-fed plants that are free from ants and have an adequate supply of beneficials may never need spraying. However, if you feel you absolutely must spray, the recommended products are BT against certain caterpillars, specific miticides against mites, Science Garden Spray against whiteflies, and Sevin against fuchsia gall mite. (Always mix Sevin with a miticide to prevent an outbreak of spider mites.) Remember that some systemics, such as Orthene, get rid of caterpillars and mites plus many other insects both pest and beneficial. Don't spray everything in the garden or you'll kill all the good guys.

Seaweed for the Garden

At regular intervals our ocean dumps quantities of kelp on local beaches. Most beach-goers find it a nuisance, but some enterprising gardeners take a little home every time they go to the beach to improve their garden soil. All that's needed for gathering is a plastic trash bag, a knife, and a sense of humor. Kelp is tough, slippery, and acts like giant spaghetti. Choose the juicy sections, not the dried-out bits.

Once home rinse off the kelp on the driveway to remove salts. Chop it up, with a spade or machete, and spade it straight into the soil or add it to the compost heap.

Kelp decomposes quickly in the ground. It's rich in trace elements. The ancient Romans worked seaweed into their fields before planting cabbages.

Ferns

Keep ferns well watered during August and September. Protect them from drying winds, which can turn fronds brown and render the plants subject to disease. Most ferns like an atmosphere comparable to the floor of a northern California redwood forest—shady, damp, and thick with acid mulch. The closer you come to it, in an atrium, shady entryway, or some other protected spot, the happier your ferns

Quick Tip

Make Seaweed Tea.
Pour boiling water into a bucket of well-rinsed chopped kelp. Leave it overnight. Decant the liquid, and spray it on plants to increase yields and discourage aphids.

Quick Tip

How to Keep a Difficult Boston Fern Alive.
When you leave for work in the morning take the fern out and hang it under a tree (like putting out the dog). Take it in when you return. One Southern California gardener used this method to keep her fern alive for seven years.

will be. Leather-leaf fern (*Rumohra adiantiformis*) and Southern sword fern (*Nephrolepis cordifolia*) are valuable exceptions to the rule. They're drought resistant, unfussy, and easy. (Sword fern is invasive but is a good filler for narrow, awkward beds.)

Many ferns are sold mainly as houseplants, but few of them can actually survive long inside most homes. (Dallas fern [*Nephrolepis exaltata* 'Dallas'] and Kimberley Queen [*N. obliterata* 'Kimberley Queen'] are exceptions; they can withstand lower light than most ferns.) The common type of Boston ferns (*N. e.* 'Bostoniensis') are among the most often bought and quickly killed of all houseplants. Indoors they die within a few months, but they thrive outdoors in semishade in coastal zones (see the accompanying quick tip). One way to have success with houseplant ferns is to grow them outdoors, but cycle them into the house for a week at a time.

Roses

Continue to feed, fertilize, water, and control rose pests and diseases. If you're following the Rose-Pro Method omit urea this month; instead, give one application of 2 tablespoons of Epsom salts and ½ cup of Milorganite to each plant. Sprinkle both over the top of the soil above the roots and water them into the ground. The Milorganite will provide slow-acting nitrogen in organic form. The Epsom salts provides magnesium. (Continue foliar feeding as described on p. 76.)

Prune Lightly. Roses usually take a rest during the heat of August while they gather strength for a great burst of bloom in fall. You can

cooperate by cutting them back lightly now to stimulate fall flowering. Remove dead twigs, spent flowers, and *hips* (the fruits of roses, which contain the seeds). Cut down a little farther than usual to make new growth for fall bloom. Remove thin, lanky growth back to a promising bud. Cut off suckers sprouting from below the bud union.

Daylilies and Agapanthus

Clean up daylilies (*Hemerocallis*) and agapanthus now by removing stems that have bloomed. On most daylilies the stems go brown after flowering; simply yank these off. But many varieties, especially the newer everblooming ones, have stems that never go brown. Instead they stay green and continue to grow; don't try to pull them off or you'll uproot the plant. After these green stems finish flowering they sprout leaves and form plantlets, called proliferates, high on the stem. As soon as the proliferates have formed one or two short roots, cut the stems off the mother plant, so they don't sap its strength. Gently snap off the pups and plant them elsewhere in the garden, or give them to friends.

Agapanthus stems have to be cut off. Some gardeners hang them upside down to dry and then use them in flower arrangements or dip them in glue and glitter for holiday decorations.

Moraea

Moraea, or fortnight lily (*Dietes vegeta* or *D. iridioides*), has white blossoms with orange blotches on them. It's good near swimming pools, and is drought resistant, easy to grow, and one of our commonest plants—some people think it's much too common. There's also a yellow type (*D. bicolor*). Both have clumps of upright narrow, pointed leaves and bear their flowers in flushes every two weeks or so, spring through fall—sometimes year-round. Keep them looking their best by feeding them lightly now and watering them well. After flowers fade from the yellow species cut off the flower stalk at the base. With white moraeas remove the seed pods to clean up the plants and promote continued flowering, but don't remove the stalks; they'll bloom for several years.

Alstroemeria

Peruvian lilies or alstroemerias (*Alstroemeria aurea, A. aurantiaca, A. psittacina, A. ligtu,* and hybrids) are members of the lily family whose azalealike blossoms and many virtues have captivated the hearts of local gardeners in recent years. The plants are considerably drought resistant; the blooms have sturdy stems, and their cut flowers last two weeks. The craze for alstroemerias began when a photograph of the Berkeley Botanical Gardens' massive display of peach, orange, and gold ligtu hybrids was published on the cover of *Sunset* Magazine. But ligtu hybrids have some drawbacks; it takes at least three years to get them going, and once established they're almost impossible to irradicate or transplant. Their tall flowers make a magnificent display, but they do so only once a year in June and July. Alstroemeria seeds are widely available though difficult to germinate. You can order the plants of ligtu hybrids from mail order houses (including B & D Lilies, 330 P Street, Port Townsend, WA 98368; 206/385-1738).

Now Fred Meyer, a San Diego hybridizer, is developing a whole new group of alstroemeria hybrids mainly for the flower industry. The Meyer hybrids are more heat resistant, easier to grow, and less invasive than the ligtu types. They also bloom longer, and can be transplanted, divided, or moved in fall. They come in many shades of white, lavender, maroon, rose, and pink with stems ranging in height from 1½ feet to 2½ feet. They're available at select nurseries throughout Southern California. If you let them go dry in summer they won't die, though they will stop blooming, but if you water, feed, and deadhead them regularly many of them will bloom on and off year-round.

Look for Meyer hybrid alstroemerias in summer and plant them in fall in loose, well-drained soil with plenty of organic matter worked in. After a few years divide and transplant the clumps, handling the tubers gently to preserve their delicate roots. After the flowers fade remove each spent stalk by giving it a sharp tug. By pulling off the stems singly you remove them cleanly and safely from the tubers, and this stimulates the plant to produce more bloom spikes. Follow up each wave of bloom with an application of complete fertilizer, and water it thoroughly into the ground.

Wisteria

Wisteria sends out long twining stems in summer. On young vines continue to train these where you want them to go, and tie them loosely in place. Catch them before they get twisted around each other. They'll eventually become a structure of thick vines from which the flower spurs will spring. If your vine is mature keep only those stems on the outer edges where you have more space for wisteria to cover. Cut all unwanted new stems back to two buds, to encourage more flower spurs to grow.

Water and feed young vines for growth. Give mature vines one deep watering in August.

Trees for August Bloom

Crape myrtle (*Lagerstroemia indica*) is an elegant, drought-resistant tree for small-space gardens in interior valleys. (It gets mildew along the coast.) It blooms in white and electric shades of pink and red from July through August. Its lovely gray-brown bark peels off yearly to soft pink. Look for the plants while they're in bloom. (People either love or hate some of the colors.)

Among the cassias that can be grown here the gold medallion tree (*Cassia leptophylla*) is the most dramatic. It's best in a warm, sheltered spot and when watered deeply and infrequently, but it will grow in lawns if it has excellent drainage.

Along the coast flame eucalyptus (*Eucalyptus ficifolia*) can grow in the teeth of the wind and still bloom magnificently. Pick out the color now, if possible. (Young ones often won't bloom in the can.) The orangy red is gorgeous viewed against the sea. Grow it with a single trunk, or, if desired, cut it back to make a huge, multibranched shrub. It blooms on and off all year. The eucalyptus beetle prefers gum eucalypts and usually doesn't attack this unless it's under stress from drought.

Control of Nematodes

Nematodes are especially active in warm weather. These are microscopic worms that bore into roots of susceptible plants, causing galls and knots and weakening the plants. Here are two ways to significantly reduce large populations of nematodes.

Solarize the Soil. Solarization—using the effects of the sun's rays—is the method to use only when nematode and fungus problems are acute and unbearable. It kills useful organisms, including worms and beneficial fungi, along with the bad ones. (This method works best where summer days are hot—90°F or 32°C—and skies are clear.)

· If nematodes and fungus have rendered a vegetable or flower area unusable sacrifice the plants now. Pull them out roots and all. (Don't compost the roots, destroy them.)

· Thoroughly soak the soil with water.

· Cover the area with clear (not black) polyethylene plastic that's 1 to 4 millimeters thick. Peg it down around the outside, and bury the loose edges. (A few round rocks in the middle will hold it down in case of strong wind.) Tests at UC Davis show even better results with two layers of clear 1-millimeter polyethylene film separated by a 6-centimeter air space. (Prop up the top layer here and there with wire hoops or bamboo frame.)

· Leave the plastic in place for six to eight weeks of hot, sunny weather. Test plots under single plastic in the San Joaquin Valley reached 140°F (60°C) at a depth of two inches and 102°F (39°C) as far down as 18 inches. Almost all traces of harmful disease organisms were destroyed, including fungi.

Plant Marigolds. Many people think marigolds repel nematodes, but the truth is they attract them. Root knot nematodes entering marigold roots are killed by a natural plant chemical before they have a chance to reproduce. Planting a single row of marigolds among vegetables won't get rid of nematodes, however. Marigolds can be used to rid the ground of these pests, but you have to start earlier in the planting season. Consider this method for next year.

- In March solidly plant the area to be treated with French marigolds (*Tagetes patula*). Space the plants in a 7-by-7-inch pattern all over the bed.
- Leave the marigolds in place for a full 120-day season of growth.
- Systematically remove all weeds at their earliest appearance.

After this treatment the ground can be planted with any desired crop. Nematodes will gradually return, but they'll be discouraged if you regularly add organic soil amendment. They don't like humusy soil.

Control of Fireblight

Fireblight is a bacterial disease of the rose family (*Rosaceae*) that infects such common garden plants as apples, pears, evergreen pear (*Pyrus kawakamii*), pyracantha, cotoneaster, California holly (toyon), plum, cherry, quince, and loquat. (Some plant varieties are resistant.) Fireblight first wilts the fresh green growth, then shrivels and blackens it as well as twigs, branches, berries, and fruit, making the victim look as if it had been caught in a flash fire. Birds and insects carry the bacteria from tree to tree during the bloom period.

Remove disfigured twigs and branches now to reduce the sources of infection. Cut out infected branches 8 to 15 inches below any visible damage, and destroy them. (Dip the pruning shears in rubbing alcohol after making each cut in order to avoid spreading the infection.)

Flower Beds and Containers

Gardeners who want to grow their own transplants of winter flowers, particularly tall rather than dwarf varieties or single colors rather than mixed, should plant seeds of cool-season flowers now. Plant in flats, small pots, or peat pots. If you can't find the seeds you want locally kick off your shoes, relax in the shade, study the seed catalogues, and send away for seeds. A few varieties may be sold out but most are still available, and service now is swift.

Seeds of such flowers as pansies, cineraria, dianthus, delphiniums, violas, nemesia, Iceland poppies, primroses, snapdragons, stock, and calendulas, planted in August, can give great numbers of transplants with which to fill beds in October. Tall varieties of stock are particularly worthwhile growing from seeds, since you can be assured of disease-free transplants. (Stock is susceptible to stem and root rots so don't plant them in the same place two years in a row.)

To grow stock disinfect flats and fill them with sterilized potting soil. Place the seeds on top of the soil, carefully spacing them where you want them; press them down gently. (Stock needs light to germinate.) Keep them moist and in semishade. Cover the flats with plastic until the seeds germinate. Then take off the plastic, protect the sprouts with netting, and move the flats in stages—over a period of two or three weeks—into increasing light, eventually into full sun. Start to feed the plants lightly when each has two real leaves. (Read catalogues carefully; some varieties have more doubles and fewer singles than others. Weaker-looking seedlings with grayer foliage are usually singles; healthier-looking, darker green ones are doubles.) The sooner you get stock in the ground the better, because early planting enables the plants to build big, strong root systems and hefty stalks. You'll reap a long-lasting and dramatic display.

Fire Protection

There's no sure way to protect your home from a raging fire, but there are some things you can do to minimize risk. If you live next to native brush or chaparral—near a canyon, for example—take these steps to protect your property.

- Keep the landscape close to your home well watered. Don't grow such flammable plants as pine trees close to your home or allow them to overhang your roof. (Shrubs and trees with lush green leaves, like pittosporum, are recommended for green belts.)

- Don't mound shrubbery close to your house. Shrubs should be spaced apart from each other and kept low. For safety from fire when houses are close together it's best to have no shrubbery between them.

- Create a buffer zone. A well-watered green area of low-growing plants can act as a firebreak between you and the chaparral. The buffer zone should be at least 30 feet wide on flat ground and progressively wider as slopes get steeper. Walls, rocks, patios, rustic seats, and wandering paths can be part of

the landscaping. Use plant materials that have proven their ability to withstand some fires, such as succulents and cacti. Coarse carpobrotus iceplant is not recommended, but rosea iceplant (*Drosanthemum floribundum*) is. (Ask your local UC Cooperative Extension Office or the California Department of Forestry for additional information and plant lists.)

- Manage the existing brush. Go right down into the chaparral and remove the fuel load from inside. (Be on the lookout for poison oak, rattlesnakes, and sudden drop-offs in the terrain.) The buildup of dead leaves, twigs, branches, and weeds in the understory is what makes the hottest fires. You may have to use a chain saw. (Keep a fire extinguisher and a shovel close at hand in case of sparks.) Cut out and haul away or chip and compost all the dead stuff that builds up inside native shrubs. Leave all the green growth, on the outside. When you're finished you'll have a wonderland of usable space for birds and other wildlife that inhabit our precious chaparral.

Tropicals

It's somewhat late for planting most tropicals this month, except in coastal zones. Among tropicals that can be planted along the coast now (or during any summer month) are papayas, bananas, and palms.

Plant Papayas and Bananas. Papayas (*Carica*) and bananas (*Musa, Ensete*) will grow and bear fruit in all frost-free zones, but they do best near the coast and thrive on sheltered, south-facing hillsides. Papayas are tall, single-trunked, succulent trees with a palmlike cluster of leaves on top. It's a common misconception that bananas, like papayas, grow on trees, but they actually grow on a large, green, herbaceous, perennial plant. The apparent trunk of a banana plant is actually formed of a group of leaf stalks. Surprisingly, the fruits themselves are technically berries.

Plant Papayas from Seed or Plants. If you compost papaya skins and seeds many papaya plants will come up here and there during the summer. Look for these seedlings now and plant a group of three to five of them in full sun, 4 to 6 feet apart. (You need both male and female plants to get fruit.) Feed your papayas for growth and provide them with good drainage and plenty of water. Or start papaya seeds in flats. For the quickest germination, rub a handful of seeds gently on a piece of screen under running water to remove the aril (protective seed covering). Sprout the seeds in the kitchen on a plate that's covered with a wet paper towel and surrounded with a plastic bag. As soon as the seeds sprout plant them carefully in a premoistened flat of fast-draining potting soil. Keep them damp in bright—not dark—shade; a warm shady spot with an hour of morning sun is ideal.

You can also purchase papaya plants at nurseries specializing in rare and tropical fruits, such as Papaya Tree Farms in Granada Hills, Exotica Seed Company in Vista, or Pacific Tree Farms in Chula Vista. The babaco papaya is a popular type because, though it's expensive, it's hardy to 28°F (-2°C), and the plant is small enough to grow in a whiskey half-barrel. Babaco papayas bear fruit when young, often while they're still in a 5-gallon can, and you only need one plant

How to Tell When Home-Grown Bananas Are Ripe

Some varieties ripen on the plant. For these, when the fruit begins to turn yellow, reach up with a long-handled fruit picker or pruning hook, and pick one banana. If it's creamy yellow inside, and is soft textured and sweet, it's ready. To harvest, cut off individual hands of fruit as they ripen or, if they're too far out of reach, cut the whole trunk down as described below.

Most varieties don't ripen on the plant. Pick their fruit when they've lost their sharp edges and indented sides; wait until they lose their angularity. When the fruit is still green but has become rounded, filled out, and fat looking it's ready to pick. (You will know if you have this type of plant because the fruit will not turn yellow on the plant.)

Once ready, cut the whole plant down by nicking the underside of the trunk with a sharp knife or giving it a single whack with a machete. It will fall of its own weight. Ask someone to stand below and catch the fruit as it falls. Cut off the entire fruit scape and hang it in a shady place to ripen, such as your front porch or patio overhang. When individual bananas go yellow they're ready to eat.

Chop up the remains of the stalk that's borne fruit; use it to mulch the rest of your bananas, or bury it and let it rot. Plant your next banana there.

* ❋ *

Don't Overprune Washingtonia Palms

Don't cut all the dead fronds from the Mexican fan palm (*Washingtonia robusta*)—the one with a thin trunk that's drought resistant—or the California fan palm (*Washingtonia filifera*)—the one with a thicker trunk and that needs more water. In nature the dead fronds of Washingtonia palms naturally hang on the tree and are the favored nesting place for hooded orioles. The orioles attach nests woven from palm threads to the undersides of the fronds. If you leave the fronds in place these beautiful birds will have a nesting place in your neighborhood. When all the fronds are cut off the birds fly frantically from tree to tree.

Highly trimmed palms also unfortunately look like long-handled chimney brushes. This treatment may be necessary in business districts, but in gardens Washingtonias look more beautiful and graceful with a natural covering of fronds on the trunk. If desired clean off the lower 8 or 10 feet of trunk and, for a neat look, cut the bottom fronds off straight.

* ❋ *

to get fruit. The fruit is large—sometimes a foot long—and equal in health-giving properties to other papayas, but it tastes more like a melon than like an ordinary papaya. The fruit starts to ripen between now and fall. Pick it when it's yellow and gives slightly to the touch.

Start Bananas from Plants You Buy at a Nursery. When growing bananas begin with a good variety, such as Ice Cream or Enano Giganti. (The plants are small but the fruit is giant.) Fertilize them often with a complete fertilizer, such as 16-16-16. Bananas are big eaters. They're also thirsty, so water them well. You can keep them barely alive with less water and fertilizer in drought years, but their growth will slow down and they won't bear fruit.

As suckers, or pups, form around the main trunk use a sharp spade to slice off all but one, and plant them elsewhere in the garden. The one pup you leave will remain to replace the mature stalk after it's borne fruit. (Each stalk of a banana plant is monocarpic and won't bear fruit again.) At thirteen to fifteen months after planting, you should have a scape covered with fruit.

Transplant Palms. Summer is a good time to plant or transplant palms, since they take off well when planted in warm soil. Before transplanting any palm be sure it's a species that can be transplanted successfully. Most can; a few cannot. Trim off all faded fronds and cut back the remaining fronds by one-third to make up for the loss of roots. Bend these upright and tie them together on top with stout twine to protect the meristem layer (the area of actively dividing cells at the bud of the plant). Each single-trunked palm has only one bud; if it's damaged the tree will die. After transplanting leave the fronds tied for a month or two to shade the bud. (Be sure to water palms well after planting and keep them well watered for at least a year, until established.)

Palms can lend a tropical atmosphere to any garden, and not all are high water users; some are drought resistant. They're incredibly interesting and varied, so before choosing a palm study the options and your requirements. Notice that some palms have fronds (leaves) shaped like feathers and others have fronds shaped like fans. Some palms form a clump while others are solitary. Some palms are self-cleaning—the fronds fall off without pruning. The fronds of others cling to the trunk after they're dead and need to be pruned off, or in some cases the old fronds look best left on the tree. Among those with persistent fronds, some have trunks that are easily cleaned off by pruning while others have leaf bases that tend to stay on the trunk for many years. An important factor to consider if you have children is that some palms are armed with formidable spikes; others are unarmed.

Cycads

Cycads (Cycadaceae) are among the most ancient plants on earth, dating from the age of dinosaurs. They're also one of nature's first attempts at making seeds. Male plants bear prominent cones that give off pollen, while female plants develop a sporophyll (a brushlike spore-bearing organ) that can produce seeds if fertilized, a rare occurrence in gardens. In appearance cycads look like ferns or palms, but they're not even closely related to either of them. The best known and most often grown cycad is often mistaken for a palm and even

Protect Canary Island Date Palms from Fungus

Before having Canary Island date palms (*Phoenix canariensis*) pruned insist that the tree pruners sterilize all pruning tools by soaking their blades for 15 minutes in a solution of 1 part household bleach to 1 part water. (Request that a saw with a reciprocating blade be used—not a chainsaw, which cannot be effectively disinfected.) Pruning with unsterilized saws causes healthy date palms to fall prey to fungus attacks, because it allows spores carried from infected palms to enter fresh cuts. As an additional precaution remove only dead and dying fronds, not fresh green growth.

bears the confusing name of sago palm (*Cycas revoluta*). In gardens cycads are long lived and slow growing. They grow well outdoors in most of Southern California, if provided with some shade.

Water cycads well now; don't let their roots dry out. When cycads are neglected their leaves may turn brown, pale, whitish, or yellow in color. Brown tips on leaves usually come from salt burn (sago palms are particularly sensitive to salts in the soil); drench the ground to leach out salts. Pale or brown patches on the leaves can come from sunburn; consider digging up the plant and transplanting it into more shade. All-over pale or yellow leaves most likely mean lack of nitrogen or trace elements; pour a complete liquid fertilizer such as Terr-O-Vite around the roots of the plant at intervals of two or three weeks throughout the growing season, and provide it with ample water. (Cycads also respond well to applications of foliar fertilizer.)

Yellowing and loss of color may also result from insect attack. Scale is the worst offender. Look under the fronds for small, round, brown bumps—these are scale insects. The safest way to get rid of them now is to painstakingly scrub them off with a brush or sponge dipped in soapy solution; they come off easily. Oil sprays kill scale, but oil can damage foliage in hot weather. Malathion is recommended against scale insects, but it works best in spring while the insects are in their crawling stage. (Spray several times in early spring at intervals of a week or two.)

Lawn Care

This is the time of year when warm-season lawns, such as Bermuda, zoysia, and St. Augustine, are looking their best, but cool-season lawns, such as Kentucky bluegrass, perennial ryegrass, and tall fescue are looking their worst. Water warm-season lawns deeply and infrequently, feed them every month to six weeks, and mow them as short as possible. Feed dichondra half-strength. Don't feed kikuyu, Futurf, or Adalayd grass (sometimes called Excalibre) in August. Continue to water cool-season lawns regularly, cut them high, and feed them lightly, if at all. (Overfeeding cool-season lawns now can stress them. See p. 161 for basic guidelines on summer care for lawns.)

Control Crabgrass When It Turns Red. Now, in August, you have yet another chance to control crabgrass—this time when it goes red in color but before it sets seed. Ask for products containing DSMA or ASMA. Be sure to follow the directions on the package and not to use these products in the middle of a hot day. Water deeply the day before use, and then avoid watering again as long as possible. For best results pull out the clumps after they die. (Another possible control is to spot-treat with glyphosate, but it will kill anything it touches.)

Control Pests and Diseases on Cool-Season Lawns. Dead or brown patches often disfigure cool-season lawns now even if you water and feed lightly. Take hold of a tuft of grass in one of the bad patches and yank up on it. If the patch is circular and grass blades pull off at the roots but the roots stay in the ground, the problem may be brown-patch fungus. Some other fungus diseases cause variously shaped brown patches; with these the grass sticks tight when you pull on it. In some cases there's a dark green or grayish green line or circle around the damaged patch. (Consult *The Ortho Problem Solver*, edited by Michael D. Smith, for pictures and descriptions.)

Treat affected grass with fungicide. Always read the entire label and follow all directions and precautions carefully. Unless you use a product that already contains fertilizer, follow up with light application of it. Water early in the morning, not late in the day. Aerate the ground to improve water penetration.

If you've noticed large numbers of moths fluttering in a zigzag pattern over the lawn in the evening and the grass blades are chewed off at ground level, look among the roots for silky white tubes with brown or gray black-spotted grubs in them. These are signs of sod webworm.

For this treat the lawn with a spray or granular product recommended for controlling webworms.

If the grass is loose and comes up like a mat, roots and all, the problem is white grubs. Roll the turf back and look for curled white grubs living under the turf and eating the roots. (In our area these are not grubs of the Japanese beetle, as is the case in the East and Middle West, but of several other beetles.) Treat with a product recommended for the control of white grubs, such as diazinon. They're easiest to kill when young, but you may have to treat more than once.

Vegetable Gardening

The main jobs in the vegetable garden this month are watering, harvesting, and pest control. All summer vegetables can be planted now, especially the heat lovers, but most gardeners prefer to wait this month out and start planting winter crops in mid-September. Most vegetable gardens in interior zones get pretty well burned up by the end of August.

Start Seeds for Cool-Season Crops. By midmonth seeds can be started in flats or peat pots for bedding plants to put in the ground in fall. (Keep them in semishade.) Good candidates are celery and all members of the cabbage family, including broccoli, cauliflower, cabbage, and Brussels sprouts. Home-grown transplants will be ready to put out in the garden in late September or October. If you need only a few it's much less trouble to buy transplants at the nursery.

Unfortunately, these plants bought at nurser-ies are usually labeled generically rather than by variety. Learn about good varieties for your zone, and ask your nursery to carry them as transplants. Patronize companies that grow "gourmet varieties." They're more expensive, but there's a good reason: the seeds cost more. If enough gardeners become informed buyers bedding plant growers and nurseries will gladly give them what they want.

Control Corn Earworm. If your corn is badly attacked by corn earworm now and you're not an organic gardener, try dusting the silks with Sevin. (Treat when the silks first emerge and continue to treat every three to five days until the silks turn brown.) Mineral oil on the silk has been tried with varying success by organic gardeners. In my garden I don't even try to combat this pest, since the worms usually don't do more than disfigure the tops of the ears. If yours are being rendered inedible perhaps you're waiting too long to pick. (Directions for when to harvest corn are given on p. 192.)

Corn needs lots of water while it's forming ears. Once you've picked them cook the fresh corn no more than three minutes after the second boil.

Continue to Harvest, and Take Stock for Next Year. This is the time of year when people who love to can and freeze are happily stashing away jars and bags of produce for winter use, and those of us who don't are giving away armloads of vegetables and perhaps vowing to plant less next year. By now first-time gardeners have learned that you don't need a whole row of zucchini to feed a family of four—three plants are plenty—but you never can plant enough corn—it goes fast.

Purchase / Plant

- [ ] Continue to plant **tropicals** in coastal zones, 152
- [ ] Transplant into the garden **biennials** you started from seed in July, when they are 2 or 3 inches high, 180
- [ ] In coastal zones continue to purchase, plant, and transplant **succulents,** including **cacti** and **euphorbias,** 185
- [ ] Replace **untidy plants** growing near swimming pools with better choices, 203
- [ ] Choose **crape myrtles** in interior zones, 208
- [ ] Purchase **cassias** and pick out **flame eucalyptus** to plant in coastal zones, 208
- [ ] Grow your own transplants by planting seeds of **cool-season flowers,** 209
- [ ] Plant buffer zones between your home and **native chaparral,** 210
- [ ] Plant **papayas, bananas,** and **palms,** 210
- [ ] Transplant **palms,** 212
- [ ] If you want to grow your own **vegetable transplants** start seeds of **cool-season vegetables** now, 215

Trim, Prune, Mow, Divide

- [ ] Stop pinching **chrysanthemums,** 79
- [ ] Cut back **petunias** in mid-August to keep them flowering, 179
- [ ] Cut off water sprouts and suckers from **deciduous fruit trees,** 203
- [ ] Prune and train **espaliers** throughout the growing season, 204
- [ ] Trim untidy **trees** and **vines** growing near swimming pools, 204
- [ ] Give **fuchsias** a light midsummer pruning, 204
- [ ] Give **roses** a light midsummer pruning; remove suckers, 206
- [ ] Clean up **daylilies** and **agapanthus** by removing stems that have bloomed, 206
- [ ] Propagate **daylilies** by planting the proliferates, 206
- [ ] Cut off bloom stalks from **yellow fortnight lilies;** take off seed pods only from **white fortnight lilies,** 206
- [ ] Prune and train **wisteria,** 207
- [ ] Clean out **native brush;** clear buffer zones, 210
- [ ] Leave some dead fronds on **Washingtonia palms** as nesting sites for orioles, 212
- [ ] Remove only dead and dying foliage from **date palms;** use sterilized tools, 213
- [ ] Pull out dead **crabgrass** if you have previously treated it with weed killer, 214

Fertilize

- [ ] Feed **fuchsias,** 55
- [ ] Feed **tuberous begonias,** 78, 177
- [ ] Feed **water lilies,** 110
- [ ] Feed **cymbidiums** with a high-nitrogen fertilizer for growth, 130
- [ ] Feed **ferns,** 132
- [ ] Feed **tropicals,** 152
- [ ] Fertilize **warm-season grasses** with the exception of Adalayd and kikuyu; feed dichondra half-strength, 161
- [ ] If **cool-season lawns** show signs of nitrogen deficiency (yellow leaves, stunted growth) fertilize lightly; otherwise not at all, 161
- [ ] Fertilize **biennials** started from seed in July with fish emulsion at weekly intervals, 180
- [ ] Feed all container-grown **succulents** with a well-diluted complete liquid fertilizer, 186
- [ ] Don't fertilize **deciduous fruit trees** now, 203
- [ ] Fertilize **roses,** 205
- [ ] Feed **fortnight lilies** lightly; follow up with water, 206
- [ ] Feed and water **cycads,** 213

Water

- [ ] Reduce irrigation of **cantaloupes** when melons start to ripen, 142
- [ ] Continue to water **succulents,** 186
- [ ] Be sure to water **plants** adequately during hot dry weather, 200
- [ ] Don't water **summer-deciduous native plants,** 200
- [ ] Water drought-resistant plants, including **Mexican fan palms** and **Aleppo pines,** 200
- [ ] Water **floss silk trees** and **coral trees** early in the month, 200
- [ ] Study your **irrigation system** to see if it can be made more efficient, 201
- [ ] Check for malfunctioning **sprinklers** and **drip emitters,** 201
- [ ] Install a new backup battery in your **irrigation control clock,** 201
- [ ] Flush filters and headers of **drip systems,** 201
- [ ] If **lawns** develop brown areas find out what's causing the problem and solve it, 201
- [ ] Renew **watering basins,** 202
- [ ] Make watering basins for **large trees** out under the drip line, not next to the trunk, 202
- [ ] Water **plants in containers,** 202
- [ ] Water **deciduous fruit trees** in accordance with their age and your soil and climate zone, 203
- [ ] Water **roses** with up to 1½ inches of water three times a week, 205
- [ ] Keep **ferns** well watered and protect them from drying winds, 206
- [ ] Give mature **wisteria vines** at least one deep watering, 208
- [ ] Keep **transplanted palms** well watered, 213
- [ ] Water **warm-season lawns** deeply at least once a week in most zones. Water **cool-season lawns** more shallowly and frequently, 214
- [ ] Water **vegetables,** 215

Control Pests, Diseases, and Weeds

- [ ] Continue to control **weeds** by mulching, cultivating, and hand pulling, 170
- [ ] Control **rose** pests and diseases, 172
- [ ] Control pests on **fuchsias,** 204
- [ ] Control serious **nematode** and **fungus** problems with soil solarization, 208
- [ ] Control **fireblight** by removing disfigured branches and twigs, 209
- [ ] Protect **Canary Island date palms** from fungus, 213
- [ ] Check **cycads** for scale, 214
- [ ] Control **crabgrass** after it goes red with a selective crabgrass killer, if desired, 214
- [ ] Control pests and diseases that cause dead brown patches on **cool-season lawns,** 214
- [ ] Look for signs of sod webworm on **lawns,** particularly **cool-season lawns;** treat if necessary, 214
- [ ] Control white grubs on **cool-season lawns,** 215
- [ ] Control **corn** earworm if desired, 215

Also This Month

- [ ] Watch **cantaloupes** for signs of ripening; pick them at "full slip," 192
- [ ] Continue to harvest **summer vegetables,** 192, 215
- [ ] Before planting in **porous containers** seal the insides with a coat of tar, 203
- [ ] Use double-potting to keep roots of **container-grown plants** cool, 203
- [ ] Gather **seaweed** for the garden, 205
- [ ] Keep **indoor ferns,** including **Boston ferns,** alive in coastal zones by giving them equal time outdoors, 205
- [ ] Order seeds and **supplies for fall planting** from mail-order catalogues, 209
- [ ] If you live next to **native chaparral** consider ways to minimize risk of fires, 210
- [ ] Harvest **bananas** when they are ready, according to type, 211
- [ ] Untie the fronds of **palms** transplanted in June, 212

SEPTEMBER

The First Fall Planting Month

September marks the beginning of the fall planting season, one of the most absorbing and busiest times of year in the garden. This is when we switch gears in preparation for winter, and winter is a great time to garden here. Beginning now, over a period of two or three months, we switch annual flowers from those that bloom in summer to those that bloom in winter and spring, and we switch vegetables from warm-season to cool-season crops. Spring-flowering bulbs fill nursery shelves, and some can be planted in September. Warm-season lawns can still be planted now, and cool-season lawns can be planted along the coast. In addition most bushes, shrubs, trees, and ground covers, other than tropicals, do best when planted in fall before the winter rains.

This great flurry of activity doesn't happen all at once. Start now to clean out faded flowers and vegetables, but leave good ones in place to enjoy as long as they're still going. Prepare the ground, begin to plant—but keep in mind that October's still ahead and it's the best planting month of the year.

Meanwhile continue to water deeply and according to the individual needs of plants. Though nights may begin to cool off along the coast and shadows are noticeably lengthening, early September is largely a continuation of summer weather. Sunny warm days are the norm. More often than not we get a blast of extremely hot weather and Santa Ana winds before midmonth. If this happens water early in the day or in the evening. Also, check drought-resistant plants, other than summer-dormant natives, for signs of stress. One deep watering now can sometimes save the life of a tree or bush that's hanging on the brink of extinction and tide it over to the winter rains. Many mature trees, like Torrey and Aleppo pines, could be saved from beetle attack and other horrors if only people would realize they need to be watered at least once now. Put a sprinkler under the canopy to the drip line and let it run for several hours, without runoff. When water supplies are curtailed because of a drought, use the precious water you have to irrigate mature shrubs, trees, and vines. Let your lawn and petunias die if you must, but save your valuable old plants—especially trees.

Bulbs

One of September's most important and exciting jobs is to start buying and planting spring-flowering bulbs. Bulbs are easy plants to grow. They have a mystique bordering on the miraculous, but growing them here in Southern California is different from growing them in the East or Middle West. Many bulbs need to undergo a cold winter in order to bloom. Some will bloom without cold weather but tend to rot during our hot, dry summers. Others can be grown here after being prechilled in the refrigerator, but in many cases they won't naturalize (come back year after year, bloom, and multiply). Countering these drawbacks, we're able to grow a huge number of charming and fascinating bulbs that are little known and rarely grown back East. Many of these naturalize readily, are drought resistant, and are almost unbelievably easy to grow.

Buy Bulbs Now to Plant Later. Begin purchasing spring-flowering bulbs in mid-September. They soon get picked over and sometimes put back in the wrong bins. A reliable local nursery is the best source of varieties that will do well in your climate zone, though some rare varieties can only be bought from catalogues. Choose the largest and fattest bulbs, because they produce the biggest blooms.

Among hardy bulbs (the kind grown in cold-winter climates) the best choices for Southern California are daffodils (*Narcissus*), hyacinths, Dutch irises (*Iris xiphium* hybrids), and tulips. In inland gardens add grape hyacinths—muscari. (*Muscari armeniacum* is best adapted to our climate.) Crocuses are difficult to grow in Southern California, though *Crocus vernus* may succeed in inland valleys. Italian species crocuses, such as *C. niveus*, are rare but can naturalize in some gardens. Most trumpet and large-cupped narcissus have to be replaced yearly, although two varieties, February Gold and Fortune, will often naturalize and eventually form large clumps.

Look for daffodils with three or more divisions. Don't pull them apart. If they're still connected, each point will produce a bloom. Feel them gently to make sure they're firm to the touch; softness means rot. Hyacinths perform best and give the most bloom if you buy large bulbs. Tulips have to be bought yearly. (You could dig them in fall and rechill them, but those who try this find that, though the bulbs can attain great size, their flowers are tiny and on short stems because of our hot summer weather.) Don't buy "naked" tulip bulbs, ones that have lost their tunics (the brown papery skin)—they might be dried out.

Take daffodils, hyacinths, tulips, crocuses, anemones, grape hyacinths, and ranunculus home but don't plant the bulbs yet. Getting them in the ground too early is a big mistake. Keep them cool and dry. The garage is usually a good place. Hyacinths, crocuses, and tulips other than the lady tulip (*Tulipa clusiana*) need to be chilled beginning next month or in November for six to eight weeks, prior to planting, but you don't have to put them in the refrigerator just yet. (Prechilled tulips are available from some mail order companies, including Breck's Bulbs: U.S. Reservation Center, 6523 North Galena Road, Peoria, IL 61632; 309/691-4610. It's best to order them in spring or summer; they arrive at planting time.) Grape hyacinths, or muscari, don't need prechilling, but they usually don't grow well in coastal gardens. In interior zones muscari sometimes come back year after year. Narcissus, ranunculus, anemones, and Dutch irises need no prechilling.

Buy Bulbs to Plant Now. Some bulbs can and should be planted in September as soon as you buy them. Among these are some superb choices from the daffodil (*Narcissus*) tribe that naturalize readily and often spread over large areas. These are known as the Tazetta and Tazetta hybrids, and they include paper whites, Grand Soleil d'Or, Golden Dawn, Matador, Chinese sacred lilies, and Geranium. Save some for forcing in pebbles later (p. 280). They're popular and sell out early.

Most important to purchase and plant now are the many captivating drought-resistant bulbs that are well adapted to our climate—so well, they'll often naturalize even in areas that receive little or no summer water. Among these are various oxalis from the Western Hemisphere and many bulbs and corms from South Africa, such as freesia, ixia, sparaxis, streptanthera, babiana, watsonia, lapeirousia, tritonia, montbretia, *Chasmanthe aethiopica*, and crocosmia. Most can take summer water if drainage is good. Some actually need it—for example *Crocosmia masoniorum* 'Lucifer', an excellent variety for June bloom. (You may have to order it

by mail.) Chasmanthe, often incorrectly called crocosmia, tritonia, or montbretia, has tall, straplike leaves and orange flowers, and it's so drought resistant it naturalizes even under invasive eucalyptus. *Ornithogalum arabicum* has long-lasting white flowers with unique, shiny-black, beadlike centers that bloom later than other spring-flowering bulbs. Chincherinchee (*O. thyrsoides*) has white blooms on 2-foot stems. Both thrive in flower beds. Spring star flower (*Ipheion uniflorum*) is great for planting around the edges of beds. Once you get it going it multiplies rapidly, comes back every year, and blooms for several months in winter and spring.

When purchasing your bulbs jot down the directions for planting as to depth and spacing. A general ☞ **Rule of Thumb** is: *Plant large bulbs at a depth that equals twice their height and small bulbs a little deeper than twice the height of the bulb.* (There are exceptions to this rule, so to be sure of correct depths and other care, refer to a bulb handbook. The best one for our area is *Bulbs, How to Select, Grow and Enjoy,* by George Harmon Scott.

Consider the Lilies. Lilies are dramatic plants in the garden but, while some gardeners swear by them, they have a reputation of being difficult to grow here. They need excellent soil, good drainage, and constant moisture—they're not good choices for drought years. There are many complicated differences among them. They're classified under nine divisions, within which there are hundreds of varieties and species. In general new varieties are easier to grow than old ones. Some may do well in one zone but not in another. The best way to find kinds adapted to your garden is through trial and error, and by purchasing your bulbs at a local nursery that has a good reputation for carrying the right things. If you live inland grow early varieties for June bloom. My own experience is that Mid-Century hybrids and the Imperial Series, classified under Division 7 (Oriental Hybrids), are the easiest. (Try growing Imperial Pink; it often succeeds where others fail.) I've also seen Regal lilies (*Lilium regale*, a species discovered by the plant explorer "Chinese" Wilson and favored by Gertrude Jekyll) with flower stems 6 feet tall. They were thriving in a semishaded bed in Altadena, and the gardener claimed they were easy to grow.

Plant lilies as soon as you get them home. They never go completely dormant and must never be allowed to dry out. All lilies need loose, humusy, well-drained, moist soil (sandy loam is best) with plenty of bone meal worked in beneath the roots. Plant them at twice the depth of the bulb, unless instructions that come with the bulb say otherwise. (*Lilium candidum* should be planted near the surface.) Feed them with 2-10-10 fertilizer when the first sprouts show. Almost all lilies like to have their heads in the sun, their feet in the shade, a cool root run, and no wind. If you can provide these conditions plus protection from snails and slugs, in pots or the ground, perhaps lilies will do well for you.

Divide Irises. If irises aren't divided every three or four years they'll stop blooming. If yours need it and you didn't divide them last summer after bloom, now, in mid-September through mid-October, is the time to tackle the job. Gardeners in hot interior valleys have no choice. It's do it now or wait another whole year. (See p. 155 for directions.)

If your irises don't need dividing this year,

clean up the bed now. Pull or cut off damaged leaves, clean up the ground, and mulch the bed. Bait for slugs and snails.

Purchase Cyclamen. In most of the country cyclamen are grown only as houseplants, but here they're one of our most aristocratic plants for cool-season bloom outdoors. Begin purchasing them now, either as tubers or as plants already in bloom. Grow them in pots, hanging baskets, or the ground.

When buying cyclamen tubers look for those that are already beginning to sprout—they're the easiest to start—and plant them so the top half of the tuber protrudes above the surface of the soil. Put them in moist, humus-rich soil and keep them damp until the tubers are well rooted. Keep the plants in semishade; they prefer a cool spot, away from reflected heat. Once they're well rooted and leaves have begun to grow begin feeding regularly with a complete fertilizer.

Don't overwater cyclamen. Wait until the leaves slightly wilt and the plant looks as if it's dry, then water it. Cyclamen plants also wilt from overwatering. You can tell if wilting results from over- or underwatering by the condition of the plant's stems. If your cyclamen's stems are soft and wet you've overwatered it, but if the stems are dry, crisp, and firm—though wilted—you've underwatered it. Also, don't clip off the faded blooms; this too can lead to rot. Pull them off with a quick downward yank.

Wake Up the Cyclamen That You Summered Over. If you summered-over some cyclamen, it's time to get their tubers to wake up and grow again. Start feeding them every two weeks with a balanced fertilizer for growth and bloom. (If

* ✹ *

When Is a Bulb Not a Bulb?

Many of the plants we call bulbs aren't bulbs at all. It's become common to lump together under this term not only true bulbs but all plants that grow from a thickened or bulbous storage organ. (Plants like daylilies, clivia, and iris are in a shady area between bulbs and perennials, so you find them discussed in books on bulbs and also in books on perennials.) Here's how bulbs differ, so you can tell them apart.

- **True Bulb.** A modified subterranean leaf bud, the true bulb has a basal plate, above which are food-storing scales (rudimentary leaves) surrounding a bud that contains the magic makings of a plant. Some bulbs, like onions, tulips, and daffodils, are tunicate—they're covered with a papery skin. Others, like lilies, are imbricate—they have overlapping scales.

- **Corm.** A thickened subterranean stem that produces a plant. The inside is just a solid piece of tissue. The buds are on top. After bloom the old corm is used up, but new ones have grown on top or at the sides to take its place. Gladioli, sparaxis, and freesia grow from corms.

- **Rhizome.** A thickened stem or branch that grows on the surface of the ground or horizontally underground, such as bearded irises and calla lilies.

- **Tuber.** A thickened stem that serves as a storage chamber but is usually shorter, thicker, and rounder than a rhizome. It grows totally or partially underground. Tuberous begonias, cyclamen, and potatoes grow from tubers.

- **Tuberous Root.** Growing underground, this differs from a tuber in that it's a swollen root rather than a thickened stem. Tuberous roots have growth buds on top in the old stem portion, from which spring the plants. Dahlias and sweet potatoes grow from tuberous roots.

* ✹ *

* ☀ *

How to Make Bulb Plantings Look Informal and Natural

Don't plant bulbs in rows, plant them in drifts (the gracefully shaped areas that flow from back to front and from side to side in a flower bed and are planted solidly with one flower). Do as nature does; put many bulbs of one kind or one color together in a single drift, and then mix one or two of another kind or color in with them. To arrange such a drift mark the outline with gypsum and toss the bulbs onto the ground. Plant them where they fall.

* ☀ *

Quick Tip

Use Bulb Covers to Mark and Shade the Ground over Bulbs.
When planting bulbs, plant low-profile cool-season flowers over them. The bulbs will grow up through them and the ground will be ornamented while you wait. Pansies, alyssum, nemesia, johnny-jump-ups, violas, primroses, dwarf snapdragons, and schizanthus make good bulb covers.

you feed only nitrogen you'll get lots of leaves and no flowers.) Meanwhile, protect the plants from slugs and snails. Colorless leaves that are twisted out of shape are caused by cyclamen mite. Spray with a specific miticide. You may have to treat them more than once.

If the roots of some of your cyclamen are crowded and you think they need potting on wait until the plants start to grow again, then move them into pots one size larger—don't drown them in soil. Often they'll stay in the same container for several years and will flower better when they're a little rootbound. Some-times the tubers grow so large they literally fill the tops of their pots. You can, if you wish, cut these giant tubers into sections to make new plants. Leave one or two eyes on each cut section; dip the cut sides in RooTone, and let them callus off for a day or two before replanting.

Tropicals and Subtropicals

This is the last month of the growing season for tropicals, so it's also the last month when they can be fertilized, if necessary, in most zones. (If you live in an interior valley it's better not to fertilize them this late in the season.) Tropicals need to slow down in October and then harden off for winter during November. If you live in a largely frost-free zone you can give them a final feeding of fast-acting fertilizer, such as a liquid, early in the month to help them increase strength during this warm month, and to eliminate any signs of nitrogen deficiency. But don't fertilize with a slow-release product. The idea is to strengthen them without triggering soft growth later in fall, when it could be nipped by frost.

In coastal zones this is also the last month for

planting tropicals, such as Natal plum, bougain-villea, philodendron, hibiscus, lantana, and tropical flowering trees. In the interior it's best to wait until spring to plant tropicals, because fall planting will make them more subject to frost. But regardless of this, many fall-blooming subtropical trees are in nurseries now, and it will be impossible to choose the colors you prefer at any other time, when the trees aren't in bloom. Trees you can find now include the Hong Kong orchid tree (*Bauhinia blakeana*), floss silk tree (*Chorisia speciosa*), and Chinese flame tree (*Koelreutera bipinnata* or *K. elegans*). Floss silk tree is one of our most spectacular large trees, and reasonably drought resistant. The whole top of the tree turns vivid pink, magenta, or bur-gundy in fall. (There's also a white species, *C. insignis*.) The trunks are green and bear prominent, weirdly wonderful spines, but if you're planting in areas where children or animals might be endangered choose a grafted kind without spines. Chinese flame tree is good near houses, is noninvasive, and doesn't grow too large, and it's quite drought tolerant. The display of salmon-colored pods in fall looks as if a bougainvillea got accidentally tangled in the top of the tree. (There's no choice of color with this tree, so you can wait if you wish and plant one next spring.)

Don't let fall-planted tropicals dry out in the almost-inevitable September heat wave; inland, hose off the area around them twice a day to raise the humidity during these spells. And come winter, remember it's important to protect them from frost.

Don't prune hibiscus this month. But in frost-free zones several other heat-loving plants that bloom all summer, such as oleanders, bougainvilleas, and plumbago, can be pruned now after bloom. They'll regrow during winter for a big burst of bloom next spring and summer. (Pruning in spring instead of fall can cut down on spring bloom, but it's necessary in areas that suffer hard frosts.) Prune oleanders by taking out whole stalks that have bloomed—down to the ground. Take off several a year to renew the plants. Don't chop off the tops like a hedge. This fails to renew the plant with fresh growth from the ground and destroys all your flowers. (You could choose a much better green hedge, if that's all you want.) Don't prune New Zealand tea tree (*Leptospermum scoparium*) now, or you'll get no winter flowers.

Citrus and Avocado Trees

Make sure citrus trees are adequately and evenly watered during September. If their roots go dry now the result can be fruit that splits. (Fluctua-tions in fertilizer levels can also cause fruit to split. Varieties with thin skins are more prone to the problem than ones with thick skins.)

Treat Lemon Trees for Brown Rot. Commercial growers pick lemons all at once, but most home gardeners leave lemons hanging on the tree until needed. If you do this you'll have fresh ones year-round whenever you want them. The only problem is that fruit left hanging on the tree after it's turned golden ripe sometimes develops brown blotches or turns brown all over. Brown skins can be caused by leaving the fruit on the tree so long that it becomes overmature. If the tree looks generally healthy and the brown fruits occur here and there all over the tree, then discoloration is most likely caused by leaving fruit on the tree too long. Pick the overripe fruit and leave the rest on the tree.

How Cymbidiums Came to California

Cymbidiums are largely terrestrial orchids native to cool tropical jungles, from the Himalayas eastward through southern Asia. For at least two hundred years they were hybridized and grown in cool greenhouses by English collectors. During the Second World War a great many varieties were sent to Santa Barbara to save them from the bombs. It soon became clear that cymbidiums flourish outdoors in Southern California. They multiplied so rapidly that when the loaned varieties were sent home after the war many more plants were left here, to continue to grow in our gardens. They've since become one of our best plants for winter and spring bloom.

But brown blotches on the rinds of lemons (or fruit that turns brown all over) may also result from a condition called brown rot, which is caused by several fungi that live in the soil under the tree. You can tell if fungus is the culprit because, in this case, fruit of all sizes will be affected but the discoloration will occur primarily on fruit that's closest to the ground. Sometimes a white mold will appear on the fruit, and sap may ooze from the trunk of the tree, near the ground. Branches may also die back. Brown rot is at its worst in wet weather, when the fungi splash up onto the tree from the ground.

If your fruit has ever been affected this way you have a chance to clear up the problem by spraying now with a garden fungicide, such as captan. Unfortunately you have to pick all the ripe fruit before spraying. Then clean up the ground under the tree and prune off any tips of branches that are brushing the earth. It's a good idea to cut out any diseased or dead growth while you're about it, and make sure there aren't any mummified fruits hanging around in the tree. Then spray the fungicide all over the ground under the tree and up into the branches, paying particular attention to the lowest 3 feet of growth. Spray in the early morning or evening to prevent burn, and use a spreader-sticker or a little summer oil to help spread the spray. (Water the trees well before spraying; oil can cause leaf drop on trees that are under water stress.)

Cymbidiums

Not all cymbidiums bloom every year. (You need three plants to be assured of annual bloom.) But some gardeners complain that none of their cymbidiums ever bloom. These plants are remarkably easy to grow, but they do have certain requirements. Here's how to make them bloom.

Switch Fertilizers in September. Beginning on the first of September switch fertilizers on cymbidiums from a high-nitrogen formula for growth to a formula higher in bloom ingredients, such as 15-30-15 or 10-30-10. (If you're feeding with high-nitrogen slow-release tablets continue their use, but once every two or three weeks treat the plants additionally with 0-10-10 or 2-10-10 liquid.) Cymbidiums continue to grow year-round so they always need some nitrogen, but a higher percentage of phosphorus and potassium now will encourage development of bloom spikes.

Keep Cymbidiums in Bright Light. Don't keep cymbidiums in too much shade. If you've sheltered yours from hot sun under a tree, during the summer, bring them out into more light now. Along the coast they can take full sun, though they'll need protection during the Santa Ana or sudden heat wave that almost always strikes sometime in September. Inland they need protection from the burning rays of midday sun—under 50 percent shade cloth or in a lath house is ideal. They often can take more sun than we give them. If your cymbidiums have dark green leaves chances are you're keeping them in too much shade. Give them enough light to turn the leaves a yellowish color. Spread the plants apart, and allow sunshine to hit those pseudobulbs. Crowded plants won't bloom as well because the leaves shade the bulbs. (Trim off dead leaves and brown tips, but don't cut off or shorten healthy leaves. Cymbidiums need all their leaves to nourish the pseudobulbs.)

How to Stop Blue Hydrangeas from Turning Pink

· Start with a hydrangea that was blue when you bought it. Some kinds never turn blue. White varieties always stay white. Some pinks turn purple instead of blue.

· Plant and grow blue hydrangeas in acid soil mix. When planting in containers use a commercial soil mix designed for camellias and azaleas. When planting in the ground amend the native soil in the planting hole with camellia and azalea mix according to package directions, or use two-thirds premoistened peat moss. Mulch with leaf mold or redwood.

· Check the root run of established plants to make sure the soil is acid. Use a soil test kit to test the pH of the soil. A pH of 4.5 to 5.0 yields blue flowers, a pH of 5.5 to 6.5 yields mauve, and a pH of 7.0 to 7.5 yields pink.

· Maintain the desired pH with aluminum sulfate. Use 1 tablespoon aluminum sulfate per foot of plant height, or ¼ teaspoon per potted plant. Mix this in water and apply it as a drench several times in spring and fall, beginning in September.

· Never use fertilizer that contains phosphorus. Phosphorus is alkaline, so the use of it will raise the pH of the soil and turn blue hydrangeas pink.

Provide a Wide Range of Temperatures.
Cymbidiums need a daily temperature range of at least 20 degrees during the hottest time of the year in order to trigger bloom. What they like best is nights that drop to 45° or 55°F (7° or 13°C) and daytime temperatures of 80° or 90°F (27° or 32°C). Our gardens provide adequately warm days and cool nights but our patios or porches often do not. They're too warm and sheltered at night. So situate your cymbidiums away from protective house walls and don't keep them indoors, or they'll never bloom.

Meanwhile water cymbidiums enough to keep the pseudobulbs from drying out and shriveling. Water should always drain right through. Cymbidium roots can't survive in a puddle. As the spikes grow stake them so they don't get broken, and protect the plants from slugs and snails.

Camellias

Keep camellias well watered this month. Letting them go dry now will make the buds go brown and drop off later, so you won't have any bloom this winter or next spring. Don't confuse this with natural bud drop. Some varieties form a great many more buds than they can open, so they always drop a lot of them of their own accord. These naturally dropped buds will be green, not brown. (Bud drop can also be caused by growing a variety that needs winter chill in a mild coastal zone where the buds can't open.)

Disbud Camellias. For the largest blooms start disbudding camellias now, by removing all but one flower bud from each tip or joint. Twist off all but one flower bud from each cluster,

being careful not to remove the growth bud. (The flower buds are round and fat. The growth bud is thin and pointed.) Drop the buds in a plastic bag and dispose of them in the trash. Some gardeners don't disbud camellias because they have too many of them or simply can't be bothered. When plants are as tall as trees it's almost impossible to disbud them. But all plants look better when they've been disbudded; the flowers become not only larger but better shaped and less prone to blossom blight.

It's a good idea to retain some forward-facing but mainly downward-facing buds, especially when plants are tall or light colored. On tall plants downward-facing flowers will be seen better. On light-colored plants they'll be less prone to sun damage. In all cases they'll last longer; when it rains, water will pour off their backs instead of soaking into the center and causing rot.

Azaleas

The time-honored method for feeding azaleas requires you to fertilize them only twice a year, once immediately after they finish flowering and again in late September. So give azaleas their second and last meal of the year during the last third of this month. (Some growers feed azaleas once a month with liquid fertilizer during the growing season. But it's possible to kill azaleas with too much kindness.) The easiest way is to use an organic fertilizer especially formulated for azaleas or camellias, following package directions exactly, or to feed with cottonseed meal or a complete organic fertilizer such as Gro Power. If the plant shows signs of chlorosis (yellow leaves, green veins) use a chelating fertilizer to correct this deficiency.

Roses

Continue to water roses with up to 1½ inches of water each time you irrigate, but reduce the number of irrigations from three times a week to twice a week. Continue to fertilize roses once a month with the commercial rose food of your choice, or if you're following the Rose-Pro Method fertilize your rose plants with 1 tablespoon of urea every week. (By giving more nitrogen now you prepare roses for a spurt of growth and flowering in fall.) Continue to control rose pests and diseases, with Orthene and Funginex or by using other methods of your choice. If you are following the Rose-Pro Method stop mixing micronutrients (Stern's Miracle Gro or Super K Gro) into your spray this month. Pick or deadhead the flowers according to your custom, but there's no need to disbud now.

Along with other fall planting, you can plant roses from nursery containers, if desired, from now through October.

Thanksgiving and Christmas Cacti

Zygocactus or crab cactus (*Schlumbergera truncata*) is an epiphyte with "leaves" (actually thickened stems) shaped like crab claws. It's often sold as Christmas cactus, but it really should be called Thanksgiving cactus because it blooms at Thanksgiving, sometimes staying in bloom until March. The true Christmas cactus (*S. bridgesii*) has smooth "leaves." The flowers usually open on Christmas day. (There's also an Easter cactus [*Rhipsalidopsis gaertneri* or *S. gaertneri*], which blooms in April and May and often again in fall.)

How to Grow Thanksgiving, Christmas, and Easter Cacti

· Grow these cacti indoors or out. (They can grow as big as 3 feet across.)

· Start by buying small ones of the same color. Plant three or four cacti in a 6-inch container in good, porous potting soil, such as Jungle Growth, to each gallon of which you add 1 cup of agricultural charcoal and 3 cups of perlite. Pot them on as necessary.

· Keep the cacti in bright but not burning light. Filtered sun is OK, but hot rays through south or west windows are not. Keep them in natural light (away from electric lights at night) for the two months prior to bloom. (During bloom, flowers last longer when plants are kept cool.)

· Fertilize the plants year-round once every two to three weeks, or with a well-diluted solution every time you water. Feed with 8-8-8 most of the year. Switch to 0-10-10 two months prior to bloom.

· Water regularly throughout the year. Keep the cacti slightly drier for a month or six weeks after bloom, but don't ever let the roots shrivel. In general water well in summer, less in fall. (Some experts withhold water for one month after the weather cools in fall; others water year-round.) Always maintain good drainage—no soggy soil allowed.

These cacti can be so gratifying that people fall in love with them. Nonetheless, because of one characteristic they all share they sometimes don't bloom; they are all *photoperiodic* (they respond to the length of the daylight hours). If you keep the plants indoors they often won't bloom, because house lights at night extend their days to a length that isn't right to stimulate flowering. So put your Thanksgiving and Christmas cacti outdoors now for six weeks or two months, in a shady place where night lighting won't strike them. Meanwhile feed them with 0-10-10 to stimulate bloom. (See the accompanying box for year-round directions.)

Flower Beds and Containers

If you were in Southern California last April, you know how delightful our spring gardens can be. If you want to achieve flower beds brimming with color—beds like those you noticed in the best gardens last spring—now's the time to plant for it. Don't wait until April and either regret not planting or try to plant then. That's one of the worst mistakes in local gardening. Start now; you have plenty of time—three whole months in most areas.

Plant Beds with Cool-Season Flowers. September is the first month when you can plant cool-season annual and perennial flowers. The earlier you get them into the ground the more likely you are to get them to bloom before Christmas. It's a race between you and the weather. Get them blooming in early December and they'll stay in bloom all winter and spring. Otherwise you'll have to wait until February or even March for flowers.

If you're a good gardener even early October will not be too late, so you have a choice. If the summer garden is still looking presentable you can keep it going through September, by removing faded flowers, grooming plants, and feeding them with fertilizer high in bloom ingredients; or if the flower beds look ratty you can tear out summer annuals now, dig up the beds, add soil amendment, and replant in mid-September with winter and spring flowers.

When planting in large tubs replace about one-third of the planting medium with fresh soil mix. When planting in small containers, or those that are chock-full of roots, replace all earth with fresh mix. Throw the old stuff in the compost.

Among good choices to plant from pony packs now are alyssum, Iceland poppy (the smaller the better), stock, snapdragon, sweet William, calendula, candytuft, foxglove, fairy or malacoides primrose, English primrose, obconica primrose, pansy, nemesia, and viola. Plant seeds of alyssum, calendula, cineraria, stock, snapdragon, johnny-jump-up, viola, annual African daisy (*Dimorphotheca sinuata*), and wildflowers. (See p. 259 for how to plant wildflowers.) Sweet peas are another good choice for planting from seeds now. You can have armloads of sweet peas (*Lathyrus odoratus*) in December if you plant them now and do the job right. (See the accompanying box.)

A word of warning. The last of the year's summer flowers, such as French and African marigolds and petunias, are sometimes on sale now. There's nothing to be gained by buying them since they'll soon be out of bloom. Petunias will live through winter in frost-free zones (without flowers) and do better than ever next summer, but marigolds will die in October. However, September is one of the best times to

Plant Sweet Peas for Christmas Bloom

· **Choose the Right Variety.** Look for the words "early flowering." ("Spring-flowering" or "summer-flowering" types won't bloom until days are more than twelve hours long.) Among tall varieties that flower early are Early Spencer, Early-Flowering Multiflora, Early Multiflora, and Mammoth. Among short varieties that require no staking are Snoopea, Supersnoop, and Jet Set. Bijou is a compact bush that flowers early.

· **Dig a North-South Trench in Full Sun.** Make your trench 1½ feet deep and 6 or 8 inches wide. (For bush types prepare the whole bed.)

· **Provide Rich Soil.** Fill the bottom of the trench with one sack of manure per 8 to 10 feet of trench. Fork it in well. Then mix the soil from the trench with one-third nitrolized ground bark or compost and a low-nitrogen fertilizer according to package directions. Backfill to 1 or 2 inches from the top. Soak this with water, and let it settle overnight.

· **Provide Strong Support.** Tall varieties need some kind of trellis to grow on. Shove metal posts or several 8-foot-tall metal plant stakes into the ground, and wire to them either hardware cloth or chicken wire.

· **Soak the Seeds in Water Overnight.** Put the seeds in a jar and pour lukewarm water over them. Leave them overnight. Plant the next day.

· **Plant the Seeds an Inch Deep.** After you sow the seeds 2 inches apart, cover them with 1 inch of potting soil—sweet pea seeds need darkness to sprout. Pat it down gently. Sprinkle daily to keep the seeds damp until they sprout. Then water regularly. Or bury a drip tube under the row prior to planting.

· **Protect Sprouts from Birds and Snails.** Cover the row with bird netting or bent aviary wire. Once the sprouts are up 6 inches, remove it; the birds won't kill larger plants. Bait regularly for slugs and snails.

· **Thin and Pinch Seedlings.** When the plants are up 6 inches, thin them to 6 inches apart. Pinch their tips to force branching.

· **Add String if Necessary.** Sweet peas have tendrils and are often better at hanging onto their supports than edible peas, but if winds and rains are strong tie twine around the row to hold up your vines.

plant euryops and marguerites because they bloom mostly in fall, winter, and spring. Plant them in full sun; they'll take off well in September's warm weather and you'll enjoy their flowers throughout the cool months.

Wake up Primroses. Did you summer-over your English primroses (*Primula polyanthus*)? As with cyclamen, which is also a member of the primrose (*Primulaceae*) family, it's time to awaken these plants and get them growing again. Clean up the plants; also separate, divide, and replant them if necessary. Primroses will often go for a couple of years in large pots without the need to be repotted or divided, but old plants eventually grow thick, tuberlike stalks and appear to push themselves up out of the ground or soil mix. If this happens repot—or replant—them in fresh soil; place the roots an inch or two deeper, but don't bury the crown.

Feed English primroses with a high-nitrogen fertilizer, such as Terr-O-Vite, to stimulate growth now, and then switch to a complete fertilizer for growth and bloom when buds show. The bigger you can get English primroses to grow now, the bigger the flowers you'll achieve later. Spray them against caterpillars with BT, if necessary, and protect the plants from slugs and snails. Colorless leaves are most likely caused by spider mites. Spray with a specific miticide; you may have to treat them more than once. Washing them off with Safer soap can also help destroy the mites and their webs. However, a regular routine of fertilizing combined with appropriate light (bright semishade now and full or partial sun in winter) will often give English primroses enough vigor to fight off mites without additional assistance.

Lawn Care

Maintain regular feeding of warm-season lawns, such as dichondra, Bermuda, and zoysia, but hold off on fertilizer for cool-season grasses, such as ryegrass, bluegrass, and fescue, for another month. (If you must fertilize make it a very light feeding, and don't feed during or just before September's usual heat wave.) Continue to water as you did during summer—deeply and as infrequently as possible for warm-season grasses, more frequently and less deeply for cool-season grasses except tall fescues (which are more drought resistant).

Plant Warm-Season Lawns. There's still enough warm weather to plant warm-season lawns now from stolons, with the exception of zoysia. It makes a much better start when planted in early summer. You can also plant warm-season lawns from seed, but it's better to wait until next spring, especially in inland areas. (Warm-season lawns can be planted from sod any month from spring through fall but not during winter dormancy.) Wait until October to plant cool-season lawns, unless you live close to the coast.

Dethatch Bermuda. If you didn't dethatch your Bermuda lawn in spring, or if the thatch was so thick it needs more than one treatment, now's the second best time of the year to do the job. If you wait too late the Bermuda won't have time to grow back and you'll have to put up with a bare muddy area all winter long. Do the job now while there's still enough warm weather to stimulate a fast recovery. (See p. 62 for full instructions.)

Vegetable Gardening

Prepare Beds for Cool-Season Vegetables. Vegetable gardening is much like flower gardening this month; it's a matter of choice. Summer vegetables often keep on producing if given food and water, especially along the coast. If that's your case, wait until October to put in the winter garden. Or if everything is dead and dying, which usually is the case inland, you can now pull up, clean up, chop up, and compost the remains and begin again, by planting the fall and winter garden on Labor Day weekend. Put in plenty of manure and soil amendment. Add fertilizer according to package directions. Use organic fertilizers if you're an organic gardener, but be sure to provide crops with adequate nourishment in winter; when the weather's cool, nitrogen is less active in the soil.

Control Migrating Pests. A number of gardeners like to start planting in some areas while continuing to harvest in others. This works well if you grow vegetables on several levels or in raised beds. The only problem is you have less of a chance to get rid of all insect pests at once. Whiteflies in particular will tend to migrate off tomatoes onto something else. It's usually best to clean out the entire vegetable garden at one time and then wait a week or two before replanting.

If you've planted flower beds with seeds of wildflowers nearby be careful when chopping up tomato vines. Tiny green worms can crawl right off them and journey across the ground to decimate your flower seedlings. If there's a very serious pest infestation—of caterpillars, say, or whiteflies—harvest all the vegetables you're going to eat, then spray the empty plants

Quick Tip

How to Make a Straight, Shallow Furrow for Seeds.
Lay the handle of a hoe flat on its back on the seedbed. Press it down evenly. Measure the furrow with a ruler for correct depth.

How to Grow Peas

Peas are a good crop to plant early this month. Get them in before the usual heat spell; warm soil sprouts seeds fast to give you an early harvest.

- **Choose a Good Variety.** There are three basic kinds to grow: Chinese pea pods (also called snow peas), snap peas, and English peas. The first two are the easiest, and you eat them pod and all. English peas are delicious, but you have to shell them, and they take up more space.

- **Prepare the Soil.** Thoroughly dig up the ground with a spade to the depth of 1 foot or at least 10 inches, adding organic amendment (no manure). Work in a low-nitrogen fertilizer, such as 5-10-10 or 4-12-12.

- **Arrange North-South Rows.** Space rows so they run from north to south and are 18 to 24 inches apart. (Each row of earth will be planted with a double row of peas.)

- **Provide Strong Support.** Even dwarf varieties need some kind of trellis to climb on. Shove metal posts or several 8-foot-tall plastic-covered metal plant stakes into the ground down the center of the row. Tie hardware cloth, chicken wire, or reinforcing wire to the stakes.

- **Make Twin Furrows.** Space twin furrows (narrow grooves in the ground) 3 to 6 inches apart, one furrow on each side of the trellis. Make the furrows 1 inch deep in coastal zones, 2 to 3 inches deep in interior zones.

- **Inoculate the Seed.** Unless you've grown peas in the same place within 3 years, or plan to fertilize with nitrogen, inoculate the seed

with rhizobia for the largest possible harvest (as described on p. 90).

- **Plant Close.** Plant the peas at intervals of 2 inches. (Or you can plant them 1 inch apart and thin them to 2 inches when the plants are 2 or 3 inches high.) Cover them with 1 inch of potting soil in coastal zones, 2 to 3 inches in interior zones. Pat it down gently.

- **Help Them Germinate.** Pea seeds germinate at soil temperatures from 40° to 75°F (4° to 24°C), but the warmer the temperature the faster they sprout. If you plant an old variety such as Mammoth Melting in early September they'll sprout fast, in three to six days. Some of the newer varieties of snap pea, such as Snappy (my favorite) and the stringless Sugar Pop, don't germinate so easily. If they fail to come up presprout more seed in the house, and put it in the ground as soon as it's sprouted. (Don't give up. Presprouting is easy—see p. 121.)

- **Foil Birds.** Cover the row with netting until the sprouts are up 5 inches.

- **Water Regularly and Deeply.** Sprinkle the row daily to keep it damp until the seed germinates. Then water deeply and regularly, or use a drip system.

- **Tie Up the Vines.** Vines will hang on to supports with tendrils, but winter rains and wind can knock them down. Once they're up 12 to 15 inches, and before the rains, wind twine around the rows periodically to hold up new growth. (See accompanying box for another method.)

to kill the pests. Wait several days for the spray to take effect before before pulling up the plants and disposing of them in the compost pile. (If you used a toxic spray be sure to wear protective clothing when you remove the plants in order not to be exposed to pesticide.)

Start a First Garden. If this is your first vegetable garden start with careful planning. Choose an area in full sun. (This is imperative for winter crops.) Prepare the soil by cultivating deeply with a spade. Don't just scratch the surface with a fork or hoe. In order to have success you must dig up the ground with a spade to a depth of 1 foot or, at the very least, to 10 inches. With the handle of the spade upright put your foot on the upper edge of the spade, and shove it all the way to the ground; then push the handle toward the ground and lift the spadeful; turn it over, and hit the resulting clod of earth with the back of the spade to break it apart. If your soil is too hard for you to accomplish this, build raised boxes on it and fill them with good soil. Add all the soil amendments you can afford, fork them into the ground, and then level the area with a garden rake. Sprinkle a complete vegetable fertilizer onto the surface of the ground according to package directions and rake it into the top 6 inches.

Plant in late September or early October, and be sure to plant cool-season vegetables, not warm-season vegetables. These are the vegetables that are planted in earliest spring in cold-season climates, such as celery and all the cole crops (members of the cabbage family), plus the vegetables that can go into the ground year-round, such as carrots, beets, turnips, and radishes. Be careful when you go to the nursery to buy the right things, because this is one of

Protect Peas from Birds and Support the Vines

Make a narrow, A-frame tent of netting by stretching a 2- or 3-foot-wide strip of Ross bird netting down each side of a planted double row. Secure them by covering the bottom of each strip with earth and tying the tops to several small bamboo stakes. (Twist-and-Tie garden twine works well.) The peas grow up inside this tent of sorts; when they reach the top untie it and let them grow beyond. Besides foiling birds this system helps the plants cling to their trellis; there's no need to wrap the row with twine to hold up sagging vines.

Interplant Peas with Lettuce

If your rows of vegetables are 18 inches apart, skip a row between every two rows of peas. Plant lettuce in the skipped row. After the lettuce is harvested out, tie bamboo or twine across the tops of two rows of tall pea varieties, allowing them to grow across the gap. Children love going through the tunnel and picking peas.

those months when you can still find transplants of summer vegetables for sale side by side with winter ones. (Check the list in the following section to be sure.)

Fall is just as good a time to start a vegetable garden as spring. In fact, there are some advantages now. Winter vegetables take less care, pest problems are fewer in winter, and irrigation water sometimes falls from heaven. Winter vegetables are fun, surprisingly easy to grow, and far more delicious than the counterparts you can buy in the market.

Begin Planting Cool-Season Vegetables. Vegetables that can be planted now include beets, broccoli, Brussels sprouts, carrots, cauliflower, celery, fava beans, kale, kohlrabi, leeks, both head and leaf lettuce, mustard greens, onions, parsley, peas, potatoes, radishes, rutabagas, spinach, Swiss chard, and turnips. (See the accompanying box for how to plant peas.) Technically, you could, if you wish, plant all these vegetables straight in the ground from seeds. In actual practice, however, it's easiest to plant broccoli, Brussels sprouts, cauliflower, and celery from transplants; plant potatoes from seed potatoes and onions from sets. (Wait until November to plant seeds of onions for slicing—the sets you plant now will give you scallions, not large onion bulbs.)

Parsley and lettuce are also often grown from plants you buy at the nursery—parsley because the seeds are slow to sprout and lettuce so you can have a quick harvest while you're waiting for the seeded rows to grow. (Lettuce seeds sprout easily.) Wait until midmonth to put in transplants of cauliflower, and wait until October to put in transplants of cabbages and artichokes.

Adventuresome gardeners might like to try growing broccoli, Brussels sprouts, cabbage, cauliflower, and celery from seeds. It requires a fuss—the seedlings need nursing along with frequent applications of weak liquid fertilizer, such as fish emulsion—but it does allow a wider choice of varieties. If you're planting the seeds straight in the ground a drip system will greatly increase your chances of success. Many gardeners grow their own transplants in flats or peat pots, but cole crops and celery actually don't like being transplanted; they form better roots when grown from seeds right where you want them. (When planting broccoli, Brussels sprouts, cauliflower, and celery from seeds, plant them early in September for best results, but plant cabbage seeds about midmonth.)

Though it's too late to plant summer vegetables, some gardeners in frost-free zones have been experimenting lately with planting a last crop of tomatoes or beans early in September. Choose an early variety, such as Early Girl tomatoes (Celebrity works too) or Venture beans. Many gardeners keep a few tomato plants going until December.

Purchase / Plant	*Trim, Prune, Mow, Divide*	*Fertilize*
☐ Transplant into the garden the **biennials** started from seed in July, 179	☐ Cut back **petunias** in late September, 178	☐ Feed **fuchsias,** 55
☐ Plant **alstroemerias,** 207	☐ Continue to mow **lawns** at summer heights, 189	☐ Continue to feed **tuberous begonias,** 78
☐ Begin purchasing **spring-flowering bulbs,** 222	☐ Divide **irises** that need division in interior zones, 154, 224	☐ Feed **ferns** for the last time this year, 132
☐ Start planting **bulbs,** especially drought-resistant ones, 223	☐ Stop pruning **hibiscus,** 227	☐ Feed all **container-grown succulents** with a well-diluted complete liquid fertilizer, 186
☐ Begin to plant **lilies,** 223	☐ Prune **oleanders** by taking out whole stalks, 227	☐ Feed and water **cyclamen,** 224
☐ Purchase plants or corms of **cyclamen,** 224	☐ Don't prune **New Zealand tea trees** in fall, 227	☐ Fertilize **tropicals** for the last time this year, only if they need it, 226
☐ Plant **bulb covers** over spring-flowering bulbs, 226	☐ Start disbudding **camellias,** 230	☐ Switch fertilizers on **cymbidiums** to a higher bloom formula to encourage flowering, 229
☐ Finish planting **tropicals** in coastal zones, 226	☐ Resume picking and deadheading **roses,** but don't disbud them, 231	☐ To maintain the color of **blue hydrangeas** start treating the soil with aluminum sulfate, 229
☐ Start planting **cool-season flowers** to bloom during winter and spring, 232	☐ Wake up **primroses,** and if necessary separate, divide, and replant them, 234	☐ Fertilize **azaleas** at month's end for the second and last time of the year; correct chlorosis if necessary, 230
☐ Plant **sweet peas** from seeds for Christmas bloom, 233	☐ Dethatch **Bermuda** if it needs it and if you failed to do the job in spring, or if you are correcting a serious problem with several treatments, 234	☐ Fertilize **Thanksgiving** and **Christmas cacti** with 0-10-10, 231
☐ **Warm-season lawns,** except zoysia, can be planted now (though it's better to wait until spring), 234		☐ Continue to feed **warm-season lawns;** don't feed **cool-season lawns** until after midmonth, 234
☐ Start planting **winter vegetables,** 235		☐ Fertilize **roses.** (Rose-Pro gardeners resume use of urea.) 231
☐ Plant **peas,** 236		
☐ Plant **cool-season lawns** in coastal zones, 261		

Water

☐ Continue to water **all garden plants** according to their individual needs (with the exception of certain natives), 200, 221

☐ Check **drought-resistant plants** for signs of stress; give them a deep irrigation, if necessary, to tide them over to the winter rains, 200, 221

☐ Don't let fall-planted **tropicals** dry out, 227

☐ Keep **citrus** evenly watered to help prevent fruit from splitting, 227

☐ Don't let **camellias** dry out now or buds will fall off later, 230

☐ Water **roses** with up to 1½ inches of water twice a week, 231

Control Pests, Diseases, and Weeds

☐ Treat **lemon trees** for brown rot, 227

☐ Control **rose** pests and diseases, 231

☐ Treat **primroses** and **cyclamen** for mites if necessary, 234

☐ Control **migrating pests,** 235

Also This Month

☐ Untie the fronds of **palms** transplanted in July, 212

☐ Start cleaning out **flower beds** and prepare the ground for fall planting, 221, 232

☐ Wake up **cyclamen** you summered-over, 224

☐ Make sure **cymbidiums** are in adequate light to produce bloom. Also see that they get the range of temperatures necessary for bloom, 229

☐ Put **Thanksgiving** and **Christmas cacti** into natural light for two months so they will bloom, 231

☐ Prepare beds for **cool-season vegetables,** 235

☐ Start new **vegetable gardens,** 237

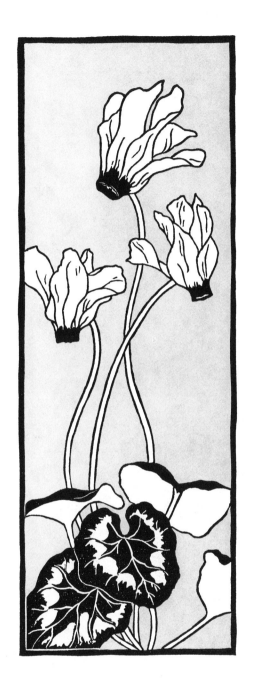

OCTOBER

The Year's Best Planting Month

October is almost always one of the pleasantest months of the year. Though we sometimes get our first rains this month and occasionally they're torrential, the rainy season doesn't officially start until next month. For the most part the weather is clear and sunny, though cooler—cool enough for working outdoors in the middle of the day even in interior valleys. That's good news for gardeners because October is probably the busiest time of the year. It's the best time to plant almost all permanent additions to the landscape; the exceptions are tropicals (a bit late for them), bare-root plants (they get planted in January), native plants, and ground covers (wait until next month and they'll do slightly better). The idea behind fall planting is to get things into the ground ahead of the major rains. Roots get established during winter and reward you the following summer with a great surge of growth. It's the time-honored, easy, water-saving way to go.

October, like March, is a pivotal month when we make the switch from one Southern California season to another. In March we switch to the summer scheme. In October we switch to winter. Gardeners who put aside extra time for gardening this month will be rewarded with better results and less work to do later. This is the time to pull up the last remnants of summer vegetables and flowers and finish planting flowers and vegetables for winter and spring. It's the best time to plant most winter vegetables. Get them into the ground as soon as possible. Cool-season lawns can be seeded now, and it's time to prune, transplant, divide, and separate a great many garden staples.

Fall Planting for Desert Dwellers

Those who live in the desert can plant a wide range of vegetables and flowers this month. Both summer and winter vegetables can be planted now, with the exception of corn and melons, which should be planted in late January or early February. (Wait until November to plant onions, but buy the seeds of short-day varieties now.) Many flowers, including ivy geraniums and petunias, which thrive in the spring and summer along the coast, can be counted on for winter color in desert areas. For further planting ideas see the selection of bedding plants at local nurseries.

Among permanent plants to put in now are oleander, flame vine (*Pyrostegia venusta*), and Easter lily vine (*Beaumontia grandiflora*). Flame vine blooms in fall and early winter so now's the time to find it in nurseries. Planted in the low desert it can curtain walls and roofs with a solid sheet of vivid, orange color for several months, climaxing at Christmas, but it will also thrive in coastal zones if given a hot spot, such as a south-facing tile roof, to tumble over. Easter lily vine needs warmth, rich soil, plenty of fertilizer, protection from wind, and lots of water. (Some desert areas have ample water supplies. Don't grow it where water is scarce.) Its white flowers bloom fragrantly spring to fall.

Trees, Shrubs, and Vines

Plant all trees, shrubs, and vines now to give them the best start possible. This is the finest time of the year to put in garden staples that

last for years and become the backbone of the landscape. Tropicals are an exception; it's better to plant them in late spring or early summer, especially in interior zones. (Very tender plants like tropical hibiscus often die with the first frost when planted in fall.) But nurseries, understandably, may carry some plants only while they're in bloom, so fall may be the only time that you can find certain flowering trees and vines.

If you do plant tropicals now don't fertilize them, do protect them from frost during winter, and ask your nursery if the plant you purchase is guaranteed to survive the winter. The reason fall planting benefits most other plants is that the soil is still warm enough to stimulate growth of roots, and winter rains will help them get established. You won't see much, if any, growth during the winter, but what you plant now will be ready to wake up and grow when the weather warms up in spring. Choose plants recommended for your climate zone, and take their eventual size and ability to withstand drought into consideration. Plant sun lovers in the sun and shade lovers in the shade, and always plant in zones, grouping plants with similar water requirements.

Among trees you might choose to put in now are all types of conifers, Chinese elm (*Ulmus parvifolia*), cork oak (*Quercus suber*—the thick-barked tree that Ferdinand the bull sat under), many melaleucas, tipu tree (*Tipuana tipu*), fern pine (*Podocarpus gracilior*), mayten tree (*Maytenus boaria*), and Australian and New Zealand tea trees (*Leptospermum laevigatum* and *L. scoparium*). Most shrubs used for hedges can be planted now, along with many shrubs used for accents and screens, including India hawthorn (*Rhapiolepis*), pittosporum, photinia, lavender star flower

(*Grewia occidentalis*), and yew pine (*Podocarpus macrophyllus*). Among vines and vinelike plants to put in now are Carolina jessamine (*Gelsemium sempervirens*), Cape honeysuckle (*Tecomaria capensis*), lilac vine (*Hardenbergia comptoniana*), and ivy. (Wait until next month to put in ground covers and California native plants.)

Fall Color

October is a good time to notice those plants that provide fall color year after year and perhaps add one to your garden. By purchasing now you can find the color that pleases you most. All of these plants can be put in now along the coast, and several can be also be planted inland. (If you live in the interior don't plant tropicals this late in the season.)

For autumn leaves choose liquidambar for its colorful pink, red, yellow, or orange foliage or maidenhair tree (*Ginkgo biloba*), which has golden leaves in fall. (In order to avoid the sticky, malodorous fruit of mature female trees plant only named male varieties, such as Fairmont or Autumn Gold.) The Hong Kong orchid tree (*Bauhinia blakeana*) has striking flowers ranging from cranberry to pink. Floss silk tree (*Chorisia speciosa*) blooms in burgundy or bright orchid to bright pink all over the top of the tree. (There's also a white species.) Markhamia tree (*Markhamia hildebrandtii*) bears golden trumpet flowers from August through October. (It's best near the coast.) Chinese flame tree (*Koelreuteria henryi* or *K. bipinnata*) is named for its salmon-colored seed pods, which follow less significant yellow flowers.

Vines include cup-of-gold (*Solandra maxima*), which grows well even on the oceanfront, and flame vine (*Pyrostegia venusta*, as discussed above in the desert section). Mexican flame vine (*Senecio confusus* or *S. angulatus*) is a yellow-to-orange vine for coastal locations. (It dies down in frost.) It may be hard to find but can be grown from seed or cuttings. Cut it back hard after bloom.

Deciduous Fruit Trees

In mild zones it's sometimes a problem to get deciduous fruit trees into winter dormancy. Don't follow the erroneous advice to feed them now in fall, though you may read it in books, magazines, and even some local newspapers. Fall fertilizing is an accepted practice in cold-winter climates but forces growth at the wrong time of year here. After midmonth hold back on water, but don't let the soil dry out completely. Dry conditions may encourage trees to drop their leaves and go dormant for the winter as is desirable.

Plants to Divide, Trim, and Mulch

October is the main month for dividing plants that tend to grow in a clump. Some of these plants—clivia, iris, daylilies, and ginger, for example—are bulblike in that they grow from thickened roots or rhizomes. Others are true perennials. The reasons for dividing are to propagate more plants, to make plants look better, to keep them to a desired size, or to encourage bloom. (When crowded, some plants bloom better but others stop flowering.) Always water thoroughly the day before dividing.

Kahili Ginger. Once the rhizomatous rootstocks of Kahili ginger crowd the top of the pot the plant will bloom less; this is a sign it needs to be

How to Divide Daylilies

Divide daylilies every three to five years to keep them blooming. Old varieties bloom longer without division than new varieties.

- Dig up the clumps. Knock off excess earth. Separate large clumps by putting two garden forks back to back and prying them apart.

- To make individual sections find the natural dividing point between two fans of leaves. Push downward between them with a large old screwdriver kept for the purpose, so that the fans break cleanly in two.

- Throw away broken parts. Trim the leaves of good divisions to 4 inches. Trim off any broken or damaged roots. Shorten overly long ones.

- Dig up the bed and loosen the soil to a depth of 1 foot; mix in bone meal, fertilizer, and organic amendments.

- For each plant make a shallow cone of earth. Replant the daylilies 12 to 18 inches apart, with their roots spread over the cone and covered with 1½ to 3 inches of soil. Mulch and water the ground. Give excess plants to friends.

either potted on or divided. Repot it, transplant it, or divide it now, to avoid destroying next year's bloom. To divide, slice down through the rhizomes with a knife or sharp spade to make large sections, 8 inches or more in diameter; trim off damaged roots only, and replant in pots or the ground, with the rhizomes just beneath the surface and the roots completely buried in humus-rich soil. Cut off faded blooms, but don't cut off the stalks or foliage; it needs its green leaves during the winter.

Clivia. October is the best time to divide clivia. They like to be rootbound, so don't divide them unless absolutely necessary. (See the box on p. 250.)

Iris. Clean up and mulch existing beds. Continue dividing and transplanting overcrowded irises (as described on p. 155). They won't bloom when crowded.

Daylily. Renew all evergreen daylilies (*Hemerocallis*) by cutting the leaves back to 4 inches. Mulch the beds and clean up dead leaves. Bait for snails and slugs. (If everblooming daylilies are still flowering wait until month's end, or even November in coastal zones.) Follow up with fertilizer to bring out fresh growth. Divide overcrowded daylilies now, in interior valleys. Along the coast do it now or wait until March. (For directions see the accompanying box.)

Moraea. Also called dietes or fortnight lilies, these eventually make huge ugly clumps with brown tips. Don't shear off the tops like rounded shaving brushes, as one often sees done; the tips will only go brown again, and new growth will stick up beyond the old in an ungainly fashion.

If you must shear moraeas cut them straight across with electric hedge trimmers 6 or 8 inches above ground. Follow up with fertilizer and water.

A much better way to treat moraeas is to dig up the old clumps now with a garden fork and divide them. (The roots aren't deep.) Cut back their tops to 4 or 5 inches and replant them. Throw away the excess. (These are too common to give away.)

Bird of Paradise. Cut off the dead leaves of bird of paradise (*Strelitzia reginae*). Pull out bloom stems after the flowers fade. Small plants can be divided with a sharp spade. They eventually make immense clumps that are almost impossible to divide. You may have to attack them with a chain saw. Replant salvageable sections.

Other Plants. Also divisible now, if necessary, are ivy geraniums, lily turf, gazanias, and all garden perennials that grow in clumps, including Shasta daisies. (Wait until November to divide and transplant agapanthus and Matilija poppies.)

Geraniums

Cut Back Zonal or Common Geraniums. Cut back zonal geraniums (*Pelargonium hortorum*) by about half. Cutting back now encourages regrowth during winter and a rest from flowering.

- Remove dead and diseased leaves and branches.
- Cut back the entire plant, making each cut straight across a branch and ¼ to ½ inch higher than a joint. Leave one or two healthy leaves on most branches. (Bare stubs won't recover.)

How to Renew Gazanias

Gazanias are one of our finest drought- and disease-resistant ground covers. Divide the clumping kinds every three or four years to keep them like new.

- Dig up the clumps. Knock off excess soil.
- Divide the clumps by pulling and clipping them apart. Trim off any damaged roots and any dead leaves or flowers.
- Refurbish the bed by spading it deeply and adding soil amendment and fertilizer.
- Replant the divisions 8 inches apart. Keep them well watered until reestablished.
- You'll have plenty of plants left over; share them with friends or discard.

How to Divide a Potted Clivia

Clivia like to be rootbound. Plants in the ground can go almost indefinitely without division. But you must divide clivia grown in pots when no soil is left and the roots push up out of the top, because then drainage becomes a problem. To divide them, take these steps.

· Use a large knife to cut around the inside of the pot or tub. Place the pot on its side. Direct strong water pressure up the drainage hole to loosen roots.

· To remove plants that stick sit on the ground with your feet on the edge of the tub, grab the stalks close to the roots, and yank the monster out.

· Cut apart the individual stalks with a knife. Trim away some of the excess roots. Repot them in potting soil, three plants to an 18-inch container.

· With potted specimens dig out some of the old soil. Replace it with fresh potting soil mixed with 1 tablespoon lime dolomite per gallon. (Geraniums don't like acid soil.)

· Feed the geraniums occasionally during the winter with 20-20-20 or 18-20-16 fertilizer.

· As the plants grow pinch back tips to make them bushy.

· Save the most succulent cuttings to make new plants. Dip them in RooTone and plant them in fast-draining potting soil with 1 tablespoon lime per gallon.

Cut Back Ivy Geraniums. If your ivy geraniums (*P. peltatum*) are in hanging baskets cut them back to 5 or 6 inches from pot level. Clean up the soil; remove dead leaves and debris. Remove a little soil and replace it with fresh mix. Feed them for growth and water them. If your ivy geraniums are growing in the ground cut them back lightly and clean up the ground around them. Then mulch, feed, and water them.

Prune Martha Washingtons. Martha Washingtons (*P. domesticum*) can become floppy if not pruned, but don't cut them back all at once. It's best to begin right after spring bloom and do the job progressively. Prune one or two leggy stems back to the lowest pair of leaves. Then cut more when regrowth begins. In coastal zones progressive pruning can be continued through October.

Coyote Bush and Other Native Plants

Coyote bush (*Baccharis pilularis*) can get tall and woody after a few years, losing the low, billowy look one desires in a ground cover. Cut it back hard now. It will sprout again from bare stubs. If you have a large area to deal with you can even mow it down with a rented heavyweight machine designed for mowing Algerian ivy. After mowing or cutting back, clean up the bed, mulch it, feed with a complete granulated fertilizer, and water the ground thoroughly. After this treatment coyote bush will come back looking much better.

These plants often die for no apparent reason, so take this opportunity to replace dead ones. (Check for drainage problems or faulty sprinklers that might have caused their demise.)

For other native plants continue to clean out the dead interiors. Cut out dead branches, and shape the plants in readiness for winter growth that begins next month.

Water Lilies

Lift Tropical Water Lilies in Interior Zones.
Tropical water lilies are the ones that hold their flowers high above the water and come in many exciting colors and a wide range of sizes. They usually can survive year-round outdoors, in coastal climates, but if frost hits your garden every year they probably won't live through winter. If you know it's going to freeze lift the tubers now, remove the soil, and store them in damp sand in a garage or cellar for the winter. Plant them again in spring. If this sounds like a bother buy fresh ones yearly. It's more expensive, but trying out new colors and sizes can add to the fun of growing these exotic plants.

Divide Hardy Water Lilies. Hardy water lilies are frequently smaller and less striking than tropical ones, but they're easier to grow and many people prefer the way they float on the surface

of the water rather than standing high above it, as tropical water lilies do. For the best bloom, divide hardy water lilies or pot them on every three years in October. (You can also plant more now.)

To repot hardy water lilies, lift the containers out of the pool. (Wear protective clothing and rubber gloves to avoid contact with algae, which can cause allergic reactions.) Inspect the roots; if they fill the container and the plants look crowded it's time to repot them. To do so, first clean up the plants by removing dead leaves and debris, and also take off any baby plants. (Plant these in separate containers as described on p. 108.) Then remove some of the old soil from the roots of the parent plant and pot it on, filling in around the roots in the new larger container with rich garden loam that contains no manure, peat moss, bone meal, perlite, or wood shavings. To keep the water from getting muddy and prevent fish from nibbling at roots, either cover the surface of the soil with a 1- or 2-inch layer of washed sand (or pebbles) or cover the soil surface with galvanized wire poultry netting.

Hardy water lilies that don't look crowded but do have yellow leaves and fewer flowers may simply need fertilizing. (The best feeding regimen is once a month beginning in April, as described on p. 110.) Feed now by pushing slow-release tablets recommended for aquatic plants beneath the soil surface, or mix 1 pound 5-10-10 slow-acting, granular fertilizer into the soil mix of every 5-gallon container. Replace the protective sand, pebbles, or wire netting on top.

Bulbs

Shop for Spring-Blooming Bulbs. If you didn't purchase bulbs and corms last month don't wait any longer. The early shopper gets the best bulbs. Always purchase bulbs at a first-rate nursery. You'll pay a little more, but it's worth it. Bargain bulbs sometimes won't even bloom. Some mail order catalogues are excellent sources of rare bulbs; a few offer the convenience of premium-size prechilled tulips, but many mail order bulbs of common varieties are just as expensive and much smaller than those you can find at the best nurseries.

You can still plant the South African bulbs, such as sparaxis, babiana, ixia, ipheion, freesia, watsonia, croscosmia, and tritonia. You can also plant oxalis and all the Tazetta types of narcissus, such as China lily, paper white, and Geranium. Lilies should be planted as soon as you get them home. (See p. 223 for more information on these bulbs.)

Buy daffodils, grape hyacinths, ranunculus, anemones, and Dutch irises now, but wait until next month to plant them. Keep them in a cool, dry place such as the garage. (Don't refrigerate them.) The temperature of the ground and of soil in containers is still too warm this month in most zones for safe planting of these bulbs. (In interior valleys daffodils and Dutch irises can be planted by midmonth, but it won't hurt to wait until November.)

Prechill Hyacinth, Tulip, and Crocus Bulbs. Hyacinths, tulips, and crocus (*Crocus vernus*) bulbs can also be bought now. The ☞ **Rule of Thumb** is: *To fool hyacinths, tulips, and crocuses into thinking they've had a cold winter put the bulbs in the lettuce drawer of your refrigerator for six to eight weeks prior to planting*. Gardeners who live in interior valleys should start chilling these bulbs now, for early December planting. Gardeners in coastal zones and air-drained,

frost-free zones should wait until November to start the chilling process. Store them in a cool, dry place until then.

Before you refrigerate bulbs put them in a brown paper bag, not plastic—it rots them. Write on the bag "Not onions, don't eat!" If your lettuce drawer takes delight, as some do, in regularly freezing lettuce, it's too cold for bulbs; store them on a low back shelf. They must not freeze. Also, beware of fresh fruits that give off ethylene gas, including apples, bananas, and pineapples. When these are stored in the same refrigerator with bulbs make sure they're in airtight bags or containers; if the gas escapes it can cause flower bulbs to rot or grow roots and sprout.

Divide Gladioli. When gladiolus stems have died, cut them off and dig up the corms. You'll probably be delighted, as I always am, to see how a new corm has grown on top of each old one. Sometimes you'll also find that several tiny new corms, called cormels, have sprouted around the edges of it. Knock off the soil and lay the entire thing, stem and all, on newspaper to dry for a few days in sun along the coast, or for a week or two in shade inland.

After they're thoroughly dry the corms will separate easily. Keep the new smaller, fatter corms that have grown on top to plant next year. Throw away the stem, the roots, and the old wider, flatter corm on the bottom. It's now worn out. You can leave the cormels attached if you wish, or separate them from the parent and either discard or plant them, but cormels are often difficult to sprout. To avoid this problem, prechill them in the refrigerator for two months, as described above for hyacinths, tulips, and crocuses. Then plant them 1 inch apart in flats or the ground in late winter, and let them grow until they're big enough to bloom; the process takes a year or two. Lift them in fall and plant them 6 inches apart the following year. (Occasionally the genetic structure of cormels will be different from the parent plant and you'll get a mutation, a flower unlike its parent.)

Roll the new corms and cormels in bulb dust containing a fungicide, like captan, and a pesticide, like diazinon or carbaryl, and store them in a cool, dry place, until next February, when once again it's time to plant glads. You can also treat the corms and cormels to control thrips before storage. To do so, soak the corms and cormels for six hours in a solution of 4 teaspoons of Lysol in one gallon of water. Dry the bulbs thoroughly before dusting with bulb dust and storing.

Divide Naked Ladies. Naked ladies (*Amaryllis belladonna*) are among our most valuable but least appreciated drought-resistant South African bulbs. Look for good hybrids now in nurseries. The cheerful pink flowers of the old wild (unhybridized) type are often seen in backcountry gardens arising in straight, awkward rows on bare stems from dusty ground. They look best massed, or mixed with aloes, aeonium, and statice (*Limonium perezii*) to cover a windswept bank near the sea, but they make a fine, informal bank cover in any frost-free zone. Once established inland they need only occasional water. Along the coast (Zone 24) they need little or no irrigation.

Eventually naked ladies form big clumps that push up out of the ground and need dividing. The ☞ **Rule of Thumb** is: *Divide naked ladies in early October, after bloom but while they're still dormant and before new roots or leaves have begun*

Quick Tip

Off-Season Bulb Storage.
For tuberous begonias, caladiums, dahlias, gladioli, and other bulb and bulb-type plants, first line a wire hanging basket with fly screen and a handful or two of sponge rock. Roll the bulbs in bulb dust, place them in the basket, and cover them with more sponge rock. Hang them in a cool, dry spot high enough to be out of the reach of field mice. (They relish most bulbs and corms.)

How to Force Poinsettias to Bloom for the Holidays

Potted poinsettias saved from last Christmas can be forced into bloom again this year, if you start now. In most cases the time involved hardly pays, but the large tub and tree-size plants produced by growers in recent years can make the trouble worthwhile, considering the plant's beauty and original cost.

- Place a healthy poinsettia plant in a warm, protected place where it will get four to six hours of direct sunlight daily. Turn it for even growth.

- Begin on October 1 to keep the plant in a totally dark, cool place (65°F; 18°C) for fourteen hours every night, for ten weeks. For example, you could place it in a closet or in the garage under an upside-down trash can or cardboard box from 5 P.M. to 7 A.M. Don't allow even the tiniest glint of light to hit the plant during the nightly dark period, or flowering will be delayed. (Temperatures below 60°F, 15°C, will also delay bloom.)

- Every morning return the plant to a place where it will get four to six hours of direct sunlight during the day.

- Meanwhile water and feed the poinsettia often with a complete liquid fertilizer high in bloom ingredients.

- When bracts on your plant begin to show good color, about the first week in December, discontinue the darkness regimen and enjoy the bloom.

to grow. If early rains stimulate growth, wait another year and dig them up a little earlier. They won't bloom for several years if divided during active growth.

Store Tuberous Begonias. Allow tuberous begonias to dry out after bloom. Slip the root ball out of the pot and let the whole thing dry in the sun. Leaves and stems will fall off by themselves. After the root ball is thoroughly dry tear off the roots, roll the tuber in fungicide, and store it for the winter in sponge rock or perlite.

If you prefer you can try keeping the tuber right in the pot or in the ground. Lay the pot on its side in a cool, dry, shady spot. Simply ignore the ones in the ground. Some may rot but a few may come back next year.

Chrysanthemums

Stop feeding chrysanthemums as soon as buds begin to open. Sit back and enjoy the flowers of your labor. Bait for slugs and snails. Visit nurseries that specialize in chrysanthemums. For example at Sunnyslope Chrysanthemum Gardens (8638 Huntington Drive, San Gabriel 91775; 818/952-4071) see how to grow chrysanthemums as spectacular cascades, hanging baskets, and bonsai. There are also annual displays at Descanso Gardens (1418 Descanso Drive, La Cañada 91011; 818/952-4400) and the Los Angeles Arboretum (301 North Baldwin, Arcadia 91006; 818/821-3222).

Roses

Give roses up to 1½ inches of water twice weekly. If you spray your roses continue the use of Funginex to control diseases, but cease spraying with Orthene this month. Fertilize roses for the last time this year if you use commercial rose food; apply it early in the month. If you're following the Rose-Pro Method, do not fertilize this month. Continue to pick and deadhead roses to set the stage for next month's flowers, often the best of the year.

Flower Beds and Containers

Cool-Season Flowers. Depending on your climate zone and the condition of your garden last month, you may or may not have started to switch flower beds and containers from summer to winter annuals, perennials, and biennials. (I am referring here to the plants that we grow as annual color and switch each season. See p. 232 for a rundown on this subject and how we grow these plants here.) October is the best month to complete this job, so if you still have flower beds and pots filled with warm-season annual flowers get them pulled out before month's end. Dig up, amend, and fertilize the soil, and transplant or sow flowers for winter and spring bloom.

Flowers to put in from transplants now for cool-season color include alyssum, calendula, cyclamen, cineraria, delphinium, dianthus, foxglove, flowering cabbage (ornamental kale), Iceland poppy, johnny-jump-up, nemesia, paludosum daisy, pansy, perennial candytuft, English or polyanthus primrose, fairy or malacoides primrose, obconica primrose, snapdragon, stock, sweet William, sweet violet, and viola. Get them into the ground as soon as possible, provide them with adequate light, and feed them well for fast growth and bloom. The ☞ Rule of Thumb is: *If you get winter annuals to bloom before the holidays you'll enjoy their flowers*

✳ ✳ ✳

Make a Ball of Primroses to Bloom All Winter into Spring

· Hang up a 14-inch wire basket. Create a neat edge by shoving premoistened sphagnum moss tightly through the two top lines of wire and clipping it into the shape of a smooth tube. Line the rest of the basket with more moist moss.

· Fill the basket with a good grade of soil mix, such as Bandini #105.

· Wrap the roots of twelve or fourteen malacoides primrose transplants in a little moist sphagnum moss (like tiny blankets). Separate two wires on the side of the basket, push in the wrapped roots of one plant, and reclose the wires. By this means plant the sides of the basket solidly with primroses, in a zigzag pattern. Reserve four to six plants for the top. (The roots of these don't have to be wrapped.)

· Keep the ball in full sun along the coast or part shade inland. Water by drip tube or hose. Feed with 20-20-20 liquid or 14-14-14 slow-release fertilizer.

✳ ✳ ✳

Keep Rabbits from Eating Pansies.
Nibbled tips on such plants as pansies,
petunias, and lettuce may be rabbit damage.
Sprinkle mothballs on the ground. (If you have a
baby, substitute moth crystals, since mothballs
might be mistaken for candy.) Cats, dogs,
opossums, and skunks are also repelled by the
odor of mothballs.

How to Make a Hanging Basket
Hang Straight.
Your hanging baskets will always hang straight
instead of crooked if, before you attach their
plant hangers, you bend all of their wires
simultaneously. Grasp a three- or four-wire plant
hanger so all the wires are held tightly together,
and bend the ends of the wires all at once into
a hook, about 4 inches from the tips. Then
spread the wires apart. Hook each plant-hanger
wire under the top basket wire or through a hole
in a wooden or plastic basket, and then bend
the plant-hanger wire back around itself.

throughout winter. If you don't, they'll just sit there
doing nothing until the weather warms up in
spring.

Even this late in the year you can plant from seeds, bring some of the flowers into bloom before Christmas, and have abundant flowers in spring; some varieties will continue to bloom through summer. Flowers to plant from seeds now include African daisy (*Dimorphotheca*), calendula, California poppy, clarkia, annual candytuft, godetia, snapdragon, sweet alyssum, Shirley poppy, johnny-jump-up, lavatera, nasturtium, phacelia, forget-me-not, hollyhock, linaria, and many wildflowers. Sweet alyssum, johnny-jump-ups, and linaria are usually the first to bloom, closely followed by calendulas. (For the most rewarding show grow tall calendula varieties such as Pacific Beauty, not the dwarf kinds.)

Permanent Perennials to Dig up, Divide, and Replant, or to Mulch. Most perennials, of course, are treated as permanent plants, not as annual color. They continue to grow and to flower in season for many years. Many gardeners combine these plants in the same bed with those treated mainly as annuals. Some permanent perennials, like the Shasta daisies already mentioned, should be lifted, divided, and replanted now (or you can throw them out and plant them again from seed). Others, like alstroemerias (Peruvian lilies) and clivia, prefer to be left in the ground undisturbed. Still others, like daylilies and irises (as already discussed), need occasional division. And chrysanthemums, which are discussed as a separate category throughout this book, are best grown on new roots from fresh cuttings taken annually in spring.

If some of these plants already grace the flower bed you're digging up and replanting for winter and spring, treat each one according to its specific requirements; either lift and divide them now or work around them without disturbing their roots. If in doubt about the correct way to handle a specific perennial refer to a good garden encyclopedia, such as Everett's *Encyclopedia of Horticulture,* Wyman's *Gardening Encyclopedia,* or the *Sunset Western Garden Book.* (Unfortunately most books on perennials give only general information on care, but they'll usually tell you if a particular plant hates to have its roots disturbed.)

I know of at least one Southern California gardener who treats his perennials in the same way that English gardeners care for their renowned herbaceous borders (flower beds planted with nonwoody plants). Every year in fall he lifts all perennial plants, digs up the bed, fertilizes and amends the soil, and then promptly replaces the plants, after first dividing those that require it. The only exceptions are those plants that detest being disturbed, and to these he gives a liberal topping of mulch.

Wildflowers

One of the greatest joys in gardening is growing wildflowers. Plant them early this month for a flower display that begins prior to Christmas and lasts through June—sometimes throughout summer.

One of the best ways to go is to buy several packaged mixes of California or Western wildflowers and add some choices of your own, such as extra linaria, California poppies, and larkspur. Put in some splashes of scarlet flax and an edging of nemophila. Notice that the labels of

How to Grow Cineraria

Cineraria are the aristocrats of the shade garden. Put in transplants now, and care for them through winter. They thrive on cold weather, as long as it doesn't freeze, then bloom fabulously in February, March, or April.

· For the finest display purchase transplants of medium or tall—not dwarf—varieties, or grow your own next year by planting seeds in August.

· Choose a spot in open shade under trees or overhangs. (Under the open sky to the north of a tall tree or house is ideal, if you protect the plants from frost.)

· Provide deep, well-drained acid soil. If that's not available, plant in 8- to 12-inch plastic pots, and sink them into the ground.

· Plant in a solid pattern all over the bed at intervals of 8 to 12 inches, depending on variety. Water regularly. Don't let the roots dry out.

· Feed every two weeks with a high-nitrogen fertilizer, such as Terr-O-Vite.

· Bait for slugs and snails, and use a systemic spray against leaf miners and aphids.

· When plants are robust and flower buds begin to show switch the fertilizer to 0-10-10 or 2-10-10. Feed once a week until flowers open.

* ✳ *

Use Pea Stakes to Protect Flowers from Heavy Rains and Wind

Use English pea stakes (originally devised to support peas) to prevent flowers from being damaged by wind or rain. Cut 2- to 4-foot-tall branches with many twigs from shrubs, such as Victorian box (*Pittosporum undulatum*). Ideally the branches are straight and strong and the twigs splay like the ribs of an upside-down umbrella. Remove the leaves.

Shove the bottoms of the sticks into the ground all over flower beds after planting. Annual and perennial flowers will grow up through the branches, lean on the twigs, and won't get knocked down by winter weather. By the time the beds are full grown the twigs should be largely hidden by foliage and flowers.

* ✳ *

some mixes indicate whether the seeds are those of annuals or perennials and whether they're easy to grow. Labels often also tell the season when you can expect the flowers to bloom, whether they need dry or moist soil, whether they prefer sun or shade, and the average height of the plants.

If you want spring flowers look for seed mixes that concentrate on spring-flowering annuals. If you'd like longer-lasting color choose seed mixes that combine annuals with perennials. If you want long-lasting bloom in a sunny bed your best bet is to choose a mixture of Western wildflowers that contains both annuals and perennials and that needs dry soil in full sun. In good years when we have adequate rains the wildflowers in these drought-resistant mixes can survive through winter and spring on little more than natural rainfall, but they perform better and last months longer when irrigated regularly once the rains cease. If you irrigate them once a week in hot weather they'll provide an ever-changing and delightful flower display from Christmas until fall, at which time you can replant. If gaps occur now and then throughout the year, fill them in with annual flowers—for example you could plant seeds of zinnias in late spring. (A word of warning: if you live in a suburban area, steer clear of wildflower mixtures that contain grasses along with the flowers. These are fine for country meadows but they look weedy in suburban gardens, and the grasses may reseed themselves in lawns, ground covers, and shrubbery.)

Another way to plant wildflowers is to make your own mix with such easily grown selections as California poppies, larkspur, linaria, nemophila, phacelia, scarlet flax, Chinese houses (*Collinsia heterophylla*), clarkia, and godetia. If desired dot

A Foolproof Way to Grow Wildflowers

· Choose a spot in full sun. Spade or rototill the ground deeply, adding organic soil amendment but no fertilizer. (If you plant wildflowers for three years in the same bed, sprinkle the ground with a light application of complete fertilizer before planting for the third time.) Smooth and level the surface with the garden rake.

· Decide on a watering system. Bi-Wall drip tubes are best. (Run the lines 12 inches apart and bury them 3 or 4 inches deep.)

· If the area you're planting is too wide for you to reach all parts of it from the edges, either make wandering paths through it or place stepping stones here and there between the drip tubes so you can walk on the bed without compacting the soil.

· Sprinkle seeds of Western wildflowers all over the bed. Sprinkle individual types in drifts, putting tall varieties at the back or in the middle and shorter varieties at the front or around the edges.

· Rake the seed lightly into the soil.

· Intersperse pea stakes throughout the bed. (See the accompanying box.)

· Protect the seeds and sprouts from birds: stretch Ross bird netting over the stakes. Fasten the edges down with rocks or wire staples. (After the plants are up 4 to 5 inches take off the netting but leave the pea stakes in place to support the plants through wind and rain.)

· Sprinkle the bed by hand twice a day until seeds germinate. Then start watering with a drip system or by soaking the bed when rains aren't adequate.

· After the plants are up and growing stand or lean on your paths or stepping-stones to weed and thin them, if necessary. Bait for slugs, snails, and cutworms.

· Use canes pruned from climbing roses to protect the bed from being smashed by skunks or other animals in spring. (See p. 29 for directions.)

✳ ✲ ✳

How to Aerate a Compacted Lawn

When the soil under a lawn becomes compacted from foot traffic or heavy equipment it loses its springy texture and becomes hard like a rock. Water puddles or runs off, and lack of air to the roots causes the turf to deteriorate in appearance and vigor; it often develops thin or bare patches. To correct this condition take these steps.

- Mow the lawn, then make holes in the sod by running a rented aeration machine over it. Or do the job by hand with a tool made for the purpose.
- Rake up the plugs.
- Spread 40 pounds of gypsum and 15 cubic feet of organic soil amendment (such as fine-grained nitrolized redwood or finely ground bark) over each 1,000 square feet of lawn. Apply a complete lawn fertilizer according to package directions. When the soil or thatch is hydrophobic (so dry it sheds water) also spread on a pelletized penetrant, such as Water In or Soil Air, according to package directions.
- Rake these materials into the holes. Follow up by watering deeply.

✳ ✲ ✳

the bed with tall orange calendulas. They'll bloom ahead of the California poppies to provide a happy contrast with the soft lavender tones of the linaria.

Lawn Care

Cool-season lawns such as ryegrass, bluegrass, and fescue are beginning to speed up now, and warm-season lawns such as Bermuda, zoysia, and St. Augustine are beginning to slow down. That means it's time to reset the blades on your lawnmower (as described below). Many lawn owners like to mulch their lawns with manure or a fine-grained soil amendment now, prior to the winter rains. This is also a good time to aerate lawns with a machine made for the purpose. (See the accompanying box.) Aeration aids growth by getting air to the roots.

Cool-Season Lawns. Reset mower blades to cut cool-season grasses shorter now, to 1½ inches. Improved varieties of tall fescue can also be cut at this shorter height now. Make sure the mower is sharp so it doesn't mangle the tips of tough fescue grass blades.

Help cool-season lawns to wake up and grow by feeding them with a complete lawn fertilizer for both root and top growth. If your lawn's been plagued with fungus and you haven't done anything about it tackle the problem now, ahead of the rains. Many products are available. Some contain fertilizer, which makes them easier to spread evenly.

Dethatch cool-season lawns and uproot any crabgrass in it in early fall. This is an annual task that can transform a lawn. (See the accompanying box.) Crabgrass can't get started in a thick, healthy lawn. It's nice to know that once you've

How to Plant a Cool-Season Lawn

If you want an instant lawn, order sod. (Be sure to prepare the ground thoroughly. Grade the soil ½ inch lower than walks to allow for the thickness of the sod, and before installing it level the ground carefully.) If you're going to plant from seed, take these steps.

· Choose turfgrass adapted to your area, such as Bonsai Supreme, a mixture of Twilight, Taurus, and Bonsai dwarf fescues or, near the coast, a blend of two or more varieties of Kentucky bluegrass and improved perennial ryegrass. (Get advice from your University of California Cooperative Extension Office.)

· Amend the soil.

· Level the ground, using a rented leveler or a handmade dragbar or leveler (as described on p. 63).

· Install a sprinkler system.

· Rent a seed sower or use a hand-held sower. Spread the seeds precisely according to the directions for the variety you're planting. Sow half the seeds while walking back and forth in one direction, the other half while walking at right angles to the original direction.

· Rake the soil lightly with a garden rake so the seed will be covered with no more than ¼ inch of soil. (Rake in one direction only so the seeds won't be buried too deeply.)

· Optional step: instead of raking the seed into the ground use a squirrel cage (a rentable mulch spreader) to cover the seeds. Cover them with not more than ¼ inch of ground bark or screened manure, or the amount directed for the seeds you're using.

· Spread a lawn fertilizer, according to package directions.

· Roll the lawn with a lawn roller one-third full of water. Erect a barrier, such as Weathashade Fence-It, to keep children and dogs out of the area.

· Use a fine spray of water to wet the soil at least 4 inches deep. (Be careful not to create puddles, because this will float the seed to the surface.) Then sprinkle lightly three or more times a day as needed to keep the surface soil moist until the grass sprouts. (Tall fescue and ryegrass germinate in about ten days. Bluegrass takes about one month.)

· When grass is about 2 inches high mow it to 1½ inches. Use a sharp mower and mow when the soil is somewhat dry, so you don't tear out young grass plants.

dethatched and started a good program of water and fertilizer your problems will mostly be confined to the edges. October is also the best time of the year to plant a cool-season lawn from seed. (See separate box.)

Warm-Season Lawns. Continue to cut warm-season lawns at the same height that you cut them throughout summer. Cutting them longer in winter, once a common practice, will simply increase thatch. Keep warm-season lawns green longer by continuing your feeding program through October.

Overseed Bermuda grass with annual winter ryegrass, if desired, for a green lawn in winter. Cut Bermuda short before overseeding, and mulch with manure or a fine-grained, dark-colored soil amendment in a ¼-inch layer over the seeds, to speed germination. Keep the ground damp until the seeds are sprouted. Be aware that in some areas, particularly warm coastal regions, there isn't enough summer heat to get the rye to completely die out in summer. The result can be a shaggy-looking summer lawn. So before overseeding with winter rye observe local lawns to see the final effects on your kind of Bermuda.

Dethatch kikuyu grass now to keep it in bounds (see the accompanying box). Collect and bag the stolons. Don't put them in compost.

Dichondra. Continue to check dichondra for flea beetles; they're most active from May through October. The round dead patches this beetle causes are often mistaken for fungus damage, lack of water, or fertilizer burn. Flea beetles can easily be seen against a white background. To see if they're attacking your dichondra put a handkerchief on the lawn or lay a

white piece of paper on the lawn and tap it; the insects will hop onto it. Inspect the cloth or paper for black, shiny beetles ½₅ inch long—about the size of a pinhead. You can also use an ordinary magnifying or reading glass to see how the lawn is damaged; flea beetles skeletonize dichondra leaves, which then turn brown. Once you've diagnosed the problem waste no time correcting it. Flea beetles work fast. Treat the lawn with Sevin, diazinon, or chlorpyrifos (Dursban). Two treatments will probably be necessary. After treatment reseed bare patches. (If some were caused by traffic patterns, stepping-stones can solve the problem and add charm.)

Continue to water dichondra when it wilts slightly and you can see your footprints in it. Then water deeply, so roots grow deep. The best time to water dichondra is just before dawn; the worst time, late afternoon.

Vegetable Gardening

It's time to put in the winter vegetable garden or, if you started planting last month, to continue the job. First, pull up and throw out or compost the remains of your summer garden. A thorough cleanup now really pays off in fewer bugs and diseases later. Dig up the soil deeply with a spade, turning it over, aerating it, and breaking up the clods as you go. Then use a garden fork to mix in such organic amendments as steer manure, chicken manure, seaweed, home-made or commercial compost, and whatever source of humus you've got. Add commercial fertilizer for vegetables according to package directions; work this into the top 6 inches of soil. If you're an organic gardener use instead blood meal, cottonseed meal, bone meal, or

How to Dethatch Cool-Season Lawns and Control Crabgrass

Some cool-season lawns, such as bluegrass and the new, finer-textured tall fescues, make lots of thatch. Others, such as ryegrass, make little or none. (See p. 61 for a description of thatch and how to gauge its thickness.)

- Dethatch cool-season lawns that need it, annually—in early fall.

- Mow the lawn short. Mow several times in different directions, adjusting the blades lower with each mowing. (This part of the process is much the same as that used on warm-season lawns in spring, as described on p. 62, but don't scalp cool-season lawns right down to the ground.)

- If the thatch isn't very thick you can dethatch a cool-season lawn by hand; rake vigorously with an ordinary metal grass rake or a special dethatching rake. Or do the job with a rented vertical mower, as described for warm-season lawns.

- Gather the piles of thatch into bags, and send them to the dump. Don't compost them, because they contain weed seeds.

- As you use a rake you may notice certain grasses standing up much higher than your lawn grass. This is usually crabgrass. It grows low and crablike, spreading out into a thick clump, but when you rake it the stolons stand up taller than the lawn grasses. Pull it up by the roots now and throw it away along with the thatch. (Use preemergent herbicides in late winter.)

- Roughen up and reseed any bare spots left by crabgrass. Cover the whole lawn with dark-colored mulch, such as manure or ground bark.

- Spread a slow-acting fertilizer such as Milorganite all over the lawn except on the parts you reseeded. (Fertilizers inhibit germination.)

- Water deeply and keep newly seeded areas moist.

Quick Tip

How to Plant a Gopher-Proof Lawn.
*Prepare and level the ground for planting.
Reserve some amended soil. Cover the ground
with chicken wire (½-inch mesh) laid flat, and
wire the sections together. Cover the chicken wire
with 2 or 3 inches of soil. Then plant the lawn
from seed. When planting from sod simply cover
the prepared ground with chicken wire, and
overlap the edges of the wire strips by one or two
inches. Lay the sod directly on top of the wire.*

* 🟎 *

How to Presprout Carrot Seeds

Some gardeners have trouble getting carrots to germinate, especially in dry or windy weather. This usually comes from not keeping them damp long enough. (It can take two to three weeks.) If you've had this problem or have difficulty at certain times of year, try pre-sprouting carrots. (Or see the tip on p. 266 for another method.)

- Mix the seeds into a handful of damp peat moss. Spread this on a paper plate.

- Put the whole thing into a ziplock bag, seal it, and freeze it for twenty-four hours.

- Remove the plate from the freezer, and leaving it inside the ziplock bag, give it bottom heat, for example on the TV or VCR (75° to 80°F; 24° to 27°C) for up to three days. Inspect it daily for sprouting.

- As soon as the seeds sprout take them out of the bag and sprinkle them, moss and all, into a prepared row. Cover this lightly with potting soil, and keep it well watered until the sprouts come through. You'll get carrots two weeks earlier than otherwise, and they'll be uniform in height.

* 🟎 *

bagged organic vegetable food. Then use a garden rake to level the ground. Use a hoe to make furrows between rows in heavy soils.

Plant tall crops to the north and short crops to the south. Full sun is needed for all winter vegetables.

Plant Vegetables from Seeds and Transplants. Plants that can be put in from seeds now include beets, carrots (see boxes), Swiss chard, kohlrabi, kale, mustard greens, parsnips, green peas, snap and other edible-pod peas, fava beans, lettuce, radishes, spinach, turnips, rutabagas, cabbage, broccoli, cauliflower, and celery. Though all of the above technically can be planted from seed, it's better to put in celery and most cole crops, including cabbage, broccoli, cauliflower, Brussels sprouts, and collards, from transplants instead of seed now. It's a little late to plant these vegtables from seed. Also plant lettuce from transplants, for an early harvest; plant it from seed for later crops. (Send away for gourmet varieties, for example a mesclun.)

Parsley grows well from seed, but it's slow to germinate. (Keep it damp for twenty days.) Most gardeners find it easier to grow from transplants. Put in a row now, feed it well, and you'll have masses of parsley all winter—so convenient for stuffing turkey and garnishing your holiday foods.

Plant curly cress, cilantro, and arugula (rocket) from seeds. All three grow rapidly, love cool weather, and are expensive to buy in markets. Garden cress tastes like watercress. Cilantro and arugula are unique, acquired tastes but delightfully addictive. Use cilantro in Chinese and Mexican cooking, salads, soups, and lamb stew. (Add it at the last minute.) Use arugula in salads, as a sophisticated garnish,

How to Grow Carrots

Carrots sprout at ground temperatures of 45° to 85°F—80° is best (7° to 29°C; best at 27°)—and thus can be planted any month year-round. (The seeds sprout slowly.)

- Choose a gourmet variety, or choose several varieties for comparison.

- Dig and prepare a bed of deep, loose, well-amended soil—sandy soil is best. A raised bed works well. Or grow carrots in a half-barrel filled with planter mix. Add bone meal and low-nitrogen vegetable fertilizer but no fresh manure—it makes carrots fork or grow many hairy roots. Water the bed deeply and allow it to settle overnight.

- Plant the seeds all over a raised bed or in a straight row next to a buried drip tube. For the latter press the back of a hoe handle into the soil to make a shallow trench.

- Carrots have tiny seeds, so mix them with a little sand in the palm of your hand to make them easier to sprinkle evenly. Pelletized seeds are available in some catalogues. You can grab these one by one and space them so they won't require thinning.

- Sprinkle the seeds thinly and evenly on the bed or down the row. Cover them lightly with ¼ inch potting soil. Pat it down gently to create good contact.

- Cover the bed with burlap strips if the weather's hot and dry.

- Sprinkle the bed once or twice daily with a fine spray for one to two weeks to keep the ground thoroughly moist until the seeds sprout. (Don't let it dry out.)

- If you're using burlap, peep under it daily. As soon as sprouts show, remove it.

- If you're not using a drip system wait until the ground is dry 4 inches down or until the sprouts just begin to wilt before watering again. Then commence regular deep watering. (This encourages a tap root to go straight down and can produce a straight carrot even in clay soil.)

- Thin the carrots according to package directions. Eat the thinnings. Carrots cannot be transplanted; it makes them grow in inedible, forked, and twisted shapes.

≺

Quick Tip

**How to Speed Germination of Seeds
of the Parsley Family.**
*Carrots, like parsley, parsnip, and the
ornamental wild carrot, Queen Anne's lace
(Daucus carota), are all members of the parsley
family (Umbelliferae), and as a group their seeds
are slow to germinate. To hasten the process
sprinkle the seeds on prepared soil and pour
boiling water over them, straight from the kettle.
Cover the seeds with potting soil. Keep it damp
until they've sprouted.*

≺

Quick Tip

How to Prevent Green Shoulders.
*Some carrot varieties tend to push up out of the
soil as they grow. The exposed portions turn
green or red and develop a bitter flavor. Prevent
this by mulching the row, or by mounding
some soil around the base of the plants
when the tops are 4 inches tall.*

≺

with Italian food, in sandwiches, and as a
flavorful raw accompaniment to oxtail soup
made from the dry mix. Both seed themselves
if you let them.

You can also plant potatoes from seed potatoes, raspberries (choose mild-winter varieties)
from plants or bare roots, globe artichokes from
seedlings or bare roots, horseradish from bare
roots, and rhubarb also from bare roots now
(though since rhubarb doesn't grow well here I
don't recommend growing it). Onions can be
put in from sets but, as explained before, you
won't get globe onions from them; you'll get
scallions.

Confine horseradish in it's own bed; it's an
invasive though culinarily useful weed. If you've
been growing it now's the time to dig up the
large roots. Peel the root, grind it (easily done
in a food processor), and then purée it with
a little water and a splash of vinegar. (Wear
gloves and don't get fumes up your nose.) Mix
a portion of this by hand with sour cream
and sugar to use right away. (Freeze the excess
purée in ice cube trays to use as needed.)

Wait until early November to plant strawberries and globe onions. Look for seeds of short-
day onion varieties, including Grano, Granex, or
Crystal Wax, now, if you didn't do it in September, so you'll have them on hand.

**Cut Down Brown Stems of Asparagus and Plant
New Beds.** Leave the stems of asparagus on the
plants as long as they remain green. When
they've turned brown, which should occur
sometime between now and January, cut them
off at ground level and top-dress the bed with
manure. Asparagus doesn't mind salty soil, but
it needs rich and preferably sandy soil, full sun,

good drainage, lots of water, and plenty of room.

Asparagus also can be planted now (as described on p. 64). It's best to plant a variety developed for this area by the University of California, such as UC 157. Asparagus is a reliable perennial vegetable, and once planted a bed of it can bear crops for as long as fifteen years if you give it good care.

Prechill Strawberry Plants for November Planting.

In mid-October cut off the runners you've been encouraging your strawberries to grow (see p. 193), thus severing them from the parent plants. Gently dig up these runners, and bare their roots by brushing or shaking off the dirt. Clip off all but two or three leaves from each new little plant. Gather them into bunches and tie them loosely together. Place the bunches in a plastic bag, and put it on a low back shelf of your refrigerator or, if your refrigerator doesn't freeze lettuce or other vegetables, into the lettuce drawer. Leave them there for twenty days prior to planting them next month, on or before November tenth. Prechilling strawberries fools them into thinking they've had a cold winter. Once the plants have become reestablished in the ground, and as soon as the days lengthen and the weather begins to warm up in late winter, they'll be stimulated to produce fruit instead of more vegetative growth. Meanwhile dig up the bed, throw away or compost all the old plants that bore this year, choose another spot for planting your new strawberry plants, and plant something else in the old bed.

Purchase / Plant

- [ ] If you grew your own transplants of **cool-season flowers** and **vegetables** plant them out in the garden now, 215
- [ ] Plant all types of **permanent landscape plants** other than bare-root plants, tropicals, and native plants, 245
- [ ] Desert dwellers can plant most **summer** and **winter vegetables** now, and many flowers, 246
- [ ] Plant **flame vine** in all mild zones; in the desert include **oleander** and **Easter lily vine**, 246
- [ ] Plant **trees, shrubs,** and **vines,** 246
- [ ] Choose and plant for permanent **fall and winter color,** 247
- [ ] Continue to shop for spring-blooming bulbs and plant the ones that can be put in now, including **South African bulbs, oxalis,** and **Tazetta** types of **narcissus,** 251
- [ ] Plant **lilies** as soon as you get them home, 252
- [ ] Buy **daffodils, grape hyacinths, ranunculus, anemones,** and **Dutch irises;** keep them in a cool dry place until planting time, 252
- [ ] Purchase **hyacinth, tulip,** and **crocus** bulbs and prechill them in the refrigerator, 252
- [ ] Plant **cool-season flowers** for winter and spring bloom, 255
- [ ] Plant **cineraria** for late winter and early spring bloom, 257
- [ ] Plant **wildflowers,** 257
- [ ] Plant **cool-season lawns;** this is the best time of year for this job, 261
- [ ] Overseed **Bermuda grass** with **annual winter ryegrass,** if desired, 262
- [ ] Plant **cool-season vegetables, year-round vegetables,** including **carrots** and some perennial vegetables, 264
- [ ] In cold low-lying gardens plant **hardy flowers** for winter color; avoid tender bedding plants, 303
- [ ] Plant **celery,** 312

Trim, Prune, Mow, Divide

- [ ] Thin out **sweet peas** and pinch them back to force branching, 233
- [ ] Divide, trim, and mulch **plants that tend to grow in a clump** and that need to be divided, including **Kahili ginger, clivia, iris, daylily, moraea, bird of paradise, lily turf, gazaneas,** and **perennials** like **Shasta daisies,** 247
- [ ] Cut back **zonal** and **ivy geraniums,** 249, 250
- [ ] Finish pruning **Martha Washing-tons,** 250
- [ ] Cut back or mow **coyote bush** that has become tall and woody, 250
- [ ] Continue to shape and clean out the dead interiors of **native plants,** 251
- [ ] Divide **hardy water lilies,** 251
- [ ] Lift, dry, separate, and store **gladioli,** 252
- [ ] Divide **naked ladies,** 253
- [ ] Dig up, divide, and replant **perennials,** or mulch them, 255
- [ ] Cut branches out of **shrubbery** to make pea stakes, 258
- [ ] Reset mower blades to cut **cool-season lawns** shorter for the winter growing season, 260
- [ ] Continue to mow **warm-season lawns** short, 262
- [ ] Dethatch **kikuyu grass** to keep it in bounds, 262
- [ ] Cut down **asparagus** stems after they go brown, 266
- [ ] Cut off runners from **strawberries,** gather them in bunches, and prechill them for November planting, 267

Fertilize

- [ ] Feed **fuchsias,** 55
- [ ] Continue to treat **blue hydrangeas** with aluminum sulfate, 229
- [ ] Fertilize **hardy water lilies** that appear to need it, but don't fertilize tropical ones, 251
- [ ] Stop fertilizing **chrysanthemums,** and enjoy the blooms, 254
- [ ] Fertilize **poinsettias** with a complete fertilizer high in bloom ingredients, 254
- [ ] Feed **roses** early this month (Rose-Pro gardeners stop fertilizing now), 255
- [ ] Feed **cool-season lawns** with a complete fertilizer, 260
- [ ] Continue to feed **warm-season lawns** to keep them green longer, 262

Water

- [ ] Water **all garden plants** according to their individual needs, your soil, your climate zone, and the weather (If rains start early reduce water accordingly.) 245
- [ ] Water **deciduous fruit trees** more sparingly in fall, 247
- [ ] Water **roses** with up to 1½ inches of water twice a week, unless rains do the job for you, 254
- [ ] Continue to water **lawns** when rains aren't adequate, 258

Control Pests, Diseases, and Weeds

- [ ] Treat **gladiolus** corms for fungus and thrips. (Don't put fungicide on those you plan to prechill.), 252
- [ ] Protect **pansies, petunias,** and **lettuce** from rabbits, 256
- [ ] Treat **cool-season lawns** with fungicide if required, 260
- [ ] Check **dichondra** for flea beetles; treat if necessary, 262
- [ ] Create a **gopher-proof lawn** by burying chicken wire under it prior to planting, 263
- [ ] Get rid of existing **crabgrass** by hand pulling, 263
- [ ] Continue to control diseases on **roses,** 254

Also This Month

- [ ] Harvest **macadamia nuts** when they fall to the ground. Cure them properly, 80
- [ ] Lift **tuberoses** and store in perlite until next May, 137
- [ ] Untie the fronds of **palms** transplanted in August, 212
- [ ] Tie up **sweet peas** and **edible peas** to prevent them from being knocked down by wind or rain, 233
- [ ] In interior zones where frost can be expected, lift and store **tropical water lilies** for the winter, 251
- [ ] If you want to try growing the cormels (tiny side bulbs) of **gladioli,** prechill them in the refrigerator, 251
- [ ] Store **tuberous begonias** for the winter, 254
- [ ] Begin forcing **potted poinsettias** for Christmas bloom, 254
- [ ] Finish pulling out faded **annual flowers** and cleaning pots and beds for fall planting, 255
- [ ] Make a ball-shaped basket of **malacoides primroses,** 255
- [ ] Straighten **hanging baskets** by attaching new wires if necessary, 256
- [ ] Aerate **lawns** that are compacted from foot traffic or heavy machinery, 260
- [ ] Thoroughly clean up the **vegetable garden;** pull up the last of the summer crops and compost the remains, 262
- [ ] Dethatch **cool-season lawns** by hand or machine, 263
- [ ] Harvest **horseradish,** 266

NOVEMBER

The First Month of the Rainy Season

Throughout most of the United States November signals the onset of cold and icy weather. After a short respite of late warm weather, the Indian summer, the sun dips low on the horizon and winter sets in for good. Gardeners throw mulch over tender roots and wrap up roses ahead of the snow. But in Southern California November heralds the return of the rainy season.

This is an active time for us and for many of our plants. Out in the backcountry, in canyons and on hillsides, the native landscape wakes up from summer dormancy and starts to green-up and grow. In our gardens we look forward to color from many flowering plants programmed by nature to bloom in winter. Roses give us some of their best blooms in November. If you did most of your fall planting in October, November is an easy month in the garden. But if you didn't plant last month don't

wait any longer—do it now. Regardless, there are a number of plants—onions, strawberries, native plants, ground covers, and many bulbs—that are best when planted in November.

Our Cyclical Rains

Ever since certain events in the 1860s it's been apparent that California's rains are not only seasonal (wet winters, dry summers), they're also cyclical (several years of ample rains followed by several years of drought). In 1861–62 California had the heaviest rains ever recorded. In Los Angeles it rained for twenty-eight days without stopping, San Francisco had 49 inches, and the Central Valley turned into a lake. This disaster was followed two years later by the worst drought in California history. Tree rings tell the story, and they have longer memories than

Pitcher Irrigation

Bury a porous clay pot and fill it with water, by hand or a pipe network, to provide controlled irrigation. Several of these in a ring under the drip line can be used to water a tree; use two or three to water a shrub, or bury a central pot to provide water for a circle of vegetables, like beans or peas. Pitcher irrigation has been used in China for more than two thousand years. According to David Brainbridge, Editor of the *Drylander* (from the Dry Lands Research Institute, University of California at Riverside, Riverside, CA 92521), recent Brazilian research finds pitcher irrigation more efficient than drip.

people—who tend to forget about bad years when the rains are good. Heavy rainfall makes them wonder, "What's all this fuss about drought?" But wise gardeners always remember first that it could happen again and second that they can never be sure how much rain there will be.

Some years the rains are torrential, smashing garden flowers and causing such bad botritus all gardeners wish they would stop. Other years there's not nearly enough rain, and gardeners have to pour on water from the hose. Every year or two there's a new scientific study that indicates the local weather pattern is changing. But it's not changing. It's the same as ever, which means never the same for very many years at a time.

Another factor, and one that's not so easy to forget, is that here in Southern California we're largely dependent on water brought from somewhere else. In the 1920s and 30s there was an overabundance of imported water. Homeowners, gardeners, and industrialists became accustomed to using water in wasteful ways. Gardens took on the grassy New England or tropical jungle look. Now we're overcrowded and there's not enough water to go around. When you combine our cyclical rainfall with the fact that irrigation water is in ever shorter supply you have a very serious problem for thirsty plants. In periods of rationing many could die. That's why we need to concentrate on establishing a basic landscape of plants that can survive drought. Now's a good time to begin.

California Native Plants

Many California native plants are well worth considering for home gardens, and November is

How to Divide and Plant Matilija Poppy

Matilija poppy (*Romneya coulteri*), one of the loveliest of California natives, has fragrant white flowers like crepe paper with large yellow centers that cover the plant all summer, complementing the handsome gray foliage. You can, if you wish, at any time of year purchase selected varieties already growing in containers from native plant nurseries (such as those mentioned above). But if you want to propagate a plant already growing in your own garden or a friend's, do the job sometime between now and January, while the plant is in its brief dormancy and just before it begins to grow again.

There are two ways to propagate this plant. The first and easiest way is to dig up a whole clump; lift it into a bucket or basket to transport it. Prepare the soil as described below for root cuttings, and plant the clump at the same depth you originally found it. The second method is to take root cuttings. (This method is best if you want to start many of these plants.)

· For root cuttings dig around the parent plant with a trowel; look for roots about pencil thick in size with small but visible buds on them. (Small pieces work fine; take several cuttings to ensure success.)

· Unless you plan to plant the cuttings immedi-ately, place them in a plastic bag filled with moist potting soil so they won't dry out. (Take them home this way if you're getting them from a friend.)

· If possible plant in well-drained soil. Loosen it first with a spade, and then plant the roots by placing them horizontally and covering them with an inch of soil.

· If you must plant in hard clay soil first spade it deeply, adding soil amendment. Then water the ground and let the area settle overnight. The next day spread a 3- or 4-inch-high layer of sand on top of the prepared area. (Use as much sand as you want; two or three bucket-fuls are ample for a good start.) Plant the roots 2 inches down in the sand. The roots will grow right between the sand and the clay. (Never mix sand with clay—this makes clay even denser. In this case you're stacking them to make a raised bed.)

· Keep the soil damp but not soggy until the cuttings sprout and you see growth begin, then water regularly until they're established. Summer water produces longer bloom.

· When the foliage dies back in late fall cut the plants down to 4 to 6 inches. New growth soon springs again from the roots.

Special Tips for Planting California Native Plants

· When purchasing a native plant, gently slide it out of its container and check the roots. Don't choose a plant with a lot of top growth and too many roots in the can. (If it's been in a container too long its roots will have become hard and taken on the shape of the can, and it won't readapt as well to the ground.)

· In clay soil plant on raised terraces or on a slope with a sleeve drain (see p. 11).

· Dig a planting hole, fill it with water, and let the water drain out.

· Water the plant in the container prior to planting.

· Carefully remove the plant from the can and gently lower it into the hole. Native plants are fragile; take care not to break the crown or roots.

· Before filling the soil in around the plant lay a stick across the hole and check how high you have placed the plant. Make sure the top of the root ball will end up 2 inches above the surrounding soil; this is especially important for native plants. Don't bury the crown in soil, or it will rot.

· Backfill the hole with native soil, gently pressing it down around the roots with your hands.

· Build a watering basin. Put a layer of loose mulch over the roots to keep them cool and moist.

· Water deeply. Thereafter water regularly to keep the soil damp but not soggy. During rains open the berm of the watering basin to let water out.

· Once the plant is established decrease irrigation. Eventually water it only as needed in summer.

Quick Tip

Pine Needles Are Precious.
When you rake fine-textured pine needles from a driveway don't throw them away. Save them to mulch acid-loving plants, such as camellias, azaleas, and blueberries, or to cover informal, woodland, or vegetable-garden paths.

the best time to plant them. Our state is blessed with a wealth of lovely wild plants, many of which have been improved by selection and hybridizing, yet they're often more widely planted in English gardens than here. Part of the reason may be that they require excellent drainage, they're difficult to raise in nursery containers, and summer watering combined with our hot temperatures sometimes leads to root rot. One way to avoid these problems is to purchase your native plants from nurseries that specialize in them, like Tree of Life in San Juan Capistrano, or find them at such botanical gardens as Theodore Payne in Sun Valley and Rancho Santa Ana Botanic Garden in Claremont. Also, prepare the ground properly, grow native plants on banks and in raised beds, concentrate on the best and easiest cultivars, and learn their watering requirements.

Not all native plants are drought resistant. Some are native to streambeds and need lots of water. Other native plants are so well adapted to our wet winters and dry summers that they can accept no summer water at all. Still others are more adaptable to garden conditions. They can take water in summer if it's given to them but will survive without it if necessary. Many drought-resistant plants from other parts of the world mix well with California natives. Bob Perry's *Trees and Shrubs for Dry California Landscapes* is an excellent book on the subject.

Among the hundreds of fine native plants that are well adapted to landscape use are toyon, or California holly (*Heteromeles arbutifolia*), Torrey pine (*Pinus torreyana*), Western redbud (*Cercis occidentalis*), St. Catherine's lace (*Erioganum giganteum*), California tree mallow (*Lavatera assurgentiflora*), monkeyflower (*Diplacus*, with lovely new hybrids coming soon), lemonade berry (*Rhus integrifolia*), sugar bush (*Rhus ovata*), Catalina cherry (*Prunus lyonii*), and Cleveland sage (*Salvia clevelandii*). Two outstanding native ground covers are trailing manzanita (*Arctostaphylos* 'Emerald Carpet'), which prefers shade inland, and Catalina evergreen currant (*Ribes viburnifolium*), which thrives in shade in all zones. Also don't overlook California lilac (*Ceanothus*), which has many fine species and named varieties to choose from. Select plants for color, growth habit, and adaptability to your soil and climate.

Seeds of California native plants, including wildflowers, can also be planted this month. The seeds of many native plants are difficult to germinate without special treatment, in some cases including subjecting them to fire beneath a handful of burning pine needles. Methods for germinating seeds of native plants are given in such books such as Lee W. Lenz's *Native Plants for California Gardens*. (Directions for planting wildflowers are given on p. 257.)

Pruning

Prevent Storm Damage. November, with its wind and rain, brings a natural cleanup, but unless you prepare for it, it can often cause damage. Open up spaces in dense trees. Allow the wind to pass through. A full tree with no gaps in it acts like a sail on a mast. A strong wind may capsize it, especially if the ground is wet. Remove dead and weak branches.

Make sure young trees are well staked. Tie them loosely, so they can move back and forth in the wind without being toppled. Trees need to flex in wind in order to develop strong trunks. When using wire for tying, run it through a section of old hose so it doesn't damage bark. Check all staked trees now to make sure no wires are restrictive. Once trees have become well rooted remove the stakes and wires, so bark doesn't grow over them.

Prune Acacias. Cut back top-heavy shrubs, such as acacia. Where necessary remove whole branches to allow wind to pass through. Head back young acacias to force branching and strengthen their trunks. With proper pruning these fast-growing, brittle but beautiful shrubs and small trees, often listed as short lived, can be kept going almost indefinitely.

Prune Cane Berry Plants. Prune selected cane berry plants, including blackberry, boysenberry, loganberry, and spring-bearing raspberry. Cut the old canes down to the ground, leaving the new ones that grew this year. On fall-bearing raspberry plants (which grow well only in the mountains) cut off the top of the cane that has borne fruit. Leave the bottom of the cane to fruit in spring.

Don't prune the canes of subtropical (low-chill) raspberries, like Oregon 1030, San Diego, Baba Berry, and Fallgold. These are the only kind of raspberry to grow in most Southern California climate zones, and all of them produce their best berries on new wood. Wait until December or January, then prune these by cutting them nearly to the ground. Dig up the suckers to make new rows (see p. 306).

Shrubs and Young Trees

Now through January is the best time to move shrubs and young trees that are growing in the wrong places. For evergreen shrubs and trees dig a deep trench around each one. Then cut through the earth under the root ball,

saving as many of the roots as possible. (You may unavoidably have to slice through some.) Ball the roots in burlap or chicken wire before lifting them from the hole. Once the plant is in its new hole remove the chicken wire, or if you have gophers it may help to leave it in place and let the roots grow through it. Burlap may be either removed or opened up and left in the hole to rot, as desired. Use a paint brush to brush some RooTone powder lightly over the root ball, to stimulate production of new roots.

Transplant deciduous plants after the leaves fall and the plant has gone completely dormant. Then dig up as large a root system as possible, knock off all soil, and replant them as for bare-roots, by holding the plant so its soil line is even with the surrounding ground and sifting the soil in with a trowel. Prune the top, to balance it with the loss of roots.

Ground Covers

November is the traditional month for planting carpetlike ground covers. Many gardeners find the name "ground cover" confusing. All plants that cover and hide bare ground are customarily lumped together under this general term. Many vines, shrubs, perennials, wildflowers, bulbs, and herbs are used for this purpose; often they're among the best choices for a particular task, but in most cases this is not the right time to plant these multipurpose plants. Here we're discussing only those low-lying creepy-crawly things generally sold in flats and used to replace lawns. Some can be walked on, others cannot. These true ground covers are among the most important plants in the landscape and the most difficult to choose.

Some nurseries carry a wide assortment of

ground covers. Before making a final choice consider the site, the conditions, and your requirements. See displays in botanical gardens, such as the Los Angeles Arboretum. Also study lists in the *Sunset Western Garden Book* and pictures in Mildred Mathias's *Flowering Plants in the Landscape* and Michael MacCaskey's *Lawns and Groundcovers: How to Select, Grow and Enjoy.*

Colorful iceplants, gazanias, pelargoniums, African daisies (*Osteospermum fruticosum*), cape weed (*Arctotheca calendula*), pork and beans (*Sedum rubrotinctum*), and lippia are among many fine choices, of varying drought resistance, for full sun. Beware of red apple iceplant (*Aptenia cordifolia*). It needs a lot of water and frequent fertilizing with a high-nitrogen fertilizer, like calcium nitrate, to look good. It's fine for quickly covering and holding a bank but builds up thick and needs replacement in about six years.

For shady spots fine-textured Needlepoint ivy, Indian mock strawberry (*Duchesna indica*), carpet bugle (*Ajuga reptans*), and star jasmine (*Trachelospermum jasminoides*) are among possible choices. (Some of these can grow also in sun if well watered.) For small spaces and between stepping-stones creeping thyme, Irish and Scotch moss (in coastal zones only), sea thrift (*Armeria maritima*), blue star creeper (*Laurentia fluviatilis*), and—in moist shade—baby tears (*Soleirolia soleirolii*) are possible choices. Asparagus fern (*Asparagus sprengeri*) is drought resistant. It's sold in cans—not flats—and it's highly invasive, but it's useful nonetheless for holding steep shady slopes.

On large slopes in full sun it's always better to combine shallow-rooted ground covers with taller, deeper-rooting plants, such as plumbago, bougainvillea, prostrate acacia (*Acacia redolens*),

and lantana. A combination of these four plants can provide a permanent bank cover with stunning color year-round. (Wait until next spring to plant all except acacia. It's too late to put in tropicals and subtropicals now except in the mildest zones, and then only during warm years.)

Bulbs

You don't have to wait any longer to put in ranunculus, anemones, grape hyacinths, Dutch irises, and daffodils (*Narcissus*). It's a fine time for planting these and all other spring-flowering bulbs you haven't yet planted, except tulips, hyacinths, and crocuses. Put the last three in brown paper bags and chill them in the refrigerator for six to eight weeks prior to planting time in late December or early January. Make sure they don't freeze, and mark the bags so you know what's in them.

Bulbs look best planted in natural drifts rather than rows. Prepare the soil, toss the bulbs on the ground, and plant them where they fall. Consult a bulb chart for proper planting depths. Put a little bone meal under every bulb you plant in the ground, and cover it with an inch or two of soil before adding the bulb. You can also plant bulbs in containers. Daffodils (*Narcissus*) of all types are especially good candidates for container planting. (For instructions, see the accompanying boxes.)

What Is a Daffodil? If you're confused by the names narcissus, daffodil, and jonquil, you're not alone. Even longtime gardeners muddle these terms, but the solution is quite easy. The words narcissus and daffodil have exactly the same meaning, but *Narcissus* is the botanical

How to Force Narcissus Bulbs in a
Basket for Holiday Bloom

· Purchase plump premium bulbs of paper whites, Chinese sacred lilies, Grand Soleil d'Or, Cragford, or Geranium.

· Choose a suitable flat basket—one approximately 6 to 9 inches in diameter and 3 to 4 inches high. Leave it plain or spray it with quick-drying paint.

· Line the basket with a circle of heavy-gauge (4 millimeter) plastic sheeting cut to fit.

· Fill the basket halfway to the top with clean pebbles or gravel. Add 6 or 8 bulbs, fitting them closely. Fill in with more pebbles to hold them upright.

· Cover the pebbles with sphagnum moss. (This is optional for a pleasing appearance.)

· Add water to the rim of the plastic. Add more every two or three days.

· Cover the basket with an upside-down cardboard box. Place it in a cool spot, such as the garage, for one and a half weeks or until sprouts are up 3 or 4 inches.

· Uncover the basket and place it in a sunny window or in the sun on your patio or porch until the flowers open. Direct sun keeps the stems from growing too long and floppy, but if you put it outside bring it in at night for warmth. Turn it daily for even growth.

· Enjoy the fragrant flowers in the house during Christmas or Chanukah, or make these baskets for gifts. If you plant six weeks before Christmas a few flowers will open that day. Allow six and a half weeks for fully open flowers.

· Discard the bulbs after flowers fade. Bulbs forced in water can't be reused.

name for a whole genus of bulbs, containing over twenty-six species and innumerable cultivars. Daffodil is the common name for all of them. (Tazetta and Tazetta hybrids, however, are seldom called "daffodils" in actual practice. Gardeners and bulb catalogues alike usually refer to these only by the botanical name "narcissus," though without italics.) Jonquil is the name of one small group of narcissus that bear a cluster of little blooms on a single stem, bloom late, and are usually yellow and fragrant. Jonquils are very hardy, and they're more common in the East and Middle West than here.

Begin Forcing Tazetta Narcissus. Tazetta and Tazetta hybrid narcissus, including paper whites, Chinese sacred lilies, Grand Soleil d'Or, Cheerfulness, Geranium, and others, have bunches of tiny fragrant flowers on each stem. They can be planted outdoors here as early as September, and they bloom in fall and winter; some of these may be already in bloom now. You can also begin now to force, in pebbles and water, the Tazetta and Tazetta-hybrid bulbs you've set aside for this purpose. By the method described in the accompanying box on narcissus you can make them bloom in six weeks and schedule them to bloom just when you want them to do so. This method of forcing bulbs is also used for indoor bloom in cold-winter climates.

Gardeners in cold-winter climates also force many bulbs by another method; they subject the bulbs to a certain period of winter chill outdoors in buried pots. They then bring the bulbs indoors and place them in a sunny window to force bloom in the dead of winter, months ahead of the bulbs' natural schedule. Here, there's no point in forcing bulbs in this manner and it's not even possible, so ignore the sections

Quick Tip

Plant Double for Twice the Show.
Plant a layer of daffodils 8 inches deep. Half-cover them with potting soil. Fit a second layer of bulbs into the spaces between the tips of the lower layer. Cover these with soil mix. The upper layer will bloom first, then the lower.

Quick Tip

How to Make Small Holes for Small Bulbs.
When planting just a few small-size bulbs, such as ranunculus, anemones, sparaxis, and oxalis, dig individual holes with a melon scoop.

How to Plant a Pot of Daffodils

This is simply a method for growing daffodils in containers so you can enjoy them on your patio or porch at their natural time for blooming. You're not forcing the bulbs, so you can keep them if you wish; they may flower again next year. (Each cultivar will bloom according to its built-in time schedule and your climate zone. The popular trumpet daffodil King Alfred usually blooms here in February or March.)

- Buy the largest bulbs you can find. Leave double- and triple-nosed bulbs whole. They'll produce a flower from each point.

- Choose an appropriately sized container. (Five to six bulbs will fit in a 12-inch pot; more, if you crowd them.)

- Cover the drainage hole in the bottom of your pot with a piece of broken crockery or plastic fly screen.

- Place a layer of fast-draining potting soil in the bottom of the container. Add a handful or two of bone meal. Cover this with more soil.

- Add the bulbs. Jamming them in as close as possible won't impair their growth, but it's wiser to leave a little space around each one so they don't touch each other or the sides of the container. That way if one rots you won't lose them all.

- Cover the bulbs with potting soil. When you've finished, the top of the soil should be 1 or 2 inches lower than the edge of the pot and the tips of the bulbs should be just below or even with the surface of the soil.

- Water the pot, and add more potting soil, if necessary.

- Place the pot in a cool, shady place, near a hose bib for convenience. Cover it with an upside-down cardboard box to keep it dark.

- Water the pot daily. When rain falls uncover the pot and let nature do your watering; then re-cover it when rain ceases.

- Once the leaves are up 3 or 4 inches remove the cover for good. Move the pot into bright light; put it in "skyshine" (under the open sky but not in full sun). Keep it there, or in cool semishade, until you see the first flower buds.

- Once buds appear move the pot into full or half-day sun. The flowers will face the sun, so put them where you can see their smiling faces. Once they open they'll last longer in part shade.

- After the flowers fade clip them off. You can then either dump the bulbs out of the pot and discard them or plant them in the ground; leave the roots and bulbs all together as a clump and keep them damp. Sometimes the leaves will stay green for several months; don't cut them off until after they go brown.

pertaining to this process that you find in most bulb books; they don't apply here. (All bulbs that have been forced, regardless of the method used, must be thrown out after the blooms fade. They'll never bloom again.)

Flower Beds and Containers

There's still time to plant spring flowers. November planting is not quite as good as October, but it's a thousand times better than waiting until spring, seeing everything in bloom, and regretting that you didn't plant in fall. First-time gardeners often fall in love with spring flowers when they see them blooming in April. They buy them and plant them then at great expense. But instead of six months of bloom from December through May they get a month or two, at the most, and decide they have purple thumbs. Not so; it's just their timing that's wrong. Remember this all-important ☞ **Rule of Thumb:** *For colorful spring flower beds, the time to plant is fall*.

Use Transplants. Annuals and perennials that can be put in from pony packs and color packs now include alyssum, calendula, cineraria, columbine, coral bells, cyclamen, delphinium, English daisy, dianthus, foxglove, flowering cabbage (ornamental kale), Iceland poppy, perennial candytuft, johnny-jump-up, hollyhock (for summer bloom), nemesia, pansy, paludosum daisy, phlox, primroses (polyanthus, malacoides, obconica, and others), schizanthus, snapdragon, stock, sweet William, and viola. Get them into well-prepared ground, feed them often with a product high in nitrogen as well as phosphorus and potassium, and, when rains aren't adequate, water them deeply. Even planting now you'll have a gorgeous

How to Plant Ranunculus

Ranunculus provide longer-lasting color than any other spring-flowering bulb. Each large-size tuberous root will give as many as fifty to seventy-five blooms.

- Choose a good variety, such as Tecolote Giants. Plant in mid-November.

- Choose a spot in full sun where ranunculus haven't grown for three or four years. (If sprinklers keep the bed soggy presprout the tubers in flats of damp sand; as soon as they've grown some roots plant them in the bed.)

- Cultivate the soil deeply, adding organic soil amendment, bone meal, and flower fertilizer according to package directions. Water the bed and let it settle overnight.

- Toss the tubers in drifts onto the bed. Rearrange them slightly so they're approximately 6 inches apart.

- Plant each tuber where it fell, making sure the points face down. Cover them with 1½ inches of soil in heavy ground or 2 inches in light, sandy soil.

- Soak the bed deeply. Except in dry, sandy soil or very dry weather, don't water again until green growth shows. Then, if rains are mere sprinkles, water often enough to keep the soil moist but not soggy. The tubers can rot if they're soaked prior to planting or if they're planted in soil that stays soggy wet. (See the note above about presprouting.)

- Protect the sprouts from birds with wire or plastic garden netting until they're up 4 inches.

* ✻ *

Tips for Success with Lupines

· Choose a Western variety, such as arroyo lupine (*Lupinus succulentus*).

· Scarify the seed (see p. 140). For a quick start also presprout the seed indoors, as for corn and beans (p. 121).

· Prepare ground that's in full sun for planting wildflowers. (See p. 257.)

· For an extra boost inoculate the seeds with rhizobia for lupines. The correct inoculant is available from the Nitragin Company, 3101 West Custer Avenue, Milwaukee, WI 53209. Be sure to indicate the species to be planted when you order the inoculant.

· Plant the seeds 4 to 6 inches apart. Cover them with ¼ to ⅛ inch potting soil.

· Thin the plants to 6 inches apart when they're 2 or 3 inches tall. Bait for cutworms, and use BT against caterpillars.

* ✻ *

display beginning for sure in February—maybe sooner—that will peak in April and last until June.

Plant Nasturtiums and Wildflowers from Seeds.
If you regret you didn't plant from seeds earlier, you can still do it, with some types. This is the best month to plant nasturtiums. Nasturtiums will grow and come back year after year if thrown, yes, simply tossed, onto a north-facing hillside—that is, they will if the hillside is just right, damp enough and earthy enough for them to take hold. But this fact shouldn't be taken to imply that this is the correct way to plant nasturtiums. Both wildflowers and nasturtiums do much better if you prepare the ground, dig deeply, add soil amendment (no fertilizer), cover the seeds according to package directions (rake wildflowers in lightly) and protect them from birds.

Wildflowers to plant from seeds now include alyssum, California poppy, clarkia, larkspur (it blooms in June), linaria, Southwestern species of lupine (see the accompanying tips for success), scarlet flax (*Linum grandiflorum* 'Rubrum'), Chinese houses (*Collinsia heterophylla*), baby blue eyes (*Nemophila menziesii*), and mixed packages of Western and Southwestern wildflowers.

Plant wildflowers in full sun. Keep the seedbed damp by sprinkling it by hand every day, or twice a day if it's dry and windy. Be patient. At November's cooler temperatures it's going to take a little longer for the seed to germinate; don't let the bed dry out or all is lost. (See p. 259 for more on growing wildflowers.)

Feed Flowers Planted Earlier. If you've already planted flower beds with wildflowers and other cool-season annuals and perennials, they should be spreading out and growing now. A few may start to bloom. Protect them from snails, bait for cutworms, and water when rains aren't adequate. Plants put into the ground when small build better roots in the ground. Iceland poppies, for example, bloom better and longer when planted early from tiny plants instead of later from more expensive 4-inch containers.

Don't forget that it's a race between you and the weather to get such winter-blooming plants as Iceland poppies, cyclamen, primroses, and pansies to bloom before Christmas; feed them for both growth and bloom. The trick with winter-blooming annuals is to fertilize them often, because nitrogen is less active in cool soil. You can use granulated or pellet-type flower fertilizer if you wish. Just toss it on the bed once every month or six weeks and water it in. But cool-season flowers respond best when fertilized every two weeks with a liquid product high in growth as well as bloom ingredients. (Liquid or slow release is always best for plants in pots.)

Continue to feed cineraria with a high nitrogen product for growth, such as Terr-O-Vite. Don't fertilize wildflowers at all—they don't need it unless you've grown them for several years in a patch of poor soil and you notice yellow leaves and an obvious decline in vigor. In that case only, fertilize after they're up and growing with a light application of granulated 6-10-5 flower food. In ordinary circumstances, fertilizer makes wildflowers grow too much at the expense of bloom. Most Western wildflowers are more drought resistant than other garden flowers. They can often survive on natural rainfall, but keep an eye on them and water when rains aren't adequate to keep them growing.

Plant Flowering Kale for Winter Color. Flowering kale, also called ornamental cabbage, is not only decorative, it's edible. It can be cooked, though the result won't win a prize for taste. A better culinary use is as a colorful raw garnish under salad greens, and with such edible flowers as violas and daylilies. Grow it in full sun as a winter bedding plant, a flower-bed edging, an unusual addition to hanging baskets, or an ornamental touch in your vegetable garden. It does well in large containers and mixes well with other flowers. Flowering kale is one of the best plants for winter color in the cold low-lying valleys that regularly get winter frost. Frost, far from fazing it, improves it by making its colors more brilliant.

Don't feed flowering kale for bloom; this stimulates bolting. Frequent applications of light nitrogen fertilizer, such as fish emulsion or manure tea, produce the best results. Protect the plants from cabbage worms with BT.

Chrysanthemums

Cut back chrysanthemums growing in the ground after bloom, leaving 6- to 8-inch stalks. New growth will spring from these stalks. In March take fresh cuttings from them, dig up and discard the old roots, and start over with the new plants.

After cutting the plants back, clean up the ground and discard dead leaves. Chrysanthemums are notorious disease carriers, so don't add their remains to the compost pile. When cutting back potted chrysanthemums after their blooms fade, never cut them back to short, bare stubs. Just take off the flowers and cut back the stalks lightly. They need their leaves to survive. When fresh growth begins, cut off the old leaves and stalk above the new growth.

Roses

In most climate zones roses will continue to grow and to flower throughout November and December. In fact, if you've taken good care of your plants November's blooms are often the best of the entire year. The flowers are rendered all the more pleasing by the lack of care roses need at this time of year. You can, if you wish, continue to pick and deadhead roses this month, but there's no need to spray them. Don't fertilize them now, and water them only until midmonth and then only if rains aren't adequate. Calculated neglect now encourages roses to slow down and get ready to drop their leaves and go dormant in December or January.

Citrus, Avocado, and Macadamia Trees

Wrap the trunks of young citrus, avocado, and macadamia trees with an insulating material of some kind, such as fiberglass, wood pulp, or corrugated paper, by mid-November, to protect them from frost damage. Thoroughly cover the trunk, from the soil line to the main scaffold branches. Tie or tape the material in place. Once the trees are two or three years old and have grown a good head of branches with a rooflike covering of leaves they usually don't need this protection.

Don't let the roots of young citrus, avocados, and macadamias—or mature trees either, for that matter—go dry in cold or frosty weather. Wilted leaves are more susceptible to frost damage.

Control of Peach Leaf Curl

Spray peach and apricot trees against peach leaf curl, an airborne fungus disease that impairs fruiting and can eventually kill a tree. This disease thickens and stunts new shoots, and it puckers, thickens, and curls fresh leaves from the time they first emerge in spring. Affected leaves are red or orange when they first emerge, and later they turn pale green or yellow. Later still, a grayish white powder appears on them, and finally the leaves drop prematurely from the tree. Affected trees bear poorly, and the fruit that survives is usually deformed by wrinkles, raised areas, and irregular lesions. Be sure to spray all your peach and nectarine trees—even dwarf ones growing in containers—against this dread disease, even if they've never shown symptoms. Since peach leaf curl is caused by an airborne fungus it's carried everywhere, though it's at its worst in wet years. Virtually all unsprayed peaches and nectarines fall prey to it eventually, and once the leaves have emerged there's no cure for the problem.

Before spraying your peach and apricot trees clean them up by removing any loose leaves or mummified fruits and by raking up and destroying all debris in, under, and around each tree. Spray the entire tree, carefully going over the trunk, the branches, and the twigs; also lightly spray the ground under the tree. Spray twice during winter while the trees are dormant, once as soon as the leaves have fallen and again before the buds swell in spring. (The exact timing will differ according to your climate zone, but usually you'll need to apply the first treatment sometime between mid-November and mid-December, and the second in late January or early February.) Use lime sulphur or chlorothalonil (Daconil), or use Volck oil mixed with a combined fungus and pest spray, such as Orthorix. Follow package directions exactly.

Lawn Care

Cool-Season Lawns. There's still time, if you didn't do the jobs last month, to plant cool-season lawns (p. 261), to overseed Bermuda with annual ryegrass (don't wait any longer; it has a short growing season, described on p. 262); and to dethatch cool-season lawns that need it, as well as to get rid of crabgrass (p. 262). Continue to feed all cool-season grasses regularly: once a month, every six weeks, or less frequently according to the product you buy. This is their best growing season. Water them when rains aren't adequate. Mow these grasses short—to 1½ inches.

Warm-Season Lawns. Warm-season lawns are starting into winter dormancy. Stop fertilizing and mowing them when their growth slows. Check dichondra for grass invasion. Treat it, if necessary, with a product recommended for grass control in dichondra that also contains a light fertilizer. Renovate kikuyu—cut it right down to the ground—if you didn't do this job last month.

Gopher Traps. Mankind's war with gophers is probably as ancient in these parts as the history of agriculture. Almost anywhere in Southern California where you grow a garden—unless it's protected by a natural barrier of underground rock—gophers will move in, push up disfiguring mounds of earth, and help themselves to the roots of your plants. For example, one local gardener who planted a new lawn woke up one morning to discover an army of gophers had invaded overnight and ruined the lawn. He tried various methods of attack, including flooding, poison bait, toxic gas, and metal traps; he even bought a cat. (His dog killed several gophers too, but did more damage digging up the lawn than the gophers had done.) This gardener finally conquered the gophers when he discovered the Blackhole, a trap made by FBN Plastics in Tulare, California.

The Blackhole trap is smaller than box-type traps, and though it's slightly more expensive than they are it's easier to use. It's shaped like a tube and contains a lethal wire snare that kills the gopher instantly. You dig down and fit it into the gopher's run. Your victim comes charging along his tunnel, sees light ahead, and runs right into the trap; that's when his light goes out. The Blackhole trap is available at many local nurseries.

Vegetable Gardening

Continue to plant carrots, lettuce, beets, radishes, kohlrabi, mustard greens, kale, spinach, and turnips from seeds to keep fresh crops coming along. If you're late in planting vegetables there's still time to put in transplants of Brussels sprouts, cabbage, cauliflower, celery, broccoli, parsley, and Swiss chard, as well as seeds of peas, fava beans, globe onions, and parsley (to speed parsley's germination see p. 266). It's best to plant earlier, but in most climate zones it's still warm enough in November to germinate seeds as long as the weather doesn't turn cold and wet. You'll just have a shorter harvest. Do plant as soon as possible, though. Among plants that are well adapted to November planting, artichoke, strawberries, and rhubarb can be put in bare root, though I personally don't recommend rhubarb. (Hot summers inland rot the roots, and along the coast there's not enough winter chill to stimulate the growth of tender, pink stalks. The leaves of all rhubarb plants are highly poisonous, and I have a hunch that the stalks, when they're overly sour, and green or brownish in color, contain too much oxalic acid for good health.) Potatoes can still be planted from seed potatoes and scallions from onion sets.

Also plant garlic now. Purchase large globes with good-sized sections in any market, or buy elephant garlic at the nursery garden or produce market. (It's a different species, and milder, but grown much the same way.) Break up the garlic cloves and plant them individually with the points facing up, in fertile soil that's rich in humus. Plant them in full sun, 4 inches apart and 2 inches beneath the soil surface. Some gardeners have told me that interplanting garlic with cabbage crops reduces problems with cabbage worms and aphids. However, test data, plus my own experience, make me doubt the efficacy of this system. Heavy rains and cold weather usually have more to do with reducing the numbers of aphids and of cabbage butterflies, whose larvae do the damage. I recommend BT against cabbage worms and Safer insecticidal soap against aphids. (Both are harmless to humans.)

The Secret Lives of Strawberries and Onions.
Strawberries and onions seem at first glance to be an unlikely pair to lump together for discussion, but they share certain characteristics that are surprisingly alike. In order to grow an abundant harvest of large, luscious strawberries,

and in order to have a harvest of premium globe onions, you have to understand some of their innate secrets. Both of them are regional crops; that is, varieties of each are designed to be grown in certain geographical areas and not in others. Both have specific temperature requirements that, for best results, require their being planted during an identical and extremely short slice of time—sometime between November first and tenth—though they require this for somewhat different reasons.

Exhaustive tests by the University of California Agricultural Extension, paid for by strawberry growers, have proved that strawberries planted between November first and tenth get winter chill at the precise moment in their growing schedule to trigger fruit production rather than foliage. When planted at the wrong time they'll put out runners but won't produce much, if any, fruit. (Watch any professional strawberry growers near you as a good indication of when to plant.)

Either plant runners from your own garden that you've already prepared as prechilled, bare-root plants (as discussed on p. 267) or plant from bare-roots purchased from nurseries now. (See the accompanying box for planting instructions.) As a general rule don't order strawberries, other than alpine varieties, from catalogues, because they usually don't carry varieties that are adapted to our climate. Strawberries are a highly regional crop—even more so than onions. Just a few hundred miles up the California coast entirely different strawberry varieties are grown, so be sure that you plant a locally adapted variety, such as Douglas, Sequoia, Tioga, Tufts, or Chandler.

Onions are photothermoperiodic; that is, they're sensitive to temperature and also to day

How to Grow Strawberries

You can if you wish grow strawberries on flat ground, or in a raised bed edged with wood, or on raised vegetable rows between furrows; you can water them individually by hand, with overhead sprinklers, or by flooding the furrows. If you want to plant and water in any of these ways follow the instructions below only insofar as they pertain to your particulars. But the mound method watered by a drip system, as described here, produces berries most successfully and with the least work in the long run.

· Plant a prechilled, locally adapted variety between November first and tenth. (If you chilled your own plants get them in the ground no later than November fifth; you'll have fruit in one and a half months.)

· Provide deeply spaded, rich, slightly acid, preferably sandy soil with a high proportion of organic matter.

· Construct mounds 6 to 8 inches high and 2½ to 3 feet wide, flat on top and with slightly sloping sides. Leave 18 inches between the mounds.

· Fertilize by mixing into the top 6 inches of soil a complete time-release fertilizer, such as Osmocote 15-15-15, according to package directions. Fertilize again in spring, and once more in summer.

· Bury a Bi-Wall drip tube (or other burial-type drip tube) 1 to 2 inches deep, down the center of the mounds.

· Set the plants in alternate positions 12 inches apart, in two rows that are 13 to 14 inches apart on top of the mound.

· For each plant make a crevice with a trowel, fan out the roots, and close up the hole so that the middle of the crown is even with the soil line. (If you plant it too deeply the crown will rot, but if you plant it too shallowly the top roots will dry out.)

· Water lightly every day for a week, or until the plants are established. After that water once a week when it doesn't rain.

· In mid-January cover the entire bed with clear plastic mulch. Carefully cut an X or a round hole 4 inches in diameter directly over each plant. Gently slip the plants up through the holes. Cut the plastic to fit the bed, and bury the bottom edges in soil to prevent it from blowing away.

· Harvest berries daily as they ripen. Cut runners off as they occur.

· Bait for sowbugs, slugs, and snails. Protect the plants from birds with netting.

· After fruiting stops let runners grow, and remove the plastic to allow them to root in the ground. Then dig up the runners, bare their roots, and prechill them (as described on p. 267). Replant them in the same bed for three years, then choose another spot.

How to Grow Globe Onions

- Choose a short-day variety, such as Granex, Grano, or Crystal Wax; plant from seed, and put the seed in the ground between the first and tenth of November.

- Prepare a row of loose, well-drained (preferably sandy) soil with a high content of humus, in full sun and with a drip tube buried down the middle. (This is the easiest way to water them, but if you wish you can use any other method commonly used for watering vegetables.)

- Add vegetable fertilizer according to package directions. Water the bed and let it settle overnight.

- Sprinkle the seeds thinly in a wide, shallow row over the drip tube.

- Cover the seeds with ¼ inch potting soil. Pat it down with the palm of your hand.

- Sprinkle the bed by hand, to make sure it stays damp, when rains aren't adequate. (Or, if possible, adjust the drip system to water daily until the seeds have germinated.)

- Once the seedlings are up, let the drip system kick in to keep the rows evenly moist throughout the growing season.

- Remove weeds when they're small, and continue to weed regularly. (Since onions have shallow roots they don't compete well; weeds will stunt their growth.)

- Thin the seedlings in late December or early January. No need to throw out all the thinnings—transplant some to another row. Leave the biggest ones in the existing row, spaced 4 to 5 inches apart.

- Give onions frequent light applications of balanced fertilizer throughout their leafy green stage in order to maintain a steady rate of growth. Stop feeding them in early- to mid-March. (Fertilizing onions with nitrogen after they begin to form a bulb makes them split.)

- The previously straight plants will suddenly grow fat. Start to pull and eat them in early May. When necks weaken and tops begin to fall over (usually before the end of May) turn off the drip system to let them cure. Dig up the remainder of the bulbs when the tops die.

- Place the onions in a shady, well-ventilated area until they're thoroughly dry. Then store them in a cool place. Mild onions don't keep as well as pungent types, but they will last several months if properly cured and stored.

length. An onion plant is stimulated to stop making leafy growth and start making a bulb not so much by temperature as by the lengthening of days, as the sun moves north in spring and summer. Each variety will form a bulb only after it's received a certain number of hours of daylight each day for a certain number of days. However, varieties vary greatly in the number of hours of daylight they need. Accordingly, all onions are categorized into long-day (northern), intermediate-day (central), and short-day (southern) varieties.

Long-day varieties, grown in northern states and in Canada, need fourteen to fifteen hours of daylight to make a bulb. Northern European and Alaskan varieties need sixteen hours or more. No long-day varieties can possibly receive enough hours of daylight in Southern California to make a bulb. If you plant them your crop will always fail, and yet you can often find seeds of long-day onions on local seed racks, and almost all onion sets are of long-day types. These sets can be used only for growing scallions (green onions). Here, in order to get the best globe onions, we must plant seeds of short-day (southern) varieties in fall, or alternatively plant intermediate varieties in late winter.

Also, once an onion has reached a certain critical size, which differs by variety, temperatures of between 40° and 50°F (4° and 10°C) will make it go to seed prematurely, or bolt. The way to grow good bulb onions here and avoid bolting is to follow this ☞ **Rule of Thumb: Plant globe onions only from seeds, never from**

sets (small bulbs). Plant only such "short-day" (southern) varieties as Grano, Granex, or Crystal Wax, and put the seeds in the ground between the first and the tenth of November.

Grano, Granex, and Crystal Wax are sweet, mild flavored, and juicy like Vidalia and Maui onions. Eat them raw in sandwiches and salads. Nothing better. Crystal Wax also makes good pickling onions when closely planted. Neither Crystal Wax nor Grano keeps well; on this score Granex is a little better. Seeds of intermediate day-length onions, including San Felipe and Pronto S, will also produce a bulb if you plant them in February; they'll ripen in summer. Onion seeds sprout extremely easily; there's no problem involved. I've often planted onions on the same day I took off for a two- or three-week vacation, and left them with an automatic drip system as a baby sitter; when I came home my onions were always up and growing. (See the accompanying box for instructions.)

By all means plant a row of onion sets now, if you want them only for scallions. For best flavor pick scallions when they're young, and plant successive crops. If you leave them in the ground too long you may eventually get a large onion, but it will be green through the middle, and it will have a thick stalk on top that won't dry out properly, so your onions will rot. Some gardeners think the way to cure thick stalks is to knock the tops over in spring when the globes are full grown, but tests have shown this practice to have no influence whatsoever on the proper ripening of onions.

Purchase / Plant

- ☐ Continue to plant **wildflowers,** 258
- ☐ Plant **California native plants,** 276
- ☐ Now through January transplant **shrubs** and **young trees** that are growing in the wrong places, 278
- ☐ Plant **ground covers,** 278
- ☐ Plant **ranunculus, anemones, grape hyacinths, Dutch irises,** all kinds of **daffodils** (*Narcissus*), and all other **spring-flowering bulbs** except **tulips, hyacinths,** and **crocuses,** 279
- ☐ Plant **daffodils** in pots, 282
- ☐ Plant a basket of **narcissus** for holiday bloom, 280
- ☐ Finish filling flower beds with **cool-season flowers** for winter and spring bloom, 283
- ☐ Plant **nasturtiums** and continue to plant **wildflowers** from seeds, including **lupines,** 284
- ☐ Plant **flowering kale** (ornamental cabbage), especially in interior zones, 285
- ☐ **Cool-season lawns** can still be planted from seeds early this month, 287
- ☐ Overseed **Bermuda** with **annual ryegrass** if desired, 287
- ☐ Continue to plant **winter vegetables,** including **garlic,** 287
- ☐ Plant bare-root **artichokes,** 288
- ☐ Plant **bare-root strawberries** between November first and tenth; use the runners you prechilled or purchase plants at a nursery, 289
- ☐ Also between November first and tenth plant **globe onions** from seeds of short-day varieties, 290

Trim, Prune, Mow, Divide

- ☐ Prune **pine trees** and other **conifers** now through February, 181
- ☐ Divide and transplant **agapanthus,** 249
- ☐ Divide **matilija poppy,** 275
- ☐ Open up spaces in **dense trees** to allow wind to pass through, 277
- ☐ Prune **acacias,** 278
- ☐ Prune **cane berries** other than low-chill raspberries, 278
- ☐ Cut back **chrysanthemums** after bloom; clean up the ground, 285

Fertilize

- ☐ Fertilize **cool-season bedding flowers;** don't feed **wildflowers,** 285
- ☐ Continue to fertilize **cineraria** for growth, 285
- ☐ Don't feed **roses** this month, 286
- ☐ Continue to fertilize **cool-season lawns;** stop fertilizing **warm-season lawns** when their growth slows, 287

Water

- [ ] Once rains arrive, stop watering **succulents** growing in the ground, 186
- [ ] Water **all garden plants** less frequently now as weather cools and rains begin, but if rains don't arrive be alert to signs of stress and water as necessary, 274
- [ ] Install **pitcher irrigation**, 274
- [ ] Water **bulbs**, especially potted ones, 279
- [ ] Water **roses** until midmonth, only when rains aren't adequate, 286
- [ ] Don't let **citrus** go dry in cold or frosty weather, 286
- [ ] Water **cool-season lawns** when rains aren't adequate. Stop watering **warm-season lawns** when they go brown, 287

Control Pests, Diseases, and Weeds

- [ ] Bait **flower beds,** especially **wildflowers,** for cutworms and slugs and snails, 285
- [ ] Spray **peach** and **nectarine trees** against peach leaf curl after leaves fall, 286
- [ ] Check **dichondra** for grass invasion; treat if necessary, 287
- [ ] Trap **gophers** on lawns and elsewhere in the garden, 287

Also This Month

- [ ] Use pine needles as **mulch,** 276
- [ ] Stake **young trees** loosely so they can develop strong trunks, 277
- [ ] Prechill **tulips, hyacinths,** and **crocuses,** 279
- [ ] Begin forcing **paper whites, Chinese sacred lilies,** and other **Tazetta hybrid narcissus** in water and pebbles, 281
- [ ] Wrap the trunks of young **citrus** and **avocado trees** with an insulating material to protect them from frost damage, 286

DECEMBER

DECEMBER

The Holiday Month

If there's one thing we can say for sure about December weather in Southern California it's that we can never be sure just what it's going to be. December is supposed to be a winter month, and sometimes it acts like one. Snow blankets the mountains and frost hits all zones. At other times there's a heat wave between Christmas and New Year's that reminds us of August—unless we go to the beach and stick a furtive toe in the icy sea. The weatherman is forever informing us that this is the coldest (or hottest) temperature ever recorded for the particular date. And we're inclined to chorus, "What unusual weather we're having!" as if that weren't the most usual thing in the world. So be alert this month: on the one hand protect tender plants from possible frost, but on the other hand continue watering if the weather's hot, dry, and windy. If you garden in an interior zone don't be fooled by this month's sunny days. An ice-cold javelin may be hidden behind December's back, ready to strike at night.

If you're too busy to give the garden much attention this month you're in luck. Most plants will roll along quite happily with only an occasional boost from you. Gardeners who prepared for winter in the fall, when time was easier to come by, can rejoice now because their gardens will cooperate in December by being less demanding. Plant lovers overwhelmed by the holiday rush can let many jobs slide. But if you're an eager beaver or were an early shopper you can get the jump on the New Year by tackling a few of January's chores, such as pruning deciduous fruit trees or planting bare-roots. Nurseries stock them beginning this month.

How to Make Poinsettias Last Indoors until March

- Purchase one to three premium plants—healthy specimens of such varieties as Eckespoint, Pixie, or Everlasting Star (which holds on to its foliage longest).

- Line a large ornamental basket with several layers of plastic cut to fit.

- Pour in a layer of styrofoam packing pellets, to hold the roots above water.

- Arrange the poinsettias in the basket on top of the styrofoam pellets.

- Surround the poinsettias with four to six low-profile green houseplants, such as Chinese evergreens (*Aglaonema* species) or Dallas or Kimberly Queen ferns, to add beauty and provide the moist atmosphere that's highly beneficial to poinsettias.

- Place the entire arrangement out of drafts in bright light, such as 18 inches to 2 feet below an electric light source, but away from direct sunlight. This should provide the required temperatures; 70°F (21°C) in the daytime and 60° to 65°F (16° to 18°C) at night are ideal. Don't subject blooming poinsettias to extremes of temperature—80°F days and 50°F nights (27° and 10°C) will make the leaves and bracts fall off. (So will drafts and over- or underwatering.)

- Water the plants when the surface of the soil feels dry to the touch, then water them enough to make excess water flow out the bottom of the container. Beginning in late December start feeding them occasionally with a weak, balanced fertilizer.

Preparing for Frost

In areas where frost is expected move tropical and other frost-tender container-grown plants under eaves, under spreading trees, or into shade houses. Don't forget to water them. Plants withstand cold weather much better when provided with adequate moisture. Some tropicals, including species often grown as houseplants and tubbed specimens of plumeria, can be brought indoors for the winter. Keep these in bright light or filtered sun, and let them go somewhat but not totally dry. Plumerias will probably go semidormant and drop their leaves but will come back when you put them outdoors again in spring. (See p. 34 for more about frost protection.)

Poinsettias

If you've been subjecting a potted poinsettia to fourteen hours of darkness nightly since October it should be in full bloom now. Stop fertilizing it for now, and bring it into the house to enjoy. For bloom that lasts several months give it the light, food, and water described in the accompanying box.

Buy more potted poinsettias early this month, if you want them to give as gifts or to decorate your home or entryway. The best plants are usually sold early. Wherever you purchase your plant, be selective. Choose a plant that hasn't already been abused. Exposure to extremes of temperature and over- or underwatering can occur before you get your plant, and these factors can make the green leaves fall off prematurely, a common fault of poinsettias. The colorful bracts should look healthy, not wilted, and the leaves should be green and firmly attached to the stalk. If several have fallen off that's a bad sign. Also inspect the flowers, the tiny little buttons in the center of the colorful bracts. Make sure they're fresh looking, not brown or mildewed.

When you get your plant home give it the location, light, and other conditions that will help it last, as described in the box. (One of the worst places to keep a poinsettia is on top of the TV.) If you leave the foil on the plant don't allow it to suffer wet feet—tear holes in the foil so water doesn't collect in it. The best way to water is to put your plant in the kitchen sink, water it thoroughly, and let it drain before putting it back on display.

Cymbidiums

Many cymbidiums start to flower in December. Some bloom as early as November. Most bloom between February and May, a few in May and June, and one or two, year-round. Choose wisely and you can have these exotic orchids decorating your home, patio, and garden for six months or more. Protect cymbidiums' bloom spikes from snails. Stake the spikes to avoid breakage, but allow each spray to maintain its natural, arching form. Allow miniatures in hanging baskets to cascade naturally. Continue to feed the plants for bloom (as described on p. 229) until buds open. Once they bloom stop feeding the plants, but keep them damp, though not soggy. For longer-lasting flowers move blooming plants into more shade and away from bees. (The flowers "blush" and fade after pollination.)

Once cymbidium spikes have set buds you can force some into bloom for holiday decoration ahead of their natural schedule. Wait until the buds on the bloom spikes are full size and look fat and ready to open. Then take the plant into the house and place it in bright light. The warmth plus the longer day will open the buds quickly. Continue to enjoy the plant indoors or, for a longer-lasting display, place it outside again.

There's one drawback, however; plants you force into bloom early won't perform as well next year. You'll get a few spikes but not as many. This is also a factor to consider when buying new varieties. Some may have been forced into bloom, and you won't get as many spikes the following year. Wait for the third year and they'll be loaded.

Sasanqua Camellias and Early-Flowering Azaleas

Choose sasanqua camellias for winter color that will return year after year. They're in bloom now. *Camellia sasanqua* 'Yuletide' is one of the best. Bright red blossoms with yellow centers dot the handsome, small-leaved foliage from November into January. Although sasanqua flowers are usually smaller and not as long lasting as those of *Camellia japonica,* the plants bloom abundantly, can take more sun, and the flowers are usually immune to blossom blight.

Also look for early- and long-blooming varieties of azalea. A collection of them can provide color fall through spring in frost-free zones. Combine them with camellias on north-facing slopes and the north side of your home. Some varieties to look for include Alaska, Albert and Elizabeth (note it rarely survives in Zone 24), Avenir, Red Wing (sometimes called Red Bird), Chimes, Carnival Time (and other members of the Carnival series), California Sunset (inland only—it dies or does poorly in Zone 24), California Peach, Eric Shame, Lucille K., Nuccio's Happy Days, Rosa Belton, and Vervaeneana Alba.

Roses

Don't fertilize or prune roses this month. Let the flowers stay on the bush, and don't water them. These steps help roses harden off for winter. Perhaps your garden isn't properly zoned and you have heavy water users like roses growing next to drought-resistant plants such as bougainvilleas. Winter is a good time for moving roses to a better spot. Prepare the new beds now; dig up the roses and move them there next month. Despite the demands of holiday activities some gardeners also find time this month to prepare the beds for January bare-root planting. To do so, spade the ground deeply and put in plenty of soil amendment. Don't be dismayed if you have clay soil. Roses thrive in it, but be sure to test the drainage, and if it's severely impaired install drains or build raised beds for your roses.

Study your rose collection with the idea of weeding out poor performers. Why struggle along with a plant that's worn out or simply not right for your climate zone? In the interest of water conservation, it's far better to grow a handful of choice roses than a great many mediocre ones.

If you are going to plant a few roses next month plan your color scheme now, and decisions will be easier later. All too often roses are planted with a shotgun approach; no thought is given to color compatibility. Don't, for instance, put one of the new brilliant oranges next to a bluish red. The best-looking rose gardens are designed like a rainbow, with a progression of harmonious colors flowing from one side to the other. Clashing colors are well separated. For a bigger display plant at least three roses of one variety together. Also consider planting one bed solidly with a single variety. You seldom see this done in a home garden, but in the right spot the effect is stunning and shows your originality.

Bulbs

Finish Planting Spring-Blooming Bulbs. If you bought bulbs this fall but didn't plant them when you should have, don't despair; you still have a little time to get them into pots or the ground. The ☞ **Rule of Thumb** is: *Finish planting spring-flowering bulbs such as daffodils on or before December 25.* When planted later the flowers will be smaller and fewer. (If you celebrate Chanukah instead of Christmas, all the better—use Chanukah as a reminder and most years you'll be ahead of the pack.) The exceptions are tulips and hyacinths (crocuses too, if you live in an interior zone). They need cold earth, so start planting them between Christmas and New Year's Day, unless there's a heat wave. If that occurs wait until early January; plant before the tenth.

Leave the bulbs in the refrigerator until you're ready to plant. If you choose to plant tulips in pots keep the planted pots in a cool place, and cover them with an upside-down cardboard box to cut out light and encourage the growth of good root systems. Water them often. When the foliage is 2 or 3 inches tall remove the covering and bring the pots out into the sun. Try to keep the roots from heating up by shading the containers in cool foliage, or by double potting. Water daily unless rains are adequate.

Tulips do well in half-barrels and in the ground to the north of trees or houses. Study the shadow pattern annually, and plant them where the ground is cool and shady in winter and then sunny beginning in February or March. Or plant them in full or morning sun and shade the ground over them with a bulb cover, such as johnny-jump-ups, paludosum daisies, or violas. They respond well to a treatment of light liquid fertilizer, such as bulb food, once at planting time and again when the leaves show.

Hyacinths grow well in the ground, planted 5 inches deep and 6 inches apart, or in shallow pots of fast-draining soil mix, planted just below or at the soil surface. Bury some bone meal under each bulb. (Keep the pots watered, cool, and darkened, as described above for tulips.) Or force them in pebbles and water or a special reusable "hyacinth glass," which keeps the roots immersed in water. Keep these forced ones cool and dark, under an upside-down cardboard box, until the tops are up 3 or 4 inches, then place them in a sunny window or outdoors in sun every day when the weather's warm (bring them in at night.) Turn the ones on window ledges to make their stems grow straight.

Plant crocuses in either low pots or the ground. Since the flowers are low they often show up better in low-level pots. Nestle them among well-placed rocks and a few pebbles to add charm and keep the soil cool.

Lift Dahlias. When dahlias have gone totally dormant, in early December, dig up the tubers. First cut back the tops to 6 or 8 inches; then use a spade to slice down through the soil and loosen it in a circle 12 to 14 inches out from each plant. Finally use a garden fork to carefully pry up the tuber, which you will find has now grown into a round clump of tubers, all attached to a central stem in the same way the spokes of a wheel are attached to the hub. Shake off the soil, cut the tops back to 2 inches, and lay the whole unseparated clump on newspaper in the sun to dry until evening. Continue the drying process for a day or two in a dry shady place, such as the floor of the garage. Then dust the clumps with bulb dust or sulfur and pack them, not touching each other, in perlite. Store them for the winter in a cool dry area, in hanging baskets lined with newspaper or in boxes.

Divide the clumps in spring when growth begins and you can see the eyes (growth buds) beginning to form; cut each clump into individual sections. Each must have an eye. (Throw out the old center stalk.) Dust the cut portions in sulfur and allow them to callus off overnight. Plant each tuber separately. You may have extras to share with friends.

Prepare Amaryllis to Bloom. Amaryllis (*Hippeastrum*) bulbs are on sale at nurseries now. (You can also purchase them from mail order companies.) Many are preplanted and already starting to grow. These are entertaining bulbs to grow for holiday color (they'll bloom for Christmas) and make excellent hostess gifts.

Place a preplanted amaryllis whose growth has begun in a sunny window and turn it daily so the stalk won't bend to the light. Keep it well watered but not overly wet. If growth has not yet begun water the plant and keep it cool and dark until growth begins, then move it into a warm, sunny location. A thick scape (stalk) will emerge from the bulb and shoot rapidly upward, often to 15 inches. Sometimes two will appear, each one bearing three or four spectacular blossoms. When the bloom begins to show color move the plant to a cooler spot, where it will last longer.

After the flowers fade cut them off, but leave the tall scape in place until you can see that the juices have gone back down into the bulb. Then cut it off. This nourishes the bulb. Put the plant outside in semishade for the summer. Feed it occasionally and protect it from snails and slugs. In September lift it from the container and let the root ball dry out. Cut off the leaves when they die. Brush the dry rootball with bulb dust or sulfur, slip it back into the pot, and allow it three months of complete dormancy, then start the process over; this time it will bloom in spring. (Once an amaryllis has been forced to bloom at Christmas you can't repeat the process.)

If you purchase a bare, unplanted amaryllis bulb now choose one that has just begun to sprout but not yet pushed up a flower scape. Plant it in rich, fast-draining soil mix in a small pot—just 4 inches wider than the bulb. Before putting the bulb in the pot, though, place a few tablespoons of bone meal in the soil in the bottom. Cover this with a little plain potting soil. Plant the bulb with its upper half above soil level. Water it and treat it as described above. Pot on amaryllis bulbs annually.

Winter Color

Permanent landscape plants that are colorful in winter enliven gardens and make good gifts. Choices include purple princess flower (*Tibouchina urvilleana*), Mexican flame vine, marmalade bush (*Streptosolen jamesonii*), Carolina jessamine (*Gelsemium sempervirens*; an attractive, evergreen, yellow-flowered vine, though unfortunately poisonous), variously hued New Zealand tea trees (*Leptospermum scoparium*), and strawberry tree (*Arbutus unedo*). The last two are among our finest slow-growing, drought-resistant plants that can be grown as shrubs and eventually become small trees. Both develop interestingly shaped trunks. Strawberry tree bears its flowers and colorful fruit now. (The fruit is edible but not flavorful.) There are striking dwarf forms that grow naturally into eye-catching shapes.

Flower Beds and Containers

Care for Winter-Blooming Plants. If you planted flower beds in September or October, by now the garden should be full of color. If not, remember the trick is to get things into bloom before Christmas and they'll bloom all winter. Once cold nights begin plants slow down and won't bloom until the weather warms up, in February or March. Of course some plants are naturally programmed to bloom in late winter, spring, or early summer. We don't expect them to bloom ahead of time. But among the flowers you can expect to be colorful prior to Christmas in most zones are alyssum, calendula, dianthus, Iceland poppy, linaria, nemesia, flowering cabbage (ornamental kale, which is grown for its colorful foliage rather than flowers), paludosum daisy, primroses of all kinds, pansy, schizanthus, dwarf stock, sweet pea, sweet William, viola, and wallflower. With the exception of linaria and sweet pea, feed these plants regularly to speed them into bloom, with a liquid fertilizer high in nitrogen and bloom ingredients such as 20-20-20.

Linaria and sweet peas can be speeded into

bloom with 0-10-10 if desired, but it usually isn't necessary. (Don't give them nitrogen; wildflowers seldom need it, and sweet peas grow at the expense of bloom if given too much of it.)

Dwarf delphiniums and dwarf foxgloves bloom in fall or early winter shortly after planting. Cut off spikes that have bloomed now, and follow up with fertilizer. Delphiniums will bloom again in spring; dwarf foxgloves will also, if they have sprouts that haven't yet flowered. (Tall varieties of delphiniums, foxgloves, and stock also bloom in spring.)

Dwarf snapdragons bloom in fall through winter but are easily decimated by caterpillars and are highly susceptible to rust. (Spray them from the outset with Bayleton against rust and with BT to control caterpillars. Next year grow taller, rust-resistant varieties, from seeds planted in September or from transplants in October.)

Deal with Frost. What if you planted early but nothing's in bloom? One possible reason is that you live in an interior zone and cold nights have held things back. If this is the case, don't worry. You'll just get flowers a little later. Some gardeners feel that frost is a natural kind of pinching, making their plants stronger and bushier in the long run and keeping things from growing too rank. Trial and error is the best way to find out which plants perform best in your climate zone, under local conditions, and with the care you give your plants.

In very cold low-lying gardens, like those in Zone 20, frosts kill some of the more tender bedding plants, like primroses, pansies, and cineraria. The best bets for winter color under such conditions are hardier plants like ornamental kale, tall calendulas, snapdragons, and

Quick Tip

A Long-Handled Scoop Keeps Fertilizer Dry. *Most powdered fertilizers contain a plastic measuring scoop. Use household wire to bind it firmly to the end of a thin, 18-inch bamboo plant stake. Use a second stake to scrape off the excess powder when measuring. Wet hands won't touch the scoop, and the fertilizer will stay dry.*

Quick Tip

How to Attach a Vine to a Smooth Wall or Fence. *To make inexpensive invisible wall hangers for vines, glob dots of clear silicone sealant where needed. Stick a short piece of twist tie into each glob. Allow it to dry overnight. Come back the next day and tie up the vine.*

bulbs, particularly paper whites and oxalis. Stock and many wildflowers will survive the cold winter and bloom in spring.

It's important even in coastal zones to protect tender annuals, especially cineraria (*Senecio hybridis*), from frost. This plant can fool gardeners because it so obviously loves cold weather and grows best and fastest in it, but frost "melts" its leaves and turns them black or brown. It actually prefers night temperatures of 45° to 50°F (7° to 10°C) with a daytime increase of no more than five or ten degrees. What place on earth would provide such a narrow range of temperatures for a wild plant? The explanation is that cineraria is not a wild plant; it's a nonhardy manmade "species" of uncertain ancestry that was developed in the nineteenth century especially to be grown in cool greenhouses. So when growing cineraria in your garden cover the beds with a tent of sheets or beach towels, supported on bamboo poles, on nights when frost is expected. Take off the covers first thing in the morning, before the sun hits the bed. (Cineraria are well worth this trouble.) Plants under a tree or overhang usually survive unharmed. Here again, trial and error is the best teacher. Continue to feed cineraria with Terr-O-Vite for growth.

Grow Plants in Adequate Light. Another factor inhibiting winter bloom is too much shade. New gardeners are sometimes unaware of how the movement of the sun creates shade to the north of trees and buildings in winter where it didn't exist in summer or fall. (See p. 173 for an explanation of the movements of shade.) If you have this problem, wait until the sun comes back in spring; your flowers will then bloom. If you have plants such as malacoides primroses or English primroses that are full grown but just sitting there doing nothing, try feeding them with 0-10-10 or 2-10-10 liquid once a week during December. This can stimulate bloom in areas that are too shady. Once flowers open switch back to a fertilizer high in both bloom and growth ingredients.

In the future, use these shady areas to plant cyclamen, cineraria, bulbs, azaleas, and obconica primroses, which will bloom in darker shade than other primroses. Under north-facing overhangs clivia and camellias are good choices for winter bloom. If plants in containers aren't blooming move them into more sun and continue to fertilize them with a product high in both nitrogen and bloom ingredients.

In Coastal Zones Plant Flowers Even Now. It's too late this year to plant flowers in most interior zones. But let's say you've just moved into a house in a mild or coastal zone, and it has some bare beds that need filling, or you were too busy in fall to tackle the job. You don't have to wait until spring to plant flowers. That's the joy of living here. Seeds that can be planted now include African daisy (*Dimorphotheca*), ageratum, California poppy, calendula, clarkia, coreopsis, larkspur, forget-me-not, gaillardia, godetia, hollyhock, lavatera, nemophila, phlox, schizanthus, sweet alyssum, Shasta daisy, and mixed wildflowers. You'll just get later bloom, and some plants, such as larkspur, may not grow quite as large. Follow the planting directions beginning on pages 255 and 283. Plant early in the month, and be sure to plant in full sun. These seeds won't germinate in partial shade, especially now.

Sprinkle the bed faithfully every morning until the seeds come up, then water as necessary. For a faster effect, in full sun put in bedding plants of alyssum, calendula, candytuft (*Iberis*), columbine, coral bells, Iceland poppy, English daisy, English primrose, pansy, nemesia, sweet William, wallflower, and viola. For semishade use cyclamen, as well as malacoides or obconica primrose. Put these in a flower bed now and much of the bed should be in bloom before April.

Pruning

A number of plants can be pruned this month, but don't prune such tender or tropical plants as bougainvillea, hibiscus, eugenia, philodendron, Natal plum, or lantana. Pruning tropicals now will stimulate growth that could be nipped by frost.

Deciduous Fruit Trees. Once deciduous fruit trees have gone dormant and dropped their leaves, they can be pruned. You can do this job now or wait until next month. Every type of deciduous fruit tree needs different treatment. Personally I study more than one reliable pruning manual for pruning Western trees before tackling this complicated and all-important job, because they all say things slightly differently and in various depths on the various trees; what is omitted in one book may be covered in another. (The pruning of deciduous fruit trees is discussed in more detail beginning on p. 22.) Follow up your pruning with dormant spray. Dormant spray is best used more than once, so even if you don't prune this month it's wise to use dormant spray now (as described beginning on p. 28) on all deciduous fruit trees and the many ornamental trees that drop their leaves in winter.

Grapes. Prune grapes this month. There are three major pruning methods, depending on the type grown. Young plants of each type must be pruned differently from those that are mature. (The *Sunset Pruning Handbook* contains diagrams and a good basic explanation of this subject.)

Save the trimmings to make ornamental wreaths and baskets. Start a wreath by wiring one bendy stem into a circle, then wind others around it. Add ribbons, dried flowers, and berries, and use the wreath in Christmas decorations. Begin a basket the same way, then weave cross-pieces to form the base. If desired attach a handle. Line the basket with sphagnum moss and a layer of plastic. Make holes for drainage, fill it with potting soil, and plant it with winter annuals. (These baskets last several years.)

Low-Chill Raspberries. Before the arrival in 1978 of the low-chill red raspberry called Oregon 1030, Southern Californians couldn't grow real red raspberries like the ones that grow in cold-winter climates. Now several additional varieties have been discovered or developed that will bear good crops here, including San Diego, Baba Berry, and Fallgold. These relatively new "subtropical" raspberries are now grown here commercially as well as in home gardens. They require different and much easier pruning than other types of cane berries.

All low-chill raspberry varieties bear their berries almost year-round on new wood that they put out almost continually. The simple pruning method for all low-chill types of raspberry is to cut all the canes down to 3 or 4 inches, now or in January. New growth will spring from the ground. Dig up the suckers to form new rows of plants; if you let your existing rows get too wide they'll become unmanageable.

Fertilize your raspberries in spring when they start to grow, with an evenly balanced fertilizer such as 16-16-16, and give them plenty of water. Spray them regularly with BT against caterpillars; they relish raspberry leaves. (If you didn't prune other cane berries, like blackberries, boysenberries, and loganberries, last month, do it now, as directed on p. 278.)

Native Plants. Native plants can be pruned any time during the winter growing season. Some gardeners prefer not to prune them at all except to remove dead and diseased branches. Other gardeners prune to show the "good bones" of certain plants. A little judicious pruning can often uncover an artistic shape that's already there but hidden by foliage.

Wisteria. If you didn't prune wisteria in summer, do it now. Observe the buds. Small, narrow buds are leaf buds. Round, fatter buds, often found on short stubby growth called spurs, are flower buds. Don't cut off the flower buds or flower-bearing spurs. Prune off long "streamers" or "twiners" (thin, young stems that grew rapidly this year). Carefully untangle them from older wood if necessary and cut them back to two or three buds to stimulate the growth of more flower spurs. Retain twiners going in desired directions and tie them loosely in place. If an established wisteria never blooms, cut into the ground around the plant with a sharp spade to prune the roots. This may stimulate bloom, perhaps not next spring but the year following.

Home-Grown Holiday Decorations

Look around the garden to see what can be used to make the house look festive for the holidays. Some gardeners recycle tubbed pine trees, bringing them indoors year after year to do the annual stint as Christmas trees. Gardens can also provide sweet-smelling evergreen cuttings from pines, firs, cedars, and cypresses. Red berries from pyracantha and toyon and the leaves and berries of English holly are naturals, though not as long lasting as conifer foliage. (Sprays such as Keeps It are available at florists' supply stores and can keep berries and foliage fresh longer.) Cuttings of succulents such as jade plant and echeveria last all month and mix well with ornaments.

Other possibilities to dye, paint, glitter, or leave plain are pine cones, strawflowers, bunches of dried herbs, thistles, agapanthus stalks, and the decorative seed pods of plants including jacaranda, certain acacias, and eucalyptus (the heavy pods of *Eucalyptus ficifolia* are especially prized for their unique shape). For a last-minute touch, tape fresh red geraniums to packages; they'll last only a day. A tall dried stalk of century plant with the seed pods still in place can be held upright by rocks hidden in an earthenware tub. Festoon it with decorations for a Christmas tree Southwest style.

Gifts for and from the Garden

Nurseries and garden supply stores are great places to do Christmas shopping. Lines are usually short, parking easy, stocking stuffers abound, and children can find inexpensive gifts, such as a rain gauge or a hummingbird feeder. Some ideas: tools of all kinds; gadgets such as thermometers that record high and low temperatures (good even for nongardeners); soil augers; tensiometers; heat cables for sprouting seeds; ornamental objects, such as bronze faucets, bird

How to Make the Classic Southern California Succulent Wreath

- Gather about a hundred cuttings and little rooted plants of various succulents. Good candidates are *Kalanchoe tomentosa* and the many different species and cultivars of echeveria, crassula, and sedum.

- Let the cuttings sit for a day or two to callus off, so they'll root and not rot.

- Purchase two wire-form rings, green florists' wire, and fern pins from a florists' supply store. You'll also need clear vinyl fishing line.

- Line one ring with premoistened sphagnum moss. Fill this with potting soil recommended for succulents mixed with 1 teaspoon slow-release fertilizer. Wad more sphagnum moss on top.

- Cover this ring with the other one and wire the two together. Clip off excess moss on the outside to make it smooth.

- Make a hole with a chopstick, through the sphagnum moss, to the same depth as the length of the stem, stick in a cutting, and secure it with a fern pin. Vary the types of succulent, the textures, and the colors as you work, fitting them together closely.

- It takes three months for cuttings to anchor themselves, so tie fishing twine to the frame and wind it around as you go to make cuttings more secure.

- Leave room for a bow at the bottom. Put a hook on the back of the wreath, and hang it.

- The finished wreath should look like a piece of Della Robbia pottery. (Rose-shaped echeverias, especially, provide this look.)

- After the holidays hang the wreath in semishade where rains will provide adequate moisture during the winter and spring. During summer and fall squirt it with a hose occasionally, or soak it in water once a week. Recycle your wreath for several years, by snipping off leggy cuttings in November or December and replacing them closer to the form, and by filling in with fresh cuttings. Feed it occasionally with a well-diluted, complete, liquid fertilizer.

How to Make a Miniature Western Ranch

- Buy two 1-gallon-size Tam junipers (*Juniperus sabina* 'Tamariscifolia'), one 1-gallon size lavender star flower (*Grewia occidentalis*), and a flat of Irish moss (*Sagina subulata*). Purchase tiny toy cowboys, a fence, a bridge, horses, and wildlife at a cake-decorating store. You'll also need red plastic plates, an old (preferably brown) plastic wastebasket, a few small rocks, and a small bag of blue gravel; it's available at aquarium supply stores.

- Make several holes in the bottom of a flat, 18-inch plastic dish designed to fit under a large planting tub. (The quick tip on p. 309 tells how. Pottery dishes are too heavy and too shallow, and it's impossible to drill holes in them.) Cover each hole with a piece of broken crockery.

- Cut the walls of a barn from the centers of the red plastic plates. Cut the roof out of the plastic wastebasket. Fix these together inside the barn with tear-proof package-wrapping tape.

- Fill the bottom of the plastic dish with a 2- or 3-inch layer of potting soil. Shape the junipers into bonsai "cypress trees" and the lavender star flower into an "apple tree" by pruning the roots and clipping off excess foliage from the trunks and branches. Plant these in the dish, and surround them with rocks.

- Plant a "meadow" of Irish moss, cut to fit. Cut a winding streambed through it and fill this with the blue aquarium gravel. Add the barn, cowboys, fence, bridge, and animals.

- Water the plants and let the dish drain. Keep it in the house for one week if desired; thereafter keep it outdoors in sun or semishade. Water it regularly, feed it occasionally, and prune as necessary. In a year or two take out the bonsai, reprune their roots, and replace them.

baths, and garden sculpture; houseplants; bare-root roses; fruit trees; kneeling pads; soil-test kits; and miniature greenhouses.

For a personal gift that doesn't need wrapping choose a sturdy basket for bringing in vegetables or flowers. Stuff it with a colorful apron, a pair of gloves, a trowel, a book or two, a few packs of seed, and a potted plant.

Make a Child's Fantasy Garden for Christmas or Chanukah. A dish garden with a playful theme can spark the imagination of a child and create an interest in gardening at an early age. Make one yourself and give it to the child to play with. Better yet, give the ingredients with a promise to help make it. Older children can be given a construction kit with a set of instructions. (If you go this route stick to succulents, and give cuttings rather than plants. They're easier to deal with.)

Arrangements using houseplants and succulents can be kept indoors for as long as a year. For these, don't make a hole in the bottom of the container; put a layer of fine gravel on the bottom mixed with agricultural charcoal, to keep drainage water pure. Some possible themes include zoo, tropical jungle, Smurf, or Mickey Mouse garden, space stations among weirdly shaped succulents, forests of ferns and miniature cycads inhabited by dinosaurs, Indians stalking cowboys in a desert scene of rocks and succulents, or a Western ranch (see the accompanying box) complete with trees and stream.

Make Homemade Gifts for Adults. Start early to pot bedding plants in baskets and containers for holiday and hostess gifts. Line baskets with dry sphagnum moss, then line the sphagnum with plastic. For outdoor arrangements make holes in

Quick Tip

How to Make Holes in the Bottom of a Plastic Container.
Hold a plastic container, upside down, steadily over a candle until a spot visibly softens; it will bubble up slightly and may change color. Then lay the container right side up on a wooden board. Use a hammer and chisel to cut a square or triangular hole.

❋ ❋ ❋

A Freewheeling Way to "Bonsai" Nursery Plants

Cut off half the roots of a well-shaped
1-gallon-size unpotted Tam juniper. Remove
unwanted branches, bare the trunk, and
clip all foliage from under the branches,
leaving the top foliage intact. Choose one
strong root near the top of the root ball, and
wind it tightly around the trunk just beneath
the soil line. Plant the juniper in a container.
As the root you wound around the trunk
grows it will slow the growth of the plant.

❋ ❋ ❋

the bottom of the plastic lining and fill it with
potting soil and bedding plants in bud, fitting
them closely together for the best effect. Keep
the basket in sun and feed the plants to get
them blooming prior to Christmas.

For indoor arrangements make no holes in
the plastic; put gravel for drainage and agricultural charcoal to absorb impurities into the
lined basket, before adding soil mix. Then fill it
with small houseplants, varying the colors and
shapes. If gray-leaved ivy is available drape it
over the side. For a finishing touch pop a red
African violet in one corner. Keep indoor
baskets in bright light but out of direct sun, and
feed them with high-bloom fertilizer. Another
idea is to make an outdoor entryway arrangement; spray paint a basket white, add chains for
hanging, and fill it with poinsettias, kalanchoe,
cyclamen, or an azalea. Or make dishes of
succulents from your garden. In a terra-cotta
pot combine driftwood with jade tree, gray-
foliaged shore juniper (draping it over the side),
and pink cyclamen. You might also fill a footed
Mexican pot with cacti and euphorbias plus a
rock or two, and cover the surface of the soil
with gravel. Or pot individual herbs, and present
them in a wooden crate.

Herb Gardening

Herbs have been cultivated, used, and treasured
by men and women for thousands of years.
Many are ornamental as well as useful. Even a
few of them can add charm, history, and mystique to any garden. You can grow enough
culinary herbs, such as parsley, rosemary, thyme,
sage, and marjoram, for your Christmas turkey,
or plant a whole garden of herbs, but wait
until spring to plant them outdoors.

You can now, if you wish, plant culinary herbs in individual pots and grow them indoors on a sunny kitchen windowsill. Pot the 2-inch nursery size into 4-inch containers when you purchase them; then pot them on into 6-inch containers as soon as their roots fill the smaller size. When you grow herbs indoors they grow fast at first, then slow down. You can keep them to size by pruning off leaves now and then for cooking. Too much fertilizer makes herbs overgrow and lose their savor, but when they're grown in containers they do need occasional light fertilizer, because potting soils are low in nutrients.

In spring plant culinary herbs outdoors in the ground in your vegetable garden, mixed in with any garden plants, in a special herb garden, or in a small space right outside your kitchen door. One organized and artful way to grow them in small space is to lay an old ladder or wagon wheel on the ground and plant in the spaces. (When you clip leaves from an herb for cooking, choose which ones you take so that you're also controlling the plant's size and shape.) Another way to grow just a few herbs is to plant them in a strawberry pot or hanging basket. (For easy care, attach containers to a drip system.)

Here are some basic facts about herbs:

· An herb is any plant used for medicine, fragrance, or flavoring. (In botany the word herb means any nonwoody plant. In cold-winter climates all these plants die down in winter, but many biennial and perennial herbs are evergreen when grown here.)

· *Not all herbs are edible. Some medicinal herbs, such as comfrey, rue, and tansy, contain toxic chemicals. They must not be taken internally by anyone and especially not by pregnant women.*

· Fresh culinary herbs from your garden are not only tastier than the dried herbs you can buy but safer. (Dried herbs purchased in markets are often imported and have frequently been sprayed with chemicals not allowed in the United States.)

· Herbs thrive in our mild climate and adapt to most soils, but they prefer good drainage, and you can provide it by growing them in rock gardens or raised beds.

· Unless you grow your herbs in containers, as described above, don't fertilize them; it makes them less flavorful. (An exception is an herb like sage that's been in the ground for several years, has often given its leaves to you, and shows an obvious decline in vigor. You can pull it out, amend the soil, and replace it; or you can feed it lightly and mulch its roots to bring it back.)

· Some herbs, such as mint and watercress, need lots of water. Others, such as rosemary and society garlic, are useful drought-resistant plants; these two are grown as ornamentals more often than as culinary herbs.

Lawn Care

Cool-Season Lawns. Feed cool-season lawns every month to six weeks during the growing season. If the grass blades turn red-brown and brown dust gets on your shoes, it's rust. Don't spray the lawn with chemicals, just feed it. The rust will clear right up. Mow weekly, and water when rains aren't adequate.

Warm-Season Lawns. Most warm-season lawns, such as Bermuda and zoysia, are dormant now and require little if any care. Once the

Grow Sweet, Crisp, Juicy Celery

When you bite into a stalk of celery grown this way, juice will squirt into your mouth and run down your face.

- Dig a trench 14 inches wide in rich, well-drained soil in full sun.
- Add manure and homemade compost or commercial soil amendment.
- Cultivate fertilizer into the top 6 inches, then water the trench.
- Plant celery transplants 6 inches apart. Water them deeply.
- Water frequently throughout the growing season to keep the celery growing fast.
- Beginning six weeks after planting, feed the celery every two weeks with liquid fertilizer.
- Control slugs; they can ruin celery.
- A month before harvest, wrap the stalks with newspaper and tie them firmly. Push earth around the bottoms of the stalks, and continue to water and feed them.

grass has gone completely brown and stopped growing you can turn off the irrigation water and stop mowing. The exception is Bermuda that's overseeded with winter ryegrass. Treat this like cool-season grasses, feed it to keep it growing, and mow it to keep it looking nice. If we have warm weather St. Augustine may continue to grow; mow it if needed. Once the weather gets cold it won't need mowing. Water dichondra as necessary, but don't mow or feed dichondra this month.

Vegetable Gardening

December is an exciting time in the vegetable garden because most winter crops are in full swing, and some are starting to produce. As crops are harvested, plant more. Among crops that can be planted this month are artichokes, asparagus, beets, broccoli, Brussels sprouts, cabbage, carrots, cauliflower, celery (see the accompanying box), kale, kohlrabi, head lettuce, leaf lettuce, peas, potatoes, radishes, Swiss chard, and turnips.

Tie the leaves over the heads of cauliflower as soon as they begin to make a head in order to prevent the curds from turning green, and watch them carefully; once cauliflowers begin to expand they grow rapidly to maturity. Purple cauliflower doesn't need this blanching. (It tastes like broccoli.) Some cauliflower is "self-blanching"—the leaves naturally cover the heads. Even so, tie the leaves together and you'll get a better product. Occasionally gardeners have a problem with cauliflower "buttoning"; a tiny little curd forms prematurely, the leaves stay small, and you never get a big head. This can result from buying stressed plants at a nursery, or from temperatures below 40°F

(4°C), insufficient nitrogen, too much salt in the soil, or letting the plants go dry.

Take off the bottom sprouts and bottom leaves from Brussels sprouts. Control aphids with insecticidal soap and beneficial insects. Cut broccoli as soon as it makes a head, and leave the stalk in the ground to produce side sprouts. (See p. 41 for more about harvesting cole crops.) Pull kohlrabi, carrots, beets, and turnips while they're still young and tender. Pick peas to keep them coming. Start harvesting the outside stalks of celery. Harvest the outside lettuce leaves as needed, or cut off the whole head. (Leave the stalk in the ground and feed and water it and it'll grow another head.) Control slugs on lettuce and celery.

Side-dress rows with fertilizer, according to the individual needs of vegetables, to keep them going. In general, if you're planting from seed begin when the plants are 2 to 3 inches high to side-dress the rows with fertilizer every six weeks, or begin then to feed them once a week with liquid fertilizer. When you're growing vegetables from transplants you should usually side-dress the rows with additional fertilizer six weeks after planting. Quick crops like radishes will need no additional fertilizer if you fertilized the soil, as you should have done, prior to planting. Give long-term crops, like broccoli and Brussels sprouts, additional fertilizer at intervals of six weeks throughout their growing season. Onions grow best with slightly more frequent and lighter doses of fertilizer. (Thin your onions by month's end and transplant the thinnings into another row. Don't neglect to weed them regularly.)

Purchase / Plant

☐ Begin planting bare-root **roses, trees, vines, berries,** and **vegetables,** if you wish, 297

☐ Purchase **poinsettias** early in the month, 298

☐ Choose and plant **sasanqua camellias** and early- and long-blooming **azaleas,** 299

☐ Finish planting all **spring-flowering bulbs,** except **tulips, hyacinths,** and **crocuses,** on or before December 25, 300

☐ Plant **tulips, hyacinths,** and **crocuses** between Christmas and New Year's Day, 300

☐ Purchase **permanent plants** that are colorful in winter, to plant or use as gifts, 302

☐ Continue to plant **cool-season flowers** in coastal zones only, 304

☐ Purchase **gifts** from nurseries and garden supply stores, 306

☐ Plant a **child's fantasy dish garden,** or give the ingredients and a promise to help make it, 309

☐ Plant **bedding plants** in baskets and pots for holiday and hostess gifts. Also use **indoor plants, succulents, herbs,** and **plants in bloom,** 309

☐ Plant **culinary herbs** in pots for use in turkey stuffing, 311

☐ Continue to plant **winter vegetables,** 312

☐ Plant **celery,** 312

Trim, Prune, Mow, Divide

☐ Stop picking and deadheading **roses;** leave the hips on the bush, 300

☐ Cut off flower spikes that have bloomed from **dwarf foxgloves** and **delphiniums,** 303

☐ Start pruning **deciduous fruit trees,** if you have time, 304

☐ Don't prune **tropicals,** 304

☐ Prune **grapes,** 305

☐ Prune low-chill **raspberries,** 305

☐ Prune **native plants,** 306

☐ Prune **wisteria** by cutting off unwanted long twiners. Prune roots of vines that fail to bloom, 306

☐ Pick **plant materials** from the garden to use as holiday decorations, 306

☐ Mow **cool-season lawns,** including **Bermuda** that's overseeded with **winter ryegrass,** 311

☐ Don't mow **warm-season lawns,** except **St. Augustine** if it continues to grow, 312

Fertilize

☐ Stop fertilizing potted **poinsettias;** bring them into the house to enjoy, 298

☐ Continue fertilizing **cymbidiums** until flowers open, 299

☐ Don't fertilize **roses,** 300

☐ Feed **cool-season flowers** with a complete fertilizer for growth and bloom, 302

☐ Continue to feed **cineraria** for growth, 304

☐ Feed **shade plants** for bloom; give them adequate light, 304

☐ Feed **cool-season lawns,** but don't feed **warm-season lawns** except for **Bermuda** that's overseeded with **winter ryegrass,** 311

☐ Side-dress **vegetable rows** according to the individual needs of plants, 313

Water

- [ ] Don't water **succulents** growing in the ground, 186
- [ ] Continue to water if the weather's hot, dry, and windy; include **California native plants** now since this is their growing season, 277, 297
- [ ] Keep **cymbidiums** damp but not soggy, 299
- [ ] Remember to keep all **bulbs,** but especially potted ones, well watered, 300
- [ ] Don't water **roses,** 300
- [ ] Water **cool-season lawns** when rains aren't adequate, 311
- [ ] Water **dichondra** if rains aren't adequate, and also water **St. Augustine grass** if it continues to grow, 312
- [ ] Turn off the irrigation systems of all other types of **warm-season lawns** once they have gone brown, 312

Control Pests, Diseases, and Weeds

- [ ] Spray **peach** and **apricot trees** for peach leaf curl if you didn't do so in November, 286
- [ ] Protect **cymbidiums'** bloom spikes from snails, 299
- [ ] Control rust on dwarf **snap-dragons,** 303
- [ ] Use dormant spray on **deciduous fruit trees** and **other woody plants** that drop their leaves in winter, 305
- [ ] Control rust on **cool-season lawns** by fertilizing and mowing them, 311
- [ ] Control **aphids** with insecticidal soap and beneficial insects, 313

Also This Month

- [ ] Prepare for frost in areas where it is expected by sheltering **tropical plants** growing in containers, 298
- [ ] Force budded **cymbidiums** into bloom for the holidays, if desired, 299
- [ ] Keep an eye on the growth of potted **bulbs;** remove covers when they reach the right height, 300
- [ ] Prepare beds for planting **bare-root roses** next month, 300
- [ ] Lift **dahlias** and store them for the winter, 301
- [ ] Prepare **amaryllis** to bloom, 301
- [ ] Protect **tender annuals,** especially **cineraria,** from frost, 303
- [ ] Tie up permanent **vines** so they don't get knocked down by rain or wind, 303
- [ ] Use the bendy stems of **grape vines** to make wreaths and baskets, 305
- [ ] Make a holiday wreath from **succulents,** 307
- [ ] Harvest **winter vegetables** as soon as they mature, 312

ROSE-PRO CALENDAR

Month	Planting	Pruning	Spraying
January	Plant bare-root roses.	Prune rose bushes and ever-blooming climbers.	Dormant spray with Orthorix.
February	Finish planting bare-root roses purchased locally.	———	Spray once a week with Funginex beginning at midmonth.
March	Finish planting bare-root roses purchased from mail-order catalogues.	Begin disbudding Hybrid Teas and Grandifloras.	Continue spraying once a week with Funginex, and add Orthene. Also mix Stern's Miracle Gro or Super K Gro into the spray.
April	———	Pick blooms or deadhead spent flowers. Also disbud Hybrid Teas and Grandifloras.	Spray once a week with Funginex, Orthene, and Stern's Miracle Gro or Super K Gro.
May	Plant roses from nursery containers.	Pick or deadhead flowers. Also disbud Hybrid Teas and Grandifloras.	Spray once a week with Funginex, Orthene, and Stern's Miracle Gro or Super K Gro.
June	Plant roses from nursery containers.	Pick or deadhead flowers. Also disbud Hybrid Teas and Grandifloras.	Spray once a week with Funginex, Orthene, and Stern's Miracle Gro or Super K Gro.
July	———	Stop disbudding. Continue picking or deadheading. Prune climbers that bloom only once a year.	Spray once a week with Funginex, Orthene, and Stern's Miracle Gro or Super K Gro.
August	Plant roses from nursery containers.	Give all roses a light pruning to encourage fall flowers.	Spray once a week with Funginex, Orthene, and Stern's Miracle Gro or Super K Gro.
September	Plant roses from nursery containers.	Pick blooms or deadhead spent flowers.	Spray once a week with Funginex and Orthene. Stop spraying with Stern's Miracle Gro or Super K Gro.
October	Plant roses from nursery containers.	Pick blooms or deadhead spent flowers.	Continue spraying once a week with Funginex. Stop spraying with Orthene.
November	———	Pick blooms if desired but stop deadheading them.	———
December	———	———	———

Month	Irrigating	Fertilizing	Other Activities
January	Water new plants every other day for the first three weeks after planting.	Give all plants 2 tablespoonfuls of Epsom salts. Also give all newly planted roses 1 cup of superphosphate and all established plants ¼ cup of superphosphate.	Apply mulch. Attend public demonstrations of rose pruning.
February	Begin watering all plants with 1 inch of water per week when rains aren't adequate.	Give each plant 1 cup of Milorganite at midmonth. (Give 2 cups of Milorganite to large established climbers.)	Early this month apply 1 cup of gypsum to the ground over the roots of each plant.
March	Apply up to 2 inches of water once a week when rains aren't adequate.	Give 1 tablespoon of sulfate of potash to each plant early in the month. Also give each plant 1 tablespoonful of sulfate of ammonia once a week.	———
April	Apply up to 1½ inches of water twice a week.	Once a week give each plant 1 tablespoonful of sulfate of ammonia.	Attend rose shows.
May	Apply up to 1½ inches of water twice a week.	Every other week give each plant 1 tablespoonful of urea.	———
June	Apply up to 1½ inches of water twice a week.	Every other week give each plant 1 tablespoonful of urea.	Attend rose shows.
July	Apply up to 1½ inches of water three times a week.	Once every other week give each plant 1 tablespoonful of urea.	Renew mulch where necessary.
August	Apply up to 1½ inches of water three times a week.	Give each plant one application of 2 tablespoonfuls of Epsom salts and ½ cup of Milorganite.	———
September	Apply up to 1½ inches of water twice a week.	Once a week give each plant 1 tablespoonful of urea.	———
October	Apply up to 1½ inches of water twice a week.	———	Attend rose shows.
November	Water until midmonth if rains aren't adequate. After midmonth withhold water.	———	———
December	Withhold water.	———	Prepare beds for bare-root planting. Remove weeds and fallen leaves.

This schedule of rose care is adapted from rosarian Richard Streeper's calendar of rose care. Detailed discussions of the steps listed here are given in the monthly chapters.

REFERENCES

Actual nitrogen. The amount of pure nitrogen in a fertilizer. To determine the number of pounds of a specific fertilizer you must use in order to give a plant 1 pound of actual nitrogen divide 100 by the first number on the package.

Air layer. To propagate a plant by growing roots from an aboveground node of a branch or trunk. The node is wrapped with sphagnum moss and kept damp (usually by covering it with plastic film). The entire portion of the plant that includes the new roots can then be severed to create a new plant. (Compare *layer*.)

Ammonic. Containing ammonia (NH4), a primary source of nitrogen in such fertilizers as ammonium sulfate, which will acidify soils as well as fertilize them. Ammonium sulfate (21-0-0) is a cheap source of fast-acting nitrogen that dissolves quickly in water, but it can burn plants if not watered in well.

Annual. A plant that completes its life within twelve months. An annual germinates, grows, blooms, sets seed, and dies all in one season. Warm-season annuals begin life in spring, and die when the weather gets cold in fall. Cool-season annuals begin life in fall, and die when the weather gets hot in summer. Some perennial plants, such as delphiniums and petunias, are grown mainly as annuals. Some perennials that are grown as annuals in other parts of the country, such as impatiens and geraniums, are grown here as true perennials.

Anther. The pollen-bearing flower part; it consists of pollen sacks and is located on the end of the stamen, the male reproductive organ of flowers.

Antitranspirants. Products sprayed on leaves that leave a film in order to slow transpiration and thus prevent wilting. They can help plants survive heat, cold, dryness, salt spray, and transplanting.

Areoles. Spine cushions. They're found on all cacti but not on any other succulents. (Many other succulents, including the cactuslike euphorbias, have spines, but they do not have spine cushions.)

Axillary bud. A bud that occurs in the leaf axil (the upper angle where the leaf joins the stem). Tomato suckers arise from axillary buds.

Balanced fertilizer. A widely used but somewhat vague term for a fertilizer that contains all three major elements (nitrogen, phosphorus, and potassium) that plants need. (See *complete fertilizer*.)

Bare-root. A plant that has had all soil removed from its roots. Many deciduous plants are sold bare root during the winter months.

Beneficials. Insects, arachnids, nematodes, and other organisms that eat or parasitize pest insects and mites. Many, such as spiders, exist in our gardens; others can be purchased for release.

Biennial. A plant that requires two growing seasons to flower and then sets seed and dies. Biennials are usually planted from bedding plants in fall or from seeds that are planted in summer to bloom the following year. Some biennials, such as the foxglove Foxy and the sweet William Wee Willie, can be grown as annuals.

Biodegradable. Capable of decomposing by natural biological means.

Bi-Wall. A type of drip tubing to bury in the ground. It's used for row crops in agriculture and home vegetable gardening, but it also works in flower borders. Double-chamber construction prevents clogging and carries water to laser-cut holes that release water.

Blossom-end rot. The black, sunken, leathery areas on the bottom of tomatoes (and also found on peppers, squash, and watermelons) that is caused by insufficient calcium in the fruit. The insufficiency in turn is caused by uneven moisture in the soil or by roots damaged from cultivation, salty soil, or extremely wet soil.

Bolt. To go to seed prematurely. Typically describes vegetables, such as onions.

Botrytis. A fungus disease characterized by fuzzy, wet filaments and the blackening and swelling of plant parts, especially flowers, leaves, and stems. Promoted by prolonged wet weather or frequent overhead irrigation.

Bract. A leaflike organ between the flower and the leaves, or one that is part of an inflorescence, or that has taken on color to look just like a petal, as on poinsettias.

Branch collar. The swollen area surrounding a tree branch where it meets a larger branch or the trunk.

Broad-spectrum pesticide. A pesticide that kills a large number of various pests rather than being designed to control one specific pest. In general, specific pesticides are better since they protect beneficials. (See *integrated pest management*.)

BT. *Bacillus thuringiensis*, a bacterial disease that kills caterpillars and is sold under several trade names (such as Attack, Dipel, and Thuricide) in liquid or powder form, to be used as a spray or dust. Caterpillars that ingest treated leaves stop eating and die in about three days.

Bud union. The location on a grafted plant where the variety was grafted onto the root stock. It may or may not be swollen. On older plants it often becomes difficult to distinguish where the bud union is, but in some cases it's easily seen. On citrus, for example, there may be a change in the size of the trunk from smaller to larger, or vice versa. On bare-root trees the bud union is often no more than a slight bend in the trunk. On roses the bud union is the knob, bump, or large swollen area from which the canes arise. (On old roses bud unions can grow to enormous size, sometimes a foot or more long.)

Bulb. A modified subterranean leaf bud; it has a basal plate above which are food-storing scales (rudimentary leaves), surrounding a bud from which comes a plant. Also used loosely to describe all plants that grow from thickened underground storage organs.

Caliche. A highly alkaline type of soil found largely in desert areas. Its high lime content may be visible as white flecks throughout or as a white crust on top of the soil, or it may occur in a hard buried layer.

Callus. The dry crust of plant cells that forms over the open cut on a cutting. (To develop the crust is to "callus over.")

Cane. The woody stem of a rose or cane berry, such as raspberries and blackberries, or a somewhat flexible, jointed, and often hollow or pith-filled stem arising from the ground, as on bamboo, sugar cane, and cane begonias.

Chaparral. A dense growth of native plants that are stiff, drought-resistant, evergreen, and sometimes-thorny shrubs of various types.

Chelate. Technically, an organic molecule that prevents iron, manganese, and zinc from being "locked up" (becoming insoluble) in alkaline soil by binding itself to them. In this combined form they stay soluble, and thus plants can use them. In *iron chelate*, *chelated iron*, or a *chelated* or *chelating* formula: a product that contains the trace elements iron, manganese, and zinc, in a form that plants can use.

Chilling requirement. The number of hours between $45°$ and $32°F$ ($7°$

and $0°C$) that a plant needs to overcome dormancy in order to grow, flower, and fruit properly. (When the temperature drops lower than freezing little action occurs within the tissues of the plant.) A plant with a *low chilling requirement* is one that needs few, if any, hours between $45°$ and $32°F$ in order to bloom and bear.

Chimney drain. A narrow drain, dug with spade, crow bar, or posthole digger, in the bottom of a planting hole on flat ground, when the cause of poor drainage is a layer of hardpan that is thin enough to break through with hand tools. The hole is then filled with sand or ground bark, to allow water to escape through the layer of hardpan down into a layer of soil that drains.

Chlorosis. Condition denoting a lack of chlorophyll (a green pigment in plant cells) often brought about by a lack of sufficient soluble iron in the soil. A chlorotic plant has yellow leaves and dark veins. Sometimes, especially in citrus, this is caused by waterlogged soil. Also, highly alkaline soil can cause chlorosis by preventing plants from absorbing enough iron, zinc, and manganese for plant health.

Clay. A fine-grained earth made up of tiny mineral particles less than .002 millimeters in size. When you grip a damp handful it holds together. Pure clay is good for little else than making bricks or pottery, but "clay soils" contain humus and may also contain some admixture of sand or silt.

Climate zone. A geographical area in which the yearly temperature range, length of seasons, average precipitation, humidity, amount of sunshine, and other factors combine to make certain plants grow better than others. The climate zones described and mapped in the *Sunset Western Garden Book* make up the zone system most widely used by Western gardeners.

Cole crop. Any member of the cabbage family, including cauliflower, broccoli, and Brussels sprouts.

Complete fertilizer. The correct term for describing a fertilizer containing all three major elements

(nitrogen, phosphorus, and potassium) that plants need. The formulas—the relative amounts of the three—may vary widely, however. A complete fertilizer high in growth ingredients has a high first number, and a complete fertilizer high in bloom ingredients has a high second number or second and third numbers.

Compost. A soil amendment made by farmers and gardeners by piling up organic materials and keeping them damp until they rot.

Cool-season flower. An annual, biennial, or perennial flower that's native to a cool climate and grows and flowers best at cool temperatures.

Cool-season lawn. A lawn variety that's best adapted to a cool climate and thus grows best and fastest during late fall, winter, and early spring.

Cool-season vegetable. A vegetable that originated in a cool climate and grows best at cool temperatures.

Corm. A thickened subterranean stem that is a solid piece of storage tissue and produces a plant from buds on top. Gladioli and freesias grow from corms.

Corolla. The collective name for the petals of a flower. The collective name for the sepals is the calyx. The corolla and calyx combined make up the perianth. (On a fuchsia the corolla is the usually downward-facing "skirt" of the flower, and it may be of any color available in fuchsias; the *sepals* of a fuchsia flare back toward the stem and they're always red, white, or pink.)

Crabgrass. An annual weed forming a thick clump of coarse grass that spreads out like a crab, turns red at the first frost, and dies out in winter.

Crop rotation. A system used by farmers and gardeners since ancient times to preserve the fertility of soil and minimize pest and disease problems. It consists of planting those crops (including flowers) that are subject to specific soilborne pests and diseases, on a particular piece of ground, no more than once every three years.

Crown. The place at soil level where a plant's roots end and its trunk or stem (or group of stems) begins. Also used to denote the top of a tree's canopy of branches.

Crown rot. A general term describing any number of fungus diseases that can attack the crown of a plant. Usually it's the result of planting too low or allowing water or mud to collect around the plant's trunk or stem (or stems).

Cultivar. See *variety*.

Curd. The white head of a cauliflower or the individual sections of a head.

Cutting. A section of a plant that's cut off for grafting or rooting.

Cutworm. A large black, brown, or gray hairless and fleshy caterpillar that curls into a C shape when disturbed. Often found underground or under fallen leaves when you dig or cultivate. Surface cutworms chew off stems at ground level overnight. Subterranean cutworms eat roots. Climbing cutworms destroy fresh shoots and young foliage.

Deadhead. To clip off faded flower heads before they can set seed.

Deciduous. Describes plants that drop all their leaves once a year.

Decollate snail. A small African carnivorous snail, introduced here to eat brown garden snails. (Their use is not legal in all counties. Check with the nearest UC Cooperative Extension Office.)

Decomposed granite. A grayish, creamy, or light-brown, granular and sometimes flaky soil composed of small particles of granite. It drains well and is high in potassium.

Diatomaceous earth. A powder made of a mined product that's filled with the sharp skeletons of tiny diatoms. It kills pests by piercing their bodies like broken glass.

Divide. To break apart the roots or to separate the bulbs of a plant that has formed a clump, in order to make new plants, to limit the plant's size, or to renew the plant.

Dormant. Describes the "sleeping" state when a plant isn't growing, though it remains alive.

Dormant spray. A pesticide, such as oil or lime sulfur, used in winter on deciduous plants that have gone dormant and dropped their leaves. Dormant sprays are usually too concentrated for use on foliage; in most cases, they would burn the leaves.

Drain. See *chimney*, *French*, or *sleeve drain* and *sump*.

Drainage. The passage of water through soil and the soil characteristics that support it. When drainage is good water passes rapidly downward through the soil. When drainage is poor water puddles on the surface or is held for a long period within the soil, traveling downward very slowly if at all. If the passage of water is seriously impeded plant roots can die from being deprived of necessary oxygen. Sandy and decomposed granite soils usually have fast drainage; in clay soils it is usually slow. Hardpan or buried rock, too, can seriously impede drainage.

Drift. A gracefully shaped area with rounded edges in a flower bed, planted with one type of plant or one color. Drifts extend from the foreground to the middle ground or from the middle ground to the background as well as from side to side in the bed.

Drip line. An imaginary line encircling a tree directly under the outermost tips of the branches. (Also, often used loosely to describe the various tubes and hoses or tube-type emitters, either buried or aboveground, that are used in drip irrigation.)

Drip system. A method of watering plants by which water at controlled low pressure is fed through a hose that in turn feeds small tubes, leading to individual plants, where emitters release water to the root zone or mist it on foliage. (In some cases emitters are attached directly to the primary hose. See *header*.)

Drought. Lack of adequate rainfall or less than normal rainfall lasting for a prolonged period: several months, a season, or several years. "Summer drought" describes our customarily dry summers.

Drought resistant. Describes plants from dry regions of the world that have developed various means and degrees of enduring drought without dying. Drought-resistant plants require less irrigation than do others, once established.

Drought tolerant. A term often used to describe a plant that, once established, can survive on natural rainfall alone, with little if any irrigation.

Emitters. Various types of plastic gadgets that release measured quantities of water. They attach to microtubing and, in some cases, to headers by simple push-pull methods. Emitters are not all interchangeable.

Epiphyte. A plant that grows by attaching itself to another plant but which doesn't sap nourishment from the host plant, as do parasites.

Espalier. To train a plant into a flat, formal shape on wires or against a wall or fence. Also the trained plant, and sometimes the framework it grows on.

Eye. The center of a flower when it has a different color from the outer petals; the bud on a tuber; a cutting that has only one bud; or an undeveloped bud, which looks like a line, bump, depression, or other demarcation on the stem of a plant.

Farm Advisor. The title that designates agricultural scientists who are representatives of the agricultural and natural resources advisory system that's supported by the state, county, and federal governments through the University of California. Reach them at local county UC Cooperative Extension Offices.

Fertilizer. Any material, either organic or inorganic, that's applied to soil or foliage to feed plants and aid their growth.

Fireblight. A bacterial disease that causes blackening and dieback of leaves, twigs, branches, and fruit on apple trees, evergreen pear (*Pyrus kawakamii*), pyracantha, and other members of the rose family.

Force. To make a plant bloom months ahead of schedule by simulating natural conditions that make it bloom.

Frass. The dust or pelletized excrement of insects, such as residues of boring left by bark beetles.

French drain. A trench in which perforated pipe has been laid, then covered with a 3-foot layer of sand or gravel. It's used to drain excess water from flat or sloping ground. The top of the gravel in the completed French drain may be level with the surface of the ground or it may be buried at any depth underground. If buried, the top of the gravel should be covered with plastic sheeting or landscape cloth prior to burying so that clay soil above the French drain can't drift down into it and clog the spaces in the gravel.

Full slip. Characterizes a ripe cantaloupe; a crack forms around the stem end so the melon slips off the vine easily, without tearing.

Furrow. A groove or trench made in garden soil for the purpose of planting, carrying irrigation water between rows, or controlling erosion.

Genus. A group of plants of one or several species that are related structurally and belong to the same family, but which differ from other genera within the family. Designated by the capitalized first word in a botanical name, which is followed by the uncapitalized species name.

Glochid. A short, barbed, almost-invisible and hairlike spine. Glochia grow from the areoles of some but not all cacti.

Glyphosate. A nonspecific weed killer made of a biodegradable salt that works by being absorbed through leaves and traveling down inside the plant to kill the roots.

Graft. To propagate a plant by inserting a section of one plant into another.

Green manure. A plant or plants, in most cases a legume, grown on a plot of land for one growing season (usually over winter) for the purpose of being plowed, tilled, spaded, or otherwise worked into the ground to improve soil fertility.

Gypsum. Calcium sulfate (CaSO4-2H₂O), a natural rock product used as a soil amendment to loosen clay soils and make them drain better when the cause of poor drainage is a high level of exchangeable sodium (alkali) rather than texture or compaction. Somewhat soluble in water, gypsum supplies soluble

calcium to replace excess exchangeable sodium (alkali). Also used to reclaim sodic (salty) soils.

Harden off. The process in a plant of gradually becoming accustomed to colder weather in fall. This includes slowing down or stopping top growth so that the foliage will be hardy. (Young leaves are most likely to suffer frost damage.) Gardeners help plants harden off by reducing water and fertilizer in fall. Also refers to gradually exposing young seedlings to outdoor temperatures and sunlight after they've been grown in a greenhouse, indoors, or under lights.

Hardpan. A layer of hard, compacted soil of any type that's cemented together by minerals and almost impenetrable by roots or water. Often buried beneath a layer of good soil.

Hardscape. Any feature in a garden that's made of a construction material, including pools, decks, hot tubs, patios, steps, walks, walls, gazebos, pergolas, and planter boxes. Most gardens include some hardscape; some have more hardscape than landscape (areas of ground with plants growing in them).

Hardy. Describes a plant that can take various degrees of frost and freezing temperatures without dying. (Does not mean a strong or easy-to-grow plant.)

Head back. To cut back the growing end of a branch or young tree in order to stimulate branching farther back on the branch or trunk, thus redirecting growth.

Header. A hose that carries water from the water source to microtubing and emitters in a drip system. Headers aren't all interchangeable; they and the various parts that are used to connect sections must be of the right size to fit.

Heel in. A way to keep bare-root plants from drying out when you can't plant them right away: laying the plants in the shade with their roots in a trench, covering the roots with soil, and keeping them damp.

Helix snail. *Helix aspersa*: our common brown garden snail.

Herb. Any plant used for medicine,

fragrance, or flavoring. (Not all herbs are edible.) In botany, any nonwoody plant that dies down in winter.

Herbaceous border. A traditional flower border planted entirely from nonwoody plants.

Humus. The organic portion of soil, made up of largely decomposed animal and vegetable matter and usually light or dark brown in color. Nitrolized sawdust, leaf mold, peat moss, and manure are organic soil amendments that eventually become humus in soils, but they're not the same as humus.

Hybrid. The offspring of a cross, by intention or chance, between two plants that are more or less unlike. Some hybrids are sterile. Seeds from a hybrid plant don't produce plants like the parent.

Insecticidal soaps. A group of biodegradable fatty acids that are sold as environmentally safe sprays (such as Safer). They kill pests, especially soft-bodied pests such as aphids, on contact (by clogging their pores).

Integrated pest management (IPM). A system of balancing pest populations with populations of beneficial insects, so that few if any chemical sprays need to be used. When sprays are used, specific sprays for the individual pest are chosen rather than broad-spectrum sprays that kill many beneficials.

June drop. Describes the dropping of many immature fruits, usually in early June but sometimes at other times. Nature's way of thinning fruit on trees that set more fruit than they can ripen.

Laterals. Side branches.

Lateral buds. Buds that are secondary to the terminal bud; they grow from the sides of stems or branches rather than the tip.

Lateral growth. Side growth; from main stems or the trunk.

Layer. To propagate a plant by bending a living branch to the ground and burying a portion of it in soil while it's still attached to the parent plant, allowing the branch to root, and then cutting off and removing the rooted portion. (Prior to burying the branch portion, a slanting cut is made halfway through it; it's then brushed with rooting compound and held open by a sliver of wood or by a pebble. Once buried it's usually pegged down on both sides or weighted down by a brick placed on top.)

Leader. The main trunk of a tree or the dominant shoot or stems of a plant, from which side growth is produced.

Leggy. Describes a plant that tends to grow too tall with long, bare stalks below.

Legume. Any member of the Leguminosae, a family made up of plants having a pod shaped like a pea pod.

Loam. Technically a soil type that is a combination of clay, sand, and silt. Loam soils vary greatly and are often described by such terms as "clay loam" or "sandy loam" depending on the percentages of their components. Also used popularly to describe any soil that's full of humus and is rich, crumbly, productive, and dark in color (as in "good garden loam").

Low chill. Describes a plant that needs few hours between 45°F and 32°F (7° and 0°C) in order to bloom and bear fruit.

Manure. Animal excrement of horses, cows, chickens, rabbits, or pigs; used for fertilizer and soil improvement. (Cat and dog droppings carry diseases and must never be used.)

Manure tea. A liquid fertilizer made by putting a shovelful of manure into a bucket of water and allowing it to stand overnight.

Microclimate. Small area within a climate zone where a plant will or won't grow because of factors of climate particular to that spot.

Microtubing. Quarter-inch plastic tubing used in drip systems to carry water to emitters. Most microtubing is of the same size, and thus interchangeable.

Mildew. Various fungus diseases (brown, powdery, and downy mildews) that grow on the surface of plant leaves and stems. They discolor and distort plant parts, sap plant energy, and can cause leaf drop.

Monocarpic. Describes a plant that blooms only once and then dies.

Mulch. A layer of loose organic matter applied to the surface of the soil to keep the ground cool, preserve moisture, stop the surface from cracking, cut down on weeds, and improve bacterial action. Also, black plastic, agricultural fabrics, rocks, pebbles, and newspapers used in the same way.

Mushroom compost. Humus in which mushrooms have been grown; an inexpensive organic amendment, largely made of manure and straw, that can be bought bagged or in bulk, sometimes direct from growers. It may have a high salt content.

Native plant (or "native"). A plant that, in its original form, grows wild in a geographic region such as California. Many native plants have been improved by selection and hybridization.

Native soil. Soil dug from a planting hole that's like the surrounding ground.

Naturalize. For a plant to multiply and come back year after year under normal garden conditions. Also for a plant to escape gardens and go wild, mixing in with and sometimes choking out native plants; examples are mustard, oxalis, pampas grass, valerian, and statice. Additionally, describes placing plants in natural looking, less artificial settings in gardens—mounting an epiphyte on a tree branch, for example.

Nematode. A microscopic, occasionally parasitic worm that lives in soil. Root knot nematodes enter the roots of plants causing swollen galls, called root knots. The plant may become yellow and stunted, and its fruit may be small. Beneficial nematodes kill various soil pests and plant pests that touch ground. They enter the pests' bodies, kill them with a bacteria, and then devour them. Some beneficial nematodes kill harmful ones by wrapping themselves around their victims and squeezing them to death.

Nitrogen. The chemical element, known by the symbol N, that is a colorless gas forming almost four-fifths of the atmosphere and is part of all living things. It's absorbed by plant tissues in the form of a soluble salt (nitrate or ammonium), makes them grow, and contributes especially to top and green growth. The first number in the trio on a fertilizer package tells the percentage of nitrogen in the product.

Nitrolized wood shavings. An organic soil amendment made of sawdust or ground wood, a byproduct of sawmills, to which the amount of nitrogen (usually from sulfate of ammonia) necessary for its decomposition in soils has been added by the manufacturer prior to sale. Also sawdust or ground wood to which sufficient nitrogen for decomposition has been added by the gardener prior to tilling it into soil. (Some wood-based soil amendments are nitrolized, others are not. Whether they are is not always stated on the labels of bagged products, but most nursery managers can tell you.) Most wood shavings used today in soil amendments are fir based, but other types of wood are also used. Nitrolized redwood consists of sawdust and ground up wood of redwood trees, to which the correct proportion of nitrogen has been added prior to sale; it's difficult to find but nonetheless available, and it's more acid than other wood products. (Also see *bark*.)

Node. The place on a plant from which leaves and axillary buds sprout.

Organic. In chemistry, any chemical compound that contains carbon. In gardening, anything that derives from plants or animals. *Organic gardeners* fertilize exclusively with organics and control pests with natural rather than chemical pesticides.

Pea stake. A plant stake, cut from shrubbery, with a straight piece to stick into the ground and many twigs to support plants as they grow.

Peat moss. A naturally occurring, usually acidic material found in peat bogs in cool wet climates where dead moss has gradually built up and partially decomposed over hundreds or thousands of years.

Perennial. Technically any non-woody plant that lives for more than two years and produces flowers and seeds for more than one year from the same roots. Some perennials are evergreen; others die down in winter. Some plants often classed as perennials will eventually make woody stems, when grown in Southern California. Some plants with fleshy roots, such as agapanthus and daylilies, are technically perennials but often classed with bulbs. Many perennials, including violas, pansies, and petunias, are customarily grown only as annuals.

Petal blight. A fungus or bacterial disease that afflicts flowers. It can ruin camellia and azalea blossoms by browning, discoloring, and rotting them to the center.

pH. A symbol that stands for degree of acidity or alkalinity, for example of soil, and which is measured on a scale numbered from 0 to 14 (7.0 is neutral). As the numbers decrease in value from 7.0 the soil is increasingly acid; as they rise above 7.0 the soil is increasingly alkaline.

Phosphorus. A nonmetallic, chemical element that's known by the symbol P and is one of the three main ingredients in fertilizers. It contributes to root and flower growth and the overall health of plants. The second number in the trio on a fertilizer package tells the percentage of phosphorus in the product.

Photoperiodic. Responding to the length of daylight hours by the onset of a physical change, such as flowering. For example chrysanthemums, which naturally bloom in fall, can be made to bloom at any time of year by artificially controlling the number of hours of daylight they undergo.

Photosynthesis. The method by which the chlorophyll in plants is acted on by sunlight, or appropriate artificial light, to change carbon dioxide and water (H_2O) into carbohydrates that feed the plant.

Pinch back. To prune off growing tips in order to make a plant bushier.

Pistil. The female organ of a flower, made up of the stigma, style, and ovary.

Pollen. A yellow dust usually produced inside the pollen sacks that make up the anther on top of the stamen of a flower; pollen grains (in seed plants called microspores) contain the male sex cells of seed plants.

Pollination. The transfer of pollen from the anthers (the male part of flowers) to the stigma (the female part). When bees, other insects, or the wind carry pollen from flower to flower on the same plant, the plants are self-pollinating. When plants need another plant, called a pollinator, to supply pollen in order for them to bear fruit, they are cross-pollinating.

Pony pack. A small, oblong, undivided nursery container customarily holding six small transplants.

Potash. Potassium carbonate obtained from wood ashes, or potassium from any salt; expressed as K_2O and used in fertilizers. A common name for potassium.

Potassium. A chemical element that occurs abundantly in nature and is one of the three basic ingredients of fertilizers, known by the chemical symbol K. It contributes to flowering and overall plant health. The third number in the trio on a package of fertilizer tells the percentage of potassium in the product.

Pot on. Successively repotting a plant into a container that's just one size larger, whenever its roots fill the pot.

Preemergent herbicide. A weed killer that kills germinating seeds.

Primary wilt. A stage when a plant barely begins to wilt, due to water stress. Signaled by a dull, lackluster look and the tips of the leaves turning down slightly. A lawn with primary wilt won't spring back when stepped on.

Pseudobulb. An aboveground, bulblike thickened stem on certain orchids, such as cymbidiums, that stores food for the plant.

Pup. A common name for the offshoots of some plants, including bromeliads and staghorn ferns, which produce side shoots that can be separated from the parent plant to make new plants.

Rhizobia. A group of beneficial soil bacteria, each of which has a symbiotic relationship with a particular species of legume. Rhizobia help legumes take nitrogen directly from the air, for nourishment.

Rhizome. A thickened stem that grows horizontally underground or on the surface of the ground, such as in bearded irises or calla lilies.

Rootbound. Describes a plant whose roots so fill a container that they've taken on its shape. The roots become thickly concentrated around the outside of the root ball, often wound around and around.

Rust. A fungus disease that attacks many plants, including snapdragons, hollyhocks, roses, and lawn grass. Yellow spots show through on the upper side of leaves where rusty pustules of brown powder occur on the underside.

Sand. A loose, gritty earth made up of tiny particles of rock. Grip a damp handful and it won't hold together. In its pure form sand contains little or no nutriment, but "sandy soils" usually contain a mixture of sand and humus and may also contain various small percentages of clay or silt.

Santa Ana. A dry wind, sometimes of gale force, that blows from the interior to the sea. High pressure over the Great Basin causes the westerly flow of air, which is heated and dried by compression as it flows over and down mountains and through canyons.

Scarify. To carefully nick or sand through the outer covering of seeds with hard seed coats, allowing them to germinate more easily.

Sepal. One section of the calyx of a flower. (The calyx is the outer covering that encloses and protects the flower while it is developing inside the bud before the flower opens.) After the flower opens the calyx usually splits into individual sepals, though with some flowers like primroses it stays in one piece. Sepals are usually green and may be small, hairy, and insignificant, but with some flowers, including fuchsias, the sepals may be colorful and look somewhat like petals, though they are not. (See *corolla*.)

Shade cloth. A landscape fabric usually made of plastic that's mainly used for covering trellises, shade houses, and other structures; it creates an appropriate environment for shade plants, which are grown under it. Shade cloth is usually black or green in color, and it's available in weaves that provide shade in varying degree, including 25 percent, 50 percent, and 75 percent shade.

Shear. To clip plants on the outside like a hedge with hedge shears or an electric hedge clipper. Shearing results in dense outer foliage which shades out inner foliage, leaving bare branches in the center of the plant, a condition that doesn't harm hedges but may harm other plants.

Side-dress. To apply dry fertilizer, as a booster, on the ground on one or both sides of a vegetable row, then water it into the soil. When black plastic mulch is in use, side-dressing is applied by pouring liquid fertilizer through holes made in the plastic, or foliar feeding is substituted.

Silk. Sticky fibers that spill out of the tops of the ears of corn and are the female flower of the corn plant. Each fiber leads to one kernel of corn and must receive one grain of pollen in order to make that kernel grow. (See *tassel*.)

Sleeve. A flexible plastic plant container that's similar to a plastic bag and elongated in shape, used like any plastic nursery container to hold the soil mix and the roots of young nursery stock. (Sleeves are often open on the bottom and can produce plants with a beneficially elongated root system, sometimes including a tap root.)

Sleeve drain. A pipe, often covered by gravel, that drains water from the bottom of a planting hole beneath the roots of a plant on a slope and releases it farther down on the slope. It is emplaced either by drilling a hole with water or machinery through hard soil, from a lower point on the hill, or by digging a trench that is later refilled.

Slow-release fertilizer. A fertilizer that's coated with a plastic or otherwise constituted in such way that small, measured amounts of plant food are released over a period of time.

Soil amendment. Anything added to soil to improve it's texture, structure, or pH. Some soil amendments are organic and break down to make humus. Others, including soil sulfur, lime, and gypsum, are inorganic.

Soil sulfur. A type of sulfur (a pale yellow, nonmetallic chemical element whose chemical symbol is S) that can be purchased in small or large bags at any nursery. It's used to acidify soil for acid-loving plants and to correct soils that have a high pH. The usual method of application is to sprinkle the recommended quantity on the ground and water it in.

Soil test. A chemical way to determine at least the pH of soils and soil mixes. More sophisticated soil tests determine some of the basic nutrients in soil.

Specialty plants. Plants that require special know-how or attention and which frequently have plant societies devoted to their culture.

Species. One kind of plant, or a group of plants, with a high number of similar characteristics that usually can interbreed only with each other. Designated by the uncapitalized second word in a botanical name. Also describes a plant in the form (or close to the form) in which it was originally found in the wild, as in "*Rosa banksiae* is a species rose."

Spike. A long, flowering stalk with flowers usually attached directly to it.

Sport. An entire plant that differs from the typical form of the plant, or a shoot of a plant that differs from the rest of the plant when it first occurs. Sports come about either from spontaneous mutation or from segregation. Many climbing roses, for example, have occurred as sports that began as one atypical shoot on a rose bush. All cole crops, such as Brussels sprouts, cauliflower, and cabbages, came from a series of sports that occurred over many centuries. They're all descendants of one ancestor, a wild plant that man segregated and grew as a crop.

Spreader-sticker. See *surfactant*.

Stamen. The male part of a flower consisting of the filament (stalk) and anther or anthers.

Stigma. The upper part of the pistil (the female part of the plant), which is sticky when receptive and which receives the male pollen during pollination.

Stolon. A stem (in some cases called a "runner") that grows aboveground or underground and that sprouts roots at the nodes, thus forming new plants. Bermuda, kikuyu, and zoysia are stoloniferous grasses; also, the runners of strawberries are stolons, as are the long shoots of currants and gooseberries that, unable to support their weight, arch to the ground and sprout roots.

Subsoil. A layer of any kind of soil lying beneath a layer of topsoil.

Succulent. Any plant that stores water in leaves or stems that are thickened for the purpose. Aloes, cacti, crassulas, and most euphorbias are examples of succulents.

Sucker. On a rose, a cane that arises below the bud union and thus comes from the rootstock rather than the variety grafted onto it. On other plants, any usually unwanted, fast-growing, upright growth from roots, trunk, crown, or main branches. On tomatoes, the sprouts from axillary buds. (See also *water sprout*.)

Sump. An inefficient drainage system consisting of a small deep hole dug in the center of the bottom of a planting hole and then filled with sand or ground bark, supposedly to drain off excess water. Not recommended; it soon fills with water and does more harm than good. (See *chimney drain* and *sleeve drain*.)

Surfactant. A chemical product used to break down the surface tension of water. Some, often called wetting agents, are used to help water penetrate soil. Others, often called spreader-stickers, are mixed into sprays to make them more effective. Sprays containing surfactants cover leaves in a smooth film rather than in droplets.

Tassel. The male flower of the corn plant that emerges from the tops of stalks and bears the pollen. (Some hybrid corn varieties sport a few distorted bisexual tassels or ears; they do no harm.)

Tensiometer. An instrument that measures soil moisture. It's made up of a handle, a probe to push down into the ground, and a dial that registers the moisture content of the soil below the surface.

Terminal bud. The bud at the tip of a branch or stem.

Thatch. In lawns, a layer of partially decomposed leaves, stems, and roots that forms between the earth and the grass blades.

Thermophotoperiodic. Describes a plant, such as an onion or a petunia, whose flowering and growth habit depend on the length of days combined with the temperature.

Topiary. The art of training plants into formalized and stylized shapes, such as circles, triangles, animals, or birds. Also the shaped plants themselves.

Topsoil. Any type of soil, whether based on sand, decomposed granite, loam, or clay, that's rich with humus and found in the top layer of soil where plant roots live. In arid regions it can take centuries for nature to create a few inches of natural topsoil. Commercial topsoil is often man-made by mixing decomposed granite, sand, or river-bottom silt with organic amendments.

Transpiration. The giving off of moisture from plant leaves into the air.

Tuber. A thickened stem, usually shorter, thicker, and rounder than a rhizome, that serves as a storage chamber and from which grows a plant. It grows totally or partially underground. A potato is a tuber.

Tuberous root. A thickened root that grows underground and has growth buds on top, in the old stem portion from which springs the plant. Dahlias and sweet potatoes grow from tuberous roots.

Variety. In taxonomy (the science of naming plants) the rank subordinate to subspecies (a name with varying meanings, usually a geographical difference) and above forma (a fifth name given to a plant by botanists to list a trivial difference). However, in actual practice the variety is generally a third italicized name that's tacked onto the usual binomial (genus and species) to indicate a particular and distinct form of a species that's found in nature. For example, in the name *Pinus mugo mugo*, the second mugo means a particular wild type of mugo pine that's different from others. All varieties first occur in nature (usually by spontaneous generation or mutation). Horticultural varieties (those that first occur under cultivation or that occurred first in nature but then persist only under cultivation by artificial means, such as propagation by cuttings) are more correctly called *cultivars*. The names of cultivars are written in plain type and enclosed in single quotes, and they follow the italicized names, however many there may be. For example, in the name *Juniperus chinensis procumbens* 'Nana,' the first name is the genus, the second name is the species, the third name (*procumbens*) is the natural variety, while the fourth name ('Nana') is the man-made cultivar. Nonetheless in common parlance most gardeners and many garden writers, including this one, often use the word "variety" loosely when referring to any plant to which a name has been given by its commercial producer or hybridizer, for example in speaking of named zinnias or roses as varieties, when actually they are more properly called cultivars. *Mandevilla splendens* 'Alice du Pont,' for example, is a particular cultivar of mandevilla.

Volunteer. A cultivated plant that comes up in a garden on its own accord and often in the wrong place, from a seed deposited by the wind or a bird, or by another wild or domestic creature.

Warm-season flower. An annual, biennial, or perennial flowering plant that's native to a warm climate and thus grows fastest and flowers best during the warmest part of the year.

Warm-season lawn. A lawn variety that's best adapted to a warm tropical or subtropical climate and thus grows best and fastest during our warm late-spring, summer, and early-fall months. Examples are St. Augustine, Bermuda, and zoysia.

Warm-season vegetable. A vegetable that originated in a warm climate and thus grows best in warm temperatures.

Water sprout. A long, whippy sucker that sprouts, usually in summer, from the tops of branches or from the trunks of trees and shoots up rapidly.

Wetting agent. See *surfactant.*

Bibliography

Ayensu, Edward S., et al. of the Ad Hoc Panel of the Advisory Committee on Technology Innovation. *Underexploited Tropical Plants with Promising Economic Value.* Washington, D.C.: National Academy of Sciences, 1976.

Bailey, L. H., and staff of L. H. Bailey Hortorium. *Hortus Third: A Concise Dictionary of Plants Cultivated in the United States and Canada.* New York: Macmillan Co., 1978.

Ball, Vic, ed. Geo. J. Ball, Inc. *Ball Red Book.* 14th ed. Reston, Virginia: Reston Publishing Co., 1985.

Bartel, Janice R., and Belt, Sage Culpepper. *A Guide to Botanical Resources of Southern California.* Los Angeles: Museum Publications, Natural History Museum of Los Angeles County, 1977.

Barton, Barbara J. *Gardening By Mail 2: A Source Book.* Sebastopol, California: Tusker Press, 1987.

Beley, Jim, ed., and Ortho staff. *All About Azaleas, Camellias & Rhododendrons.* San Ramon, California: Ortho Books, 1985.

Blackmore, Stephen, and Tootill, Elizabeth, eds. *The Facts on File Dictionary of Botany.* Aylesbury, United Kingdom: Market House Books Limited (simultaneously published in United States by Facts on File, Inc., and in London by Penguin Books), 1984.

Blomberry, Alec, and Rodd, Tony. *Palms: An Informative, Practical Guide to Palms of the World: Their Cultivation, Care and Landscape Use.* London, Sydney, Melbourne: Angus and Robertson Publishers, 1984.

Capon, Brian. *Botany for Gardeners: An Introduction and Guide,* Portland, Oregon: Timber Press, 1990.

Carr, Anna. *Rodale's Color Handbook of Garden Insects.* Emmaus, Pennsylvania: Rodale Press, 1983.

Carson, Rachel L. *Silent Spring.* Boston: Houghton Mifflin, 1962.

Chamberlin, Susan. *Hedges, Screens and Espaliers.* Tucson: HP Books, 1983.

Clausen, Ruth Rogers, and Ekstrom, Nicolas H. *Perennials for American Gardens.* New York: Random House, 1989.

Courtright, Gordon. *Trees and Shrubs for Temperate Climates,* 3rd ed. Portland, Oregon: Timber Press, 1988.

————. *Tropicals.* Portland, Oregon: Timber Press, 1988.

Cullmann, Willy; Gotz, Erich; and Groner, Gerhard. *The Encyclopedia of Cacti.* Sherborne, Dorset, England: Alphabooks, 1986.

Creasy, Rosalind. *Cooking From the Garden.* San Francisco: Sierra Club Books, 1988.

————. *The Complete Book of Edible Landscaping.* San Francisco: Sierra Club Books, 1982.

Everett, Thomas H. *The New York Botanical Garden Illustrated Encyclopedia of Horticulture.* 10 vols. New York and London: Garland Publishing, 1981.

Farrell, Kenneth R., and staff. *Agricultural Publications Catalogue, University Of California Division of Agriculture and Natural Resources.* Special publication 3020. ANR Publications (University of California, 6701 San Pablo Ave., Oakland, CA 94608-1239), 1989.

Feathers, David, and Brown, Milton, eds. *The Camellia: Its History, Culture, Genetics, and a Look Into Its Future Development.* Columbia, South Carolina: The R. L. Bryan Company, 1978.

Fell, Derek. *Annuals: How to Select, Grow and Enjoy.* Tucson: HP Books, 1981.

————. *Vegetables: How to Select, Grow and Enjoy.* Tucson: HP Books, 1982.

Graf, Alfred Byrd. *Exotica Pictorial Cyclopedia of Exotic Plants from Tropical and Near-tropic Regions.* E. Rutherford, New Jersey: Roehrs Co., 1976.

Harper, Pamela, and McGourty, Frederick. *Perennials: How to Select, Grow and Enjoy.* Tucson: HP Books, 1985.

Harrington, Geri. *Grow Your Own Chinese Vegetables.* Pownal, Vermont: Garden Way Publishing, 1984.

Hoyt, Roland Stewart. *Checklists for the Ornamental Plants of Subtropical Regions: A Handbook for Ready Reference.* Los Angeles: Livingston Press, 1938.

Hunter, Beatrice Trum. *Gardening Without Poisons.* Boston: Houghton Mifflin Company, 1964.

Jekyll, Gertrude. (Intro., Richard Bisgrove.) *The Illustrated Gertrude Jekyll.* Boston, Toronto: Little, Brown, 1988.

Jekyll, Gertrude, and Mawley, Edward. *Roses.* Rev., Stuart Graham Thomas. Salem, New Hampshire: The Ayer Company, 1983.

Johnson, Huey D., and Robie, Ronald B. *Plants for California Landscapes: A Catalogue of Drought Tolerant Plants.* Bulletin 209. Sacramento: California Department of Water Resources, 1979.

Koehler, C. S. *Insect Pest Management Guidelines for California Landscape Ornamentals.* Publication 3317. Berkeley: The University of California Division of Agriculture and Natural Resources, 1987.

Labadie, Emile L. *Native Plants for Use in the California Landscape.* Sierra City Press, Oakland: 1978.

Lathrop, Norma Jean. *Herbs: How to Select, Grow and Enjoy.* Tucson: HP Books, 1981.

Latymer, Hugo. *The Mediterranean Gardener*. New York, Toronto: Barrons, in association with The Royal Botanic Gardens, Kew, 1990.

Lenz, Lee, W. *Native Plants for California Gardens*. Claremont, California: Rancho Santa Ana Botanic Garden, 1977.

Lenz, Lee W., and Dourley, John. *California Native Trees and Shrubs for Garden and Environmental Use in Southern California and Adjacent Areas*. Claremont, California: Rancho Santa Ana Botanic Garden, 1981.

Levick, Melba, and Prentice, Helaine Kaplan. *The Gardens of Southern California*. San Francisco: Chronicle Books, 1990.

Lindsay, Lowell, and Lindsay, Diana. *The Anza-Borrego Desert Region*. Berkeley: The Wilderness Press, 1985.

MacCaskey, Michael. *Lawns and Ground Covers: How to Select, Grow and Enjoy*. Tucson: HP Books, 1982.

———. *The Complete Guide to Basic Gardening*. Tucson: HP Books, 1986.

Martin, R. Sanford. *How to Prune Fruit Trees*. 10th ed. Van Nuys: The Press of Document Engineering, 1978.

———. *How to Prune Western Shrubs*. Culver City, California: Murray & Gee, 1947.

Mathias, Mildred, ed. *Flowering Plants in the Landscape*. Berkeley, Los Angeles, London: University of California Press, 1982.

Milne, Lorus, and Milne, Margery. *The Audubon Society Field Guide to North American Insects and Spiders*. New York: Alfred A. Knopf, 1980.

Munz, Philip A. *A Flora of Southern California*. Berkeley, Los Angeles, London: University of California Press, 1974.

———. *California Desert Wildflowers*. Berkeley, Los Angeles, London: University of California Press, 1962.

———. *Shore Wildflowers of California, Oregon, and Washington*. Berkeley, Los Angeles, London: University of California Press, 1964.

Padilla, Victoria. *Southern California Gardens*. Berkeley, Los Angeles, London: University of California Press, 1961.

Patent, Dorothy Hinshaw, and Bilderback, Diane E. *Garden Secrets: A Guide to Understanding How Your Garden Grows and How You Can Help It Grow Even Better*. Emmaus, Pennsylvania: Rodale Press, 1982.

Paul, Anthony, and Rees, Yvonne. *The Water Garden*. New York: Viking Press, 1986.

Perry, Robert C. *Trees and Shrubs for Dry California Landscapes: Plants for Water Conservation*. San Dimas, California: Land Design Publishing, 1981.

Peterson, Tru, ed. *The New A to Z on Fuchsias*. San Francisco: The National Fuchsia Society Inc., 1981.

Picart, François. *Escargots from Your Garden to Your Table: How to Control, Raise and Process the Common Garden Snail*. F. Picart Snails (1550 Ridley Ave., Santa Rosa, CA 95401), 1978.

Quiros, Alice, and Young, Barbara. *The World of Cactus and Succulents and other Water Thrifty Plants*. San Francisco: Ortho Books, 1977.

Ray, Richard, and MacCaskey, Michael. *Roses: How to Select, Grow and Enjoy*. Tucson: HP Books, 1983.

Ray, Richard, and Walheim, Lance. *Citrus: How to Select, Grow and Enjoy*. Tucson: HP Books, 1980.

Redfield, Margaret. *The Southern California Month-by-Month Flower Gardening Book*. Los Angeles: J.P. Tarcher, 1976.

Reilly, Ann. *Park's Success with Seeds*. Greenwood, South Carolina: Geo. Park Seed Co., 1978.

Relf, Diane; Schwab, Judy; Steeves, Elissa; and Nathan, Virginia, eds. *The Virginia Master Gardener Handbook*. Petersburg: Virginia Cooperative Extension Service, 1987.

Robinson, William. *The English Flower Garden*. Rev., Graham Stuart Thomas. New York: The Amaryllis Press, 1984.

Rodale, J. I., ed. *How to Grow Vegetables and Fruits by the Organic Method*. Emmaus, Pennsylvania: Rodale Press, 1976.

Scheider, Alfred F. *Park's Success With Bulbs*. Greenwood, South Carolina: Geo. Park Seed Co., 1981.

Schmidt, Marjorie. *Growing California Native Plants*. Berkeley, Los Angeles:

University of California Press, 1980.

Scott, George Harmon. *Bulbs: How to Select, Grow and Enjoy*. Tucson: HP Books, 1982.

Sinnes, A. Cort, and Ortho staff. *All About Fertilizers, Soils and Water*. San Francisco: Ortho Books, 1980.

Smaus, Robert. *Los Angeles Times California Gardening: A Practical Guide to Growing Flowers, Trees, Vegetables and Fruits*. New York: Harry N. Abrams,1983.

———. *The Los Angeles Times Planning and Planting the Garden*. New York: Harry N. Abrams, 1983.

Smith, Ken. *Western Home Landscaping*. Tucson: HP Books, 1978.

Smith, Michael D., ed. *The Ortho Problem Solver*. 2nd ed. San Francisco: Ortho Information Services, 1984.

Spellenberg, Richard. *The Audubon Society Field Guide to North American Wildflowers, Western Region*. New York: Alfred A. Knopf, 1979.

Sunset Books and *Sunset* magazine. *Garden Pools, Fountains and Waterfalls*. Menlo Park, California: Lane Magazine and Book Company, 1974.

———. *Sunset Introduction to Basic Gardening*. Menlo Park, California: Lane Publishing Co., 1981.

———. *Sunset Pruning Handbook*. Menlo Park, California: Lane Magazine and Book Company, 1975.

———. *Sunset Western Garden Book*. 5th ed. Menlo Park, California: Lane Publishing Co., 1988.

Taylor, Norman. *Taylor's Guide to Annuals*. Rev. ed. Edited by Gordon P. DeWolf, Jr. Boston: Houghton Mifflin, 1986.

Tekulsky, Mathew. *The Butterfly Garden*. Boston: The Harvard Common Press, 1985.

Uber, William C. *Water Gardening Basics*. Dragonflyer Press (2460 N. Euclid Ave., Upland, CA 91786-1199), 1988.

UC publications. See Farrell, *Agricultural Publications Catalogue*. (Many publications also available from local county Cooperative Extension Offices.)

Walheim, Lance, and Stebbins, Robert L. *Western Fruit, Berries and*

Nuts: How to Select, Grow and Enjoy. Tucson: HP Books, 1981.

Waters, George, and Harlow, Norah, eds. *The Pacific Horticulture Book of Western Gardening.* Boston: David R. Godine, Publisher, in association with The Pacific Horticultural Foundation, 1990.

Wright, John I. *Plant Propagation for the Amateur Gardener.* Poole, Dorset, England: Blanford Books, Ltd. (distributed in the United States by Stirling Publishing, New York), 1983.

Wyman, Donald. *Wyman's Gardening Encyclopedia.* (expanded second ed.). New York, Macmillan Publishing Company, and London, Collier Macmillan Publishers, 1986.

Yepsen, Roger B., Jr. *The Encyclopedia of Natural Insect and Disease Control.* Emmaus, Pennsylvania: Rodale Press, 1984.

Born into a family of garden lovers in Yorkshire, England, Pat Welsh spent her teen years on a Pennsylvania farm until her family moved west in 1945. Pat's love of gardening eventually led to a career as a garden lecturer, writer, and television communicator. She lectured at garden clubs and the UCSD Extension, and when *San Diego Home/Garden* was founded in 1979, she became its first Garden Editor. She later spent five years as the Emmy-award-winning "Resident Gardener" on the San Diego NBC station. Pat has written dozens of magazine articles and columns on local gardening. She is the host of two how-to garden video tapes for *Better Homes & Gardens*. Her work has won several gardening awards, including four Quill and Trowel Awards from the Garden Writers of America. Above all, she is a Southern California gardener with her hands in the soil.